ANSWERING
JEWISH
OBJECTIONS
to
JESUS

Also by Michael L. Brown

Go and Sin No More: A Call to Holiness

Let No One Deceive You: Confronting the Critics of Revival

From Holy Laughter to Holy Fire: America on the Edge of Revival

Israel's Divine Healer

It's Time to Rock the Boat: A Call to God's People to Rise Up and Preach a Confrontational Gospel

Our Hands Are Stained with Blood: The Tragic Story of the "Church" and the Jewish People

Whatever Happened to the Power of God: Is the Charismatic Church Slain in the Spirit or Down for the Count?

How Saved Are We?

The End of the American Gospel Enterprise

Compassionate Father or Consuming Fire: Who Is the God of the Old Testament?

Michael L. Brown is a Jewish believer in Jesus and has a Ph.D. in Near Eastern Languages and Literatures from New York University. He is the president of the Brownsville Revival School of Ministry in Pensacola, Florida, and has served as a visiting professor at Trinity Evangelical Divinity School and Fuller Theological Seminary. He has written over ten books and is a contributor to the *Oxford Dictionary of Jewish Religion*.

ANSWERING JEWISH OBJECTIONS *to* JESUS

Volume 1

General and Historical Objections

MICHAEL L. BROWN

BakerBooks

A Division of Baker Book House Co
Grand Rapids, Michigan 49516

Published by Baker Books
a division of Baker Book House Company
P.O. Box 6287, Grand Rapids, MI 49516-6287

Third printing, January 2001

Printed in the United States of America

Library of Congress Cataloging-in-Publication Data

Brown, Michael L., 1955–
    Answering Jewish objections to Jesus : general and historical objections / Michael L. Brown.
        p.   cm.
    Includes bibliographical references (p.) and indexes.
    ISBN 0-8010-6063-X (paper)
    1. Apologetics. 2. Jews—Conversion to Christianity. 3. Jesus Christ—Messiahship. I. Title.
    BV4922.B76 2000
    239—dc21   99-046293

The material from Basilea Schlink, *Israel, My Chosen People* is © 1988 by Evangelical Sisterhood of Mary and is used by permission of Baker Book House and Evangelische Marienschwesternschaft.

For current information about all releases from Baker Book House, visit our web site:
http://www.bakerbooks.com

In memory of my beloved father,
Abram Brown (1914–1977)

Contents

Part 1   General Objections

Part 2   Historical Objections

Preface

In November of 1971, as a rebellious, proud, heroin-shooting, rock-drumming, Jewish sixteen-year-old, I discovered something I was not looking for, and the course of my life was completely altered. I found out that Jesus was the Jewish Messiah! I learned that he was the one spoken of in the Hebrew Scriptures, that he was God's way of salvation for Jew and Gentile alike, and that through faith in him my life could be transformed—even though I didn't want it to be transformed. I loved my sinful ways! But God's goodness overcame my badness, and in a matter of weeks, I was a brand-new man.

My parents were thrilled—and relieved—to see the tremendous change in my life. I had fallen so far, so quickly, since my bar mitzvah at age thirteen, and my parents had been deeply concerned. But the positive transformation was more radical and dramatic than was the fall. The only problem for my parents—especially for my father—was that in their opinion I had joined a foreign religion. So my father, thrilled with the change in my life but very much wanting me to come back to our traditions, brought me to the local Conservative rabbi in early 1972 (I was still not yet seventeen). But rather than attacking my beliefs, this twenty-six-year-old rabbi befriended me. He told me that in his opinion he was not as spiritual a person as I was, although his beliefs were right and mine were wrong. In his view, Judaism, meaning traditional, Orthodox, observant Judaism, was the only true faith for our people, and he felt that the key for me would be to meet some very religious—and zealous—traditional Jews. And so the journey began!

In the summer of 1973, the rabbi brought me to Brooklyn to spend an afternoon with some ultra-Orthodox rabbis. It was a real eye-opener for me! I was impressed with the devotion and kindly demeanor of these men, and I was challenged by their scholarship. How could I, just eighteen years old and barely able to read the

Hebrew alphabet, tell them what our sacred Hebrew texts meant? They had been studying the Scriptures all their lives; I had been a believer less than two years, although by then I had read the Bible cover to cover roughly five times and memorized more than four thousand verses. But they had memorized the original; I was dependent on English translations. What business did I have telling them that Jesus was actually the fulfillment of the prophecies of our Hebrew Bible?

This was my predicament: I was sure my faith was sound and that Jesus really was our Messiah, but I could find almost no literature (and almost no people) to help me. When I did find solid academic works by Christians dealing with Messianic prophecy and related subjects, they tended to be insensitive to the traditional Jewish objections I was hearing. On the other hand, the few books (really, booklets) I found specifically addressing Jewish objections tended to be popular, short, and nonscholarly in their approach. I was in a quandary!

How could I effectively answer the questions of the rabbis and refute their objections? And what about my own conscience? Could I really be at peace with myself without being able to provide intellectually solid responses to my own people, especially when the rabbis told me that if I could read the original texts, I would never believe in Jesus? So it was that I began to study Hebrew in college, ultimately making it my major and continuing with graduate studies until I earned a doctorate in Semitic languages. And all through my college and graduate years, I was constantly dialoging with rabbis and religious Jews, sometimes in public debates, other times one on one. I wanted to understand exactly why my own people rejected Jesus—Yeshua—as Messiah, and I wanted to answer them with truth as well as with love.

In the providence of God, I became somewhat of a specialist in Jewish debate and dialog, and in the late 1980s and early 1990s, my Messianic Jewish friends and colleagues began to ask me, "When are you going to put all this in writing?" In fact, one friend in particular, Sid Roth, lovingly badgered me for years, asking me almost every time we talked, "So Mike, when are you going to write *the* book"—implying that everything else I was writing was of secondary importance! Finally, in 1996 I felt the release to begin the work in earnest, and as word started to get out, I was amazed at the level of interest expressed by many of my Christian friends: "I want to read your book and then give it to one of my Jewish friends who doesn't believe in

Jesus! When is it coming out?" At last I can answer, "Now," with only one caveat. It's no longer a book; it's a series of three books. There was simply too much material to cover, and after all this time—especially given the fact that no comparable work exists—I felt that it was better to be too thorough than not thorough enough.

Following this volume, two more volumes should come out in six-to-nine-month intervals, meaning that, God willing, by the end of 2000 or the beginning of 2001, all three volumes should be in print. If there is sufficient reader interest, these three volumes will then be combined into a one-volume reference edition, with some special studies and further notes added. It is with great joy that I release this first volume to you. May you be blessed, edified, strengthened, and stretched as you read, study, think, and pray. Perhaps this will be the beginning of an important spiritual and intellectual journey for you too!

I would encourage you to read through the introduction, after which you can go through the objections in any order you choose. They are complete in themselves and extensively cross-referenced. If you choose, however, to read through the material from cover to cover, you will find that the objections often follow a logical order, so you will notice that one answer tends to build on the previous responses. You will also notice that the endnotes tend to be more extensive when dealing with especially controversial material. Of course, the notes could have been expanded almost without limit, and I was sorely tempted to provide extensive documentation for almost every statement I made throughout the book. But this was clearly unnecessary, and all interested readers will find more than ample documentation and references for further research. I trust that even the most staunch critic will agree that I have done my homework.

It is my prayer that the publication of this series, representing the fruit of more than a quarter of a century of dialog with my own Jewish people, will provide encouragement first and foremost to every Jewish believer in Jesus around the world. My dear brothers and sisters in the Messiah, this is for you!

To every Jewish reader who does not yet believe that Jesus (Yeshua) is the Messiah, it brings me great joy to know that you have this book in your hands. Read it with an open heart and an inquisitive mind! I pray that our God would reveal his truth to you in the pages that follow, which have been written with much toil and with many tears, because of my love for you.

To every Christian reader of this book, I am glad to know that you are interested in sharing the good news of the Messiah with my people. If not for a small group of Italian American Christians who took an interest in my wayward soul in the early 1970s, I might not be alive today. I am forever indebted to them. So I pray that God would help you, my Christian friends, to make the Messiah known to my Jewish people!

My thanks are extended to all of my friends and co-workers who have encouraged me and prayed for me during these years of research and writing. Thanks also are due to Jim Weaver, Academic Editor at Baker Books, for so enthusiastically getting behind the publication of this work, to Melinda Van Engen for her excellent editorial work, and to Baker as a whole.

I have dedicated this book to my beloved father, Abram Brown, who died many years before he could see the full impact of his wonderful influence in my life.

Note on citations and sources: Rabbinic literature is cited using standard conventions (e.g., the letter "m." before a Rabbinic source means "Mishnah," "b." stands for "Babylonian Talmud," "y" stands for "Palestinian Talmud," and "t" stands for "Tosephtah"). When there is a difference in the numbering of biblical verses between some Christian and Jewish versions, the Jewish numbering is in brackets (e.g., Isa. 9:6[5]). Bear in mind, however, that the actual verses are identical; only the numbering is different. Also, in keeping with the stylistic conventions of the publisher, all references to deity are lowercase. However, I have capitalized terms such as *Messianic, First Temple,* and *Rabbinic* to be in harmony with most popular Jewish conventions.

Introduction

The history of Jewish objections to Jesus is a long one, dating back almost two thousand years. It is not surprising, therefore, that for many centuries Jews and Christians alike have accepted without question the statement "Jews don't believe in Jesus." In fact, many have become so accustomed to this way of thinking that few realize such a statement is actually quite ironic, not to mention somewhat bizarre.

Consider for a moment that Jesus (or as he would have been known to his contemporaries, Yeshua) was born a Jew, raised in a Jewish community, lived and worked as a Jew among Jews, worshiped at the temple as a faithful Jew, attended synagogue regularly, taught as a Jew, and ultimately died as a Jew with the Hebrew Scriptures on his lips. He spent almost his entire life in constant interaction with fellow Jews, and all his immediate followers were Jewish. He was welcomed by many of his Jewish contemporaries as the promised Messiah, he pointed to the words of the Israelite prophets to explain his mission, and he spent virtually all his time—with precious few exceptions—preaching to Jews, healing their sicknesses, and meeting their deep spiritual and emotional needs. Out of the countless thousands of people whose lives he directly touched, few of them were non-Jews.

When reports circulated that he had risen from the dead, Jewish women were the first eyewitnesses and Jewish men announced this good news to crowds of interested, religious Jews. It was Jews who told other Jews about his resurrection and Jews who healed other Jews in his name. Of the large numbers of those who first put their faith in him, *all of them were Jews*. In fact, it was several years before any Gentiles became part of this community of believers.

"Jews don't believe in Jesus!" How can this be? No one would be surprised that many Jews did not and still do not believe Jesus was the Messiah. After all, there is a saying, "If you have ten Jews in a room, you have eleven opinions." Yes, we do have our points of view!

No one expects us to agree on everything, especially when it comes to religion. But how can it be that of all the peoples on the face of the earth, the Jewish people are known *in particular* as the ones who do not believe in Jesus? While most Indians are Hindus and most Arabs are Muslims, you would not expect to hear the blanket statement "Indians (or Arabs) don't believe in Jesus." Yet for many it is a simple, accepted fact that *Jews* do not believe in Jesus.

The purpose of this book, then, is fourfold: to understand why this strange turn of events has occurred, to list the major objections Jewish people have had (and do have) to Jesus being the Jewish Messiah, to clearly answer these objections, and to show why Jews (more than any other people) *should* believe that Jesus is the Jewish Messiah. Only then can they be completely true to the God of Abraham, Isaac, and Jacob and in harmony with the Hebrew Bible.

The good news is that there have always been Jews who have believed in Jesus as Messiah, even if they have been in the great minority. In every century, thousands of Jews have recognized and followed Jesus as the promised Messiah of Israel. Today, many tens of thousands of Jews believe in Jesus, possibly even hundreds of thousands.[1] The majority reside in the United States and the former Soviet Union, but more and more are now living in Israel. And one day, the Scriptures declare, there will be a great *national* change of heart. On that day, of all the peoples on the face of the earth, the Jews will be known in particular as those who *do* believe in Jesus the Messiah. That day will soon come!

For now, however, we need to tackle the objections Jewish people have to Jesus in an honest, fair, and comprehensive manner. Surprisingly, although through the years there have been a number of Jewish works written attacking the Messianic credentials of Jesus, no major work has ever been written to refute and answer these varied objections.[2] It is high time for us to categorically refute the refutations and decisively answer the objections.

Of course, most Jewish believers in Jesus are unaffected by the materials produced by the so-called "anti-missionaries" (Jewish leaders who actively work to bring Jews out of cults, Christianity, or other religions and into Judaism, especially traditional Judaism). The faith of these Jewish believers is too vibrant, their experience with God too real, their confidence in the unity of the entire Bible—the "Old" and "New" Testaments—too strong, their relationship with Jesus the Messiah too precious. They're really not worried about what a devoted rabbi or active anti-missionary has to say. Some, however, do become confused and troubled, while traditional or secular Jews who are seeking the truth about Jesus often must overcome the arguments of the anti-missionaries and rabbis.

As a result, this series of books needed to be written.[3] The anti-missionary arguments are here, the Messianic answers are here, and the evidence is in. The verdict should be clear to all: Jesus *is* our Messiah and King!

The Facts and Nothing but the Facts

In this volume and the two to follow, we will list more than 150 Jewish objections to the messiahship of Jesus, some of them serious, others slight, and a few so superficial they are actually silly. The objections are divided into six sections.

General Objections

These are in many ways the most common, least sophisticated, and often, most emotional objections. They contain broad generalizations, make sweeping statements, and are based on the perception of what Jews "as a whole" believe and do. The heart of these objections is simply this: "Jesus is not for Jews! Our religion is Judaism, not Christianity. No true Jew would ever believe in Jesus." To a great extent, answering these objections is a matter of correcting misconceptions as well as getting people to stop and think about the emotional—and sometimes irrational—nature of what they are saying.

Historical Objections

Historical objections tend to be more substantial and deal with the very purpose of the Messiah (in other words, the claim that the Messiah was to bring peace to the world) or the alleged failure of the church ("Christian" anti-Semitism and the state of the church worldwide, including its divisions and scandals). The heart of these objections is this: "Jesus cannot be the Messiah because we are obviously not in the Messianic age." In answering these objections, we need to define clearly the purpose and mission of the Messiah; provide a biblical picture of the Messianic age; explain the difference between a New Testament, Messianic Jewish expression of faith versus a later, corrupted "Christian" form; admit to the failures of the church while pointing to glorious and profound changes brought about by the gospel and giving shining examples of true Messianic faith.

Theological Objections

These objections are the most serious and cut to the heart of the differences between traditional Judaism and the Messianic Jewish/Christian faith. They revolve around the nature of God (the Trinity, the deity of Jesus, the person of the Holy Spirit), the continuity of the law (Is it still binding in total, or was it abolished by Jesus or Paul?), the nature of mankind and the need for salvation, and sin and the means of atonement. In sum, these objections support the claim that the religion of the New Testament is a completely foreign religion that is not only un-Jewish but is also unfaithful to the Hebrew Bible. Thus, issues of Messianic prophecy are secondary, since Jesus is viewed as a false prophet and the founder of an alien faith. Our answers here seek to distinguish between what the Hebrew Bible actually says (in distinction from later Jewish traditions), what the New Testament actually says (in distinction from later church traditions), and how Jewish tradition at times underscores the essential Jewishness of Christian beliefs.

Objections Based on Messianic Prophecies

Traditional Judaism strongly rejects the standard Messianic prophetic "proof texts," either denying they have anything to do with Jesus, claiming they have been mistranslated, misquoted, or taken out of context by the New Testament authors or traditional Christian apologists, or arguing that none of the *real* Messianic prophecies—the so-called provable prophecies—were ever fulfilled by Jesus. In short, people who hold these objections say, "We don't believe Jesus is the Messiah because he didn't live up to the biblical description of the Messiah." We answer these objections by looking back to the Hebrew Scriptures and rediscovering that the Messiah's mission was both priestly (involving atonement for sin) as well as royal; by noting that Scripture points to a twofold coming of the Messiah, whose first arrival had to be before the Second Temple was destroyed in the year 70 c.e.; and by examining the alleged misinterpretations of biblical prophecies and pointing out different ways of understanding the words of the New Testament authors. Where relevant, supporting evidence is adduced from the Rabbinic literature.

Objections to the New Testament

Objections to the New Testament can be broken down into several categories: The New Testament misquotes and misinterprets the Old Testament, at times manufacturing verses to suit its purposes; the genealogies of Jesus given by Matthew and Luke are hopelessly contradictory (at best) and entirely irrelevant anyway; the New Testament is filled with historical and factual errors (especially Stephen's speech); the teachings of Jesus are impossible, dangerous, and un-Jewish; and the New Testament is self-contradictory. To sum up rather bluntly: "Only a fool would believe in the divine inspiration of the New Testament." To counter these objections, we compare similar problems (with their solutions) from the Hebrew Scriptures, show the Jewishness of the thought patterns and ideas of the New Testament, and provide answers to apparent contradictions and/or distortions. Because many of these types of objections are treated in standard works on Bible difficulties, we deal here with those that are most frequently raised by the anti-missionaries and that are especially relevant to our topic.

Objections Based on Traditional Judaism

Some of these objections are highly emotional and underlie much of the gut-level reaction of hostility to the gospel. They also explain why so many Jews—especially the Orthodox—are unwilling to think for themselves on these issues. The two key points here are: (1) "Judaism is a wonderful, fulfilling, and self-sufficient religion. There is no need to look elsewhere." (2) "God gave us a written and an unwritten tradition. We interpret *everything* by means of that oral tradition, without which the Bible makes no sense." To answer these objections, we refute the notion that there is an unwritten, unbroken, binding tradition going back to Moses—demonstrating that the *written* Word provides the foundation for our faith—and we explain why all people (including Jews) need the Messiah.

Each of these six sections follows a similar format: (1) a concise statement of the objection; (2) a concise answer to the objection; and (3) an in-depth treatment, including citations of important sources where needed and consideration of possible objections to our answers. Although the objections are divided into different thematic chapters, they all tend to flow from a few problem areas. It will be helpful, therefore, to keep the following thoughts in mind while reading.

A Summary of the Major Issues

The principal problems include:

1. Most Jews are not familiar with the Jesus of the New Testament or with the true Christian (or Messianic Jewish) faith. This means that many of the objections they raise are based on misunderstanding. The best refutation of these objections is simply to set the record straight. We must not forget that many Jews don't even realize that Jesus Christ is Yeshua the Messiah (in other words, "Christ" was not Jesus' last name!). And just as most Christians are almost totally ignorant of what real Muslims believe, so also most Jews are almost totally ignorant of what real followers of Jesus believe.

Sadly enough, the more religious a Jewish person is and the more time that person spent learning in a yeshiva (a school for traditional Jewish studies), the more biased and distorted that person's views will be concerning who Jesus is, what he taught, and how he and his followers lived. This gives us all the more reason to set the record straight with the facts and nothing but the facts.

2. What we call "traditional Judaism" today was only in its formative stage two thousand years ago. Therefore, the Messianic Jewish faith is basically as old as the Rabbinic Jewish faith, and in some ways, it is older.[4] Both of these religious expressions were thoroughly Jewish faiths that went different ways. Therefore, they have much in common. However, since it was the Rabbinic faith that became recognized as "mainstream Judaism," and since this faith stood in opposition to belief in Jesus, it became dogma that belief in Jesus and true Judaism were incompatible.

But the question must be asked: Who determined that Rabbinic Judaism was the true Judaism? Who decided that the teachings of the rabbis were Jewish while the teachings of the disciples of Jesus were not Jewish? That is almost like the apples saying to the oranges, "Only apples are fruit, therefore oranges are not fruit." Says who? The real question is, What do the Hebrew Scriptures teach? Which Jewish expression follows the Bible? That must be the rule of Jewish faith and practice.

Regardless of what anyone tells you today, no Jew keeps the Torah as it was originally given. It is simply not possible. Changes have had to be made in our relationship to the law since we have had no temple, no functioning priesthood, and no sacrifices for more than nineteen hundred years, during which time most Jews have been living outside of the land of Israel. This means some things *must* have changed. According to the rabbis, we now have the Talmud and Rabbinic writings as our guide. According to Jewish believers in Jesus, we have the writings of the new covenant (New Testament). Which of these is to be followed? The answer: that which is faithful to the Hebrew Scriptures and recognizes the true Messiah.

In dealing with many of the objections raised in this book, you will see that the traditional Jewish side assumes what it wants to prove, namely, that it alone represents true Judaism. Therefore, it is important to point out that not everything that claims to be Jewish is biblical. It is true that Orthodox Judaism rejects Jesus and his teachings, but is it right in God's sight to do so? It may be Jewish in the traditional sense to deny that Jesus is the Jewish Messiah, but that is only because that particular form of Jewishness deviated at some key points from the Hebrew Scriptures. It is better to be biblical than Jewish—when and if that choice arises.

There is another side to the story as well. In the last few decades, Jewish scholars have increasingly recognized that Jesus and his followers were faithful Jews. In fact, many scholars—both Jewish and Christian—argue that if you really want to understand the New Testament, you must read it against its first-century Jewish background. Many Jewish traditions are actually in harmony with the teachings of the New Testament, regardless of which came first and which came second. Also, Jewish traditions concerning important subjects such as the nature of God, how he reveals himself to man, and the atoning power of the death of the righteous shed light on fundamental Christian teachings. In other words, Christianity is a lot more Jewish than many people realize!

Putting this all together, when answering some objections we must respectfully say, "I appreciate your traditions and interpretations, and I know you think they are authentically Jewish, but in fact they are not in harmony with the Hebrew Scriptures." At other times our answer is very different: "Look at your own traditions. They are my traditions too! They say the same thing I'm trying to say. Maybe you just never considered them in the context of belief in Yeshua and the New Testament."

3. As the Messianic Jewish faith developed and grew, it began to fulfill one of its key, biblical functions, namely, making the God of Israel known to the nations. As a result, there was a great influx of Gentiles into the community of believers, and because the Messiah had given his life for Jew and Gentile alike, the Gentiles were not

required to become Jews in order to join this community of faith. Soon enough, the Gentiles made up the vast majority of Messianic believers, and so to all outward appearances, the faith began to look like a new, Gentile religion and certainly not a faith for Jews. This was one of the factors that made it easier for the rabbis to conclude that belief in Jesus was a Gentile rather than a Jewish thing. In other words, Jesus is not for us!

Along with this historical chain of events, many Gentile believers began to sever their ties with the Jewish people, cutting off the Jewish roots of their faith. Soon, Christianity had lost all connection with its Jewish heritage, and the Jesus of Christianity hardly resembled the Messiah of the Bible. In fact, new teachings were brought in and new practices developed, some of them with pagan roots. This made it even harder for Jews to recognize Jesus as the Messiah of Israel, making the gap between Jesus and the Jewish people even wider.

Thus, many Jewish objections to Jesus are actually objections to Christendom—by which I mean the diluted and often polluted faith that began to develop several hundred years after the New Testament was completed. Real Christianity is completely biblical, and in that way, "Jewish" in the best sense of the word. It has plenty of room for Jews to live as redeemed Jews and Gentiles to live as redeemed Gentiles. But most Jews today don't know what real Christianity (or true Messianic Judaism) is. To answer their objections, it is important to shatter some of the myths and explain what we really believe. In some cases, we don't believe in "Christianity" either.

When considering fundamental doctrines that are unacceptable to Jews—such as the divinity of the Messiah or atonement only through his blood—we must separate what we really believe from what our Jewish friends and adversaries perceive we believe, always going back to Scripture and asking, What does the Word of God say? You would be amazed to see how many times basic doctrines of our faith, beliefs that seem so fundamental to us, are grossly misunderstood or caricatured by our opponents.

4. Tragically and pitifully, as the church became powerful in society, beginning in the fourth century c.e., it began to persecute those who refused to believe in its version of Jesus—by this time a distorted, hardly Jewish Jesus—leading to centuries of bloodshed and atrocities committed against the Jewish people by those who claimed to be Christians. The horrible story of "Christian" anti-Semitism, one of the great tragedies in human history, settled things completely for many Jews. "This Jesus is the cause of most of our troubles in the

world today, and Christianity is a religion of hate not love. It is anything *but* the true Messianic faith."

Through the centuries, many Jews have chosen to be tortured, exiled, and even killed rather than become Christians. For them, this was the noble, Jewish way to die. For them, this was the deepest act of loyalty to the God of Israel and the people of Israel. As a result, many Jewish objections to Jesus are shot through with emotion. "I won't betray my ancestors! I won't apostatize!" Even the Holocaust is perceived by many Jews as a "Christian" event—or at least an event made possible by historic "Christianity." It is important to fully acknowledge the terrible crimes committed by so-called Christians in Jesus' name, to utterly renounce them, and to explain that our goal is not to get Jewish people to convert to a foreign, alien religion but rather to be faithful to the God and Messiah of the Hebrew Scriptures.

It is also important to point out something that very few Jews know: Genuine Christians have been and continue to be the truest and best friends Jewish people will ever have. How I wish I could bring rabbis and anti-missionaries from around the world to meet Christians in India, Korea, Finland, Kenya, Bolivia, Guatemala, Germany, the Netherlands—the list goes on and on—who have a supernatural, sacrificial love for the Jewish people. This love was placed in their hearts by the Holy Spirit, in many cases as soon as they believed in Jesus and received new life through him. As a young Malaysian Christian woman said to me in 1992, "We don't know much about the Jews. [Remember that Malaysia is predominantly Muslim.] We just know that we love them!" Little by little, the true church is showing its true colors, and those true colors will one day produce a rainbow of light, love, and hope for the Jewish people.[5]

This Book Is for You!

I have written this book for several potential readers. I'm sure you fit in somewhere.

First, this is a resource book for everyone who is interested in reaching the Jewish people with the good news of Jesus the Messiah. While it is both our mandate and privilege to tell the whole world about Jesus, and while it is true that hundreds of millions of people have never even heard his name, we must not forget about the Jewish people. The Scriptures actually encourage us to make Jewish evangelism a priority. This is not because we get some special prize for our efforts—as if a born-again Jew were some kind of trophy—nor is it because winning a Jew to the faith proves we are "right,"[6] nor is it because God loves the Jews more than any other people. But the Jews are the ones with whom the ancient covenants were made, the people from whom the prophets came, and the nation from which the Messiah traces his earthly origin. If anyone needs to hear the truth about Jesus, it is his own Jewish people. So while we continue to actively and sacrificially reach out to all the nations, we must continue to reach out in love to the lost sheep of the house of Israel.

Reading this book will sensitize you to various Jewish perspectives and encourage you to share your faith with wisdom. In the process of reading and learning, I believe you will also find some aspects of your own beliefs that need fine tuning and adjusting. That's all right too. None of us have totally arrived in terms of our understanding of God and his Word.

Second, this book is written for those Jewish believers who have been confused and befuddled by the anti-missionaries. The answers here will combat the apparent truth of the anti-missionaries with the real truth of Scripture.

Some of you were once fervent, committed believers, telling others about Jesus without hesitation or doubt. Now you're not sure who's right. You want to be a faithful Jew, and now you're wondering if your belief in Jesus is idolatrous. Have you become part of a foreign religion? Are all your prophetic proofs as reliable as a rope of sand? Do the New Testament writings that once seemed so precious to you now appear to be full of holes? Have you betrayed your family, your ancestors, and worst of all, your God by believing in Jesus? Are the rabbis really right when they tell you they have an oral tradition of interpretation going all the way back to Moses? Do you find it difficult even to pray? After all, maybe if you don't pray in Jesus' name, God won't hear you. On the other hand, maybe if you *do* pray in Jesus' name, he won't hear you! What do you do?

Well, there's no need to be afraid or uptight. God is near, and he is not worried about religious formulas. He's looking at your heart. If you're sincere, he knows it, and that's what matters most. Have an honest talk with him. Tell him you want to follow him and serve him and obey him with all your being, no matter what the cost. Then read through this book carefully with your Bible in hand and get ready to have your faith restored. If you can read Hebrew, better yet. You will see even more clearly that there are answers—sound answers—for every objection raised.

The truths stated in the pages that follow have helped numerous struggling believers recover their faith. They have also been used by God to help bring open, seeking Jews into a knowledge of the truth about Jesus our wonderful Savior and to enable some Orthodox Jews to embrace the one whom they had rejected all their lives. Prepare to be encouraged!

This leads me to address the last—but certainly not the least—group for whom this book was written, namely, Jews of every background—Reform and Hasidic, Humanist and Conservative, Orthodox and Reconstructionist—who do not yet believe that Jesus is Israel's promised Messiah.

I want you to know that I'm really glad you're reading this book, whatever your motivation might be. Even if you want to use it to strengthen your convictions and beliefs *against* Jesus, I'm still glad you have the book in your hands. It is my fervent prayer for every reader, Jew or Gentile, Catholic priest or Orthodox rabbi, nominal Christian or atheistic Israeli, that each one see the truth clearly. As one of the world's most influential Jews wrote almost two thousand years ago, "We cannot do anything against the truth, but only for the truth" (2 Cor. 13:8). Who would knowingly fight against the truth?

Maybe you feel sure of your position, or maybe you have secret, inner questions and doubts. Maybe you're seeking answers, or maybe you're looking for ammunition. I ask you this one thing: Are the responses provided in the pages that follow the truth? Are they in accordance with the Hebrew Scriptures? Are they fair and honest? I'm sure you will agree as you read this book that I fully understand the objections. Maybe I've even articulated them for you! But what about the *answers* to the objections? What about the case *for* the messiahship of Jesus?

For years I was told there was no validity to the Christian claim that Jesus fulfilled the Messianic prophecies of the Hebrew Scriptures. Sincere rabbis explained that after Jesus lived and died, the authors of the New Testament went back and found so-called Messianic prophecies in the Hebrew Bible and made them fit the life of Jesus perfectly, and, where necessary, they adjusted the facts about Jesus' life and death to make him fit the prophecies.

"So you see," the rabbis explained, "there's no truth to your claims at all. It's like a man who shot arrows at a target and then afterward painted bull's eyes around the arrows. Someone just made it seem as if Jesus hit the bull's eye of prophetic fulfillment." Wrong! Jesus hit the bull's eye perfectly, but someone moved the target. I can show you this is true. Will you be bold enough to find out for yourself?

For years I was told, "There is no substance to your arguments. You give lots of proofs, but all of them are false, so zero plus zero plus zero equals zero." Well, what if I can show that it is the *objections* to the messiahship of Jesus that have no weight? What if you begin to see that all the objections listed here have the sum total of zero? What excuse will you give then for not believing in Yeshua?

Just because you were born into a certain religion does not make that religion right. Hundreds of millions of people are born Hindus, which means they are born into a religion that worships thousands, even millions, of gods. Let's say you approached a sincere Hindu and said, "These idols are not gods. A monkey or cow is not a god. A snake is not a god." And he responded, "For countless generations, all my ancestors have believed in these gods. Who are you to say they have all been wrong? And who am *I* to question *them?* These traditions are sacred. Our beliefs are holy and very deep." How would you react to that kind of reasoning? You would say, "The poor soul! May God open his eyes to the truth."

Well, let's put the shoe on the other foot now. I'm telling you that Jesus is the Messiah prophesied in the Hebrew Bible and that there are definitive answers to the many Jewish objections lodged against him. How do you know I'm wrong? Pause for a moment and give it some honest thought. Maybe you weren't born into an idol-worshiping family, but what makes you so sure that all your traditions are right? What makes you so sure that the sentiments you have against Jesus are correct? Could it be that the reason you claim my position is illogical or stupid or unworthy of serious consideration is precisely because you never gave it serious consideration? Could it be that all you know is a gross caricature of the real Jesus?

Consider what many people believe about the Jews. Millions of Japanese today actually think that Japan's economic problems are the fault of the Jews. "But," you say, "the vast majority of Japanese people have never even met a Jew."[7] Exactly! That's the problem. In the same way, during the Middle Ages, some people actually thought Jews had horns. How could they believe something so preposterous? Simple. Reliable people told them it was so, and more importantly, they didn't know any Jews personally (or they didn't know one whose head wasn't covered—obviously to hide those horns!). The only Jew many people around the world today actually know is a gross caricature of the real thing, whose montrous image is based on rumor, innuendo, misunderstanding, and lies.

It's the same thing with Jesus. The only Jesus many Jews know is a monstrous figure, a false prophet, a liar and deceiver, a traitor and the founder of a terrible, counterfeit religion, one whose followers are the cause of worldwide anti-Semitism and even the Holocaust. That is not the real Jesus! That is not the Yeshua of history or the Yeshua of the New Testament or the Yeshua of reality. It is an ugly, distorted, and warped picture that bears no resemblance to the actual person. Could it be that you have the same biased, unfounded views of Yeshua the Jew that other people have about you as a Jew? The only way to overcome this kind of ignorance and bias is by exposure to the truth, even if that truth hurts.

What if you find the very problems you have had with Jesus solved on the pages that follow? What if your strongest objections are answered—even if you don't want them to be answered? What will you do with the truth? No doubt, you might be confronted with some difficult choices. You might encounter tremendous opposition and misunderstanding if you recognize Jesus as Messiah. If you are Orthodox you might suffer extreme rejection and even persecution. It will be worth it all. You will have the blessing of the Messiah and the favor of God. You will be a brand-new person through him. You will have a message of fresh hope—the very message of true redemption—for your fellow Jews. The burden of your sin and guilt will be removed, and you will experience a genuine change of heart. You will begin to have a real, deep relationship with God your Father, and you will enjoy his favor forever.

So read on! You never know what you might learn and who you might encounter along the way. The Messiah—the *real* Messiah—is nearer than you think.

PART 1

GENERAL
OBJECTIONS

1.1. Jews don't believe in Jesus.

That is a serious misconception as well as a gross over-statement. Jews have always believed in Jesus. In fact, in the beginning, it was *only* Jews who believed in him, and today, there are probably more Jewish believers in Jesus than ever before.

Although you may not be aware of this (I certainly wasn't for the first sixteen years of my life), it is common knowledge to both Jewish and Christian historians that all of Jesus' original followers were Jews, and within a few years after his death and resurrection, thousands of Jews believed in him. At first the question was, "Can you be a Gentile and believe in Jesus?" That's how Jewish this whole thing was! (Read Acts 15 for more information.)

Since then, in every generation there has been a faithful remnant of Jews who have followed Jesus the Messiah, numbering from the thousands into the tens of thousands, and they have maintained their faith in spite of often difficult consequences. Right now, there are as many as 150,000 to 200,000 Jewish believers in Jesus worldwide (this is probably a conservative estimate), including American Jews, Russian Jews, South American Jews, and Israeli Jews. Many of them are highly educated, and some are ordained rabbis. Jews *do* believe in Jesus, and their numbers are growing by leaps and bounds.

1.2. I was born a Jew and I will die a Jew!

You're absolutely right! You were born a Jew, and whether you believe in Moses, Jesus, Muhammad, Sigmund Freud, or Rev. Moon, you'll always be a Jew. The question is, Will you be a faithful Jew in God's sight? That's what really matters. You must never forget that as a Jew you have a special calling and responsibility. Will you fulfill the purpose for which God made you? Being a Jew is no small thing. Will you live and die in right relationship with God? Will you love him with all your heart and soul and strength? And if what we're telling you about Jesus being the Jewish Messiah is really true (and we're quite sure it is), will you be a faithful Jew who follows your Messiah or an unfaithful Jew who rejects him?

Can I ask you a simple question? Who is a Jew? If you give the traditional answer, namely, you are Jewish if your mother is Jewish, you really haven't answered anything. What makes your mother Jewish?

Is being a Jew simply a religious matter? If so, are atheistic Jews still Jews? Are humanistic Jews still Jews? And what of Reform Jews who deny that the Torah is literally the Word of God and who don't believe in a physical resurrection or a literal Messiah? Are they still Jews? Is being a Jew simply a matter of ethics? If so, is an unethical, corrupt Orthodox rabbi still a Jew? Is being a Jew a matter of solidarity with the people of Israel? Then what of antinationalist Israelis? Are they still Jews? Is being a Jew simply a matter of ethnicity? If so, then one's religious beliefs can't change one's Jewishness.

Again, the question must be asked, Who is a Jew? It's important not to use a double standard here. For example, if you're a secular Jew and you do not live by the Torah or the Rabbinic traditions, how can you tell me that I'm not Jewish because I believe in Jesus? You might say, "But you have joined another religion!" I answer: No, I'm following the religion of the Scriptures. And according to the Torah, the issue is not one of "different religion" but of lifestyle and faith. God is not so much concerned with what "religion" we identify ourselves with—the word *religion* doesn't even occur once in the entire Hebrew Scriptures—as much as with what we believe and how we live. In fact, from a biblical viewpoint, being an atheist or a materialist or a sensualist constitutes infinitely more of a departure from the faith than entering into disputes about who the Messiah is.

I follow the Word of God and love the Lord with all my heart and soul. Do you? If not, how can you tell me I'm not a Jew? (By the way: Both my mother and father are Jewish.) I have given my life to make the God of Israel known to the nations. Have you? If not, how can you tell me I'm not a Jew? I worship the God of Abraham, Isaac, and Jacob every day, praying to him and studying his Scriptures constantly. Is that your lifestyle too? If not, how can you tell me I'm not a Jew? I have turned away from living for self-gratification and sinful pleasure, seeking to be holy because the Lord is holy. What about you? You must ask yourself whether you are really living as a faithful Jew in God's sight.

If you are Orthodox, you probably have no problem recognizing me as a Jew. In fact, you might even identify me with the special—but hardly flattering—label "apostate Jew."[1] Even anti-missionaries recognize that Jewish followers of Jesus are still Jews, targeting us in particular with their outreach efforts. They certainly aren't investing this kind of time and effort in reaching *Gentile* Christians!

In the end, the real question is *not* whether Jews who follow Jesus are still Jewish. Rather, the crucial question is whether Jesus is the Messiah predicted by Moses and the prophets. If he is, then you, as a Jew, must do some real soul-searching and answer a difficult, challenging question: How can you call yourself a Jew and yet reject or ignore our God-sent Jewish Messiah? Following the Messiah is part of the fabric of our soul, touching on the very reason for our existence as a people.[2]

You see, one of the key reasons the Lord put the Jewish people on this earth was so that we could be a nation of priests *(kohanim)*, spreading the light of the knowledge of God to the rest of the world. In other words, instead of keeping the truth to ourselves, we were called to declare the glory of the Lord to the Gentiles and educate them in his truth.[3] The Scriptures speak of this clearly:

> You yourselves have seen what I did to Egypt, and how I carried you on eagles' wings and brought you to myself. Now if you obey me fully and keep my covenant, then out of all nations you will be my treasured possession. Although the whole earth is mine, *you will be for me a kingdom of priests* and a holy nation.
>
> Exodus 19:4–6

> Sing to the LORD a new song;
>   sing to the LORD, all the earth.
> Sing to the LORD, praise his name;
>   proclaim his salvation day after day.
> *Declare his glory among the nations,*
>   *his marvelous deeds among all peoples.*
> For great is the LORD and most worthy of praise;
>   he is to be feared above all gods.
>
> Psalm 96:1–4

Yes, the people of Israel were to be a light to the world. This is part of our destiny and calling as Jews, and it is only through the Jewish

Messiah that we can fulfill this God-ordained task.[4] This is something you need to consider. In fact, it may help you to understand why you sometimes have wondered about your very identity and purpose in life. What does it mean to be born a Jew? Why are we here? Why have we experienced so much trouble with so little positive fruit? What is our mission after all? Is there something we have been missing—or *someone* we have been missing?

I know this may be a hard pill to swallow, but it's really important that you give this some careful thought. Is it possible that this Jesus-Yeshua whom you so strongly reject is the key to bringing the knowledge of the only true God to the inhabitants of this planet? Is it possible that true Jewishness is directly tied in with following him?

Think about it. It will do you—along with many others too—a world of good.

1.3. A person is either Jewish or Christian. I'm Jewish.

You're mixing apples with oranges. People are born Jewish or Gentile, but in order to become a Christian (or "Messianic") you must be born anew. This new birth comes through putting your faith in Jesus the Messiah. Your sins are forgiven, you receive a new heart, and you become a follower of the Messiah. That's what it means to be Christian, or Messianic. But no one is born Christian. That's where the misconception lies. Nor is Christianity (or Messianic Judaism) merely another religion. Rather, it speaks of a living relationship between God and his people— both Jews and Gentiles—through the Messiah. Through physical birth you are either Jew or Gentile; through spiritual birth you become a follower of Jesus the Messiah.

It might help you to remember that the word *Christian* comes from the word *Christ*, which is derived from the word *christos*, the Greek equivalent of the Hebrew word *mashiach* (Messiah). Interestingly, it was a good number of years before the first followers of Jesus were called Christians (or Messianics), a term apparently coined by outsiders and critics (Acts 11:26; see also 1 Peter 4:16). No one is born a Christian, although children can obviously be born into Christian homes. As one preacher said: Just because the kitten was born in the cookie jar doesn't make it a cookie! So also, just because someone was born in a Christian home that doesn't make him a Christian. It is only when someone completely identifies himself with the Messiah Jesus that he becomes Messianic, or Christian.

In a similar way, someone may be born Jewish, but that does not make that person a practicing or religious Jew. A person becomes practicing or religious by choosing to live a certain lifestyle. That's how it is—although in a more profound way—with following Jesus the Messiah (i.e., Christ) and becoming Messianic (i.e., Christian). Whether you're Jewish or Gentile, you must be born anew through faith in him. The ultimate question, therefore, is not whether you're Jewish or Gentile but whether you are of the Messiah or not.

1.4. Doesn't belief in Jesus mean you're no longer Jewish? As I understand it, belief in Jesus and Jewishness in any form are incompatible.

> You have unknowingly repeated one of the great lies of the Inquisition, namely, that one can be faithful to Jesus only by totally repudiating one's Jewishness. To the contrary, everything about belief in Jesus was and is Jewish, in the purest and most biblical sense of the word.

I understand what you're thinking. You obviously believe that Jesus was the founder of a new religion called Christianity, a religion for the Gentiles. And so, if a Jew follows this "goyyische" (Yiddish for "Gentile") religion he is no longer a Jew. Right? This would be like a Hindu becoming a Muslim. We wouldn't call him a Hindu for Muhammad, would we? Why then do we call ourselves Jewish believers in Jesus, something our critics call a contradiction in terms? The answer is simple: Jesus is the Jewish Messiah, the one spoken of in our Hebrew Bible. Believing in him is the most Jewish thing a Jew can do.

Let's think this through for a moment. Although Yeshua came into the world that all people might be saved from their sins and brought into right relationship with God, he came first and foremost for his own Jewish people. It was only when we rejected him *as a nation*— just as, centuries earlier, we rejected the Torah and the prophets as a nation—that his message was taken to the Gentiles, who embraced him by the thousands. In time, there were so many Gentile believers in the Messiah—many of whom forgot the Jewish, biblical roots of their faith—that it almost seemed as though Christianity was a new, foreign religion, something not for Jews at all.[5]

What made matters even worse was that the emerging Rabbinic Jewish community began to disassociate itself from the many thousands of Jews who were followers of Jesus the Messiah. These Messianic Jews now found themselves between a rock (the increasingly Gentile church) and a hard place (the increasingly unfriendly Rabbinic community). Over the course of the next thousand years, Gentile Christians began to welcome Jews into their midst only if they renounced all ties to their Jewishness, while the Rabbinic community would welcome them only if they renounced all ties to Jesus. You need to see this for what it is: a monstrous perversion of the truth and a tragic twist of history.

Do you remember what happened after the Vietnam War? It was bad enough that we fought a war we had little intention of winning. It was bad enough that so many lives were lost. But there was something even worse: As these courageous veterans returned from the jungles of Vietnam—many of them mentally and physically scarred, others now addicted to drugs—we gave them almost no welcome. We were embarrassed about the war, and we took out our shame on them. Rather than welcoming them back as heroic Americans (as we did with our previous veterans), we almost disassociated ourselves from them, and many of them never recovered from that emotional wound. They of all people should have been embraced by their fellow Americans, in whose name they went to Vietnam and under whose flag they fought.

Now, there is something strangely similar about the fate of Jewish followers of Jesus. The Jewish apostles brought the message of the Jewish Messiah to the Gentile world, and yet, centuries later, these Gentile Christians told Jews who wanted to know more about Jesus, "If you want to believe in him, you must abandon everything Jewish!"[6] Jews who were baptized during the Middle Ages even had to promise to eat pork.[7] Talk about forgetting your roots! In fact, when it was alleged that one of the medieval popes was actually Jewish, Bernard of Clairvaux exclaimed, "To the shame of Christ, a Jew now occupies the seat of St. Peter." Really! (By the way, this "St. Peter" is none other than Shimon Kepha, the *Jewish* fisherman who became one of the first disciples of Jesus.) So it was that, figuratively speaking, Jews helped build the house from the foundations up, and then they were told that as Jews they were not welcome.

After the forced conversions of the Crusades, some Jews outwardly professed faith in Jesus while secretly practicing Judaism. It was one of the purposes of the Inquisition to weed out and destroy these people even if, in theory, there were sincere Jewish Christians who believed that faith in Jesus and being Jewish were compatible. Unfortunately—and I'm sure, quite unknowingly—you have repeated the lie of the Inquisition.[8]

As in the case of the Vietnam veterans, Jewish people have often treated Jewish Christians as if there is something wrong with us, as if, by being loyal to our God and our Messiah, we are sinning. Instead of recognizing that we have had to go against the grain of tradition (both Jewish and Christian) for the sake of the truth, and instead of understanding that our faith in Jesus has caused us to rediscover just how Jewish we are (see below, 1.5, for more on this), Jews have called us deceivers, mercenaries, and apostates. In fact, by the end of the first century, there is evidence that religious Jews were taught to curse Jewish Christians three times daily in their prayers, a practice that persists (in some circles) to this day. (This practice was instituted at least two centuries before the persecution of Jews by so-called Christians. At some point toward the end of the first century, some of the Rabbinic leaders either composed or adapted a prayerful curse to be recited against believers in Yeshua—specifically Jewish believers in him.)[9]

Of course, we are willing to suffer these things and we embrace them gladly (see Matt. 5:10–12; Acts 5:41; Phil. 1:29; Heb. 13:12–14). Jesus even told us that we would be put out of the synagogues and that whoever killed us would think he was doing God a service (John 16:2). The fact is, however, that belief in the *real Jesus* (i.e., the Yeshua of the Bible and not the one of later, man-made tradition) and *true Jewishness* (which does not always equate with *traditional Jewishness*) are compatible, and when a Jew embraces Yeshua the Messiah, he becomes more Jewish than ever before. Just ask any of a thousand Jewish followers of Jesus what happened in their lives once they believed in him. You'll be amazed at what you hear.

The bottom line is this: Being a faithful Jew and believing in Jesus the Jewish Messiah are totally compatible.

1.5. Messianic Judaism, or Hebrew Christianity, is just one big deception, designed to lure unsuspecting

Jews into Christianity. Half of the people involved are not even Jewish. Most of those who are Jewish were Christian ministers who changed their names to sound more authentic.

> Maybe a bad experience with a Messianic Jew has given you a wrong impression of the whole. Is it possible you have misjudged our hearts and motives without knowing the facts? Most Jews who have come to know Jesus as Messiah have experienced a deep reawakening of their Jewishness. Many have recovered aspects of the biblical Jewish lifestyle, while others have made *aliyah* (i.e., emigrated to Israel) for life. In fact, their children now attend Israeli schools and fight in the Israeli army. It is because these people have so deeply recovered their Jewishness that some of them have changed their names—e.g., from Martin to Moishe. Others changed their names so as to refute the lie of past "Christian" anti-Semitism, which said, "You can't be Jewish and believe in Jesus." As for the Gentile believers who have joined Messianic Jewish congregations, they have done so out of love for Israel and Jewish life. Is this wrong?

I'm a little surprised that you're repeating the standard party line about Messianic Jews being deceptive. It would be one thing if, for example, we tried to lure newly emigrated Russian Jews into a "Jewish education program" without identifying ourselves as believers in Yeshua, or tried to present ourselves as traditional synagogues with a distinct approach to Torah and nothing more. Such practices would be deceptive, and I (along with all Messianic Jewish leaders whom I know personally) would never think of engaging in such dishonest activities.

But is it true that Jews who believe in Jesus call themselves Messianic Jews, Hebrew Christians, or Jews for Jesus because they don't want other Jews to know they are really just Christians masquerading in Jewish garb? Are we merely trying to hide the fact that, in actuality, we have committed what Rabbi Aryeh Kaplan called "an act of religious treason"? Of course not! We put our cards right on the table for everyone to see. We say that we are Jewish followers of Jesus the Messiah because that is who we are. We find being Jewish and believing in the Jewish Messiah to be compatible (see above, 1.5). As a result, we make every effort to communicate this clearly.

Let me turn it around and ask you this: If you as a Jew discovered that Jesus was the Messiah predicted by Moses and the prophets and you believed in him, experiencing a glorious personal change, a renewed love for the God of Abraham, Isaac, and Jacob, a passion for the Hebrew Bible, and a fresh attachment to the people and land of Israel, would it occur to you to say, "I'm no longer Jewish"? What if you came to realize that Christianity in its root form is actually Jewish, or, as some modern scholars have expressed, another of the first-century Judaisms?[10] As a brand-new follower of Jesus the Messiah, wouldn't you feel deeply that as a Jew, you had really come home?

Even if you accept what I'm saying *in general,* you might still question specific Messianic Jewish practices. I want to address these issues honestly. First, however, as an "insider," let me tell you that there is constant discussion among many Messianic Jews about subjects such as how to observe the Sabbath in light of the new covenant, the ongoing relevance of the dietary laws *(kashrut),* or whether to incorporate some of the Rabbinic liturgy into weekly worship services. Such themes are discussed at our annual Messianic Jewish conferences as well as in Messianic periodicals and books.[11]

Messianic Jewish leaders wrestle with these issues because they feel a responsibility to do so as Jews. They are not engaging in theological, biblical, and practical debates among themselves so as to win Jews to their faith. They would continue to deal with these issues even if there were not another Jew on the planet. I know this firsthand because I have often talked with Messianic Jewish leaders about these very things, telling them they are spending too much time on them. Loyalty to God, not deception, is their goal.

Here is a description of why many Messianic Jews do what they do, both in their corporate worship services as well as in their private and family lives. I do not necessarily agree or disagree with all the particulars but simply state the facts.

1. We often use terms such as *Messiah* instead of *Christ,* or *Yeshua* instead of *Jesus* because for many Jews, *Jesus Christ* represents a non-Jewish religious figure, namely, the founder of the Catholic Church and the inspiration behind the Crusades. It is because we want Jews to think about the *real* Jesus—the one who came in fulfillment of the Hebrew prophets, the Jewish Redeemer, and the founder of the Mes-

sianic faith for all peoples—that we call him Yeshua the Messiah. It is done for the sake of clarity, not duplicity.

2. We often use Hebrew songs and prayers in our services because many of the songs are taken directly from the Hebrew Bible and many of the prayers date from the days of Jesus and earlier (e.g., the Shema). These elements are not merely borrowed from later Rabbinic tradition. They serve to remind worshipers that our faith is indeed the continuation of the faith of our fathers—Abraham, Moses, David, and the Messiah. Also, while Christians frequently sing the same words from the Old Testament in English in their worship services, many Jewish believers enjoy singing them in Hebrew. One reason—among many—that Gentile Christians often form a large part of Messianic Jewish congregations is because they enjoy the Messianic Jewish style of worship.

3. Some Messianic Jews also include later Rabbinic prayers in their services because they agree with the content of the prayers and find no reason to reject this part of their heritage. These Jewish believers in Yeshua do not believe they are part of a new, foreign religion but rather consider themselves to be part of the true Jewish remnant that is faithful to both their Jewish roots and their Jewish Messiah. Thus, some of them put on *tefillin* (phylacteries) for their private prayers, believing that Jesus prayed with them too, and wear the *tallit* (prayer shawl) and *yarmulke* (*kipa*, or skullcap) in their public services. (Some Messianic Jews wear a *yarmulke* all the time, just as Orthodox Jews do, and for similar reasons, namely, as a constant reminder that they walk before God.)

4. The traditional Jewish calendar is followed because its general accuracy is accepted.[12] (We do not automatically reject everything Rabbinic.) Virtually all Jews worldwide follow the same calendar—regardless of whether they agree with traditional Judaism on other points of faith and practice—and so we participate in the same life cycle as does the rest of the Jewish community. Similarly, some Messianic Jewish congregations follow the same weekly Torah reading schedule as do traditional Jews (apparently, it was already established in the time of Jesus), likewise reading the synagogal portion from the Prophets, but adding a reading from the New Covenant Scriptures.

5. Because the title "pastor" often sounds foreign to a Jew, and because many Jews are in the habit of calling their congregational leaders "rabbi," there are some Messianic Jewish leaders who also call themselves "rabbi." Since these leaders do not want to mislead

people, however, they sometimes use the title "Messianic rabbi." This way people know they are leaders of a Messianic congregation, i.e., a congregation that believes Jesus is the Jewish Messiah. I should point out, however, that many leaders refuse to use this title, calling themselves either "congregational leader," "Messianic pastor," or simply "pastor." They understand that the title "rabbi" conveys something very specific to a Jewish person, and they want to stay clear of any charge of deception. While they want to communicate to interested Jews that they are not a traditional church, they also want to communicate that they are not a traditional (or Conservative or Reform) synagogue either. One reason many of these congregations use the term Messianic *synagogues* is because the Greek word *synagoge* is actually used in the New Testament to describe a meeting place of believers in Jesus. In James 2:2 (actually, Jacob 2:2 in its original Greek title), the word *synagogue* simply means "a place of assembly."

6. In a similar fashion, some Messianic Jewish Bible colleges or seminaries call themselves *yeshivas,* indicating to potential students that their emphasis is in Messianic Jewish studies and ministry. However, since it has been pointed out that only Orthodox Jews use the term *yeshiva* (other branches of Judaism generally avoid this term), many Messianic Jewish leaders prefer to abandon the term as well, lest it seem they are being intentionally misleading. (In my capacity as head of such a school from 1987 to 1993, I chose—with the unanimous approval of our Messianic Jewish board—to change our name from Messiah Yeshiva and Graduate School of Theology to Messiah Biblical Institute and Graduate School of Theology, for the very reasons in question. We wanted all Christians to know that this school was for them too.)

7. The most famous change of names among Jewish believers in Jesus was that of Martin Rosen, an ordained Baptist minister, to Moishe Rosen, the founder and longtime leader of Jews for Jesus. But Moishe always put his cards on the table for all to see. While still holding to his basic Baptist beliefs, he recovered his Jewish roots and wanted everyone to know that being Jewish and believing in Jesus were compatible. (In fact, Moishe was the childhood name his mother called him.) Another famous Martin changed his name too. Martin Kahane (famous as Meir Kahane) was a militant rabbi assassinated for his political and religious views. Obviously, he recovered his Jewish roots too, only his were traditional and staunchly Zionistic. The question, therefore, is not whether such name changes are valid but

whether Jesus is the Jewish Messiah and belief in him is something authentically Jewish. If it is, then changing one's name to emphasize one's Jewishness is hardly dishonest.

Having said all this, I should point out that there is a good deal of diversity among Jewish believers in Jesus regarding the above seven points. Some are happy to be in traditional churches, while not forgetting their solidarity with Israel and their Jewish people, while others are happy to be in Messianic congregations, while not forgetting they are part of the universal Christian faith. Some are at home wearing *yarmulke* and *tallit*, while others are at home wearing a cross around their neck. Some prefer to be called Messianic Jews, others, Jewish Christians, others, Jewish believers, and some, just plain Christians. You see, what we call ourselves is not that important (although some of our detractors certainly make a big issue out of it). It is what we believe that is of central importance, and that is what we prefer to discuss.

I have just a few closing thoughts. First, I have met plenty of strange and even dishonest Orthodox and ultra-Orthodox Jews. Some yeshivas are famous for padding their attendance rolls with nonexistent students to get more money from the government, and they do it in the name of Talmud study. Yet they are totally devoted to their Talmud studies! It would be wrong, however, to judge all Rabbinic Jews by the bad example of a few. In the same way, if you did have the unfortunate experience of meeting a dishonest Messianic Jew (or worse still, a misguided Gentile Christian posing as a Messianic Jew), don't judge the rest of us by that encounter. And even among the sincere and honest, some errors have been made.

Second, 1 Corinthians 9:19–22 does not mandate deception as standard missionary practice—in spite of the statements of the anti-missionaries.[13] Paul wrote:

> Though I am free and belong to no man, I make myself a slave to everyone, to win as many as possible. To the Jews I became like a Jew, to win the Jews. To those under the law I became like one under the law (though I myself am not under the law), so as to win those under the law. To those not having the law I became like one not having the law (though I am not free from God's law but am under Christ's law), so as to win those not having the law. To the weak I became weak, to win the weak. I have become all things to all men so that by all possible means I might save some.

What Paul was talking about—and what *is* standard practice for missionaries and Christian workers around the world, regardless of what people group they are trying to reach—was the issue of cultural sensitivity. Our goal is to present the good news of the Messiah to everyone—Jew and Gentile alike. That is why many Jewish believers in Jesus have sacrificially given their lives to reaching people in India, Africa, and China. (See below, 1.12, for a few examples.) A missionary to China would learn the Chinese language and customs, adopt the dress of the people in the region, and take on as much of their lifestyle as possible (without compromising his faith). As a result, he would have more of an open door to tell them about the one true God and Jesus his Son. In the same way, a Jewish believer trying to reach Orthodox Jews might adopt the traditional food laws *(kashrut)* so as to be able to sit down at the same table with his Orthodox neighbors and tell them about Yeshua—without offending them over food issues.

Remember, the man who wrote, "To the Jews I became like a Jew, to win the Jews," *was* a Jew—and no one questioned it for a second.[14] He was saying, "In order to reach some of my people, I will take on myself traditions and practices that I don't have to—without violating my fundamental beliefs and convictions—rather than be looked on as an outsider. Is it a sacrifice? Sometimes it is, but I do it gladly because I feel I am obligated to reach everyone. I will submit myself to their customs and ways if I can help bring them into the knowledge of God." Really now, what's so terrible about this? When you look at it impartially, it's quite commendable.

I leave you with this. Our Jewish friends and critics constantly remind us of the horrible history of "Christian" anti-Semitism (see below, 2.4–2.8). On our part, we distance ourselves from this ugly history, utterly repudiating its roots and its fruits, clearly separating ourselves from any hint of such religious, "Christian" hatred. And in the process of renouncing "Christian" anti-Semitism in any and every form, we clearly reaffirm our Jewish identity. Is it fair then to call us deceptive for saying that we are *still* Jews, that we are not part of *that* church, and that we refuse to deny our solidarity with our people? Would our critics rather have us call ourselves modern-day Crusaders, burning down synagogues and persecuting Jews?

1.6. You have your religion, and I have mine. Jesus is for the Gentiles, and if he helps them, great. In

fact, Judaism teaches that the righteous of all nations have a place in the world to come. But for us, the Jewish people, we have the Torah. That is our portion.

> What an insult to the Gentiles! If Jesus did not fulfill biblical prophecy, if he is not the promised Messiah of Israel, if he was not born of a virgin, if he did not die for the sins of the world and rise from the dead, if he is not coming back as King of all kings to rule and reign here forever, then he is the Messiah and Savior of nobody. He is a false prophet and the writers of the New Testament were either deceivers or deceived. If he did do all these things, then he is the Messiah and Savior of everyone—both Jew and Gentile. As for the Torah, it remains our portion, but it is only through the Messiah that we can truly interpret it and live it out.

At the risk of repeating myself, I want to remind you that if Jesus the Messiah—Yeshua HaMashiach—is not for the Jews, then he is for nobody. The argument that Jesus is for the Gentiles is not only insulting and demeaning to them, but it is historically absurd. In fact, the life and ministry of Yeshua occurred in such a deeply Jewish context that for as many as ten years after his resurrection, his followers told only other Jews the good news that the Messiah had come and died for our sins. They thought this message of the Jewish Messiah was for Jews only! It was quite a shock for many of them to accept the possibility that Jesus was for the Gentiles too. This is basic, historical truth.[15]

Maybe an analogy will help. Let's say that the Lubavitch movement—an ultra-Orthodox Jewish movement that spans the globe but originated in Eastern Europe—continued to grow, proclaiming to Jews around the world that the Rebbe (their spiritual leader and Grand Rabbi) was the Messiah, gaining a positive hearing from some Jews and a negative hearing from others. Now, let's say that twenty years later, the Lubavitcher rabbis began to feel that they should also tell the Gentiles about the Rebbe, and millions of Gentiles began to follow him, totally eclipsing the hundreds of thousands of Jews who believed in him. Then, let's say that the rest of the Jewish community began to ostracize the followers of the Rebbe, claiming that he was not really the Messiah and saying glibly, "Look, if he helps the *goyyim* ("Gentiles" in Yiddish), that's fine, but the Rebbe is not for Jews!"

What would a surprised Lubavitcher say in response? Something like: "You've got to be kidding! If the Rebbe is not for us Jews, then he is for no one." The same is true in regard to Yeshua our Messiah.

"But," you respond, "your analogy breaks down. Jewish followers of the Rebbe continue to live a Jewish lifestyle, whereas Jewish followers of Jesus don't." A moment ago you were criticizing Messianic Jews for maintaining their Jewishness, calling us deceivers (1.5). Now you attack us for *not* maintaining our Jewishness! The facts are undeniable and indisputable: Jesus and his followers were thoroughly Jewish in the most biblical sense of the word, and Jews who have followed him through the ages have often experienced a deep reawakening of their Jewishness.[16]

As for the traditional Jewish concept that the righteous of all nations are accepted by God—regardless of their religion—it is important to remember that our Hebrew Bible gives a very dismal picture of the moral state of the human race (see vol. 2, 3.15), and it would be a real mistake to exaggerate the number of "righteous" people in the world today. Even if we use Jewish tradition as our measuring rod—remembering that this tradition is often much more liberal than the Bible when it comes to dealing with human sin—we see that the vast number of people on the earth are unrighteous. How so? They regularly violate the so-called seven laws of Noah, laws that Judaism believes are binding on all peoples of all nations.[17]

These laws, derived by the rabbis from Genesis 9:1–6 in particular, are considered to be universal in nature and forbid (1) blasphemy, (2) idolatry, (3) sexual immorality, (4) murder, (5) robbery, and (6) eating a portion of a living animal. The seventh law calls for the establishment of courts of justice. The prohibition against idolatry alone eliminates the majority of the human race throughout history along with more than two billion people today (Hindus, tribal peoples, etc.). If we add in atheists—including all of the communist world (that includes China)—then almost one billion more are contained in the number of nonrighteous.[18] If we focus on just one more law, namely, sexual immorality, it is clear that most of the human race falls seriously short of even the Rabbinic standard of righteousness. Using the Hebrew Bible as our guide, virtually no one makes the mark without divine help.

So while it is nice to make apparently broad-minded statements such as, "Judaism teaches that the righteous of all nations have a place in the world to come," the fact is that hardly anyone ends up being righteous enough! It is like the owner of a professional basketball team saying to a group of people who are under five feet tall, "We are an equal opportunity employer. We will not restrict you on the basis of color, creed, or education, and we will give a lucrative contract to any of you who can make the team." Thanks for nothing! That kind of generosity we can do without.

The simple truth is that all of us—both Jews and Gentiles—fall far short of God's mark, and that is why he was kind enough to send Jesus the Messiah to all of us.[19] Instead of condemning us for our sins, he sent the Messiah to save us from our sins. How? By living a perfect life, showing us the way to God by his deeds and words, and then dying in our place as the ransom that paid the debt we could never pay. It is through Jesus that both Jews and Gentiles become righteous. Without him, all of us are in trouble. With him—and with him alone—we have hope.

As you read on, you will be surprised to learn how the Torah, along with the rest of our Hebrew Scriptures, points to Jesus the Messiah, coming to full realization, application, and meaning through him (see, e.g., vol. 3, 4.1). Thus, it is not only the Torah that is our portion but the Torah and the Messiah that belong to us. It is our privilege to share these unspeakable treasures with the nations of the world. As Jews, we have a unique relationship to the Torah and the Messiah, but not an *exclusive* relationship. And through Jesus, we can all become children of the living God, Jew and Gentile alike, each with our special callings and gifts, yet all sinners redeemed by the same Savior. And so in the end, there will be one God, one Messiah, and one family.[20] Who could object to that?

1.7. The fundamental problem with Christianity is that it is not Judaism. Therefore, all your so-called proofs from the Hebrew Scriptures are meaningless. They are simply your interpretation not ours.

Who says Judaism is the faith that is in harmony with the Hebrew Scriptures? Who says Christianity (or Messianic Judaism) is not for Jews? Who says your interpretation is right? If Jesus is indeed the successor of Moses and the prophets, the Messiah spoken of in our Hebrew Scriptures, then the faith that acknowledges him is the proper faith for those who claim to adhere to those Scriptures. Of course, much that has been called Christianity through the years has hardly been either Christian or biblical—let alone

Jewish. But there is an authentic Christianity that is thoroughly biblical and amazingly Jewish. It is the right faith—meaning right in the sight of God—for you and for every Jew without exception.

We've already covered some of these points in our previous answers (above, 1.4–1.6), but the following thoughts should prove helpful.

As Jewish believers in Jesus we are convinced that our fore-fathers made a tragic mistake in rejecting Jesus as Messiah. To say that Christianity is not Judaism, therefore, is to miss the key question, namely, Which faith is the true, biblical faith? It is also highly misleading to say that Christianity is not Judaism, because it gives the false impression that we are dealing with two completely separate religions, when in reality we are dealing with two faiths that have much in common. For example, both faiths believe in the authority and inspiration of the Hebrew Scriptures, both faiths believe in one God, both faiths believe in the coming of a Messiah, both faiths believe in an afterlife with reward and punishment. As I mentioned previously (above, 1.5) many scholars today—both Jewish and Christian—point out that Christianity in its New Testament form was actually quite Jewish, or, as other scholars have expressed it, another of the first-century Judaisms. For this reason, some Jewish believers prefer to speak of Messianic Judaism vs. traditional Judaism—two different *Jewish* expressions of faith (see again, 1.5). This way, the key issues of dispute come into focus: Are the Jewish followers of the Messiah correct, or are the Jewish followers of the traditional rabbis correct?

Having made this broad statement, it is important to emphasize that there is much in Judaism that is positive and from God, and there is much in Christianity that is negative and man-made. This is because many Jewish traditions are based on the Scriptures or at least breathe the spirit of the Scriptures, and other traditions in Judaism are full of wisdom, beauty, and ethical value. Our people, after all, have many unique, God-given qualities and gifts. On the other hand, as Christianity departed from its biblical roots (meaning its roots in the Hebrew Bible and New Covenant Scriptures, as discussed briefly in the introduction and in 2.7), it strayed from its purity and spiritual power. In fact, while the New Testament authors emphatically reaffirmed that the Jews, of all peoples on the earth, were chosen in a special sense, teaching that God would ultimately redeem them on a national scale,[21] "Christian" authors writing centuries later taught that the Jews, of all peoples, were specially *un*chosen!

That's why it's not even accurate—let alone constructive—to say Christianity is not Judaism, because (1) not everything that calls itself Christianity is truly Christian; (2) true Christianity is very Jewish; and (3) Judaism itself is a mixed bag, with some biblical, heavenly roots and some unbiblical, earthly roots. The question is, Which faith is ultimately right and true in the sight of God?

All of us know that for more than fifteen hundred years, most Rabbinic Jews have rejected Yeshua and the New Testament. But what makes them right? Who says their interpretation is the correct one? The only thing we can do is take an honest look at the Scriptures and see what God really says.

You might say, "But who am I to differ with what my rabbi teaches and believes?" Good question! We'll answer that at some length later (see vol. 3, 6.1–6.3). For now, let me make one, simple point. I'm sure you're familiar with the Dark Ages, a time when knowledge, creativity, and learning were greatly suppressed. In those days, the church banned the translation and distribution of the Bible in the language of the people. The Bible, church leaders claimed, was not for the masses. It could be understood only by the priests. People who fought against this mind-set—men such as William Tyndale and John Wycliffe, who translated the Scriptures into the language of the people—were hunted like criminals, imprisoned, and even killed.

"That's abhorrent!" you say. "The Bible is God's Word for everyone, in particular, the Jewish people."

I agree wholeheartedly! How is it then that you as a Jew don't feel free to read the Bible on your own? Why are you dependent on someone else's interpretation? Isn't God able to lead you into the truth as you seek him with an open mind and an honest heart? In fact, isn't that the only way you can be sure you're on the right track?

If traditional Judaism is the faith of Moses and the prophets, the true and only faith for the people of Israel, then as a Jew you must follow it. But if traditional Judaism (in its overall direction) has strayed from its biblical roots, if it has made a terrible mistake throughout history in rejecting Jesus the Jewish Messiah, then you must reject those errant traditions and go back to the Word of God, the God of the Word, and the Messiah sent by God and foretold in the Word.

1.8. If Jesus is the Jewish Messiah, why don't more Jews believe in him?

Actually, there are tens of thousands of Jews who have believed and do believe in him. The problem is that most Jews have not bothered to check into the facts about Jesus, and the only Jesus most of them know is either the baby Jesus of Christmas, an emaciated figure hanging on a cross in churches, or the Jesus of the Crusades and Inquisitions. The question is, Why don't *you* believe Jesus is the Messiah? Do you really know who he is?

I encourage you to consider the following points.

1. Most Jews have never seriously studied the issue. Many of those who have decided to find out who Jesus is have been quite surprised by what they have learned. The greatest scholars and scientists in the world once believed the earth was flat—until firsthand investigation and discovery altered their outlook. It's the exact same thing with Jews who honestly investigate the Messianic claims of Jesus. Everything changes—to put it mildly.

2. If most religious Jews learn anything about Jesus in their traditional studies, it is quite biased and negative.[22] Thus, they do not entertain even the possibility of the messiahship of Jesus.

3. Many so-called Christians have committed atrocities against Jews in the name of Jesus, helping to drive Jews away from their true Messiah. (See below, 2.7, for more on this, along with my book *Our Hands Are Stained with Blood.*)

4. These same Christians have often put forth a distorted picture of Jesus that bears little resemblance to the real Messiah who walked the earth two thousand years ago. Can Jews be blamed for thinking that Christians worshiped idols when the churches were filled with worshipers bowing before large, beautiful statues depicting Jesus as a babe in his mother's lap?

5. There is often great pressure on those Jews—especially religious Jews—who put their faith in Jesus the Messiah. Some succumb to the fear, the pressure, the intimidation, the separation, and the loneliness, and they deny with their lips what they know to be true in their hearts.

6. Traditional Jewish teaching gives a slanted portrayal of who the Messiah is and what he will do. Since the description is faulty, peo-

ple are looking in the wrong direction for the wrong person. No wonder relatively few have found him.

7. Once a learned Jew does believe in Yeshua, he is discredited, and so his name is virtually removed from the rolls of history. It's almost as if such people ceased to exist. (Do you remember reading the novel *Animal Farm* in school? Revisionist history goes on to this day—even in traditional Jewish circles.) The story of Max Wertheimer provides one case in point. In the last century, Wertheimer came to the States as an Orthodox Jew, but over the course of time, he became a Reform Jew and was ordained a rabbi upon graduating from Hebrew Union College in Cincinnati in 1889. (He also received a Ph.D. from the University of Cincinnati the same year.) He then served as the greatly loved rabbi of B'Nai Yeshurun Synagogue in Dayton, Ohio, for the next ten years. When he became a fervent believer in Jesus, however, pastoring a church as well, his name was literally removed from the rolls of the school—a school of alleged tolerance at that. Why was his name dropped? According to Alfred A. Isaacs, cited in the November 25, 1955, edition of the *National Jewish Post,* Wertheimer was disowned by Hebrew Union College solely because of his Christian faith.[23] And to think, this happened in a "liberal" Reform Jewish institution!

8. Although this may be hard for you to accept, because our leadership rejected Jesus the Messiah when he came, God judged us as a people (just as he judged us as a people for rejecting his law and his prophets in previous generations), and as a result, our hearts have become especially hardened toward the concept of Jesus as Messiah.[24] Paul explained this in his important letter to the believers in Rome: "What Israel sought so earnestly it did not obtain, but the elect did. The others were hardened, as it is written: 'God gave them a spirit of stupor, eyes so that they could not see and ears so that they could not hear, to this very day'" (Rom. 11:7–8; the quote here is taken from Deut. 29:4 in our Torah and Isa. 29:10 in our Prophets).

If you stop to think about it, isn't it strange that as a people we have almost totally lost sight of the fact that Jesus-Yeshua is one of us, actually, the most influential Jew ever to walk the earth?[25] Yet most of us think of him as if he were some fair-skinned, blue-eyed European. The good news is that Israel's hardening was only partial: There have always been Jews who followed Jesus the Messiah, and in the end, our people will turn back to him on a national scale. Paul explains this a few verses later:

I do not want you [Gentiles] to be ignorant of this mystery, brothers, so that you may not be conceited: Israel has experienced a hardening in part until the full number of the Gentiles has come in. And so all Israel will be saved, as it is written: "The deliverer will come from Zion; he will turn godlessness away from Jacob. And this is my covenant with them when I take away their sins."

Romans 11:25–27; the quote is taken from Isaiah 59:20–21; 27:9; and Jeremiah 31:33–34, all in our Prophets

Hopefully, you will be one of those Jews who is determined to find out the truth about the Messiah right now, determining to follow him at any cost. In the end, you must decide for yourself, and the bottom line question is one that only you can answer: Why don't *you* believe Jesus is our promised Messiah?

What if more Jews—including your rabbi—did believe in him? Would you? Of course, that wouldn't change the facts. Either Jesus is or is not the Messiah of Israel. Public opinion can't affect the truth. But many times, when people find out that it's okay to hold to a certain opinion, they come out of the closet.

Maybe it would help you to know that many of us in Jewish work have spoken with Orthodox and even ultra-Orthodox Jews who have told us in private that they believe Jesus is the Messiah, but they are afraid to go public for fear of what could happen to them. Maybe if a number of these religious Jews—some of whom are rabbis—showed up one day on your doorstep and told you their views, it would get you to think seriously about the matter.

As we grow and mature—from infants to children to teens to adults—we find out that not everything we have been told is true. Sometimes we just have to learn for ourselves. And even as adults, we often have skewed perspectives on many things. Just look at what Democrats believe about Republicans (and vice versa) or what Palestinians believe about Israelis (and vice versa) or what Black Muslims believe about Jews (and vice versa). Our perspectives, opinions, and convictions are not always right—no matter how strenuously we argue for our position. Common sense tells us that all of us can't be right about everything all the time.

Even on an interpersonal level, how often have you met someone only to find out that all the bad things you heard about that person were greatly exaggerated or false? It happens all the time. As for the matter at hand, I assure you in the strongest possible terms: *As a Jew, most everything you have heard about Jesus has been untrue.* You owe it to yourself to find out just who this Jesus really is—and I say this to you whether you are an ultra-Orthodox rabbi reading this book in secret or you are a thoroughly secular, wealthy Jewish businessman who was given this book by a friend.

This much is certain: We have carefully investigated the claims of Jesus and can testify firsthand that Yeshua is who he said he was. What do you say?

1.9. I won't betray my ancestors! I won't forsake the faith of my fathers!

> That is a noble sentiment, and God appreciates the fact that you honor the memory of your forefathers. But the Torah is very clear: When we have to choose between loyalty to our families and loyalty to God, we must choose to be loyal to him—no matter what the consequences. If we truly love our family and our heritage, then the most noble thing we can possibly do is be faithful to God and the Messiah at any cost. In the end, we will be the shining lights in our family history. And when you say, "I can't forsake the faith of my fathers," I remind you, Abraham did.

First and foremost, each of us must obey the Lord; it is to him alone that we must give account. The prophets were often misunderstood and rejected by their families and friends. God even said to Jeremiah, "Your brothers, your own family—even they have betrayed you; they have raised a loud cry against you" (Jer. 12:6). But today, whom do we admire, the prophets who stood their ground in the midst of intense opposition or those who sided with the crowd?

Go back to Exodus 32. While Moses was still on Mount Sinai, the Torah records that the Israelites made a golden calf and worshiped it as the representation of God. When Moses came down from the mountain ablaze with holy anger, he knew that those who had sinned had to be judged.

> So he stood at the entrance to the camp and said, "Whoever is for the Lord, come to me." And all the Levites rallied to him. Then he said to them, "This is what the Lord, the God of Israel, says: 'Each man strap a sword to his side. Go back and forth through the camp from one end to the other, each killing his brother and friend and neighbor.'" The

Levites did as Moses commanded, and that day about three thousand of the people died. Then Moses said, "You have been set apart to the Lord today, for you were against your own sons and brothers, and he has blessed you this day."

Exodus 32:26–29

The Levites were honored because they stood *with* God and *against* their own families. That is the kind of allegiance he requires—not, of course, to take up swords against our loved ones, but to follow the Lord even if it means standing in opposition to our own families and friends. In fact, this was established as law in ancient Israel:

> If your very own brother, or your son or daughter, or the wife you love, or your closest friend secretly entices you, saying, "Let us go and worship other gods" (gods that neither you nor your fathers have known, gods of the peoples around you, whether near or far, from one end of the land to the other), do not yield to him or listen to him. Show him no pity. Do not spare him or shield him. You must certainly put him to death. Your hand must be the first in putting him to death, and then the hands of all the people. Stone him to death, because he tried to turn you away from the Lord your God, who brought you out of Egypt, out of the land of slavery.

Deuteronomy 13:6–10

You might want to pause for a moment and read this passage again. It demands radical loyalty and ruthless love, and it is reminiscent of the words of Jesus, although he never spoke of putting to death those who didn't follow him.[26] As the Messiah of Israel, however, he too called for absolute devotion: "Anyone who loves his father or mother more than me is not worthy of me; anyone who loves his son or daughter more than me is not worthy of me; and anyone who does not take his cross and follow me is not worthy of me" (Matt. 10:37–38).

The bottom line is that God is not waiting for our approval. Rather, we are in need of *his* approval. Are we showing ourselves worthy of him?

Do you know that in the Scriptures some of our leaders were condemned for walking in the way of their forefathers while others were commended for *not* walking in the way of their forefathers? Of the Israelite king Ahaziah, son of Ahab and Jezebel, it is written: "He did evil in the eyes of the Lord, because he walked in the ways of his father and mother and in the ways of Jeroboam son of Nebat, who caused Israel to sin" (1 Kings 22:52).

Josiah, king of Judah, was different. His father, Amon, was a proud sinner and was assassinated by his own officials. But Josiah, as a very young man, began earnestly to seek the Lord. And he was commended! Rather than walking in the ways of his father, Amon, he followed the example of his ancient forefather David: "He did what was right in the eyes of the LORD and walked in the ways of his father David, not turning aside to the right or to the left" (2 Chron. 34:2). Notice also Joshua's words to the people of Israel:

> This is what the LORD, the God of Israel, says: "Long ago your forefathers, including Terah the father of Abraham and Nahor, lived beyond the River and worshiped other gods. . . . Now fear the LORD and serve him with all faithfulness. Throw away the gods your forefathers worshiped beyond the River and in Egypt, and serve the LORD. But if serving the LORD seems undesirable to you, then choose for yourselves this day whom you will serve, whether the gods your forefathers served beyond the River, or the gods of the Amorites, in whose land you are living. But as for me and my household, we will serve the LORD.

> Joshua 24:2, 14–15

If your forefathers did not follow the Lord, if they were atheists or lawbreakers or crass materialists or followers of a strange religion, then you must break with their example—the sooner the better. And what if your parents and grandparents were devoted people? What if they were not "wicked sinners" and they did not live undisciplined and reckless lives? What if they were (or still are) religious, practicing Jews? How can you dare to break with some of their cherished beliefs? Consider this: It is possible that you have much more light than they had. Maybe they never heard the real news about the Messiah. Maybe all they heard was some dead Christian tradition masquerading as the gospel. Who knows? If they had known in their day what you know today, they might have been the first in your family to put their trust in Jesus the Messiah.

What if your ancestors were incorrect in some of their positions and traditions? What if, while seeking to be faithful to God by observing their customs, they were unfaithful to God in rejecting Jesus as Messiah? What if they realized their error when they died? More than anything else in this world, they would wish that you would not perpetuate their error. If they could watch your life right now, they would be pleading for you to do the right thing, hoping that someone in their family line would finally become a follower of the Messiah. They would be the first to tell you that being loyal to your deceased fam-

ily members is commendable but being true to the living God is infinitely more important—and absolutely indispensable. Can you violate the truth for the sake of deep sentimental ties? Will you betray
God rather than Grandma?

Maybe you lost loved ones in the Holocaust. Should those horrible, tragic days of darkness stop *you* from embracing the light? Should
yesterday's sorrows and pains hold *you* back from walking in today's
blessings? It is true that as a people we have been without the Messiah for many generations. Is that a good reason to be without him
in this generation? Or, to give an analogy, if your grandparents lived
and died in the desert, insisting with their last breath that there was
no water to be found, should *you* go thirsty as well even when you
discover a vibrant spring? If all of your honest seeking and studying
leads you to conclude that Yeshua is the prophesied Redeemer, will
you deny your convictions for the sake of your companions? Will you
put feelings before facts and emotion before evidence?

Always remember that you will have to live with your choices forever, and when you die and stand before God, no one—not your
mother or father, or sister or brother, or son or daughter—will be
there to hold your hand. Will you be able to look God in the face and
say, "I felt deep down in my heart that Jesus was our Messiah, but I
didn't want to seem disloyal to my family. Instead, I chose to be disloyal to you."

Three centuries ago, a man called the Baal Shem Tov developed a
new expression of Judaism that came to be known as Hasidism. It
was soundly rejected by the traditional leaders of the day, and his followers were even excommunicated and physically attacked.[27] Today
his adherents, called Hasidim, number in the hundreds of thousands
and are considered to be among the most traditional Jews alive. The
Baal Shem Tov is now regarded as one of the great leaders in modern Jewish history. In the beginning he was an outcast! History does
have a way of correcting itself.

To all Hasidic Jews who are reading these words, I ask each of you,
Could it be time for you to make another fresh break with the crowd
and develop a new expression of Judaism—a Messianic, new covenant
expression? How will future generations judge each of you who have
the courage to forge this new path of obedience to God at any cost?

One hundred years ago, when Theodor Herzl prophetically proclaimed the formation of a modern Zionist state, his ideas were
rejected by Jewish leaders worldwide. Fifty years later, the nation of
Israel was born. Who was right and who was wrong? When the young

Polish boy Eliezer Ben Yehudah became convinced that Hebrew was to be used as the everyday language of the Jewish people, even beginning to read secular books in his home, his own family put him out. How many millions of Hebrew-speaking Jews are there now?

From this we learn that what seems radical and outlandish to one generation often becomes regular to the next. I would urge you, therefore, not to let family pressure or the fear of breaking with the crowd stop you from pursuing the truth. One day the soundness of your choice will be evident to all.

1.10. What happens to Jews who do not believe in Jesus—especially those who never heard about him? What happened to my wonderful Jewish grandmother who never hurt anyone in her entire life? Is she in hell?

These are not questions to be answered lightly, as if heaven and hell were mere figures of speech. And, to be perfectly frank, we're not just talking about your grandmother; we're talking about my grandmother too. Still, the bottom line is this: While I don't know your grandmother and I am certainly not her judge, I do know that countless millions of Jews and Gentiles have lived lives that have displeased God (and this includes at least some of our grandmothers), countless millions of people have condemned their souls through their words and deeds, and countless millions of people will be pronounced guilty on judgment day. It wouldn't be fair to you if I failed to warn you in advance. Of course, I will be the first to say that the New Testament does not explicitly address the issue of what happens to those who never heard the message of forgiveness of sins through Jesus, but of this much we can be sure: God is both a compassionate and righteous Judge, there are consequences to breaking his commandments, his standards are high, and if we reject his ordained means of atonement, we are in trouble.

As I said, I don't know your grandmother and I am not her judge, but I can give you some guidelines that should help you evaluate the state of your own soul before God (and, possibly, think through some issues regarding Grandma too).

For starters, I would encourage you to ask yourself a couple of basic questions: What happens to Jews who do not follow the Torah? On what basis are we judged at death? According to the Five Books of Moses (specifically, Leviticus and Deuteronomy), our people would be blessed or cursed in this lifetime based on our faithful allegiance to God's laws and commands. It is an indisputable fact of history that, for the most part, we have been cursed through our disobedience rather than blessed through our obedience. (Read the Scriptures, and then keep on reading through our long, painful history.) If we have suffered such things in this world because of our sin, what does this indicate for the world to come?

Someone might argue that we suffer for our sins in this world rather than in the world to come. That, however, is not only speculation without clear biblical support, it is downright dangerous speculation. You are playing a risky game with your soul! First, suffering and punishment, in and of themselves, are not necessarily remedial or beneficial. How many incarcerated murderers are released from prison only to murder again? How many alcoholics keep on drinking even as they degenerate through alcohol-related diseases? Second, many people commit ugly, heinous sins in this life and do not suffer for them, living to a ripe old age. When will they be punished? Third, the same God who judges us here and now will be the one who judges us then and there, and his standards are lofty and uncompromising. The only legitimate question to ask yourself is this: Using God's Word as the rule, how do I measure up?

Consider the Ten Commandments. You can use them as a checklist, a kind of pre-judgment exam. How do you stand? Maybe you don't worship the silver statue of an idol, but greed and materialism are just another form of idolatry. (Gods of silver and gold take many forms!) Maybe you haven't slept with someone other than your spouse, but if you lust and fantasize after other people, you have committed adultery with them in your heart.[28] Maybe you haven't murdered anyone, but if you have hated someone, then you have committed murder in your heart. The possibility of future judgment is something you need to think about. As surely as God judged our people in the past for our sins, he will judge us in the future for our sins.

This leads to another important issue. You may make light of the concept of hell and future punishment, but I wonder if you take seriously the intensity and scope of the horrible judgments that have already fallen upon us in the past. Do you realize that the Torah and Prophets warned us that God would send terrible punishment on us if we disobeyed—yet we sinned and the judgments were poured out? And they will happen again if we follow a similar course of behavior.

These prophetic warnings are not just words on a page. The Book of Lamentations describes actual history when it says, "Young and old lie together in the dust of the streets; my young men and maidens have fallen by the sword. You have slain them in the day of your anger; you have slaughtered them without pity" (Lam. 2:21). This happened because of our sin!

In Deuteronomy 28, the Lord promised that terrible, horrific things would take place if we persistently sinned against him.

Even the most gentle and sensitive man among you will have no compassion on his own brother or the wife he loves or his surviving children, and he will not give to one of them any of the flesh of his children that he is eating. It will be all he has left because of the suffering your enemy will inflict on you during the siege of all your cities. The most gentle and sensitive woman among you—so sensitive and gentle that she would not venture to touch the ground with the sole of her foot—will begrudge the husband she loves and her own son or daughter the afterbirth from her womb and the children she bears. For she intends to eat them secretly during the siege and in the distress that your enemy will inflict on you in your cities. If you do not carefully follow all the words of this law, which are written in this book, and do not revere this glorious and awesome name—the LORD your God—the LORD will send fearful plagues on you and your descendants, harsh and prolonged disasters, and severe and lingering illnesses. He will bring upon you all the diseases of Egypt that you dreaded, and they will cling to you. The LORD will also bring on you every kind of sickness and disaster not recorded in this Book of the Law, until you are destroyed.

Deuteronomy 28:54–61

You may say, "I don't believe it!" But it happened nonetheless.

You might reply: "Well that's not the kind of God I serve." But that *is* the kind of God he will be if you scorn him and reject his Word. If you choose to go your own way and do your own thing, you *will* suffer his wrath.

Consider also Daniel 12:2: "Multitudes who sleep in the dust of the earth will awake: some to everlasting life, others to shame and everlasting contempt." This gives us a picture of what will happen to the human race in the future. And getting back to Grandma, certainly, of the multitudes who will arise to "shame and everlasting contempt" there will be countless women, many of whom were someone's grandmother—possibly mine or yours—as well as someone's mother and someone's daughter. Those are the painful, tragic facts. All the sentimentality in the world will not change this.

Like it or not, Israel's history suggests that judgment has been the norm—at least in this world. Some of our "grandmothers" died during the fall of Jerusalem in 586 B.C.E. (described so graphically in Lamentations) and during the fall of Jerusalem in 70 C.E., and both of these falls were because of our people's corporate sin.

You see, there is such a thing as wickedness before the Lord. The Hebrew Bible speaks of sinners multiplied hundreds of times, using descriptive terms such as the "wicked," the "ungodly," and the "unrighteous," just to name a few relevant terms. In other words, in God's sight, it is not just the Adolf Hitlers of the world who are unrighteous. Rather, by his standards, most human beings (including most Jews) are unrighteous (although very few are as sinful as Hitler). And this again leads me back to Grandma.

It is possible that we all tend to sentimentalize about Grandma and Grandpa—as if they never had any grievous sins in their lives and as if there wasn't even a hint of spiritual or moral corruption behind those tender eyes or within that kindly, gray head. Could it be that they seem so saintly to us because we knew them only in their old age, in a somewhat idealized relationship, and now, only from distant memories? Is it possible that when they were younger, many of them sinned too, while even in their elderly years, some of them were filled with anger, bitterness, and ugly, critical spirits?

Of course, you might say that you really did know your grandparents (or parents) well, and they were devoted Jews, living the most scrupulous, godly lives that could be lived, quick to repent when they fell short of the mark. The thought of them being in hell seems utterly incomprehensible—not to mention totally absurd—to you. That's perfectly understandable, and I remind you again: I am not their judge, nor do I set the standards for their judgment. God alone will determine their ultimate state, and my beliefs or your beliefs can't alter the facts. Either they *were* righteous in his sight or they were *not* righteous in his sight. All the arguing in the world won't change that. Either they will be resurrected to eternal life or they will be resurrected to eternal death, regardless of what you and I say. I can only point out again that, based on our performance as a people in this world, we should not be too optimistic about our fate in the world to come.

Do you agree with the biblical view that all people are not righteous but sinful? If you do agree with God's Word, then that means many of the readers of this book, along with many people whom we know personally, are in danger of suffering God's anger.

This is why Moses and the prophets warned our people about coming judgments (but we didn't listen), it is why Jesus and his disciples warned our people about coming judgments (but we didn't listen again), and it is why some Jewish leaders warned our people that the Holocaust was on the immediate horizon, urging European Jews to flee for their lives—but again we didn't listen.[29] The notion that mass murder could be carried out in sophisticated, cultured Europe was completely unthinkable. Yet it happened!

Today, we warn all people of all backgrounds that there will be a final judgment, a great day of accounting. This too will certainly happen. How will you fare on that day? Are you ready to meet the Lord?

I should also caution you here against putting your hope in some of our traditions that indicate that even the worst of us will suffer only eleven months of punishment in the world to come. Where do our Scriptures teach such a thing? The fact is they don't. Rather, as we saw from Daniel 12:2, they teach the opposite.[30]

You may be thinking, "Okay, I may not be as righteous as I sometimes claim to be (especially when I'm attending synagogue), and I admit that I may have an overly sentimental view of my forefathers. But why do you claim that it is only those who believe in Jesus who go to heaven? It just sounds like some kind of magic formula to me, and it hardly seems fair to say that people will go to hell just because they don't believe the same way you do."

That's a good point, and it deserves a good response. Here it is: All of us have sinned, all of us need a savior, and Jesus alone is that savior. All of us are guilty, all of us have become separated from God, and Yeshua alone can wipe away our guilt and bring us into a right relationship with God. Either this is true or it isn't. It's not a matter of just saying the right words ("I believe in Jesus! I believe in Jesus!"). It's a matter of true repentance, true faith, and a true change of life through the Messiah. (See below, 2.15, and vol. 2, 3.7, for more on this.) And that's why it's so urgent that we tell everyone the good news of his coming. People are literally perishing without him.

Of course, everyone will be judged according to the light that they have, but for the most part, this is more a matter of severity of guilt as opposed to acquittal. Yeshua gave a parable to this effect:

Who then is the faithful and wise manager, whom the master puts in charge of his servants to give them their food allowance at the proper time? It will be good for that servant whom the master finds doing so when he returns. I tell you the truth, he will put him in charge of all his possessions. But suppose the servant says to himself, "My master is taking a long time in coming," and he then begins to beat the menservants and maidservants and to eat and drink and get drunk. The master of that servant will come on a day when he does not expect him and at an hour he is not aware of. He will cut him to pieces and assign him a place with the unbelievers. That servant who knows his master's will and does not get ready or does not do what his master wants will be beaten with many blows. But the one who does not know and does things deserving punishment will be beaten with few blows. From everyone who has been given much, much will be demanded; and from the one who has been entrusted with much, much more will be asked.

Luke 12:42–48

According to this parable, those who knew their master's will and disobeyed will be judged more severely than those who did not know his will and disobeyed. But take notice of this: Jesus did not speak about those who simply did what was right without knowing their master's will. Rather, he exhorted us by these examples of *disobedience*. This tells us something about human nature, since the two examples given deal with different levels of disobedience and different levels of punishment, not with obedience in contrast with disobedience. Left to ourselves, we do wrong!

How then should we view the state of those (both Jews and Gentiles) who have never heard about the Messiah and Savior?[31] We should see them as people about to get on a plane we know will soon crash. It is remotely possible that one or two of the passengers will survive, but for the most part, we can assume that just about everyone who gets on board will soon die. Therefore, we should warn them not to get on that particular flight, urging them to go another way.

In terms of those who never heard about Jesus, we believe that virtually all of them are in a fallen, lost state, although there might be someone somewhere who has longed for true salvation through the one true God, finding it and finding him without a human being telling him the message. Such things can and do happen.[32] But there is no question that our responsibility as children of the one true God is to tell everyone that there is a judgment, there is a hell (Hebrew, *gehinom*), and there is a way of escape: Jesus the Messiah has paid for our sins.

Will God be fair to those who had no opportunity to believe in him or obey him? Certainly he will. (Note what Saul of Tarsus, better known as Paul, wrote about his own life: "Even though I was once a blasphemer and a persecutor and a violent man, I was shown mercy *because I acted in ignorance and unbelief*" [1 Tim. 1:13].) Speculating about specific details, however, is sheer guess work, and in point of fact, it changes nothing and profits little. Why not deal with what we know right now?

Do we believe God is being fair at this very moment? Do we believe his past judgments on our people (as recorded in his Word) were fair? If we agree he *has been* fair and he *is being* fair, then we can be confident he *will be* fair. For those who are not so sure about his past and present fairness, what makes us think our perspective is right with regard to his *future* fairness?

The bottom line is that truth is truth. To deny it does not change it. Sometimes people choose their religious beliefs so as to comfort themselves after the death of a loved one, even going to séances with the hope of talking again with their dear, deceased relative or discovering "new hope" in some kind of doctrine such as reincarnation. Anything to avoid the finality of death! But think for a moment: What if I tried to convince you that your deceased loved one didn't die, that the doctors were wrong and it was another body in the coffin? You would tell me I was crazy! You would accuse me of living in a dream world. It's the same with hell and future punishment. Changing our beliefs will not change the facts. Denying that there is a real hell will not diminish its reality.

Only God knows where our forefathers are now, and what you say or what I write can't change that one bit. This much is sure (and excruciatingly true): If our grandmothers have perished in unbelief, then their deepest desire, their most fervent, agonized request is that we do not join them, and their worst nightmare would be that we too would reject the only hope of salvation.

I certainly hope that our parents and grandparents somehow lived and died in good standing with the Lord and that they managed to receive mercy and atonement from him. But you must answer for yourself alone, and so I ask you again: What about you? Are you ready to face God? Will you be judged righteous or wicked when you die? Are you sure of your atonement? Do you know your sins are forgiven? How much do you have to suffer (in this world or the next) to pay for your misdeeds? Are you positive there is no life after death or that the traditional Jewish teaching on limited suffering in the afterlife is really true? I urge you to give serious consideration to these questions. They really are matters of life and death.

1.11. What would happen to a Nazi murderer who believed in Jesus before he died? Would he go to heaven, while the Jewish men, women, and children he killed, many of whom were God-fearing people, would go to hell?

Based on the teaching of the Hebrew Bible, *if* the Nazi could truly repent before he died, then God would accept him as righteous, but merely "believing"—without true repentance—is meaningless. As for the Jews killed by that Nazi, if they died in right relationship with God, then they would go to heaven; if they died out of favor with him, they would perish. One thing is very important to remember: The fact that these Jews died in the Holocaust does not necessarily make them "saints" (even though we often speak of the six million Jewish "martyrs" of the Holocaust). Our people were indiscriminately exterminated by the Nazis simply because of their ethnic background—even if they were atheists or God-haters. Their tragic suffering in the Holocaust did not, in and of itself, transform them into godly people. To the contrary, many actually *lost* their faith during that time, while a large number of secular and irreligious Jews became overtly hostile to God.

I know that any question regarding the Holocaust can be charged with emotion, but it's important that we think through the issues calmly and with clear heads. It will also be useful to treat the different aspects of the above questions one by one. Let's look first at the larger issue of true repentance for the worst of sinners before we deal with the specific relationship between "believing in Jesus" and "repenting."

Over twenty-five hundred years ago, the Lord spoke these words to our people through the Jewish prophet Ezekiel:

Say to them, "As surely as I live, declares the Sovereign LORD, I take no pleasure in the death of the wicked, but rather that they turn from their ways and live. Turn! Turn from your evil ways! Why will you die, O house of Israel?"

Therefore, son of man, say to your countrymen, "The righteousness of the righteous man will not save him when he disobeys, and the wickedness of the wicked man will not cause him to fall when he turns from it. The righteous man, if he sins, will not be allowed to live because of his former righteousness." If I tell the righteous man that he will surely live, but then he trusts in his righteousness and does evil, none of the righteous things he has done will be remembered; he will die for the evil he has done. And if I say to the wicked man, "You will surely die," but he then turns away from his sin and does what is just and right—if he gives back what he took in pledge for a loan, returns what he has stolen, follows the decrees that give life, and does no evil, he will surely live; he will not die. None of the sins he has committed will be remembered against him. He has done what is just and right; he will surely live.

Ezekiel 33:11–16[33]

According to the Hebrew Scriptures, if a wicked man truly turns from his wicked ways, God will completely forgive him. Of course, this doesn't mean there are no consequences for his actions. For example, a rapist who truly repents will still have to go to jail for his crime; however, God will forgive him if his repentance is real. In the same way, a Nazi could be forgiven should he genuinely turn back to God, asking God for mercy and turning from his wicked ways, although he would still be accountable for his deeds on a human level.

The Lord also spoke these words of exhortation through Ezekiel:

Repent! Turn away from all your offenses; then sin will not be your downfall. Rid yourselves of all the offenses you have committed, and get a new heart and a new spirit. Why will you die, O house of Israel? For I take no pleasure in the death of anyone, declares the Sovereign LORD. Repent and live!

Ezekiel 18:30–32

Commenting on this text, the revered medieval rabbi Jonah of Gerondi—known especially for his books on repentance—wrote that these words applied to

a man who transgressed and sinned and then came to take refuge under the wings of the divine Presence [i.e., the Shekinah] and to enter into the paths of repentance [as God said in Ps. 32:8], "I will instruct you and teach you in the way you should go." On that day he will cast away

all the transgressions he has committed and he will make himself as if
he were born on that very day, with neither guilt nor merit in his hand.

Yesod HaTeshuvah, 1:1, my translation

And lest he say, "I have sinned and sinned over and over again and
my guilt is beyond counting. I'm too ashamed to appear before God
and ask for mercy, and I could never keep his commandments," Rabbi
Jonah strongly urges him not to speak that way. Rather, he should
recognize that it is the nature of the Creator to receive penitent ones
with open arms, and therefore, he should be encouraged to repent
and reform his ways. Such is the teaching of the Hebrew Bible and
Jewish tradition.

In fact, the Talmud contains an extraordinary statement to which
a leading authority on Rabbinic Judaism, Professor Jacob Neusner,
draws attention: "Grandsons of Haman studied Torah in Bene Beraq
[a well-known city of Torah study in Israel]. Grandsons of Sisera
taught children in Jerusalem. Grandsons of Sennacherib taught Torah
in public. And who were they? Shemaiah and Abtalion [teachers of
Hillel and Shammai]" (b. Gittin 57b).

Neusner then comments:

> to understand the power of this statement, we have only to say, "Hitler's
> grandson teaches Torah in a yeshiva of Bene Beraq," or "Eichmann's
> grandson sits in a Jerusalem yeshiva, reciting prayers and psalms and
> learning Talmud." Not only so, but, to go onward with Sennacherib—
> who can stand for Himmler—and Shemaiah and Abtalion, the great-
> est authorities of their generation—who can stand for the heads of the
> great yeshivas and theological courts of the State of Israel—Himmler's
> grandsons are arbiters of the Torah, that is to say, Judaism, in the State
> of Israel. . . . The message declares that sinners who repent and seek
> reconciliation are to be forgiven. The nation that repents is to be wel-
> comed back into the company of civilization, as Germany has regained
> its honor in our day.[34]

Our Scriptures also give us examples of two extraordinarily wicked
men, Ahab king of Israel, and Manasseh king of Judah, both of whom
repented and were accepted by God. Of Ahab the Bible says: "There
was never a man like Ahab, who sold himself to do evil in the eyes of
the Lord, urged on by Jezebel his wife. He behaved in the vilest manner by going after idols, like the Amorites the Lord drove out before
Israel" (1 Kings 21:25–26).

Because of Ahab's sins, God promised to utterly destroy him, saying, "I am going to bring disaster on you. I will consume your descendants and cut off from Ahab every last male in Israel—slave or free" (1 Kings 21:21). However, Ahab repented and grieved when he heard the Lord's sentence of judgment:

> When Ahab heard these words, he tore his clothes, put on sackcloth and fasted. He lay in sackcloth and went around meekly. Then the word of the Lord came to Elijah the Tishbite: "Have you noticed how Ahab has humbled himself before me? Because he has humbled himself, I will not bring this disaster in his day, but I will bring it on his house in the days of his son."
>
> 1 Kings 21:27–29

God accepted his repentance!

The case of Manasseh is also dramatic:

> He sacrificed his sons in the fire in the Valley of Ben Hinnom, practiced sorcery, divination and witchcraft, and consulted mediums and spiritists. He did much evil in the eyes of the Lord, provoking him to anger. . . . Manasseh led Judah and the people of Jerusalem astray, so that they did more evil than the nations the Lord had destroyed before the Israelites. The Lord spoke to Manasseh and his people, but they paid no attention. So the Lord brought against them the army commanders of the king of Assyria, who took Manasseh prisoner, put a hook in his nose, bound him with bronze shackles and took him to Babylon. In his distress he sought the favor of the Lord his God and humbled himself greatly before the God of his fathers. And when he prayed to him, the Lord was moved by his entreaty and listened to his plea; so he brought him back to Jerusalem and to his kingdom. Then Manasseh knew that the Lord is God.
>
> 2 Chronicles 33:6, 9–13

I encourage you not to read these accounts lightly. Ahab and Manasseh were among the most notorious sinners spoken of in the Bible. In fact, not only were they both idol worshipers, leading the nation astray by their example, but they were both murderers! And as if Manasseh's sin of sacrificing his own sons in the fire was not awful enough, consider the fact that "Manasseh also shed so much innocent blood that he filled Jerusalem from end to end" (2 Kings 21:16). This man was wicked! He was responsible for *mass murder.* Yet the Lord had mercy on him.[35]

And so, if the Lord could accept the repentance of murderous, wicked men such as Ahab and Manasseh, could he not accept the repentance of a murderous, wicked Nazi?

At this point, you might say to me, "To tell you the truth, I don't really disagree with what you are saying. The problem is that you keep talking about repentance—which is the hallmark of *traditional Jewish* spirituality—whereas my question had to do with believing in Jesus, which is the hallmark of *traditional Christian* spirituality."[36] Well, you've made a good point. The only problem is that it is not valid, since *both* repentance and faith are hallmarks of true Christian spirituality.[37] In fact, *repent* is really the first word of the gospel message.

When John the Immerser (known in Christian circles as John the Baptist) came preaching in the wilderness of Judea, his message began with the call to repent (see Matt. 3:2). Jesus began his public preaching with the very same message of repentance (Matt. 4:17), and when he sent his disciples out to preach, they too called people to repent (Mark 6:12). After his resurrection, Jesus taught his apostles (i.e., emissaries) that repentance and forgiveness of sins formed the heart of the message they were to bring to the world, beginning at Jerusalem (Luke 24:47), and this is exactly what they declared to their Jewish people (see Acts 2:38; 3:19; 5:31; 11:18; 17:30; see also Heb. 6:1; 2 Peter 3:9). Paul—famous for his teaching on "justification by faith"—summarized his message as follows:

> I have declared to both Jews and Greeks that they must turn to God in *repentance* and have *faith* in our Lord Jesus. . . . First to those in Damascus, then to those in Jerusalem and in all Judea, and to the Gentiles also, I preached that they should *repent* and turn to God and prove their *repentance* by their deeds.
>
> Acts 20:21; 26:20

It is true there is a tremendous emphasis on faith (i.e., genuine trust) in the New Testament (see vol. 2, 3.7 and vol. 3, 4.2 for more on this), but this goes hand in hand with repentance. To repeat Paul's words, God calls all men to "turn to God in repentance"—meaning they must turn away from their disobedient ways and turn back to him—"and have faith in our Lord Jesus"—meaning they must believe in him as Savior and Messiah, trusting that his death in our place paid the penalty for our sins, just as the sacrificial animals offered up on the Day of Atonement paid for the sins of our people.[38]

Such teaching is not new or strange. Just read the Torah and the Prophets. The former emphasized the sacrificial system of atonement, the latter emphasized repentance. They are two sides of the same coin, and both called for explicit faith in the Lord as well as total obedience to his commands. The New Testament makes these very same points, adding the distinctive emphasis that our Messiah *has come* and provided both Jews and Gentiles with complete atonement through his blood. That's why the call to believe in him is so pronounced (see also vol. 3, 4.2). It is utterly impossible from a New Testament standpoint, however, to separate true faith from true repentance just as it is impossible to separate faith in the one true God from obedience to his laws from an Old Testament standpoint.

All of this means that this entire objection is based on a gross misunderstanding of the New Testament teaching on faith. Jacob, Yeshua's brother,[39] wrote about this in his letter to other Jewish believers, stating that it was pure folly to claim that one could have faith without accompanying action: "As the body without the spirit is dead, so faith without deeds is dead" (see James 2:18–26).

Simply stated: Neither Jesus nor the writers of the New Testament ever taught that someone could be saved by simply repeating a little prayer or reciting some formula.[40] Rather, they stressed that putting one's faith in Jesus meant asking God to forgive the sinner through the death and resurrection of the Messiah, thereby setting him free from bondage to sin, giving him a new heart, and starting him on a brand-new life with God as his Father and Yeshua as his Master. To "confess Jesus as Lord" (Rom. 10:9–10) without following him as Lord is as useless as reciting the Shema—that Yahweh alone is our God—without serving him as God. True faith in God and his Messiah means a true *relationship* with God and his Messiah.

So, back to the first part of your question ("What would happen to a Nazi murderer who believed in Jesus before he died?"), the answer is clear. If by "believing in Jesus" you simply mean, "believing that he is the Lord and Savior," then that Nazi would be judged for his sins and condemned to hell. If, however, by "believing in Jesus" you mean putting his trust in the Lord Jesus to cleanse him from his sin and guilt, repudiating his evil deeds with his whole heart and turning to God in true repentance, asking for mercy and pardon, then he would be forgiven, just as Ezekiel declared. The only difference—according to your scenario—is that he would have died before he was able to demonstrate the reality of his repentance and faith (the New Testament calls this "producing fruit in keeping with repentance";

see Matt. 3:8; Acts 26:18), so only God would have known the condition of his heart. If he truly had a change of heart, however, heaven would be his home.

However, lest you get the idea that deathbed repentance is something worth waiting for (in other words, why not sin now and repent later?) I remind you of the counsel of Rabbi Eliezer in the Mishnah: "Repent one day before you die!" This means, of course, that since you don't know the day of your death, you should repent every day (cf. m. Avot 2:10; Avot d'Rabbi Nathan 15, end; see also Ben Sira 5:7). Death may overtake you suddenly, before you have the opportunity to get right with God, or, by the time of your death, you might have become so hard-hearted that repentance is the farthest thing from your mind. The more we sin, the harder we get!

Thus, in the case of a resolute, murderous Nazi, it is doubtful that someone who had hardened his heart so deeply by slaughtering so many people could spontaneously, at will, bring about some last minute change, although God has, on occasion, granted this kind of deathbed repentance. Thank the Lord that such a slender thread of mercy exists, but don't hang your eternal well-being on it! As Augustine, the early church leader, wisely remarked (with reference to the thief who was crucified next to Jesus and repented before he died): "There is one case of death-bed repentance recorded [in the Bible], that of the penitent thief, that none should despair; and only one that none should presume."

As for the Jews killed by that Nazi, obviously, I am not their judge, and, of course, I can give you only my educated opinion. It is God alone who determines their final destiny. Still, I would reiterate that just because one of our people suffered the terrible tragedy of dying in the Holocaust doesn't automatically make him or her a saint.[41] Many of our people were irreligious before and during the Holocaust, right up to the time of their deaths. Does simply dying because one is a Jew—especially when that one would have gladly ceased to be Jewish—atone for one's godless life up to that moment? If so, do traditional Jews believe that the Jewish Christians who died in the Holocaust are guaranteed a place in heaven—in spite of their so-called idolatry?

But there's something more: Some Jews (both traditional and Messianic) believe that the Holocaust had at least some elements of divine judgment in it. In other words, our terrible corporate suffering was partly due to corporate sin. This would be similar to the destruction of Jerusalem in the years 586 B.C.E. and 70 C.E. At those times, our city was destroyed and people mercilessly butchered because we had sinned against God (read Lamentations for more on this, and see below, 1.17). Would a sinful Jew who was killed then by the Babylonians or Romans automatically become a saintly martyr? Why then should Jews who died in the Holocaust automatically be considered martyrs? I know the parallels are inexact (especially because of the specifically racial dimensions of the Holocaust), but they are similar.

Some ultra-Orthodox rabbis would tell us today that the Holocaust occurred because of our people's apostasy, and if we don't repent, the same thing could occur again, even in America.[42] (As to the question of traditional Jews who died in the Holocaust, faithful to their traditions, and, to the best of their knowledge, faithful to their God, I refer you back to 1.10.)

This much is sure: While we cannot go back in time to the horrific days of the Shoa—as the Holocaust is known among many Jews today—or sit here and pronounce judgment on people whose lives ended more than a generation ago, we know that our God will accept those who come to him according to his terms—and we might be surprised to see some of those whom he accepts and some of those whom he rejects.

1.12. No religious or educated Jew would ever believe in Jesus.

This statement is an absolute falsehood. There have been prominent rabbis along with brilliant Jewish scholars who have become believers in Jesus, but you rarely hear about them because they are generally discredited by their own people once they prove unshakable in their faith. Whereas they were revered as saintly giants before they believed, they are reviled as ignorant sinners after they believe. The fact is that Jews who are more religious than you and more highly educated than you do believe Jesus to be the Jewish Messiah.

Have you ever heard of Daniel Zion, the chief rabbi of Bulgaria during the Holocaust? He was instrumental in helping to save hundreds of Jewish lives during that horrific time in history, settling in

Israel after the war. Yet, his name is unfamiliar to almost all Jews today. Why? Simple. He was a believer in Yeshua!

He was so highly respected by the Orthodox leaders in Israel that in 1954 the newly appointed chief rabbi, Samuel Toledano, offered him the position of judge in Jerusalem's Rabbinic court. The only obstacle was Zion's faith in Yeshua, a problem that Toledano suggested could be overcome if Zion kept his beliefs to himself. To this, Zion could not agree, and he presented the evidence for his faith in a meeting with the leading rabbis, concluding with these words: "I give up all earthly honor for the sake of the Messiah, my mate."

Stripped of the title of "rabbi" by the Rabbinic court, he was still looked to as rabbi by the Bulgarian Jews and officiated in the Yeffet Street Synagogue in Jaffa until October 6, 1973. In addition, every Sabbath afternoon, he would teach about Yeshua and the New Testament to a group he would bring home with him in between the morning and evening synagogue services. He died in 1979 at the age of ninety-six, firm in his commitment to the Messiah. And—to break another stereotype you might have—he never considered himself a "Christian," living a traditional Jewish life until his dying day.

During the days of Nazi occupation, he was publicly flogged and humiliated, and all this time he was a believer in Jesus! On one occasion, he received a vision from Yeshua, in which the Lord told him to warn Boris, the Bulgarian king, not to submit to Nazi pressure to deliver the Bulgarian Jews over to the Polish and German death camps. This warning was delivered to the king in writing just one day before Boris left for Germany to meet with Hitler. The king refused to comply with the Führer's demands! A beloved chief rabbi, through his close relationship with Jesus the Messiah, was used by God to save Jewish lives in the Holocaust.[43]

An example of a different kind is that of Auguste Neander (born David Mendel), the outstanding historian of early Christianity who was a leading professor at the universities of Berlin and Halle last century. Respected for his great erudition as well as his godly, sacrificial lifestyle, he helped slow the rising tide of German theological rationalism that was spreading rapidly in the early 1800s. Neander had become a believer in Jesus while studying in high school, influenced by two of his Christian friends. (His parents gave him a secular education with the hopes of him becoming a lawyer.)

In complete contrast to Daniel Zion, the Orthodox rabbi, Neander came from a less observant home but distinguished himself as a learned scholar, lecturer, and author, also giving away the bulk of his income to help others in need. Do you think he was smart enough to think for himself?

If you say, "But Neander wasn't raised in a strict religious environment," I reply, "Then what about Daniel Zion?" If you say, "But Daniel Zion came from an Eastern European, Orthodox background, not having sufficient contact with secular scholarship," I reply, "Then what about Auguste Neander?"

The fact is there are Jewish believers in Jesus (both past and present) who break every one of your preconceived molds. For every objection you raise, I can introduce you to a Jewish believer whose testimony refutes that very objection (see also below, 1.13–1.14). In fact, I'll introduce you to one more Jewish believer in Jesus, a man who was *both* very Orthodox and very educated: Samuel Isaac Joseph Schereschewsky.

Born into an Orthodox home in Lithuania, he excelled as a student of Talmud, demonstrating an exceptional proficiency in language studies from an early age. When he was given a copy of the New Testament in Hebrew, however, he studied it carefully for himself, becoming convinced that the prophecies in the Hebrew Scriptures about a coming Messiah were fulfilled in Jesus. Then, after graduating from the University of Breslau, he openly confessed his beliefs, which until that time he had kept secret. After further studies in preparation for ministry, he determined to go to China to translate the Bible, and this is where he left his mark.

"But I've never heard of him," you say. Of course you haven't! You see, if he had continued on his path of excellence in Rabbinic studies, he might be hailed today as one of our great rabbis—even if he had rarely left the confines of the yeshiva, spending all his hours learning and teaching and writing about the intricacies of Jewish law and tradition. Instead, because he poured out his life for multitudes of Gentiles who had never heard about the God of Israel—serving as a light to the nations, which is the very thing we Jews were called to do—his name is unknown to you.

By the time Schereschewsky arrived in China after a long journey by ship, he was already writing good classical Chinese—to the astonishment of the local people. But it was not always easy for him. Not only did he spend countless thousands of hours meticulously translating the Hebrew and Greek Scriptures into Mandarin and Wenli, he did so in spite of a severe illness that left him almost completely paralyzed for the last twenty-five years of his life. He was also mute for a time and in constant pain. Yet he persevered, training the middle finger of his right hand to strike the typewriter one agonizing character at a time. When he could not use his finger, he would grasp a small stick in his fist and use it to strike the keys.

So great were his accomplishments that Max Müller, the Oxford University philologian, considered him to be one of the six greatest Oriental linguists in the world, while Rabbi Dr. Max Margolis said of him, "Among the men and women who consider it their blessed work to bring the Word of God within the reach of far-off tribes by means of translations in their native idioms we may single out Bishop Schereschewsky, the Christian Jew."[44]

Rabbi Daniel Zion, Professor Auguste Neander, Bishop Joseph Schereschewsky—the list of illustrious Jewish believers in Jesus is really quite impressive. When you stop and consider the facts, you'll have to admit that one of your excuses is erroneous: Educated and religious Jews *have believed* in Yeshua the Messiah and *do believe* in Yeshua the Messiah. It is not education and learning that stop people from believing in Jesus but rather ignorance as to who he really is and what our Scriptures really say about him.

1.13. Those educated or religious Jews in the past who did convert to Christianity did so for monetary gain or because of social pressure. It had nothing whatsoever to do with intellectual arguments or honest theological convictions.

Were the shoe on the other foot and I were making such statements about the motivations of secular Jews who became traditional, I would be labeled anti-Semitic! No doubt, Christianity, along with every other major religion (including Judaism), has had its share of "convenience conversions." These counterfeit conversions, however, in no way diminish or negate the fact that there have been highly educated or very religious Jews who have followed Jesus unflinchingly, even though it cost them their reputations, their livelihoods, their careers, and even their inheritances. There have been many such Jews throughout history and to this very day.

To allege that Jews believe in Jesus for monetary gain is not only a ludicrous lie, it also smacks of anti-Semitism, implying that Jews will do anything for money. It is also a prideful judgment that says, "Because I don't believe in Jesus, I'm sure no one in his right mind would ever believe in him. Therefore, any Jew who believes in Jesus must have some ulterior motive."

In point of fact, history is filled with Jews who forsook all to follow the true Messiah. Rather than being mercenaries, these men and women were some of the noblest people our race has ever produced. Of course, it is true that some Jews through the centuries "converted" to Christianity in order to improve their social status and/or professional opportunities, but it is unfair and inaccurate to question the sincerity of those many Jews who have followed Jesus as Messiah despite enormous personal cost just because others were insincere.

I made reference earlier to Rabbi Dr. Max Wertheimer whose name was dropped from the rolls of his alma mater, the Hebrew Union College in Cincinnati, because of his faith in Jesus. Was Wertheimer a mercenary? Hardly! According to Nahum Brodt, as rabbi of B'Nai Yeshurun Synagogue at the end of the last century, Wertheimer "received a salary of $2,000 a year, plus house, fees from weddings, bar mitzvahs, and the like. When he became a believer in the messiahship of Jesus he went back to school, after which he became pastor of the First Baptist Church, Ada, Ohio. What salary did he get then? The magnificent sum of $500 a year!"[45]

How about Richard Wurmbrand, the Romanian Jew, who, together with his wife, Sabina, experienced almost unspeakable torture and hardship under the communists because of his faith in Jesus? Was Wurmbrand a mercenary? He had been a brilliant, secular, pleasure-loving Jew who was confronted with the truth about the Messiah and was dramatically changed, becoming the pastor of a Hebrew Christian congregation. He preached fearlessly, refusing to conform to the godless standards of the communists, and, as a result, suffered fourteen years of brutal imprisonment, including three years in solitary confinement in an underground cell. During those three dark years, the only faces he saw were the faces of his torturers, while his wife, of whose whereabouts and safety he knew nothing, languished in a slave labor camp. And there was always an easy way out: Renounce your faith in Jesus!

Such a thought was never an option for him. In fact, Wurmbrand was imprisoned *three different times* for his preaching. If he wanted to live a "normal" life with his family, he could have. Instead, he chose to be loyal to his Lord.

Wurmbrand endured many tortures, including being frozen to the edge of death (then revived by the doctors), burned with red-hot irons, viciously beaten all over his body, clubbed and whipped on the soles of his feet, often daily (because of the damage done to his feet he has never been able to stand for long periods of time). He was locked in a carcer (an upright, casket-sized box with razor sharp spikes protruding from every side) until he passed out from bleeding or pain, he was doused with ice water while his body burned with tubercular fever, he was made to live in his own excrement and urine—the list goes on and on. It is no exaggeration to say that he was subject to almost every imaginable indignity and abuse, never denying his Savior.

This is just a two-paragraph snapshot of some of his sufferings for the Messiah, expressed in his own words:

> The tortures and brutality [while in solitary confinement] continued without interruption. When I lost consciousness or became too dazed to give the torturers any further hopes of confessions, I would be returned to my cell. There I would lie, untended and half dead, to regain a little strength so they could work on me again. Many died at this stage, but somehow my strength always managed to come back. In the ensuing years, in several different prisons, they broke four vertebrae in my back, and many other bones. They carved me in a dozen places. They burned and cut eighteen holes in my body.
>
> Doctors in Oslo [after his release from prison], seeing all this and the scars of the lung tuberculosis which I also had [during some of the prison years], declared that my being alive today is a pure miracle! According to their medical books, I should have been dead for years. I know myself it is a miracle. God is a God of miracles.[46]

When he testified before Congress about his treatment under the communists, the congressmen were shocked when he removed his shirt to reveal more than a dozen major holes on his torso. This was Wurmbrand's reward for his faith in Jesus! To this day (at the time of this writing, Pastor Wurmbrand is ninety and Sabina eighty-eight), since his release from prison, he has served the Lord tirelessly, never taking even a single day of vacation (I mean this literally) and never owning a home of his own.[47]

What makes this all the more surprising is that Wurmbrand is a prolific author—in fact, his books are the most translated religious books written this century—yet he has never taken a dime from his writings for personal profit, using all the money from the sales of these books to help the families of martyrs around the world, also reaching out to communists, Muslims, and most recently, terrorists. As a Jew, you should be honored to know that someone like Richard Wurmbrand—the most famous tortured believer of our time—is actually "one of us."

As you listen to him share the love of God with friend and foe alike—speaking to them fluently in English or Russian or German or French or Hebrew or Romanian (to name a few)—you realize that the half has not been told about some of the wonderful, pious Jewish believers in Jesus who have kept the faith through thick and thin. What a shame it is that such saints have been reviled, ridiculed, and rejected by our people as apostates and mercenaries. Clearly, it is not the Jewish believers who were tarnished and untrustworthy; it is the people who so falsely accused them who have been stained.

I'll close with a final example, that of Haham Ephraim. (Haham is the colloquial expression for "rabbi" in certain Oriental Jewish communities.) He was born in Tiberias in 1856, which is important when you remember that the lie that Jews believe in Jesus for the sake of monetary gain was much more prevalent last century than this century. (Of course, it is sadly true that such libelous rumors are still fairly common in Israel to this day, but this proves just one thing: Old rumors die hard!) His full name was Ephraim ben Joseph Eliakim, and he was the son of a Tiberias rabbi, eventually becoming recognized as Haham and serving as *dayyan* (a Rabbinic judge). What's more, he married the chief rabbi's daughter.

It seemed he was set for life, spiritually, socially, and even economically. Furthermore, he had a strong aversion to Christianity, and as he himself later noted, he had "never permitted his wife or children to go near the hospital department of the Church of Scotland Mission [located in their area in Tiberias], however ill they might be." Yet, as he began to study the prophecies of our Hebrew Bible, talking honestly with the local leader of that very same Church of Scotland, he became convinced beyond a doubt that Jesus was our Messiah—but only after much soul-searching and inner turmoil, spending countless hours with his brother rabbis, none of whom could answer his questions.

What did he "gain" from his newfound faith? On the one hand, he entered into an intimate relationship with God the likes of which he had never known, enjoying abundant peace until his death at age seventy-four. On the other hand, he was seized and beaten by his own people, falsely accused of theft and confined in a filthy cell, and then flogged and starved, incurring lifelong health problems as a result. After being forcibly relocated to a Jewish colony at the Lake of Huleh—his name utterly renounced by former friends and companions—he worked long, hot hours doing manual labor in the fields. When he finally returned to Tiberias, his wife and children were taken from him.

W. M. Christie, a Christian leader who knew the Haham throughout this period of time, actually heard his relatives and in-laws say, "Had he been an ordinary Jew, we could have understood it. But that a rabbi, and one of his standing, should change, why, we never heard of such a thing."[48] Does this sound familiar?

Of course, you might be wondering, "Well, once it became known that this rabbi—the son-in-law of the chief rabbi—believed in Jesus, he must have made a fortune off his story." Not so! For years he worked in Jerusalem as a day laborer, carrying stones and mortar. As Christie relates:

> His income was that of an ordinary worker, but he never complained. He was content with the simplest of living and clothing, and anything he could spare from his meager resources he used to help the poor whom he met through his continual testimony to the Gospel. . . . During this time he came much in contact with the rabbis in Jerusalem, many of whom had been his pupils in Tiberias. They were troubled and vexed to find him doing such lowly work, and pled with him: "We beg you to have regard for your age and to abandon this hard and menial labor and return with us to be our father and chief as you were formerly."[49]

He remained steadfast, in spite of these overtures. Eventually, he was sponsored by a Christian group who enabled him to give all his time to sharing his faith with his people, resulting in some real fruit (even among a few fellow rabbis), along with some violent attacks, including occasional stoning by his fellow Jews. He died profoundly thankful to his Savior and Messiah, never regretting his decision for a moment, in spite of the hardships he endured.

Examples such as these could be multiplied, but enough has been said to set the record straight. It is true that, especially in eighteenth- and nineteenth-century Europe, where cultural Christianity dominated the society, a number of Jews "converted" to the faith with the sole purpose of gaining social or economic advancement. This is similar to situations that sometimes exist today in Orthodox Jewish circles, when, for example, a secular Jewish man will become observant in order to marry a (newly observant) Jewish woman. But this, of course, does not negate the fact that many Jews become observant without mixed motives. In the same way, the fact that some Jews "converted" to Christianity with insincere motives does not negate the fact that true conversions took place as well.

And when you think in terms of a Jewish person—especially a religious Jew—becoming a Messianic Jew, what utilitarian motivation could there be for such an act? Why go against the grain and risk the loss of everything unless you are moved by sincere conviction? As one dear Orthodox man once said to me, "Why believe in Jesus? It's hard enough just being a Jew in this world with all the problems we have. Why ask for more trouble by believing in Jesus too?" But I can do no other. I *know* that Yeshua is our Messiah, and I must follow him and be loyal to our God regardless of the consequences.

For your part, you are going to have to wrestle with the fact of the messiahship of Jesus for yourself—even if it costs you everything. The decision will be well worth it. Richard Wurmbrand, Haham Ephraim, and a host of other Jewish believers in Jesus who have suffered much for their faith would add a hearty "Amen."

1.14. Those religious Jews who did become followers of Jesus always had the tendency to stray. If you study their lives, you'll see that most of them threw out their traditional values and beliefs before they ever considered nonsense like Christianity.

Who told you that? How many of these people have you interviewed? Are you aware that many of the religious Jews who put their faith in Jesus were absolutely shocked to learn that he was the Messiah? They were living traditional lifestyles and were very much against anything Christian, but they couldn't resist the truth of the Scriptures, in spite of the consequences of believing. As for those religious Jews who did begin to question their traditions before believing in Jesus, there is nothing illogical about this. They found problems with their spiritual foundations and sought the truth elsewhere.

There have been plenty of religious Jews who were happy with their traditions and beliefs before they came to the inescapable conclusion that Jesus is the Messiah, deciding to follow him no matter what their teachers, peers, or family said.

As for those Jews who did, in fact, question their traditions before hearing the good news about Jesus the Messiah, I'd like to ask you something: What's wrong with questioning one's traditions? Not all traditions are true. Not all beliefs are trustworthy. Not all holy books are holy. Why shouldn't an honest student think through the things he is taught? Is the traditional Jewish faith so fragile that it cannot withstand scrutiny? Must an ultra-Orthodox Jewish teenager be kept in an environment so secluded that he is not allowed to think for himself? Is there something his teachers have been hiding from him, or will his faith stand the test? Is the appeal of the New Testament so strong and the power of the Talmud so weak?

It's one thing to educate our children according to our convictions and seek to keep them from sinful, polluting influences. It's another thing for Orthodox parents to tell their children that if they read the New Testament, they will have no place in the world to come![50] Many of the traditional Jews who left some of their traditions would never have been exposed to the gospel message if they had continued to live a cloistered, yeshiva lifestyle. It was their honest, inquisitive minds and their searching questions—questions that often went unanswered by their traditional teachers—that helped lead them to a true knowledge of God and the Messiah. Keeping people from honest inquiry is never healthy.

In 1987, I invited a leading anti-missionary from Monsey, New York, to come to Maryland for a public debate. This rabbi was well known through his cable TV show and newspaper columns, and he had claimed that no Messianic Jew would ever debate him. It was in response to his claim that I offered to debate him publicly in the Baltimore area, guaranteeing that he would have at least three hundred Messianic Jews in the audience. I also told him that on the next day he could address a class of my top college and graduate students. He would be allowed to speak to them without rebuttal from me. All I asked was that he make the debate known to the Orthodox community as well, so they could hear both sides. In spite of all his rhetoric, he refused the offer, claiming that it would take the traditional Jews away from Torah study, also adding that he was afraid they might be influenced.

I was completely willing for the local Messianic Jewish community to hear this very strong, highly educated rabbi do his best to convince them that Yeshua was *not* the Messiah. I knew the truth was on our side and we had solid answers for every question he would raise. Yet he was afraid I might plant a seed of doubt in his constituency's minds about their own faith.

To this day, our ministry (called ICN Ministries, standing for Israel, the Church, and the Nations) actively distributes unedited audio and video copies of debates we have had with leading rabbis and anti-missionaries, encouraging people to hear both sides of the issues.[51] We have nothing to fear. We do not believe in brainwashing (contrary to what some uninformed person may have told you), nor do we need to rely on heavy-handed peer pressure. We are confident that if a Jewish person earnestly and honestly seeks God and his truth, he will find them. Is the open pursuit of truth a virtue or vice?

It was disclosed recently that Muslim children in certain strict schools in Pakistan were kept chained, ostensibly to shelter them from evil, outside influences. The practice was so harsh that it even offended some local Muslim leaders. Now what if some of those children grew up with religious questions, and when they had the opportunity, they began to seek answers to those questions? What if they ultimately saw that the Koran was not, in fact, divine truth, and instead they began to read the Scriptures? Would this be wrong? Wouldn't their spiritual struggle and religious odyssey be for their ultimate good?

Are you a Reform or Conservative Jew? If so, do you realize that the only reason such branches of Judaism even exist is because several generations ago some traditional Jews began to question aspects of what they were taught, eventually becoming the leaders of a new expression of Judaism? (The same could be said of Hasidic Judaism; see 1.13.) Stop for a moment and think. It can only do you good.

1.15. Missionaries like you target the sick, the elderly, the ignorant, and the young and uninformed.

Actually, we don't target any one group in particular—although many of us are especially interested in having exchanges with rabbis and religious Jews whenever we have the opportunity, and we especially appreciate interaction with well-informed Jews. We won't, however, withhold the good news about the Messiah from anyone, young or old, healthy or sick. Everyone should know about the mercy of God that is available through repentance and faith. As for those who have lived their entire lives without the knowledge of the Messiah and now are nearing death through sickness or old age, isn't it only fair to reach out to them? This is the time that many of them are finally doing some serious thinking about the meaning of life and their relationship with God. Is it right to neglect them?

Some anti-missionaries specialize in rumormongering—spreading unfounded, often vicious allegations about Jewish believers in Jesus—and they don't stop even when they know the truth.[52] They also delight in calling every Jewish believer in Jesus a "missionary"— and they don't mean it as a compliment either. Unfortunately, these tall tales filter down to the Jewish community at large, so by the time you hear them, you think there must be some credibility to them. It's time to put these rumors to rest. The facts are as follows:

1. There is no such thing as targeting specific groups. Jewish believers in Jesus consist of young people and old people, rich people and poor people, married people and single people. We are not all part of one organized group (any more than American Jews in general are part of one organized group), nor do we have some kind of systematic, standardized program of evangelism that we all follow.

2. Because we are excited about our faith, we often speak freely to those with whom we have contact, so students speak to students, housewives speak to housewives, businessmen speak to businessmen. This is the primary way in which our faith is spread.

3. It is common to see Jewish believers in Jesus active on college campuses. This, however, is the norm for many religious groups and organizations. The traditional Jewish group called Hillel is found on campuses throughout America, as is the Catholic group named after Cardinal Newman, and the evangelical group known as InterVarsity Christian Fellowship. You can also find Buddhist groups, Hare Krishna groups, New Age groups, and many other religious groups on campuses. Students are asking lots of questions at this formative time of their lives. They are thinking through the major issues of life and looking for serious interaction. That's why groups such as the Lubavitcher Hasidim often have campus rabbis involved with Jewish students. If it's right for them to have a presence in our colleges and universities, then it's right for us to be there too.

4. As for the elderly, even if we had some kind of universal, organized outreach (which we don't), it is preposterous to suggest that we target them in particular. Have *you* ever tried to change the thinking of an older person? However, some of them only think about the purpose of life and the reality of death when they are in their final days, and it is only then that they are willing to talk seriously about these issues. Also, all of us who have parents who do not believe as we do try our best to share our faith with them before it's too late, before they pass the point of no return only to find out that their rejection of the Messiah was wrong. Should we leave them to die in darkness? And don't forget that ministers of all persuasions—rabbis and priests and pastors alike—are called on by friends and relatives to visit ailing or dying parents, aunts, uncles, and so on. Many times, the elderly in our society are left to suffer alone, separated from their loved ones while they waste away in hospitals or nursing homes. If it's right for a Catholic priest or an Orthodox rabbi to visit a hospital or nursing home, praying and talking with an old dying patient, why is it wrong for one of our ministers to do so?

There is one last point that should be made. The false accusation that we target the young and the uninformed becomes even more ironic when you realize that a strong case could be made that it is *traditional Judaism* that especially targets the young and the uninformed. Don't "missionary" groups such as Lubavitch spend a good deal of time reaching out to "ignorant" Jewish young people who were raised in nonobservant homes? I can tell you personally that Lubavitch rabbis—very kind and sincere men—were willing to spend hours with me *before* I knew Hebrew and had done any Rabbinic study but refused to study with me once I was established in my learning. (They said they were afraid I would use my studies against them, or that I would secretly influence others in the group.)

Statistics show a large percentage of *ba'alei teshuvah* (Jews who become traditional) are young people, often college age, and most all of them have become *ba'alei teshuvah* through the influence of other traditional Jews (campus rabbis, Lubavitch outreach groups, and specialized yeshivas).[53] Other surveys indicate that a far larger percentage of *women* become observant than men.[54] Does this then indict traditional Judaism? Does it mean that traditional Judaism preys on uninformed young people and vulnerable women? (My exaggerated stereotyping is intentional!)

Actually, *neither* traditional Judaism nor Messianic Judaism targets any one group. People are more likely to make major changes in their younger years, so it is only natural that the largest single group of converts (either to traditional Judaism or to Messianic Judaism) come from Jews in their mid-teens to early twenties, and there seem to be some sociological reasons for the high percentage of female *ba'alei teshuvah.* Thus, the objection about targeted outreach is inaccurate and untrue.

1.16. I'm not a very religious person, but I'm certainly not a bad person. I'm basically a normal, middle-of-the-road, good person.

> By whose standards? Did you know the Hebrew Bible does not even recognize a "not too good and not too bad" class of people? You are either a sinner or you are righteous, a servant of the Lord or a transgressor.

The Talmud recognizes three classes of humanity: the righteous, the wicked, and the average (literally, "between, in the middle," in Hebrew *benoni* (pronounced bey-no-nee); see, e.g., b. Rosh Hashanah 16b). The Bible does not recognize this "middle" class.

Look in the Torah: There are blessings for obedience and curses for disobedience, with nothing in between. Look in Psalms: There are righteous people and wicked people, with no middle-of-the-road people. Look in Proverbs: There are fools and there are wise. That's it! And look in Daniel 12:2: There are those who are raised to everlasting life and those who are raised to everlasting shame, in other words, heaven or hell (1.10–1.11). Where do you fit?

When the flood came in Noah's day, only eight people were spared. Where were all the middle-of-the-road, basically good people? Throughout the Scriptures, the nonreligious—those who did not take God and his Word seriously—were judged by him as sinners. Why should you be any different?

Unfortunately, we tend to justify ourselves, pronouncing ourselves pretty good in comparison with others. So the thief is pretty good in comparison to the murderer, and the onetime killer is pretty good in comparison to the serial killer.

Once, my wife, Nancy, had to go to court because of a problem with the license plates on her vehicle. We had moved to another state, and we assumed the plates were good for one year after registration, as they had been where we previously lived. We found out that wasn't the case, even though we never received a notice in the mail. In court, Nancy waited as people were called up on all kinds of charges—including stalking and contempt of court—but most of the violations were for infractions such as DWI (Driving While Intoxicated).

One man stood up and, pleading for leniency, said to the judge, "But sir, I have a good driving record." The judge replied, "What are you talking about? Look at all these violations," proceeding to list *many* driving infractions. "But," the man said, "I've never been arrested for DWI!" Isn't that the way we are? "I'm not as bad as the next guy," or, "By my standards—which tend to shift according to convenience—I'm a pretty good person!"

It is with good reason that the Book of Proverbs says, "All a man's ways seem right to him, but the Lord weighs the heart. . . . All a man's ways seem innocent to him, but motives are weighed by the Lord. . . . There is a way that seems right to a man, but in the end it leads to death" (Prov. 21:2; 16:2; 14:12).

Beware that you do not play the role of judge and jury in the trial of your own life. It's all too easy to acquit yourself, whereas the Lord might pronounce you guilty. How do you think he would rate you as a Jew and as a human being? By what standard? Irreligious Jews are condemned by their neglect of the law; religious Jews are aware of their shortcomings and sins. You had better make sure you know how to receive forgiveness of sins and how to live a life that the Lord Almighty accepts. This is nothing to take lightly.

Many years ago, Billy Graham appeared on the *Tonight Show* with Johnny Carson. As the two of them talked, Carson said, somewhat apologetically, "You know, I can't even quote all of the Ten Commandments." Dr. Graham gently but firmly replied, "Yes, but you have broken all of them." Does this apply to you?

1.17. If Jesus really is the Messiah, why are there so many objections?

The number of objections that exists is not important, since there are solid answers to each and every objection, and actually, there are far more arguments *for* the messiahship of Jesus than *against* it. In fact, it would take hundreds of books to document the various proofs. But even if there

were more Jewish arguments against Jesus than for him
(and there are not), what would that prove? Most Jews today
don't even take the Ten Commandments seriously. Do their
objections disprove the truth of the Bible or God's law?

It would be easy to give you proofs from Messianic prophecy, from
history, from contemporary miracles, or from my own life that point
clearly to the messiahship of Jesus, but let's be honest. Most Jews
today—including the great majority of Reform and Conservative rabbis along with Jewish professors and scholars in general—don't even
believe that the Hebrew Scriptures are the literal Word of God. Many
of them don't believe in the divine origin of the Torah or the binding
nature of the Ten Commandments. For most contemporary Jews,
therefore, the real problem is not so much with believing in Jesus and
following him but rather with truly believing in God and obeying him.

The only thing that our objections to Moses and the prophets—
and Jesus—prove is that as a people (including our religious leadership) we tend to stray from the path of truth and obedience. We fought
with Moses and Aaron and scorned the words of the prophets. We
even disregarded the voice of God himself days after he spoke from
Mount Sinai. Why should it be so surprising that we rejected the Messiah when he came? We have a track record of rejecting God's
prophets and laws from the beginning of our history until now.

Just think: Within days of receiving the Ten Commandments on
Mount Sinai, we broke the very first commandment and fell into idol
worship. In the following years, we often spoke about stoning Moses
and Aaron, appointing new leaders, and going back to Egypt. We fell
into all kinds of sexual sin and pagan practices and regularly disobeyed and disbelieved the Lord. In fact, out of the entire generation
that came out of bondage in Egypt, only *two* men made it into the
Promised Land. This is painful but true.

After centuries of disobedience and rebellion, this is how the biblical authors summed things up:

The LORD warned Israel and Judah through all his prophets and seers:
"Turn from your evil ways. Observe my commands and decrees, in
accordance with the entire Law that I commanded your fathers to obey
and that I delivered to you through my servants the prophets." But they
would not listen and were as stiff-necked as their fathers, who did not
trust in the LORD their God. They rejected his decrees and the covenant
he had made with their fathers and the warnings he had given them.
They followed worthless idols and themselves became worthless. They

imitated the nations around them although the LORD had ordered them, "Do not do as they do," and they did the things the LORD had forbidden them to do. They forsook all the commands of the LORD their God and made for themselves two idols cast in the shape of calves, and an Asherah pole. They bowed down to all the starry hosts, and they worshiped Baal. They sacrificed their sons and daughters in the fire. They practiced divination and sorcery and sold themselves to do evil in the eyes of the LORD, provoking him to anger. So the LORD was very angry with Israel and removed them from his presence. Only the tribe of Judah was left, and even Judah did not keep the commands of the LORD their God. They followed the practices Israel had introduced. Therefore the LORD rejected all the people of Israel; he afflicted them and gave them into the hands of plunderers, until he thrust them from his presence.

2 Kings 17:13–20

In light of a history like this, is it any wonder we failed to embrace *the Messiah* when he came? Is it surprising we still reject him to this day? If most Jews around the world today don't even follow *Moses* (or are just plain ignorant of what he taught), should it surprise us that most Jews today don't follow Jesus (or are just plain ignorant of who he was)? Should it seem odd to us that Gentiles in general are more inclined to put their faith in Jesus than are Jews, even though they often have to leave their family religion—Hinduism, Buddhism, Islam, nominal Christianity—and frequently suffer great persecution or even martyrdom as a result?

Take a good look at what the Lord said to the prophet Ezekiel:

Son of man, go now to the house of Israel and speak my words to them. You are not being sent to a people of obscure speech and difficult language, but to the house of Israel—not to many peoples of obscure speech and difficult language, whose words you cannot understand. Surely if I had sent you to them [in other words, to the Gentiles], they would have listened to you. But the house of Israel is not willing to listen to you because they are not willing to listen to me, for the whole house of Israel is hardened and obstinate.

Ezekiel 3:4–7

This is quite a statement. Maybe the fact that Gentiles, more so than Jews, have historically followed Jesus the Jew is actually a major argument *in favor* of him being Israel's Messiah! Maybe if more of us took the words of *God* more seriously we would take the words of *his Messiah* more seriously too, as the Lord said to his prophet: "But the

house of Israel is not willing to listen to you because they are not willing to listen to me." Is that the root of the problem?

To you who would classify yourself as a religious Jew, I ask you to
think about whether the Rabbinic, oral traditions—as beautiful as
many of them may be—have sometimes obscured the words of God
written in the Scriptures. To which do you give more attention, the
words of God or the words of men?[55] Are you sure you are listening
to the Lord? As for Jesus being the Messiah, have the numerous objections to him with which you were raised made it difficult for you to
honestly and openly look at the evidence? These are questions worth
considering.

1.18. Christianity simply doesn't work. It doesn't pro-duce what it promises. Deep down, you know what I'm saying is true.

Actually, the reverse is true. To speak personally, I have
been overflowing with almost indescribable blessing since
I found new life through Jesus, and I can give you in-
numerable proofs that he is the true Messiah, that he is alive
today, and that he is at work in the earth and in my life.
Could it be *your* tradition that cannot produce intimacy
with God and the assurance that your sins are forgiven?
Could it be that deep down you know what I'm saying is
true? In fact, I would like to ask you a question: What is the
clear evidence of the presence of the living God in *your* life?

Through the years, I have had the privilege of speaking with Jewish believers in Jesus who were raised Orthodox or Hasidic or had
even been ordained as rabbis. They testified to the great joy they now
have in serving God and his Messiah, and they spoke of the wonderful changes that have taken place in their lives since they put their
faith in Yeshua. They strongly contrasted their past experience as traditional Jews with their present experience as Jewish believers in
Jesus. The differences were pronounced! They went from being loyal,
devoted, diligent Jews who had no sense of real intimacy with God
and no definite assurance of forgiveness of sins to being Jews who
now serve God out of love, enjoying a close, personal relationship
with him. (I should point out that in most cases the process of change

in their lives generally began with honest, intellectual study of the Scriptures, leading them to definite faith in Yeshua. In other words, this was not just a matter of feelings.)

While they sometimes spoke of the fine, sincere Jewish friends and colleagues they had had in the traditional world (in other words, they didn't demonize religious Jews and Judaism), they were quick to point out that in spite of all their study and effort as traditional Jews, they always fell short. Things changed dramatically once they were "born again," and rather than becoming lazy, careless believers, they were all the more zealous to please the Lord.

Now, let me contrast this with four representative examples taken from my years of interaction with traditional Jews. (By the way, I speak here of my interaction with traditional Jews simply because they take their Judaism more seriously than most other Jews.)[56]

First, there was Aaron the yeshiva student. Thinking that I had dialed the number of a different Jewish school, I found myself talking with a congenial man in his twenties. He was a *ba'al teshuvah*—i.e., a Jew who became religious later in life. He became observant for two reasons: (1) He wanted to be assured of his place in the world to come, and (2) he wanted to have a relationship with God in which he could pray to his heavenly Father and have his prayers answered.

Years had gone by, he explained, and he had become a devoted student of Talmud, living a very traditional lifestyle, but there were two problems he found along the way: (1) According to his studies, only the super-righteous, like Moses, could be assured of their place in the world to come. For the rest, it was a matter of hoping in the mercy of God. Why then, he wondered, should he bother keeping all the commandments if he was just as dependent on the mercy of God now as he was when he was not religious? (2) According to his observations, answers to prayer are apparently random, coming to the observant and nonobservant just the same. Again, he thought to himself, what's the use of all my praying and studying and keeping the laws?

Yes, his candid confession was amazing—and tragic. But even more amazing and tragic was this: Where was his sense of fellowship with God? Where was his sense of walking with him, loving him, worshiping him, and enjoying him? (Yes, according to our Scriptures, we are to enjoy God!) How could he *know* that his beliefs were right? Obviously, he couldn't.

In 1975, I spent a couple of days with a Lubavitch family in Brooklyn, attending Yom Kippur (Day of Atonement) services with them. When the father and I talked, he could hardly relate to any questions

I asked him in terms of his *personal relationship* with God. Finally, when I asked him why he lived the way he did, he replied (to my shock): "It's pretty d—n good. My grandfather lived like this, my father lived like this, and my children will live like this." That was it! Of course, he could offer me all kinds of intellectual and mystical reasons for his practices, but our orientations to God were worlds apart. As incredibly devoted as he was, he hardly seemed to have the love relationship of a bride with her groom, even though this is how the ancient rabbis described Israel's relationship with her God.[57]

Again, to my amazement, I found similar attitudes among the other Lubavitchers with whom I spoke during my stay there (including many hours of talks before and after 1975). They tried so hard, they strove with all their might, and they were so sincere—but they did not *know* the Lord. I have never forgotten those conversations. What a contrast their experience was to the words of the Lord in Jeremiah 9:23–24, where we are called to an intimate knowledge of God:

> This is what the LORD says: "Let not the wise man boast of his wisdom or the strong man boast of his strength or the rich man boast of his riches, but let him who boasts boast about this: that he understands and knows me, that I am the LORD, who exercises kindness, justice and righteousness on earth, for in these I delight," declares the LORD.

In the early 1990s, I spent an afternoon with another Hasidic Jew in Brooklyn. He was a distant relative of Yoel Teitelbaum, the late Satmar Rebbe (the Satmar are another Hasidic group, even more observant than Lubavitch). Our talk was cordial and honest, and I found him to be most pleasant as well as learned. We began to discuss the issue of atonement: After Yom Kippur each year, was he *sure* his sins had been forgiven? After his hours of fasting and his countless prayers of repentance, did he *know* he had been cleansed? Not quite! Instead, he explained that it was hard for him to be sure if he had *fully* repented, if his sincerity had been *total*, if his turning from sin had been *complete*, if he was *sincere* about not wanting to commit the same sins again.

Of course, this kind of honest introspection was commendable, but his lack of assurance of forgiveness was pitiful. This dear man did not know the blessedness of which the psalmist spoke: "Blessed is he whose transgressions are forgiven, whose sins are covered. Blessed is the man whose sin the LORD does not count against him and in whose spirit is no deceit" (Ps. 32:1–2). Nor were the promises in the Torah relating to the Day of Atonement (promises that were predicated on the proper blood sacrifices being offered in conjunction with repentance) real to him:

> This is to be a lasting ordinance for you: On the tenth day of the seventh month you must deny yourselves and not do any work—whether native-born or an alien living among you—because on this day atonement will be made for you, to cleanse you. *Then, before the Lord, you will be clean from all your sins.*

Leviticus 16:29–30

Do your own random survey of ten or twenty Jewish believers in Jesus and ask them what *their* experience has been in terms of assurance of forgiveness, removal of guilt, and a new ability to break away from sinful habits. You'll have trouble restraining their enthusiasm! Ask them if they *know* they have been cleansed and if they *know* they are clean.

"But," you say, "I don't know if I can believe them. Maybe they're making it up!"

Actually, *that* would be hard to believe. Why in the world would they knowingly make up a story on which they've based their very lives? Why would they give themselves to something they know is not true? Why would many of them make difficult personal choices (often at great personal sacrifice; see above, 1.12–1.14) to follow a system that really didn't deliver the goods—and then lie to you to try to recruit you too? Honestly and truly, I tell you that we who have put our faith in Yeshua—both Jews and Gentiles—have been gloriously transformed, and we walk in wonderful fellowship with our God and Father, "having our hearts sprinkled to cleanse us from a guilty conscience and having our bodies washed with pure water" (Heb. 10:22). It is for this reason that we can "draw near to God with a sincere heart in full assurance of faith" (Heb. 10:22). Does such a relationship with the Lord appeal to you? It is available through the Messiah!

This leads me to my last illustration. In September of 1995, I received a highly unusual sixteen-page letter. It was from an ultra-Orthodox Jew who had been raised as a Gentile in an Episcopal home before converting to Judaism. He had listened to a tape of my 1991 radio debate with Rabbi Tovia Singer, and, while volunteering the fact that Rabbi Singer shot himself in the foot with some of his poor arguments (in particular, when he misstated the traditional Jewish position regarding the Davidic Messiah and Isaiah 53), he wanted to challenge me on my views concerning Jesus.[58] I called him, and we spoke for some time.

While he admitted that he had never been "born again" in his prior church experience, he had been serious about his Episcopal faith as a teenager, leading him to research the Jewish roots of Christianity. As a result, he became convinced that Judaism was the true religion, and he converted, spending many years in yeshiva study. Was his experience in Judaism what he expected? Not quite. In fact, he confessed to me that he often went through times of deep spiritual darkness.

Then he began to tell me about his wife, with whom I soon spoke. She was a Jewess but had been raised in a family of committed Jewish Christians. Through her own study, coupled with a feeling of unusual peace she experienced when staying with a traditional Jewish family one Sabbath, she became traditional, ultimately meeting and marrying her now very observant husband. She zealously worked to bring Jewish believers in Jesus into traditional Judaism and was quite firm in her convictions as we talked.

Still, since she had made such an issue of her initial Sabbath experience, I had to ask her about her ongoing walk with the Lord. Her response? She had to admit that her experience with God as a Christian had often been brighter and more vibrant than her experience with him as a traditional Jew. (This reminds me of the candid confessions of two Jewish women who had once been believers in Jesus, then became very observant Jews, only to return in the end to their faith in Yeshua. Both of them told me of the inner agony they felt— and from which they could never fully escape—when they denied Jesus during their years in Orthodox Judaism. Something was always gnawing at them.) What would a Sabbath-observing, Torah-keeping Messianic Jew say to this dear, misguided woman? You can have Yeshua, who is Lord of the Sabbath, and the Sabbath too! You can walk in real light, truth, and fulfillment. It's not either/or. Unfortunately, for the present, she could not see this.

Of course, you may read these accounts and think to yourself, "I'm sure I can find a religious Jew who will claim to have a wonderful relationship with God, along with a Messianic Jew who will admit to his deep spiritual frustrations." I agree! There are exceptions to every rule, and there is some subjectivity to people's individual experiences. Also, you never know exactly what happened in the life of any given person.

For example, one Jew who once believed in Jesus may have had a personal dispute with someone in his congregation, becoming embittered. Soon enough, his bad feelings and disappointment became an unconscious indictment against Jesus. He threw out his faith in the Messiah because someone rejected him! (I know of at least one case in which a weak, Jewish believer in Jesus turned against the faith because he wasn't given a prominent position in the congregation and his pride was injured. I'm sure you could give me a few examples of weak *ba'alei teshuvah* who left Orthodoxy because the person they wanted to marry jilted them, and so on.) Other Jews may have heard about Jesus through a contemporary, made-for-TV version of Christianity that was so superficial that its results were only skin deep. It presented such a hyped-up, phony Christianity that it was bound to disappoint sooner or later. (The sooner the better, in my opinion!) Yes, you may find some disgruntled Messianic (or former Messianic) Jews out there.

Plus, many of us who have been transformed through the death and resurrection of the Messiah are hungry for even *more* of God— to walk even more closely with him, to worship him and adore him and know him even more. This, however, is a healthy hunger, not an admission of emptiness or failure. This is the kind of loving longing that newlyweds experience when they're separated even for a few hours. They can't wait to see each other again! That's how we feel toward our Messiah. We just can't get enough of him. That's how we feel toward our God. We love to spend time with him and obey his commands. In contrast to what you will normally hear from your average traditional Jew, if you probe these hungry, Jewish believers, they will tell you of their vibrant relationship with the Lord.

Of course, we have our ups and downs, our struggles and frustrations, our trials and tests, our good times and bad times. But I tell you without any exaggeration or hype, knowing Jesus the Messiah and having God as my Father is the most wonderful thing I could ever imagine—in this world or in the world to come.

Don't just take my word for all this; do your own survey. Talk with as many traditional Jews and Messianic Jews as you possibly can. (Don't tell them *why* you're asking your questions; just probe them for honest answers. If you can talk with some born again Gentile Christians too, by all means do so.) You'll see that what I'm saying is absolutely true. Then, just act on the truth that you find. You'll join multitudes of Jews and Gentiles who have been cleansed from their sins, delivered from every imaginable vice (from sinful pride to sexual perversion, from uncontrolled anger to unbridled adultery), healed of every conceivable physical and mental disorder (from blindness to bulimia, from AIDS to arthritis), and who now have peace with God through Jesus the Messiah. The door is still open for you.

1.19. You missionaries always use the same old arguments and proofs. Your faith can't be very deep!

To be perfectly honest, I've been getting a little bored with the standard arguments of the anti-missionaries. New or old, however, truth is truth. We don't need to come up with some novel, new proofs for the messiahship of Jesus any more than we need to come up with novel, new proofs for the existence of God. What *you* need to do is carefully examine the evidence. I think you'll discover that there is a lot more to our position than you ever imagined, and as we continue to study and tap into the rich mine of biblical truth, we are more than happy to provide you with further arguments and proofs. For now, I've provided you some real food for thought. Read, study, reflect, and pray. As the Messiah said to Jewish forefathers who believed in him, "If you hold to my teaching, you are really my disciples. Then you will know the truth, and the truth will set you free" (John 8:31–32). It's time for you to experience that freedom for yourself.

PART 2

HISTORICAL
OBJECTIONS

2.1. If Jesus is really the Messiah, why isn't there peace on earth?

According to the biblical timetable, things are right on schedule, and Jesus has been doing everything the Messiah was expected to do up to this point. The problem is that you have an incomplete understanding of the biblical picture of the Messiah. According to the prophet Malachi, the Messiah would bring purification and purging before he brought peace. He would execute judgment before he established justice. Many would not be able to endure the consequences of his coming. This is written in our Hebrew Bible! For many of our people, his coming would be bad news not good news. Our Scriptures also teach that the Messiah was to be a priestly King, like David. As a royal Priest, he came to make atonement for sins and offer forgiveness and reconciliation to Israel and the nations. As King, his dominion expands every day, as he rules over those who embrace him as Messiah. Soon he will return and establish his kingdom on the earth, destroying the wicked and bringing worldwide peace. So, what you expected to be the *first act* of the play will actually be the *final act*.

If there is one standard objection to the messiahship of Jesus, it is this one, and on the surface, it appears to be logical: "The Messiah will bring peace to the earth; Jesus did not bring peace to the earth; therefore, Jesus is not the Messiah." Could anything be more plain?

Of course, I could answer this objection with a question: "Why should there be peace on the earth if we *rejected* the Messiah, the bringer of peace?" (We will, in fact, return to that issue later; see below, 2.6.) But there is actually a serious flaw to the very premise of the objection: The reasoning is circular. It states what it wants to prove. In other words, it presupposes that the Messiah will usher in an age of peace ("That is part of the very concept of the Messiah"), and because Jesus did not literally do this on the earth, he is dis-

69

qualified from being a legitimate Messianic candidate. What is really being said is this: "According to *our description* of the Messiah, it cannot be Jesus."

But who says your description is right? That is the crux of the problem. In point of fact, the Hebrew Scriptures give us a much wider description of the Messiah and the Messianic age, and it is only Jesus who fits the bill. Thus, *from a biblical perspective*, it is not true to say the sole purpose of the Messiah was to bring about peace on earth. That is only part of the biblical portrait. In fact, nowhere in our Scriptures does it explicitly say, "When the Messiah comes there will be peace on earth." Rather, it speaks of an era of peace at the end of the age (see Isaiah 2:1–4, without any mention of a Messianic figure there), tying this in with the reign of a descendant of David, a greater David (see, e.g., Isaiah 11), and it is this glorious Davidic King whom we call Messiah. Jewish tradition, however, has forgotten that this Davidic Messiah will be like David, both priestly and royal, while there are other significant biblical prophecies that speak of the Messiah's sufferings and his atoning death on our behalf (see below, as well as the relevant discussion in vol. 3 dealing with Messianic prophecies). The bottom line is this: The Messiah first came to make peace between God and man, bringing the hope of reconciliation and forgiveness to the world. The ultimate effects of his first coming will lead to his return and an era of complete peace on earth.

Before considering some important verses from our Hebrew Bible, I want to share with you a fascinating Talmudic tradition along with an even more fascinating interpretation of that tradition from the writings of the Vilna Gaon, the greatest Rabbinic scholar of the eighteenth to nineteenth centuries. The Talmud says: "The world will exist six thousand years. Two thousand years of desolation [meaning from Adam to Abraham]; two thousand years of Torah [meaning from Abraham to somewhere around the beginning of the Common Era]; and two thousand years of the Messianic era [roughly the last two thousand years]; but because our iniquities were many, all this has been lost" (i.e., the Messiah did not come at the expected time; b. Sanhedrin 97a–b). According to this well-known Jewish tradition, the Messiah was supposed to come about two thousand years ago! As explained by Rashi, "After the 2000 years of Torah, it was God's decree that the Messiah would come and the wicked kingdom would come to an end and the subjugation of Israel would be destroyed." Instead, because Israel's sins were many, "the Messiah has not come to this very day"—now two thousand years later. Interesting, isn't it?

Let's take a closer look at the actual dates involved. Most traditional Jews follow Rashi's dating, putting the expected time of the Messiah's arrival at roughly 200 c.e. However, Rashi based his figures on a significant chronological error in the Talmudic tradition, probably the most famous error of its kind in Rabbinic literature. It is a miscalculation of almost two hundred years! You see, when the Scriptures were not explicit in dating times and events, the rabbis had to rely on other sources and traditions to figure out how long certain periods were, sometimes getting these historical periods wrong.[1] In the case in point, they believed that the Second Temple stood for only 420 years, whereas it stood for approximately 600 years. Adjusting Rashi's calculations by roughly 180 years, therefore, we find ourselves right in the middle of the time of Yeshua. *He* was the one who came at the time the Messiah was expected to come, and this according to a *Rabbinic* tradition.[2]

Now, the Vilna Gaon examined one of the more obscure stories of the Talmud in which a famous sage, Rabbi Yehoshua ben Chananyah, was confronted by the elders of Athens. These Greek intellectuals, living at the beginning of the second century c.e., asked Rabbi Yehoshua, "Where is the midpoint of the world?" In reply, he raised his finger and said, "Here!" When asked to prove his point, he asked for ropes and measure (b. Bechoroth 8b). What does this mean?

According to the Gaon, the Athenian elders were aware of the Talmudic tradition we just cited from Sanhedrin 97a–b and were arguing with Rabbi Yehoshua that

the present should be the midpoint between the two productive eras of the world, the eras of Torah and Mashiach. But obviously he has not come, for you Jews have certainly not been redeemed. We have crushed you and turned you into a nation of ruin, disaster, and despair. The "midpoint of the world" has manifestly passed by and the Era of Mashiach has not begun. Why, then, do you persist in hoping for his arrival? Why should he come in the future if he did not come at his appointed hour? Is it not clear that the time for his arrival has passed you by forever?[3]

The problem, according to the Vilna Gaon, was that the Athenian elders were unaware of another Talmudic tradition that stated, "The son of David [i.e., the Messiah] will not come until all the government has turned to heresy" (b. Sanhedrin 97a), interpreted to mean that there would be a worldwide turning *away* from God before the Messiah would establish his kingdom. And so, the Gaon explains,

> When the Elders asked, "Where is the midpoint of the world?" Rabbi Yehoshua raised his finger and said, "Here!" He was saying that although the Jews had not merited Mashiach's coming by their deeds, nevertheless the Era of Mashiach had indeed arrived at its appointed time. At "the midpoint of the world" God began turning the wheels of history to insure the ultimate arrival of the scion of David. (p. 149)

In other words, God began a process of giving the human race over to its spiritual darkness and sin so as to eventually bring it to a place where "mankind will realize that the only way to convert himself back into a true human, a God-like being filled with wisdom, love, kindness, and an exalted spirit, is by the acceptance of God's dominion. And when God demonstrates all this and man recognizes it, Mashiach will finally come" (p. 150).

And when did this process begin? It was "with the advent of the last third of human history: the Era of Mashiach may not be apparent, but it is 'here.'"[4] Yes, even though the Messiah himself has not come, the Messianic era began right on schedule, only not in the way most were expecting.

What about Rabbi Yehoshua's request for ropes and measure? The Gaon interprets this with reference to 2 Samuel 8:2, where King David measured out Moabite captives with lengths of rope, putting two-thirds of them to death while only sparing the last third (and see Zech. 13:8–9, also cited in the discussion). He explains that,

> The ropes of King David are the measure of human history. The two-thirds of world history which did not choose to recognize God's dominion refused to choose life. But the last third will be directed towards eternal life by a Providence which will lead the Jews step by step to the recognition of God.
>
> What is the basis of your assertion, asked the Elders, that "here," in the last third of human history, God's mercy is at work and we are in the Era of Mashiach? Answered Rabbi Yehoshua: Remember the ropes of King David and you will learn the ways by which God directs His world. They teach us that God will never abandon his world, that ultimately the good for which God created it will be realized.[5]

Note again those words "we are in the Era of Mashiach," spoken more than eighteen hundred years ago. Yes, according to the Vilna

Gaon's interpretation of this Talmudic account, the Messianic era began more than eighteen hundred years ago. When you make the adjustment for his error in chronology (as pointed out above with regard to Rashi's calculations), he is telling us in effect that the Messianic age began at the time of Jesus.

I remind you, of course, that the Vilna Gaon did not believe in Jesus any more than he believed Muhammad was the first Pope (note also that in all probability the Gaon did not have an accurate picture of who Yeshua was and what he did). It is striking, however, that this great Jewish scholar recognized that the Messianic era actually began at its appointed time and that this era was first a time of *transition*. Shades of "Christianity"! The biggest differences between the Gaon's position and Christianity's position are these: (1) The Gaon saw the present, transition age as one of universal, increasing darkness and apostasy. We see it as an age of ever increasing awareness of the Messiah in the midst of great darkness and apostasy. (2) He believed the Messianic era began *without* the coming of the Messiah. We believe it began *with* his coming.

Is it possible the Messiah *did* come two thousand years ago, but "because our iniquities were many" we did not recognize him? Isn't this a more logical position than that posited by the Vilna Gaon? In fact, we will see in a moment that this position is not only more logical but is actually more *biblical*, since according to the Hebrew Bible, the Messiah was to arrive before the Second Temple was destroyed— in other words, more than nineteen hundred years ago.

Interestingly, the respected Jewish scholar Abba Hillel Silver pointed out that there was great expectation among our people that the Messiah would come "about the second quarter of the first century c.e., because the Millennium was at hand."[6] Thus, according to Silver, "When Jesus came into Galilee, 'spreading the gospel of the Kingdom of God and saying the *time is fulfilled* and the kingdom of God is at hand' [Mark 1:14–15], he was voicing the opinion universally held that the year 5000 in the Creation calendar, which is to usher in the sixth millennium—the age of the Kingdom of God—was at hand."[7] When the Temple was destroyed in 70 c.e., however, and when the Messianic hopes surrounding the false messiah Simeon Bar Kochba were dashed to pieces in 135 c.e., many of the Talmudic rabbis needed to figure out why the Messiah hadn't come at the appointed time, ultimately revising their chronology.

What was the solution to which these rabbis came? Silver summarizes the Rabbinic response as follows: "The Messianic age has actually begun with the destruction of the Temple [i.e., in 70 C.E.], but before its final denouement 365 or 400 years or more may elapse."[8] Silver argues that the only way for these early rabbis to reconcile their Messianic expectations with their view that he did not come as expected was to postulate that the Messianic era actually *did* begin on time—according to this chronology in the year 70 C.E.—but it could be several more centuries before its conclusion. Shades of the Vilna Gaon's interpretation!

Once more, it is not the Messianic Jewish position that is faulty but rather the Rabbinic position that is lacking. Messianic Jews say the Messiah came right on schedule and one of the signs that our people failed to acknowledge his coming was that the Temple—the central place of prayer and sacrifice for our nation—was destroyed forty years after he offered himself as the final sacrifice for sins. The Rabbinic view would be that the Messiah did *not* come on schedule and that the destruction of the Temple—leaving our people without an official, national means of atonement—signified the beginning of a Messianic era *without* a Messiah (the traditional Jewish Messiah *still* hasn't come) and *without* a replacement for the Temple system.[9]

Here are some related Talmudic traditions worth considering about the time and nature of the Messiah's coming.

The Talmud states, "If they [i.e., the people of Israel] are worthy [the Messiah] will come 'with the clouds of heaven' [Dan. 7:13]; if they are not worthy, 'lowly and riding upon a donkey' [Zech. 9:9]" (b. Sanhedrin 98a).[10] Just days before he died, Yeshua entered Jerusalem riding on a donkey, with the crowds hailing him as King Messiah. But then the people turned on him. Is it possible that he came "lowly and riding on a donkey" because we were not worthy of his coming, and in the future, when we recognize him as Messiah, he will return in the clouds of heaven?[11]

According to b. Yoma 39b, God did not accept the sacrifices that were offered on the Day of Atonement *for the last forty years before the destruction of the [Second] Temple* (this was known to the people by means of a series of special signs, all of which turned up negative for those forty years; see b. Yoma 39a). The Temple was destroyed in 70 C.E., so from 30 to 70 C.E., a period of forty years, the annual atonement sacrifices were not accepted. What great event happened in the year 30? Jesus was rejected and nailed to a cross! Is it possible that God no longer accepted the atonement sacrifices because the Messiah had offered himself as the perfect, final sacrifice?

Here is one more Rabbinic text to think about: "Why was the Second Temple destroyed, seeing that the people were engaged in Torah, [keeping] commandments, and [performing] charitable deeds? Because at that time there was hatred without a cause" (b. Yoma 9b). Jesus himself said that Israel's leaders had hated him without a cause (John 15:18–25). Is it possible that *this* was the great sin that led to the destruction of the temple, hating *the Messiah* without a cause? And it was from the very year of his death, 30 c.e., that the atonement sacrifices ceased to be accepted.

Of course, we must remember that in the Talmud, these statements are cited only as several opinions among many, and none of them are absolutely binding or final. Yet these traditions had their origins somewhere, and it is not hard to see that they preserve an important belief: *The Messiah was expected to come twenty centuries ago, but something terrible happened.* Every Jewish person, therefore, must ask the question: If we have been waiting for thousands of years and still our expected Messiah has not come, is it possible we have been waiting for the wrong Messiah? Is it possible that twenty centuries ago the real Messiah did appear and we did not recognize him? Is it possible that without even knowing it, the Talmud has left us hints that point us in this very direction?

"Well, all that's fine and good," you might say. "And it's certainly something to think about. But you keep stressing that what really matters is what the Hebrew Scriptures say, *not* what the Jewish traditions say. Is there clear evidence in our Bible that the Messiah came two thousand years ago?" Absolutely! Let's take a look.

We'll begin by putting three powerful pieces of evidence together. The conclusion is inescapable, especially in light of the Rabbinic traditions that preserve the memory that the Messiah was expected in the days of the Second Temple.

First, we'll look at Haggai 2:6–9. These verses were recorded in the days of the building of the Second Temple, somewhere in the last third of the sixth century b.c.e.:

This is what the Lord Almighty says: "In a little while I will once more shake the heavens and the earth, the sea and the dry land. I will shake all nations, and the desired of all nations will come, and I will fill this house with glory," says the Lord Almighty. "The silver is mine and the gold is mine," declares the Lord Almighty. "The glory of this present house will be greater than the glory of the former house," says the Lord

Almighty. "And in this place I will grant peace," declares the LORD Almighty.

The rabbis wrestled with these verses, asking, "In what way was the glory of the Second Temple greater than the glory of the First Temple?" You see, even though Persian kings helped fund the initial rebuilding of this Temple, and even though Herod elaborately beautified it about five hundred years later, fulfilling God's words that the silver and gold were his, some rabbis realized that the "glory" of the Temple meant more than a splendid building. This is especially clear when we think of the biblical account of the dedication of the First Temple, a dedication marked by the glory of the Lord:

> The priests could not perform their service because of the cloud, for the *glory* of the LORD *filled* the temple of God. . . . When Solomon finished praying, fire came down from heaven and consumed the burnt offering and the sacrifices, and the *glory* of the LORD *filled* the temple. The priests could not enter the temple of the LORD because the *glory* of the LORD *filled* it. When all the Israelites saw the fire coming down and the *glory* of the LORD above the temple, they knelt on the pavement with their faces to the ground, and they worshiped and gave thanks to the LORD, saying, "He is good; his love endures forever."
>
> 2 Chronicles 5:14; 7:1–3; cf. also Exodus 40:34–35,
> where an almost identical scene took place and the Lord *filled*
> the tabernacle with his *glory*—meaning his manifest presence

Where was this glory at the dedication of the Second Temple? It was nowhere to be seen! In fact, the rabbis noted that there were at least five important items missing from the Second Temple that were present in the First Temple: the ark with the mercy seat and cherubim; the (divine) fire (see immediately above, 2 Chron. 7:1); the Shekhinah; the Holy Spirit; and the Urim and Thummim (b. Yoma 21b). It must be asked, therefore, in what way the glory of the Second Temple was greater than the glory of the First Temple. The standard answers given by the leading Rabbinic commentators are: (1) the Second Temple stood for a longer period of time than did the First Temple, or (2) the Second Temple, as beautified by Herod, was a more splendid building.[12] Neither of these answers, however, is satisfactory in light of the awesome presence of the glory of God that marked the dedication of the First Temple.

In addition to this, the Lord declared in Haggai 2:9 that in the Second Temple he would grant peace. However, while there were several peaceful eras during the days of that Temple, its overall history was marked by war and turmoil, much more so than the First Temple.[13] How then was this Temple to be specially marked by "peace," and, more important, how was its glory to surpass the glory of the First Temple? To answer these questions, we turn to the next piece of prophetic evidence, coming from the Book of Malachi, written somewhere around 400 B.C.E. (i.e., less than 150 years after the rebuilding of the Second Temple). Here we have a more explicit statement: There was to be a divine visitation at the Second Temple—and for many of our people it would be bad news, not good news, a time of judgment rather than joy.

As rendered in the New Jewish Publication Society Version, Malachi 3:1–5 states:

> Behold, I am sending My messenger to clear the way before Me, and the Lord whom you seek shall come to His Temple suddenly. As for the angel of the covenant that you desire, he is already coming. But who can endure the day of his coming, and who can hold out when he appears? For he is like a smelter's fire and like fuller's lye. He shall act like a smelter and purger of silver; and he shall purify the descendants of Levi and refine them like gold and silver, so that they shall present offerings in righteousness. Then the offerings of Judah and Jerusalem shall be pleasing to the LORD as in the days of yore and in the years of old. But [first] I will step forward to contend against you, and I will act as a relentless accuser against those who have no fear of Me: Who practice sorcery, who commit adultery, who swear falsely, who cheat laborers of their hire, and who subvert [the cause of] the widow, orphan, and stranger, said the LORD of Hosts.

We see from this passage that the Lord (in Hebrew, *ha'adon*, always used with reference to God in the Hebrew Bible when it has the definite article),[14] preceded by his messenger, would visit *the Second Temple*, purifying some of his people and bringing judgment on others. That is to say, there would be a divine visitation of great import that would occur *in the days of the Second Temple*. How are these verses to be understood?

According to the famous medieval Jewish commentaries of Radak (David Kimchi) and Metsudat David, "the Lord" refers to none other than "King Messiah." However, neither of these commentators took sufficient note of the fact that the Messiah was to come to the Temple that stood in Malachi's day (and note also that it is called "his Temple"—pointing clearly to the divine nature of the "Lord" spoken of here). I ask you, did this happen? If it did, then the Messiah must have come before the Temple was destroyed in 70 C.E.; if not, God's Word has failed.[15]

After reviewing the prophecy we just read from Haggai 2, we can now put two big pieces of the puzzle together: The glory of the Second Temple would be greater than the glory of the First Temple because the Lord himself—in the person of the Messiah[16]—would visit the Second Temple! And in this place he would grant peace because the Messiah, called "the Prince of Peace," would come there in person and open the way for peace and reconciliation between God and man.[17]

"But," you object, "I thought you said the Messiah did *not* come primarily to bring peace during his so-called 'first coming.' Now you seem to be saying that he *was* some kind of a peacemaker."

That's a good observation! Actually, although the Messiah's main purpose two thousand years ago was not to establish peace on the earth (see also objection 2.6, below), since he knew that he would be rejected as King at that time, he is still rightly called the Prince of Peace in the Scriptures. How so? First, he *offers peace* to all who will embrace him and turn from sin; second, he *makes peace* between hostile sinners and a holy God; and third, he *brings peace* to his people who follow him. It is his sacrificial death on the cross that will ultimately lead to worldwide peace when he returns to establish the kingdom of God on earth.[18] It is clear, then, that we have a perfectly good explanation of the meaning of Haggai's prophecy (namely, that in the days of the Second Temple God would grant peace), since the Messiah himself visited there and offered peace to all who would hear his voice. For those who say that the Messiah did *not* come to the Second Temple, where then was the *shalom*, the promised peace?[19]

Now we turn to our third piece of evidence, found in Daniel 9:24–27, one of the most widely discussed prophecies in the Tanakh.[20] While scholars disagree as to when this chapter was actually composed, everyone understands the historical background presupposed by the text. In other words, the Bible wants us to place Daniel 9 at the end of the period of the Babylonian exile, somewhere in the 530s B.C.E. Daniel had been asking the Lord when the exile would end, having understood from the words of Jeremiah that the captivity in Babylon would last for seventy years (see Jer. 25:11–12; 29:10). According to Daniel's understanding, the seventy years were almost over, signaling the time of Judah's restoration. So he gave himself to prayer and fasting, repenting before the Lord for his people's many sins, and asking God to fulfill his promise and bring to an end Judah's exile.

Surprisingly, the answer that came from the angel of the Lord dealt with a period far beyond the period of 70 years. In fact, it spoke of a period of 490 years, literally 70 sevens (or 70 weeks, meaning weeks of years, as opposed to weeks of days, an understanding that is almost universal among both Jewish and Christian commentators). But this is where the agreement ends, and the questions and differences of interpretation are myriad. For example: When does this period of 490 years begin? How should the years be divided? What events will transpire in the last week of years? How many anointed ones (Hebrew, *mashiachs*) does the text describe?

Actually, for our present discussion, it is not important to have definitive answers for all these questions because the biblical text makes one thing perfectly clear: *Final atonement for Israel's sins had to be made before the Second Temple was destroyed.* (Remember that Daniel's prophecy was received shortly *before* the rebuilding of the Temple and describes the future destruction of the Temple in 70 c.e.) Let's read Daniel 9:24–27 in the New Jewish Publication Society Version:

> Seventy weeks have been decreed for your people and your holy city until the measure of transgression is filled and that of sin complete, until iniquity is expiated, and eternal righteousness ushered in; and prophetic vision ratified, and the Holy of Holies anointed. You must know and understand: From the issuance of the word to restore and rebuild Jerusalem until the [time of the] anointed leader is seven weeks; and for sixty-two weeks it will be rebuilt, square and moat, but in a time of distress. And after those sixty-two weeks, the anointed one will disappear and vanish.[21] The army of a leader who is to come will destroy the city and the sanctuary, but its end will come through a flood. Desolation is decreed until the end of war. During one week he will make a firm covenant with many. For half a week he will put a stop to the sacrifice and the meal offering. At the corner [of the altar] will be an appalling abomination until the decreed destruction will be poured down upon the appalling thing.

You might say, "Some of these verses are difficult to understand." Maybe so. But what is *not* difficult to understand is that a period of extraordinary significance in our people's history was about to unfold in which the Temple and the city of Jerusalem would be rebuilt and during which, among other things, iniquity would be expiated and eternal righteousness ushered in—all *before* the destruction of the Temple and the city. There it is again! God's solution for sin would be set in place before the year 70 c.e.

To review: The Hebrew Scriptures teach that while the Second Temple was standing, there would be a divine visitation to that Temple of great import, bringing purification and judgment. Sin would be atoned for and everlasting righteousness ushered in, and the events associated with this Second Temple would be so great that its glory would surpass that of the glorious First Temple. If the Messiah, the Son of God, did not come and visit the Temple, if he did not pay for our sins and establish a new way of righteousness, if he did not bring the glory of God to the house of God, if his coming did not purify and purge the Jewish people in his generation, then how were these prophecies fulfilled? What divine visitation *did* take place if not for the coming of the Messiah? When else *did* God visit the Second Temple in a "personal" way?

The answers to all of the above are simple: Either the Messiah came almost two thousand years ago or the biblical prophets were false prophets—in which case we can throw the Bible out and go join some other religion (or abandon religion completely). Thankfully, we don't need to lose confidence in the Scriptures for one second: The Messiah came, died, and rose from the dead right on schedule and in strict conformity to the biblical prophecies (see vol. 3 for more on this), doing all he was scheduled to do during his first visit to earth. The problem is not with him but with us, and in that light, we must consider a grim prophecy delivered by the prophet Hosea more than twenty-seven hundred years ago:

> The Israelites will live many days without king or prince, without sacrifice or sacred stones, without ephod or idol. Afterward the Israelites will return and seek the LORD their God and David their king. They will come trembling to the LORD and to his blessings in the last days.
>
> Hosea 3:4–5

This is the period in which we have been living since the coming of the Messiah twenty centuries ago: Most of our people have been without God and the Davidic Messiah, without king or prince or sacrifice; but we are now returning to the Lord and his Messiah, and he is being found by us.

"That's really interesting," you say, "but is there any other evidence in the Bible that there would be some kind of large gap in God's dealing with his people? You seem to be arguing that there is a long interval between the Messiah's initial coming into the world and his return."

Exactly. And there *is* further biblical evidence to support this. In fact, it is found in the calendar God gave to our people.

In biblical days, the New Year began with the month of Nissan (see Exod. 12:1–3; 13:4–5; b. Rosh Hashanah 2a–b), and the first major holy day was the Passover, followed by Firstfruits (the first day after the very next Sabbath), followed fifty days later by Shavu'ot (the Feast of Weeks), meaning that there is a cluster of activity at the beginning of the calendar year. When does the next holy day occur? Five months later! At that time there is an even more intense cluster of religious activity: first, Rosh Hashanah, the traditional New Year, falling on the first day of the seventh month; second, Yom Kippur, the Day of Atonement, occurring ten days later; third, and finally, Sukkot (the Feast of Tabernacles), occurring just four days after Yom Kippur. So, there are *no* holy days for five long months, and then, quite suddenly, three major spiritual events in just fourteen days.

What's the connection between the calendar and the Messiah? Simply this. These holy days, which have been so important to the life cycle of our people through the generations, are filled with prophetic meaning and significance, only some of which have been recognized by the rabbis. This is because it is only through the Messiah that we can fully understand the meaning of these special days.[22] Let me explain.

When Jesus began his public ministry, he was recognized as "the Lamb of God, who takes away the sin of the world" (John 1:29). The reference was to the annual ceremony of the slaying of the Passover lamb, looking back to the time when our forefathers were delivered from Egypt and commemorated every year in the Passover Seder. Even irreligious Jews have heard the story of the ten plagues that God sent on the Egyptians, culminating with the death of every firstborn male in the land, a horrible plague from which the Israelites were spared. How were our forefathers protected from the angel of death when he went through the land? It was through the blood of the Passover lamb.

The Lord instructed his people to slaughter an unblemished lamb, one for each family. Then they were to take the lamb's blood and smear it on the door frames of their homes, and when God saw the blood, he would pass over them:

> When the LORD goes through the land to strike down the Egyptians, he will see the blood on the top and sides of the doorframe and will pass over that doorway, and he will not permit the destroyer to enter your

houses and strike you down. Obey these instructions as a lasting ordinance for you and your descendants. When you enter the land that the Lord will give you as he promised, observe this ceremony. And when your children ask you, "What does this ceremony mean to you?" then tell them, "It is the Passover sacrifice to the Lord, who passed over the houses of the Israelites in Egypt and spared our homes when he struck down the Egyptians." Then the people bowed down and worshiped.

Exodus 12:23–27

Passover derives its name from the fact that the Lord passed over our people in Egypt when he saw the blood of the lamb on the doorframes of their homes. Yes, it was the blood of that sacrificial lamb that saved them from death. When was it that the Messiah laid down his life as a sacrificial lamb to save us from sin and death? At the time of the Passover! While our people were preparing their lambs for slaughter throughout the land, God was preparing *his* Lamb for slaughter.

But this is only the beginning. Three days later, on the first day after the Sabbath, Jesus the Messiah rose from the dead. What day was this on the Jewish calendar? It was the day of the Festival of Firstfruits, as described in Leviticus 23:16, "Celebrate the Feast of Harvest with the firstfruits of the crops you sow in your field."[23] This is what Paul, the great Jewish teacher, wrote about as he reflected back on these wonderful events roughly twenty-five years after the Messiah's resurrection:

> But [Messiah] has indeed been raised from the dead, the firstfruits of those who have fallen asleep [i.e., died]. For since death came through a man, the resurrection of the dead comes also through a man. For as in Adam all die, so in [Messiah] all will be made alive. But each in his own turn: [Messiah], the firstfruits; then, when he comes, those who belong to him.

1 Corinthians 15:20–23

Israel's calendar began with the sacrifice of the Passover lamb, followed by the celebration of the firstfruits of the harvest. The Messiah fulfilled both of these, laying down his life for us and then being the first to rise from the dead—a token of the resurrection of the righteous at the end of the age. What was next on the biblical calendar? It was the Feast of Weeks, fifty days after Passover, a time when, according to Jewish tradition, our people received the law on Mount Sinai.[24] Significantly, it was on the first day of this feast, exactly fifty days after Yeshua's resurrection, that the Holy Spirit was poured out on his followers, fulfilling the prophecy of Joel (see Joel 2:28–32 [3:1–4]).[25] This is more than coincidental!

It gets even more interesting from here. As mentioned above, this cluster of religious and spiritual activity on our calendar is followed by almost six months of silence—no special festivals or holy days other than the weekly Sabbaths and the monthly New Moons. Then the cluster of activity begins again—the Feast of Trumpets (Rosh Hashanah), Yom Kippur (the Day of Atonement), and the Feast of Tabernacles, all filled with prophetic meaning.

Several New Testament authors, mirroring the words of Jesus himself, wrote that the Messiah would return with the blast of the trumpet (i.e., the shofar or ram's horn; see Matt. 24:30–31; 1 Cor. 15:51–52; 1 Thess. 4:16; Rev. 11:15), the piercing wake-up call that will be heard around the world. Interestingly, Moses Maimonides wrote that the shofar blast on Rosh Hashanah signified, so to say,

> Wake up from your sleep, you sleepers! Arise from your slumber, you slumberers! Examine your deeds! Return to God! Remember your creator! Those of you who forget the truth in the futilities of the times and spend all year in vanity and emptiness, look into your soul, improve your ways and your deeds. Let each of you abandon his evil ways and his immoral thoughts.[26]

So it will be when the Messiah returns! In fact, many biblical interpreters believe that the prophet Zechariah described this event, speaking of a day when our people would look to the Lord's Messiah and mourn, recognizing him for who he really was—the one pierced for their sins—and then deeply repenting for having rejected him for so long:

> And I will pour out on the house of David and the inhabitants of Jerusalem a spirit of grace and supplication. They will look on me, the one they have pierced, and they will mourn for him as one mourns for an only child, and grieve bitterly for him as one grieves for a firstborn son. On that day the weeping in Jerusalem will be great, like the weeping of Hadad Rimmon in the plain of Megiddo. The land will mourn, each clan by itself, with their wives by themselves: the clan of the house of David and their wives, the clan of the house of Nathan and their wives, the clan of the house of Levi and their wives, the clan of Shimei and their wives, and all the rest of the clans and their wives.
>
> Zechariah 12:10–14[27]

What will happen after this time of mourning and repentance? Atonement will come to our people, as it is written in Zechariah 13:1, the very next verse in that book: "On that day a fountain will be opened to the house of David and the inhabitants of Jerusalem, to cleanse them from sin and impurity."

This, then, will be the sequence: First, the sounding of the trumpet and the Messiah's return, then, the Day of Atonement—spoken of in consecutive verses in the same prophetic book. Then, as if the picture needed to be made any more clear, the very next chapter in Zechariah states that Yahweh himself will come to Jerusalem and fight for his people, destroying the nations that have attacked the city (Zech. 14:1–5), after which the survivors of these nations will come up to Jerusalem to worship the Lord—*in fulfillment of the Feast of Tabernacles* (Zech. 14:16).[28] Our very calendar lays it all out!

This is the order: Passover (speaking of the Messiah's death and our deliverance through him); Firstfruits (Yeshua is the first to rise from the dead); and Shavu'ot or Pentecost (the Holy Spirit is poured out on the Messiah's followers). All this took place in conjunction with Yeshua's first coming, corresponding to the beginning of the biblical calendar. Now, after a gap of almost two thousand years—corresponding to the five-month gap between holy days on Israel's calendar—we are about to enter into the final phase of holy days and celebration: Trumpets (the Messiah's return with the blast of the shofar); Yom Kippur (national atonement coming to our people as we recognize the Messiah and repent); and Tabernacles (all peoples coming to Jerusalem to worship the Lord). What a wonderful, scriptural picture!

What's more, Israel's calendar revolved around the cycle of harvest, so that even during the intervening months, when no special days or celebrations were held, things were moving toward the time of ingathering, represented by Tabernacles. That's exactly where we stand today: During these intervening years between the first coming of the Messiah and his return, everything is moving toward the final ingathering of souls—both Jewish and Gentile—into the kingdom of God.

The tragedy is that as a nation we missed the time of the Messiah's visitation, failing to realize that he would come to give himself as a righteous martyr, an atoning sacrifice for our sins, before exerting his rule over us, functioning not only as a king but also as a priest.[29] We failed to see that he came first to make expiation for our sins. Yet the Hebrew Scriptures have much to say about the priestly role of the

Messiah, although traditional Judaism has virtually eliminated any vestige of this concept from its laws, lore, and liturgy.

This becomes even more interesting when we realize that the Jews who wrote the Dead Sea Scrolls were looking for *two* Messianic figures, called the Messiahs of Aaron and Israel.[30] In addition to this, the important first-century C.E. document called the Testaments of the Twelve Patriarchs, in particular the Testaments of Levi and Judah, also had much to say about this priestly Messiah, speaking of him in highly exalted terms.[31] These concepts were undoubtedly derived from the Hebrew Bible itself. In fact, a good case can be made for the argument that Rabbinic Judaism excised the concept of a priestly Messiah in reaction to Yeshua's priestly Messianic work.[32] This is so important!

"What's the big deal?" you ask. "I really don't see it. So what if the Messiah was to be a priestly King. The bottom line is that the Messiah did *not* bring peace to the earth and establish God's kingdom."

That's where you're missing the point! When our own Hebrew Bible states that the Messiah was to be a *priestly King*, it means that he had to deal with our sins once and for all as well as establish peace on the earth. First, he had to rule in our hearts and bring us into right relationship with God; when he returns he will establish God's reign over all the world. This is the very point stressed in the passage we just examined in Daniel 9: God would deal decisively with sin before the Second Temple was destroyed, and he would do this through his Messiah. Isn't this the logical order? First, the root of the problem—human sin—must be addressed. Then, after people repent of their sins and receive forgiveness from the Lord, his kingdom can be established.

What then is the biblical background to this concept of a priestly Messiah? According to Psalm 110:4, the Lord made an emphatic oath that the Davidic *king* in Jerusalem was to be a *priest* forever after the order of Melchizedek, the ancient priest-king of that city: "The LORD has sworn and will not change his mind: 'You are a priest forever, in the order of Melchizedek'" (Ps. 110:4; see also Genesis 14 and Hebrews 7). According to one interpretation, this divine oath was spoken to David by an inspired court poet, in which case David himself was declared to be a priest-king. According to another interpretation, the whole psalm was spoken by David about the Messiah. Thus, the opening words, "The LORD says to my Lord: 'Sit at my right hand until I make your enemies a footstool for your feet'" (Ps. 110:1), are understood to be those of David, declaring God's promise to the Messiah, David's lord.[33] And it is the royal Messiah who is designated a priest forever like Melchizedek, the first priest-king mentioned in the Scriptures.

In either case, it is interesting to note that David *did* perform priestly functions such as offering sacrifices (see, e.g., 2 Sam. 24:25), a divine service that only priests could perform,[34] while according to 2 Samuel 8:18, David's *sons* were priests (*kohanim*, always translated as "priests" throughout the rest of the Hebrew Bible).[35] Thus, David, *the biblical prototype of the Messiah*,[36] was to be a priestly king. In keeping with this, the Messiah is explicitly typified by a priest ruling on a throne in the Book of Zechariah.

According to a prophetic vision recorded in Zechariah 3:8, the Lord said, "Hearken well, O High Priest Joshua, you and your fellow priests sitting before you! For those men are a sign that I am going to bring My servant the Branch" (NJPSV). And who is the Branch? He is none other than the Davidic Messiah, as widely recognized by biblical commentators.[37] Thus the New Jewish Publication Society Version simply explains in a footnote, "I.e., the future king of David's line. See 6.12; Jer. 23.5–6; 33.15–16; cf. Isa. 11.1." So, the High Priest and his fellow priests are a sign that the Branch—the Davidic Messiah—is coming.

In the very next chapter of the book, the prophet sees another interesting vision and asks the angel, "'And what . . . are those two olive trees, one on the right and one on the left of the lampstand? . . . What are the two tops of the olive trees that feed their gold through those two golden tubes?' He asked me, 'Don't you know what they are?' And I replied, 'No, my lord'" (Zech. 4:11–13 NJPSV).

What did these double symbols stand for? "Then he explained, 'They are the two anointed dignitaries who attend the Lord of all the earth'" (4:14), again explained by the NJPSV to mean, "I.e., the high priest and the king (cf. 3.8–9 with note); lit. 'sons of oil.'"[38] Once again these two key figures are joined together.

But the clincher is found in Zechariah 6:11–13, where the prophet is commanded to

> take silver and gold and make crowns. Place [one] on the head of High Priest Joshua son of Jehozadak, and say to him, "Thus said the LORD of Hosts: Behold, a man called the Branch shall branch out from the place where he is, and he shall build the Temple of the LORD. He shall build the Temple of the LORD and shall assume majesty, and he shall sit on his throne and rule. And there shall also be a priest seated on his throne, and harmonious understanding shall prevail between them" (NJPSV).

I don't know about you, but these words strike me as absolutely amazing. Once again, it is the *High Priest,* crowned as *king,* who serves as a symbol of *a man called the Branch*—the nickname of *the Messiah.* I'll say it again: The Messiah was to be a priestly King, and as a priestly King he came to atone for our sins. Thus, the prophet Isaiah tells us that this Servant of the Lord would suffer for our sins (see Isa. 53:4–6), be stricken for our transgressions (53:8), be offered as a guilt offering (53:10), and bear our iniquities (53:11). God says, "Therefore I will give him a portion among the great, and he will divide the spoils with the strong, because he poured out his life unto death, and was numbered with the transgressors. For he bore the sin of many, and made intercession for the transgressors" (53:12).[39] How wonderful our Messiah is! He is not only our glorious King but our great High Priest.[40]

This much is certain: Since the Messiah had to come almost two thousand years ago—according to the testimony of our own Scriptures—if Jesus is not the Messiah, we will never have a Messiah. It is either Yeshua or no one. Tragically, for two thousand years now, most of us Jews have chosen the latter option, although we have pinned our hopes on many false messiahs along the way, from Bar Kochba to Shabbetai Zvi to the Lubavitcher Rebbe.

Isn't it time we realize what almost one billion Gentiles, along with countless tens of thousands of Jews around the world, have already recognized? Jesus *is* the Messiah of Israel and the nations, and it is high time we reverently receive him as such, for the good of our people and the glory of our God. In the words of a famous letter written to first-century Jewish followers of Jesus, "Just as man is destined to die once, and after that to face judgment, so [Messiah] was sacrificed once to take away the sins of many people; and he will appear a second time, not to bear sin, but to bring salvation to those who are waiting for him" (Heb. 9:27–28).

Many of our people missed him the first time around. Let's be sure we're waiting for him when he returns!

Yeshua the Messiah did what he had to do according to our Scriptures, coming right on schedule and offering himself for our sins. Therefore, we can be sure he will return and do everything else prophesied of him. In fact, whereas traditional Judaism is still waiting for the Messiah to come and make the first and last installments in the plan of redemption in one fell swoop, the real Messiah already came twenty centuries ago and made the down payment for our souls, giving us total confidence that he will come back to finish the work, claim his redeemed people for himself, and settle the score with the wicked and the godless of the world.

Whose position is more secure? One position says, "Although he was supposed to come almost two thousand years ago, our sins prevented him from coming. But we're still waiting for him!" The other position says, "He was *supposed* to come almost two thousand years ago, he *did* come almost two thousand years ago, and he paid for our sins and rose from the dead—just as it was written of him. We have no doubt he'll be back at the scheduled time, just as soon as everyone in the world has had an opportunity to believe in him, repent, and receive forgiveness for their sins." Which position do *you* embrace?[41]

As you'll see in the next answer, there's something significant about the times in which we are living, times that could well usher in the Messiah's second coming to earth. The clock is ticking and the transition age is almost over! While we might think we have been waiting for the Messiah for two thousand years, he has actually been waiting for us! Don't wait for him another moment. The hour is late and the time of his return is drawing nearer by the day.

2.2. Why have wars, famines, and human suffering only *increased* since Jesus came?

As we explained in the previous answer, we are in the transition age, the age when God's kingdom is being established throughout the earth, one life at a time. During this era, because the population of the world has increased and technology has advanced, there are now more evil people capable of doing more evil things, causing an increase in human suffering. Also, Jesus told his disciples that before the end of this age, there would be great turmoil and upheaval, the final birth pangs before God's kingdom was fully established on the earth. But this is only part of the picture. Throughout the world, the knowledge of the one true God has also increased dramatically since Jesus came. This was one of the key roles of the Messiah—to spread the knowledge of God to the nations of the world—and it is certainly no small matter that hundreds of millions of people who once would have lived and died in spiritual darkness have now come into the light of the Messiah.

As we noted in the last objection (2.1), most Jews think that when the Messiah comes, universal peace will be established on earth—immediately and almost automatically—and all suffering will end. Actually, these things will take place when the Messiah *returns*. It is only then that he will destroy the wicked from the earth and usher in that time of total peace for which we all long. But this will not simply be a dramatic, world-changing event that comes out of the blue. Rather, it will be the culmination of a process that has been taking place for the last two thousand years. In fact, it will bring about the culmination of a process that has been unfolding for four thousand years or more.

You see, even though we humans have failed over and over again by sinning against God and doing our own thing, he has refused to give up on us. Instead, he has given us countless opportunities to come into a right relationship with him. From the time of Abraham on, he has been working in a public way to bring us back to himself. That's why, when God called Abraham (then Abram), he said to him, "I will make you into a great nation and I will bless you; I will make your name great, and you will be a blessing. . . . All peoples on earth will be blessed through you" (Gen. 12:2–3). The reason God chose Abraham and his descendants was so that the *whole world* could be blessed. As expressed by the Jewish biblical scholar Nahum M. Sarna, "God's promises to Abram would then proceed in three stages from the particular to the universal: a blessing on Abram personally, a blessing (or curse) on those with whom he interacts, a blessing on the entire human race."[42]

This expresses the heart of our heavenly Father and Creator: He did not and does not want people to die in their darkness and misery. He wants people to know him, serve him, and enjoy his goodness.

Therefore, after choosing Abraham, he singled out Abraham's son Isaac, and then he selected Isaac's son Jacob, whose name was changed to Israel. Thus, all the people of the world were to be blessed through the descendants of Israel. Then, out of the twelve sons of Jacob/Israel, he chose the tribe of Judah, and out of the tribe of Judah, he selected the family of Jesse, and out of that family, he made David his choice, promising to bring the Messiah through David's line.

The time period from Abraham's calling to David's calling was roughly one thousand years, and the time period from David's calling to the coming of the Messiah into the world was also about one thousand years. This was certainly a pretty slow process of development, especially when you consider that during this entire time—and even more so in the years before—very few people on this planet had a personal relationship with God or really knew him as Father. Instead, they worshiped all kinds of idols, spirits, and strange gods, living without a clear spiritual purpose and dying without a certain hope.[43] Even among the people of Israel, the Scriptures tell us that the great majority of our nation did *not* walk with the Lord or obey his commandments (for more on this, cf. above, 1.10).

"But that's just the way things are today," you say. "Not much has changed since your so-called Messiah has come into the world."

Really? Do you know what is taking place around the world at this very moment? The knowledge of the one true God—through Jesus the Messiah—is spreading around the globe in ways that would boggle your mind. This wonderful story of the advance of Messiah's kingdom, especially in the last one hundred years, is almost too wonderful to believe. But it's all true!

You see, it is not only technology that has increased by leaps and bounds this century.[44] It is not only weapons of mass destruction that have been invented and devices of mass communication that have been developed. The kingdom of God has been established in more than *one billion* lives worldwide—to the tune of one hundred thousand or more every day.[45] The Messiah is finishing his work at an exponential pace and bringing God's blessing to the nations!

Just consider this: In the time it takes you to read this page, more than two hundred people will have turned from darkness to light, from bondage to spiritual freedom, from sexual lusts to purity of heart, from idol worship to the service of the Creator, from hatred to love, from dead religion to living faith, and they will do it through Jesus the Messiah, who paid for our sins through his death on the cross, rose from the dead, and sent his Spirit to help us along the way. Yes, extraordinary things are happening, and they have been on a dramatic, wonderful increase since the beginning of the twentieth century.

Of course, you may be wondering why things haven't happened even more quickly. I've wondered about that too! Still, there are some concrete answers I *can* give you, although the Lord in his wisdom hasn't seen fit to tell us everything.

1. God is accomplishing his plan of redemption with our cooperation. To the extent that we obey his Word and spread the good news about the Messiah, his work is being done. To the extent that we procrastinate and compromise, his work is being delayed. After all, we have a responsibility one to another, and we must cooperate with the

Lord to help reach our fellow brothers and sisters here on this earth. It doesn't happen automatically. As a Hasidic rabbi once commented, "Why has the Messiah not come either yesterday or today? Because we are today just as we were yesterday." The same applies to his return.

2. There is something significant about the end of a millennium and about the twentieth century as a whole. It seems that the Holy Spirit is turning up the heat and increasing the pace. Things are happening that have never happened before.[46]

3. Wars and atrocities have only increased around the world to the extent that the teachings of Jesus the Messiah have been rejected. The notorious mass murderers of this century—Hitler, Stalin, Mao Tse Tung, Pol Pot, and Idi Amin, to name some of the worst—are perfect examples of sinful human beings who did not bow their knees to the God of Israel or receive a new heart through his appointed Messiah. How then can Jesus—whom they scorned—be blamed for the bloodshed? You might as well point a finger at God and say, "If there really is a God, then why is there so much suffering in the world today?"[47]

I should also point out that it is only to the extent that the church has rejected the Messiah's teachings of love, compassion, and sacrifice in favor of violence, hatred, and strong-armed persecution that Jews—and non-Jews as well—have suffered at the hands of these people. In fact, the entire Christian world suffered. In other words, one key reason that the Dark Ages were so dark was because the church departed from its biblical foundations and embraced human traditions that contradicted and negated the precepts of the Old and New Testaments. How then is Jesus responsible for actions committed by those who followed him in name but not in deed?

Our focus, however, should not be on what hypocritical, false followers of the Messiah have done in the past or on what sinful, God-rejecting rebels are doing in the present. Rather, we should step back and see exactly what the Lord has been doing through Jesus the Messiah. We should note carefully how wonderfully Yeshua has worked on behalf of our rebellious planet, in particular in the last one hundred years as the time of his return draws nearer. You see, he taught his followers that the message about God's kingdom had to be proclaimed throughout the entire world, to every nation and people, and then the end would come (Matt. 24:14). That end is getting closer!

Let me put this in perspective for you: By the year 100 c.e., the Bible had been translated into only a handful of languages (less than a half dozen, to be exact). By 200 c.e.—one hundred years later—the number had grown only to seven. By the year 500, it had increased only to thirteen, and by 1000, to just seventeen. Nine hundred years passed with less than twelve new translations! And all this time people were dying without the knowledge of God as contained in the pages of the Holy Scriptures. Thousands of lives were being touched, but the going was slow.

By 1500 c.e., the number of languages with the Word of God had grown to 34 (that's still a pretty slow pace), then, picking up a little speed, by the year 1800, there were 67 translations, and then, by the year 1900, the number had swelled to 537. By the year 2000, the number will exceed the 2000 mark. Isn't this incredible? It sounds like the knowledge of the kingdom of God is spreading. It sounds like the work of the Messiah is making awesome progress. (Remember: People are coming to God through the message of Jesus the Messiah brought to them by the followers of Jesus the Messiah. Without that message of light, they would continue to live and die in spiritual darkness.)

Missiologists (scholars who study contemporary and historical trends among those spreading the message of the Messiah) tell us that roughly 70 percent of all growth in the Messianic kingdom has taken place during this century. (In other words, 70 percent of all those who have believed in Jesus the Messiah and received a new heart through him have done so in the twentieth century alone.) Of that phenomenal growth, 70 percent has taken place since World War II. And—brace yourself—of that incredible increase, 70 percent has taken place since the mid-1980s! These overwhelming statistics tell us that *one-third* of twenty centuries of the expansion of the kingdom of God has taken place *in a period of less than twenty years*—and most of it is occurring among the most impoverished, oppressed, and downtrodden peoples of the world. This means that millions of people have come to believe in the God of Israel and the Messiah of Israel in the last decade alone. Something unique is happening in the days in which we live!

Writing in the November 1990 issue of *Missions Frontiers,* Dr. Ralph D. Winter stated that in the year 100 there was approximately one genuine follower of Jesus for every 360 people on the earth; by 1900, there was one true follower for every twenty-seven people; by 1989, one for every seven; and by the year 2000, he projected that there will be one in three. The end is drawing near! The time of Messiah's return is approaching.

To look at this from another angle and with a small variation in statistics, consider the chart showing milestone dates in the growth of true Christianity (bearing in mind that "true Christianity" is Jewish in the most biblical sense of the word; see above, 1.4–1.7). According to the compilers, the chart offers "at the dates indicated, a comparison of: (1) the number of Bible-believing Christians [people who have come to know the God of Israel through the Messiah]; and (2) the total number of people in the world." You will see that it is *not* just a matter of an increase in numbers alone (since world population in general has also greatly multiplied in this century); rather, phenomenal growth has come to the people of God in terms of *percentage* of world population as well. The statistics are as follows:

One [true follower of Jesus] per hundred (1%) by A.D. 1430 (1 to 99 after 1430 years)
Two per hundred (2%) by A.D. 1790 (1 to 49 after 360 years)
Three per hundred (3%) by A.D. 1940 (1 to 32 after 150 years)
Four per hundred (4%) by A.D. 1960 (1 to 24 after 20 years)
Five per hundred (5%) by A.D. 1970 (1 to 19 after 10 years)
Six per hundred (6%) by A.D. 1980 (1 to 16 after 10 years)
Seven per hundred (7%) by A.D. 1983 (1 to 13 after 3 years)
Eight per hundred (8%) by A.D. 1986 (1 to 11 after 3 years)
Nine per hundred (9%) by A.D. 1989 (1 to 10 after 3 years)
Ten per hundred (10%) by A.D. 1993 (1 to 9 after 4 years)
Eleven per hundred (11%) by A.D. 1995 (1 to 8 after 2 years)[48]

What this means in practical, down-to-earth terms—and it is staggering—is that there are approximately 100,000 to 150,000 people coming to the Messiah *each day* and more than 16,000 *new congregations* being established *each week*. Spiritually speaking, there can be no doubt: It's harvest time, and this transition age is almost over.

Zechariah 10:1 reads, "Ask the LORD for rain in the springtime [literally, in the time of the spring rains]; it is the LORD who makes the storm clouds. He gives showers of rain to men, and plants of the field to everyone." You see, there is a time for sowing and a time for reaping, a time for the fall rains and a time for the spring rains, and just as surely as there are agricultural times and seasons established by God, there are spiritual times and seasons established by God. The unprecedented, worldwide influx of souls into God's kingdom in these last few decades means that, without doubt, it is spiritual harvest time.

You might say, "But Islam is growing rapidly too, and that certainly has nothing to do with the God of Israel, the Messiah of Israel, or the Scriptures of Israel."

I agree! But the message of Jesus has *everything* to do with the God of Israel, the Messiah of Israel, and the Scriptures of Israel—not to mention the fact that true Christianity is growing far more rapidly than Islam, and its growth today is completely devoid of the use of force or coercion, something that cannot be said for Islam.[49] In fact, as soon as you recognize that the gospel message is Jewish from start to finish, you will get excited. That is to say, when you realize that the word *gospel* means "good news," and the good news is that the Messiah has come to set us free from our sins and bring us into right relationship with God, then as a Jew you will be thrilled with the progress that the gospel of Jesus (the good news about our Messiah) is making. The Lord is bringing lost sinners into his kingdom in unprecedented measure around the world, and that is something to get excited about. I tell you again: The Messiah's return is drawing near.

But all will not be rosy before he comes. He warned his followers twenty centuries ago that before the end of this age came there would be terrible times:

You will hear of wars and rumors of wars, but see to it that you are not alarmed. Such things must happen, but the end is still to come. Nation will rise against nation, and kingdom against kingdom. There will be famines and earthquakes in various places. All these are the beginning of birth pains.

Matthew 24:6–8

Of course, these kinds of things have happened before, but Jesus predicted they would be on the increase before his return.[50] He also predicted that there would be a great increase in *persecution* for the faith: "Then you will be handed over to be persecuted and put to death, and you will be hated by all nations because of me. At that time many will turn away from the faith and will betray and hate each other" (Matt. 24:9–10).

This, too, has happened before, but in recent decades, persecution of Christians has increased a hundredfold, and church statisticians tell us that tens of thousands of followers of Jesus are killed *each year* for their beliefs—some would say as many as three hundred thousand annually—figures that are absolutely overwhelming.[51] The final conflict is coming to a close!

There are two other factors that should also be considered relative to human suffering in our day. First, God is beginning to judge the world for centuries of sin and disobedience, and the earth itself is vomiting out its inhabitants. (This does not mean that every weather-related disaster is a judgment from God on sinful people, but it does mean that some of the problems we are facing are a result of this planet beginning to react to countless generations of sinful abuse.)

In Leviticus 18:28, the Lord warned our people not to defile the Promised Land with sexual immorality, since "if you defile the land, it will vomit you out as it vomited out the nations that were before you." Just as the physical body reacts to alcohol and drug abuse by breaking down and degenerating, it seems from the Bible that the earth itself reacts to moral and spiritual pollution (not to mention ecological pollution), "vomiting out" those who live on it. In keeping with this, Scripture tells us that in the end God will shake everything that can be shaken (see Heb. 12:25–29 and Hag. 2:6), an event that will bring the entire universe into upheaval. The end of the age will be anything but tranquil!

Second, we need to recognize that there is a destructive, malevolent figure, called Satan in the Hebrew Scriptures, who is on the warpath against our race.[52] He is a fallen celestial being who is in complete rebellion against God and hates the human race because we are created in the image of God. To make matters worse, the New Testament Book of Revelation speaks of a time when Satan's destructive fury against humankind will be especially great "because he knows that his time is short" (Rev. 12:12). This describes a time at the *end* of this transition age, indicating that there will be a conflict between good and evil right up to the climax of this era, and great darkness will coexist right next to great light. (See Isaiah 60:1–3 for a picture of such a time as this.) The battle will only intensify until Jesus returns.

You need to remember that it was Hosea, an Israelite prophet, who predicted that there would be a *long period* of spiritual decline for our people, a time in which we would be without our Messianic King (see immediately above, 2.1). In other words, there would be many years of darkness before the outworking of the final redemption. Since we learned from the Hebrew Bible that the Messiah had to come before the Second Temple was destroyed, Hosea's words about this long time *without* a Davidic king must refer to the period we are in now. That is to say, his prophecy of our spiritually desolate condition must refer to the period in between his first and second comings, the period in which we presently live.[53]

Therefore, I can tell you again that things are right on schedule, proceeding exactly as our Scriptures said they would. On the one hand, the knowledge of God is spreading like holy fire around the globe, and masses of people are coming into his kingdom through Jesus the Messiah. On the other hand, sinful, God-rejecting humanity continues to shake its fist at its Maker, and the world is in a state of upheaval.[54] The transition age is just about over, and the Messiah is soon to appear.

Does this help you to see things more clearly? If you're still struggling, perhaps the following thoughts will sharpen the picture even more.

According to one stream of thought in traditional Judaism, in each generation there is a *potential Messiah*, and, since no Messiah has yet been revealed, that must mean no generation has been worthy of him (or recognized him, which is the flip side of the same coin).[55] Our view is that there was *one Messiah,* foreknown by God and described in advance in his Word, who came at the appointed time and has been accepted by some and rejected by many. Thus, we believe that every generation has had to make up its mind about the same, one Messiah, God's only Messiah, who came as predicted—as opposed to the traditional Jewish view that speaks of a different, never-revealed, potential Messiah in every generation. Moreover, this so-called "potential Messiah" is one who is *not* explicitly described in the Hebrew Scriptures (since he is a different person every few decades) and the time of his coming is not predicted (how could it be predicted, since it keeps changing?).

For our part, there is no reason to engage in such speculation, since the real Messiah *was* revealed and millions of people—Gentiles and Jews alike—have recognized him and embraced him. At some point in the not-too-distant future, there will be one generation of Jewish and Gentile people who will recognize the Messiah in a significant enough way that he will return.

In contrast with this is some of the recent "the Rebbe is Moshiach" fervor (i.e., the belief that the Lubavitcher Grand Rabbi, Menachem Mendel Schneerson, who died in 1994, is the Messiah). Explaining this concept of a potential Messiah in each generation, one of the Rebbe's followers wrote:

> The first thing we have to know is—surprise!—the Messiah is already here. He's been here all the time, walking the same streets as you . . . or I. Now, two things have to take place: God must reveal the Messiah

to the Jewish people and the Jewish people have to accept the Messiah. But not necessarily in that order. It can very well be that, at first, the Jewish people have to acclaim a holy man as the Messiah and then God will give His own thumbs-up—*but in God's time.*[56]

With all due respect to the author's sincerity, where in the Bible is there support for such a position? And how can he possibly question *our* belief, namely, that the Messiah came at the time predicted by the prophets, died for our sins and rose again as predicted by the prophets, and awaits our recognition as a people, also predicted by the prophets?[57] Again I ask, whose beliefs are scriptural and whose beliefs are speculative?

Interestingly, when the Rebbe died in 1994 without being revealed as the Messiah, many of his followers announced that his death served as an atonement for our sins, and they eagerly awaited his resurrection.[58] In fact, some Jewish leaders criticized them, stating that their views about the Rebbe sounded like Christian teaching about Jesus. They replied: "Not at all! The Christians got their ideas from us. These beliefs are really Jewish!"

There was only one ingredient lacking from the story: the hope that the Rebbe would one day *return.* Here, too, the Rebbe's followers have followed suit, with one of his disciples concluding his biographical sketch of Rabbi Schneerson by writing, "May we merit his immediate return, even before going to press."[59] (By the way, it strikes me as only fair to ask: If traditional Judaism is right and there is a potential Messiah in each generation, why do we need the Rebbe to return? Why not simply identify and welcome this new generation's Messiah?)

So, it is "kosher" for this dear, religious Jew to believe that his rebbe is the Messiah who will one day return even though he did not rise from the dead and even though he is unknown by 99.9 percent of the people of the world (let alone by millions of Jews who have never heard of the "Lubavitcher Rebbe"). At the same time, however, it is *not* okay for us to believe that Yeshua, who fulfilled the Scriptures, who did rise from the dead, and who has brought the knowledge of God to more than one billion people, *is* the promised Messiah!

Doubtless, Rabbi Schneerson was a brilliant, devoted leader who brought thousands of Jews into a traditional expression of their faith, but contemporary scholars did not even deem him worthy of mention in a voluminous work like the *Cambridge Biographical Encyclopedia* (while religious figures such as Mother Teresa, scientists such as Dr. Jonas Salk, and rock stars such as Jimi Hendrix were discussed), and the *Encyclopedia Judaica* gave him only one line, while contemporary Jews such as Bob Dylan and Woody Allen had entire paragraphs written about them!

In fact, to help put this in even clearer perspective, a recent book listing the one hundred "most influential Jews of all time" ranked Jesus of Nazareth second, following only Moses (because of the influence of the Mosaic traditions on Judaism, Christianity, and Islam), with Saul of Tarsus (Paul) ranked sixth (right after Abraham) and Mary (i.e., Miriam), Yeshua's mother, ranked ninth. The Rebbe was not even ranked in the top one hundred. In fact, he was referred to only once, and that in the article on Bob Dylan (who was ranked ninety-seventh).[60] Yet, somehow, for many Jews, it is legitimate to consider Rabbi Schneerson to be the Messiah while it is illegitimate to consider Jesus to be the Messiah.

We don't need to look for any other candidate or Messianic pretender. The real Messiah came twenty centuries ago, and he is preparing to return. Are you ready? The stage is being set.

2.3. There was no Jewish expectation in the first century that the Messiah would be a great miracle worker, so all of Jesus' alleged miracles were of no interest to the first-century Jewish leaders, and they are of no interest to me.

> I think you are misinformed, and I don't believe you are being honest with yourself. First, there most definitely *was* first-century Jewish expectation concerning a miracle-working Messiah, in keeping with the predictions of the biblical prophets. Second, if you understood that Jesus the Messiah really did heal the sick, open blind eyes, and raise the dead, and that he is still performing miracles, I think this *would* be of considerable interest to you.

On several occasions, it is recorded in the New Testament that when Jesus healed the sick and performed miracles, the people wondered out loud as to whether he could be the Messiah. For example, Matthew tells us that on one occasion people "brought Jesus a demon-possessed man who was blind and mute, and Jesus healed him, so that he could both talk and see. All the people were astonished and said, 'Could this be the Son of David?'" (Matt. 12:22–23; remember that "Son of David" meant "the Messiah"). Why did they respond in this way? Because it was commonly believed at that time that the Messiah would be a miracle worker![61]

On another occasion, the disciples of John the Baptist came to Yeshua and asked him, "Are you the one who was to come, or should we expect someone else?" (Luke 7:20). How did the Messiah respond to this question? Luke records,

> At that very time Jesus cured many who had diseases, sicknesses and evil spirits, and gave sight to many who were blind. So he replied to the messengers, "Go back and report to John what you have seen and heard: The blind receive sight, the lame walk, those who have leprosy are cured, the deaf hear, the dead are raised, and the good news is preached to the poor. Blessed is the man who does not fall away on account of me."
>
> Luke 7:21–23

Do you see the significance of this? A number of religious Jewish men came to Jesus and wanted to know if he was really the Messiah. He responded by saying, "Watch this! I'm doing the works that the Messiah was expected to do." In other words, "I'm the one!"

In fact, a lengthy description of the Messiah in the Dead Sea Scrolls—written even before the New Testament—describes God's miraculous activity in conjunction with the reign of his anointed one in words almost identical to those just cited from Luke 7:21–23:

> [For the hea]vens and the earth will listen to His Messiah, [and all] that is in them will not turn away from the holy precepts. . . . For the Lord will observe the devout, and call the just by name, and upon the poor he will place his spirit, and the faithful he will renew with his strength. For he will honour the devout upon the throne of eternal royalty, free-ing prisoners, giving sight to the blind, straightening out the twisted. . . . And the Lord will perform marvelous acts such as have not existed, just as he sa[id] for he will heal the badly wounded and will make the dead live, he will proclaim good news to the meek, give lavishly [to the need]y, lead the exiled and enrich the hungry.[62]

Where did these different Jewish groups get such ideas? From the Hebrew Bible![63] There are several well-known passages in the Tanakh that speak of healings and miracles in conjunction with the Messianic age. For example, we read in Isaiah 35, a well-known Messianic prophecy, that when God visits his people, "Then will the eyes of the blind be opened and the ears of the deaf unstopped. Then will the lame leap like a deer, and the mute tongue shout for joy. Water will gush forth in the wilderness and streams in the desert" (Isa. 35:5–6). These were signs that God's kingdom was arriving. Those who had been captive to oppressive sickness and disease were set free.[64]

So, when Yeshua began to preach and teach in his hometown synagogue one Sabbath, it is written that he outlined the purpose of his mission by quoting from Isaiah 61, reading these words: "The Spirit of the Lord is on me, because he has anointed me to preach good news to the poor. He has sent me to proclaim freedom for the prisoners and recovery of sight for the blind, to release the oppressed, to proclaim the year of the Lord's favor" (Luke 4:18–19, quoting portions of Isa. 61:1–3). Healings and miracles were thus part and parcel of the Messiah's mission, and they formed some of his most impressive credentials.

Similar descriptions of the miracles of the Messianic age (whether performed by God himself or by his Messiah) are also found in the Talmudic literature (see, e.g., b. Sukkah 52a, where Messiah ben David raises Messiah ben Joseph from the dead), and a special token of divine favor believed to accompany some of the most saintly Talmudic sages was their miracle-working ability (in particular Honi the Circle Drawer and Hanina Ben Dosa).[65] In fact, throughout the ages— right up to our own day when the Lubavitcher Hasidim pointed to the alleged miracles of their rebbe as possible proof of his messiahship—Jews have commonly viewed the Messiah as a miracle worker of sorts.[66] Also, according to the fourth- to fifth-century Christian scholar Jerome, the false Messiah Bar Kochba (influential from 132 to 135 c.e.) performed counterfeit miracles to delude the people.[67]

In any case, if there ever was a time when miracles were freely associated with the Messiah, it was the first century, when no such things as atheistic rationalism or secular humanism existed. You may have gotten your facts wrong because later Rabbinic teaching put more emphasis on the Messiah as a teacher or warrior.[68]

As for not caring about miracles yourself, give it some thought the next time you or someone you love is faced with a serious illness or life-threatening condition. Perhaps the gracious healing power of Jesus the Messiah will seem more relevant to you then.[69]

This is simply the reality of human nature: We are weak, frail, prone to sickness, and, as a race, riddled with terrible suffering and disease. Even though followers of Jesus are not exempt from sickness and pain—hardly!—they often experience the Messiah's powerful and real touch, receiving healing and deliverance in some pronounced and wonderful ways. Many Jews have actually turned to God in repentance and put their faith in Yeshua the Messiah after they received healing from a serious physical or mental disorder.

Just ask David Yaniv about this. Born in Tel Aviv in 1936, he injured his back while working on a kibbutz, only to become paralyzed because of a neurosurgeon's error during a spinal operation. For seven and a half years, he could move around only with the help of a wheelchair or crutches and heavy leg braces. After becoming terribly depressed, he finally resigned himself to follow his doctor's advice to "learn to live with it" because the damage to his nerve was irreparable. Then he had two experiences that changed his life forever.

First, as a result of watching Christian programming that was aired on a Lebanese station, he met Yeshua as his Savior, receiving forgiveness of sins and a new heart. His wife soon met the Messiah too. Then, to David's utter amazement, after a Christian woman received a "word" that someone watching that same Christian program was being healed of long-term paralysis from the waist down, he awoke the next morning to find his legs responding to stimuli. He was healed! Within days, he was walking on his own, having completely recovered from an incurable condition, to the absolute amazement of twenty-five doctors, neurosurgeons (including the surgeon whose error crippled David in the first place), and neurologists who came from across Israel to examine him.[70] More than fifteen years later, he is as healthy and fit as ever.

This modern-day, documented miracle is just another reminder that the Messiah came to set the captives free—in keeping with the prophecies of our own Hebrew Scriptures. When he returns to fully establish the kingdom of God on earth, he will perform even greater miracles than those we have seen to date.

2.4. Jesus cannot be the Messiah because more Jewish blood has been shed in his name than in any other name or for any other cause.

Certainly, much Jewish blood has been shed in Jesus' name by violent and ungodly men who have been a total disgrace to Christianity. This is reprehensible and completely inexcusable. Still, your statement is quite exaggerated and also misses a crucial point. First, more Jews have been killed by people who professed no faith at all in Jesus than by those so-called "Christians" who persecuted our people in Jesus' name. For example, the atheistic Stalinists who slaughtered our people did not do so in Jesus' name, nor have the militant Islamic terrorists. Second, there is something important we must recognize, even though it is terribly painful even to consider. From a biblical perspective, the most common reason Jewish blood has been shed is that we Jews have strayed from God, violated his covenant, broken his laws, and failed to heed his prophets. Just look at the curses for disobedience promised in the Torah of Moses. We could not have suffered so much if we were guiltless as a people. As for hypocritical *goyyim* (Gentiles) shedding Jewish blood in Jesus' name—no true follower of Jesus could ever murder in his name—this terribly sinful act is also alluded to in the Torah.

In the next few answers, I'll address in detail the difficult subject of "Christian" anti-Semitism, discussing the relevant issues with complete honesty and candor. Right now, I want to ask *you* a question. Honestly, why do you think so much Jewish blood has been shed through the years? Do you believe this was what God intended for us, that this is the demonstration of his love to us and the proof of his blessing upon us? Or do you think something went wrong and that the Lord did not intend for us to suffer as we have? Do you *really* believe Jesus is the cause of our suffering?

Let me take this one step further and ask you an even more difficult question: What if Jesus really was our Messiah and we were given a choice to receive him or reject him? What would be the consequences of our saying no to our God-sent deliverer?

Almost two thousand years ago, when Jesus the Messiah came to the city of Jerusalem for the last time before his death, he wept over the city, foreseeing the terrible suffering that was about to come:

As he approached Jerusalem and saw the city, he wept over it and said, "If you, even you, had only known on this day what would bring you peace—but now it is hidden from your eyes. The days will come upon you when your enemies will build an embankment against you and encircle you and hem you in on every side. They will dash you to the ground, you and the children within your walls. They will not leave one stone on another, because you did not recognize the time of God's coming to you."

Luke 19:41–44

He had longed to do good to his Jewish people, but as a nation, we were not willing. Forty years later Jerusalem was sacked by the Romans. Yeshua knew it was coming. Listen to his words of lamentation:

O Jerusalem, Jerusalem, you who kill the prophets and stone those sent to you, how often I have longed to gather your children together, as a hen gathers her chicks under her wings, but you were not willing. Look, your house is left to you desolate. For I tell you, you will not see me again until you say, "Blessed is he who comes in the name of the Lord."

Matthew 23:37–39

Right up to the moment of his crucifixion, even after he had been severely whipped and beaten, Yeshua was more concerned with the suffering that was about to come to his people than with his own physical and emotional agony:

A large number of people followed him, including women who mourned and wailed for him. Jesus turned and said to them, "Daughters of Jerusalem, do not weep for me; weep for yourselves and for your children. For the time will come when you will say, 'Blessed are the barren women, the wombs that never bore and the breasts that never nursed!' Then 'they will say to the mountains, "Fall on us!" and to the hills, "Cover us!"' [quoting Hosea 10:8] For if men do these things when the tree is green, what will happen when it is dry?"

Luke 23:27–31

Tragically, this was part of a pattern: Just as we repeatedly rejected the Torah and the prophets, we rejected the Messiah when he came (see also above, 2.1–2.2). Look at how one of the ancient biblical authors described our history during biblical times:

The LORD warned Israel and Judah through all his prophets and seers: "Turn from your evil ways. Observe my commands and decrees, in accordance with the entire Law that I commanded your fathers to obey and that I delivered to you through my servants the prophets." But they would not listen and were as stiff-necked as their fathers, who did not trust in the LORD their God. They rejected his decrees and the covenant he had made with their fathers and the warnings he had given them.

They followed worthless idols and themselves became worthless. They imitated the nations around them although the LORD had ordered them, "Do not do as they do," and they did the things the LORD had forbidden them to do. They forsook all the commands of the LORD their God and made for themselves two idols cast in the shape of calves, and an Asherah pole. They bowed down to all the starry hosts, and they worshiped Baal. They sacrificed their sons and daughters in the fire. They practiced divination and sorcery and sold themselves to do evil in the eyes of the LORD, provoking him to anger. So the LORD was very angry with Israel and removed them from his presence. Only the tribe of Judah was left, and even Judah did not keep the commands of the LORD their God. They followed the practices Israel had introduced. Therefore the LORD rejected all the people of Israel; he afflicted them and gave them into the hands of plunderers, until he thrust them from his presence.

2 Kings 17:13–20

(Remember: This is the historical summary provided for us in our own Hebrew Bible. Yes, God's Word is ruthlessly honest.)

The fact is, we were warned. Few sections in the Torah—or the Bible as a whole—are more clear than Leviticus 26 and Deuteronomy 28, the chapters promising blessings for obedience and curses for disobedience. There, in explicit detail, God promised our people prosperity and well-being *in this world* if we were careful to obey his commandments, and threatened us with terrible judgments if we refused to obey (see also the discussion above, 1.10). Unfortunately, as the Lord foretold Moses, our history was to be marked by national disobedience and curses as opposed to national obedience and blessings:

And the LORD said to Moses: "You are going to rest with your fathers, and these people will soon prostitute themselves to the foreign gods of the land they are entering. They will forsake me and break the covenant I made with them. On that day I will become angry with them and forsake them; I will hide my face from them, and they will be destroyed. Many disasters and difficulties will come upon them, and on that day they will ask, 'Have not these disasters come upon us because our God is not with us?'"

Deuteronomy 31:16–17

At this point you might be asking, "What does this have to do with my objection? What does this have to do with all the suffering our people have endured at the hands of Christians who persecuted us in Jesus' name? What is the connection?"

The connection is simply this: We have suffered primarily because of *our* sins not the sins of those who persecuted us. In other words, while every hypocritical Christian or fanatical Muslim or murderous Nazi who has done harm to a Jew will be judged by God for his or her own sins, there must have been something wrong on our part as well for us to have suffered so terribly on a national level. This is absolutely explicit in our Scriptures.[71] If we were in good standing with God on a national level, we would be blessed not cursed. Therefore, even though you may find this difficult to swallow, in reality, your argument is with the Torah, not with me. In fact, the Orthodox Jewish author Meir Simcha Sokolovsky, examining Israel's history in light of the blessings and curses of Deuteronomy 28, makes an interesting observation:

> The uniqueness of the Jewish People—the Chosen People—is evident not only in the miracles and the marvels which are an integral part of its history, but also in its chronicles of unmatched suffering and travail. No other nation in the world has been so persecuted, so beleaguered by evil decrees, so victimized by libels, so repeatedly expelled from so many lands as the Jewish nation. . . . This alone would constitute clear proof that the suffering and agonies which have been visited upon the Jewish people are not mere chance, but the inevitable consequence of the unique relationship between God and his people Israel, whom he has chosen to draw near to himself, meticulously meting out both its reward and punishment. In the words of the prophet:
> Only you have I known (befriended) of all the families of the earth: therefore I will punish you for all your sins. (Amos 3:2)
> A son whose father rebukes him for unseemly conduct senses his father's love and closeness to him even as he is punished. He realizes that his father would not have bothered to punish a strange child who behaved similarly since the matter would have no import for him.
> Thus it is with the Jewish People: the irrational nature of its suffering demonstrates that it comes from Heaven. It is a sign and a wonder testifying to the everlasting bond of love between the people of Israel and their God.[72]

What I am urging you to consider is that even our suffering at the hands of the church—an agonizing subject that I have written on in depth[73]—is *partially* due to the fact that our continued rejection of God's messengers, from Moses to Jeremiah to the Messiah, took us out from the place of blessing and protection and made us vulnerable to an onslaught from hell. It seems that the Torah prophesied about this too.[74]

Look at Deuteronomy 32:19–21 as rendered in the New Jewish Publication Society Version:

The LORD saw and was vexed
And spurned His sons and His daughters.
He said:
I will hide My countenance from them,
And see how they fare in the end.
For they are a treacherous breed,
Children with no loyalty in them.
They incensed Me with no-gods,
Vexed Me with their futilities;
I'll incense them with a no-folk,
Vex them with a nation of fools.[75]

The principle here seems to be one of tit-for-tat punishment, and it really does apply to the question at hand: Because we rejected the Messiah when he came, the door was opened for us to suffer atrocities at the hands of his false followers. In other words, since we sinned against God (and our rejection of the Messiah was certainly a sin against God), people sinned against us.[76]

"But why do you keep saying that the Christians who tortured and killed our forefathers were false followers of Jesus? It seems to me they were the most devoted and zealous followers of all!"

Not at all. The words of Jesus and the rest of the New Testament are absolutely clear: Anyone persecuting, torturing, or killing another human being in Jesus' name—especially with the goal of converting that person—is *not* one of his. To the contrary, Yeshua pronounced blessings on the *meek* and on the *peacemakers,* praising those who joyfully endured persecution and insult for his sake (see Matt. 5:3–12). He taught his followers to love their enemies, to pray for those who persecuted them and do good to those who hated them (see Matt. 5:44; Luke 6:35). He made it absolutely clear that his people were *not* to take up the sword in an attempt to defend him or extend his kingdom, warning that "all who draw the sword will die by the sword" (Matt 26:52; see also John 18:36). In fact, the earliest Christians were so committed to nonviolence that they refused even to serve in the Roman army.

Paul taught the believers to "bless those who persecute you; bless and do not curse," calling on them not to "repay anyone evil for evil" and counseling them not to be "overcome by evil" but rather to "overcome evil with good" (Rom. 12:14, 17, 21). Peter reiterated this, reminding his readers that they were called to patient suffering, even when it was completely unjust. Why?

> . . . because Christ suffered for you, leaving you an example, that you should follow in his steps. "He committed no sin, and no deceit was found in his mouth." When they hurled their insults at him, he did not retaliate; when he suffered, he made no threats. Instead, he entrusted himself to him who judges justly. He himself bore our sins in his body on the tree, so that we might die to sins and live for righteousness; by his wounds you have been healed.
>
> 1 Peter 2:21–24

That is the example every Christian is to follow.[77]

So emphatic was this teaching that John, one of the men closest to Jesus during his days on earth, could actually write, "We know that we have passed from death to life, because we love our brothers. Anyone who does not love remains in death. Anyone who hates his brother is a murderer, and you know that no murderer has eternal life in him" (1 John 3:14–15). That is what the New Testament says!

In point of fact, I could cite dozens of similar New Testament passages, along with thousands of moving stories of followers of Jesus being imprisoned, tortured, and slaughtered for their faith—true followers of Jesus will be the persecuted, not the persecutors[78]—but I can sum up my point here with one statement from the Messiah: "Not everyone who says to me, 'Lord, Lord,' will enter the kingdom of heaven, but only he who does the will of my Father who is in heaven" (Matt. 7:21). In other words, not everyone who calls himself a Christian or Messianic Jew really is one. Rather, all those who do not do God's will are *not* followers of the Messiah—even if they perform miracles in his name (Matt. 7:22–23). They may call him Lord, but they deny him by their evil deeds.

To summarize, because we rejected the Messiah when he came (the rejection of no other person could cause such suffering for us as a people), we forfeited the blessings of God and inherited his curses instead, one of which included being persecuted and hounded by godless people, some of whom could even be professing Christians. This is in keeping with a pattern we find several times in the Scriptures: When we sinned against God and were deserving of his punishment, he gave us over to the hands of other godless nations to afflict us, nations such as

Assyria or Babylon.[79] The problem is that these nations then went *too far* in their actions and became themselves the objects of judgment. Consider God's words to Assyria:

> Woe to the Assyrian, the rod of my anger, in whose hand is the club of my wrath! I send him against a godless nation, I dispatch him against a people who anger me, to seize loot and snatch plunder, and to trample them down like mud in the streets. But this is not what he intends, this is not what he has in mind; his purpose is to destroy, to put an end to many nations. . . . [Therefore] when the Lord has finished all his work against Mount Zion and Jerusalem, he will say, "I will punish the king of Assyria for the willful pride of his heart and the haughty look in his eyes."
>
> Isaiah 10:5–7, 12

Some of Israel's suffering was due to her own sin, and some was due to the sin of her oppressors. As the Lord declared in Zechariah 1:15 (after Judah suffered at the hands of Babylon, Edom, and others), "I am very angry with those nations that are at ease; for I was only angry a little, but they overdid the punishment" (NJPSV). Or, as rendered in the NIV, "I was only a little angry, but they added to the calamity."

This has been the pattern throughout history, from the Old Testament period until today. To one extent or another, we have often deserved punishment as a people, but the punishment was often too extreme, and God then had to punish the punishers too. Yeshua warned us that the Romans would inflict terrible judgment on Jerusalem and its people because we missed the time of our visitation, but the Romans no doubt were far too ruthless and as a result were judged by God as well. So it has continued to this hour. Until we return to God in repentance and acknowledge the Messiah, we remain vulnerable to the malicious attacks and malignant devices of those who hate the Jewish people, and these Jew-haters, who by their very actions prove that they too do not know the Messiah, will be judged by God as well.

This much is clear: The consequences of our rejecting the Messiah certainly cannot be used as a criterion to deny his messiahship!

Wouldn't it be tragic to perpetuate the error of rejecting him, remaining ignorant of his teachings, and blaming him for the atrocities committed by his false followers, instead of coming to him in faith and reversing the pattern of judgment? I tell you with complete confidence: Jesus is the *cure* of our every problem, individually and nationally, not the *cause* of our every problem.

2.5. Christianity is actually a religion of hate not love. Its bad fruit proves that it is a bad tree, even according to Jesus' own criteria (see Matt. 7:15–20; Luke 6:43–45).

> Years ago, some Orthodox rabbis told me that I didn't know what real Judaism was. Could it be that you don't know what real Christianity is? The fruit that has been produced through the coming of Jesus into the world—in the lives of his true followers—has been wonderful and extraordinary. Anyway, your reasoning about Christianity being a bad tree is faulty. Let me explain.

When I was in graduate school at New York University, I met and interacted with students and professors from many religious backgrounds, and since then, as I have traveled around the world telling people the good news about Jesus the Messiah, I have spoken with even more people representing a wide range of spiritual beliefs, including Muslims, Buddhists, Hindus, Sikhs, and animists. To this day, when I discuss religion with people who are educated in what they believe, I always ask them what their religion really teaches. In other words, I say, "I have heard that you believe such and such. Is this true?" And then they explain, "Yes, that is correct," or, "No, that is a common misconception." Whenever it is possible, I ask them to support their statements with citations from their holy books. This way I can learn what they really believe (and not just what someone told me they believe), and I can more effectively share my beliefs with them. Wouldn't you agree this is a fair approach?

In the same way, when it comes to what Christianity really teaches and what ideals it actually expresses, we must go back to the words of Jesus and his followers as recorded in the New Testament. That alone is authoritative for those professing to be his disciples today.

"But," you say, "there is often a big difference between what a religious book says and what the followers of that religion do."

That's a good point—but it doesn't change my argument. First, when the so-called followers of a religion fail to adhere to the clear teaching and standards of that religion, then they are rightly branded hypocrites. But their hypocrisy certainly doesn't detract from the truth of the religion itself.

Second, in a religion such as Islam there are, in fact, explicit passages in the Koran and the early Muslim traditions that advocate physical violence and war in order to propagate the faith. This stands in complete contrast to the teaching of the New Testament, which categorically rejects the use of force in order to propagate the faith. Therefore, when Muslims launch a holy war to spread Islam, they are often *being true to their faith;* when Christians do such a thing, they are always *denying their faith.*

Third, we Jews rightly react when an anti-Semite uses the Talmud to prove that the rabbis advocated such perversions as, for example, having sex with children.[80] We point out that the only way anyone could come to such a conclusion would be through the complete *misuse* of the Talmud, and we are zealous to defend the real meaning and intent of the Talmudic scholars. In the same way, when Christianity is mischaracterized (in this case, branded a religion of hate), it is necessary to go back to the New Testament sources and see what they really say.

Fourth, the overall fruit produced by true faith in Jesus breeds anything but hate. (I'll say more about this last point in a moment.)

Let's first review what Jesus and his followers taught regarding treatment of those who oppose the faith, attitudes to one's enemies, and the use of force to spread the faith. As we saw before (2.4), Yeshua pronounced blessings on the *meek* and on the *peacemakers,* praising those who joyfully endured persecution and insult for his sake, instructing his followers to love their enemies, to pray for those who persecuted them and do good to those who hated them. This is what he taught:

> Do to others as you would have them do to you. If you love those who love you, what credit is that to you? Even "sinners" love those who love them. And if you do good to those who are good to you, what credit is that to you? Even "sinners" do that. And if you lend to those from whom you expect repayment, what credit is that to you? Even "sinners" lend to "sinners," expecting to be repaid in full. But love your enemies, do good to them, and lend to them without expecting to get anything back. Then your reward will be great, and you will be sons of the Most High, because he is kind to the ungrateful and wicked. Be merciful, just as your Father is merciful. Do not judge, and you will not be judged. Do not condemn, and you will not be condemned. Forgive, and you will be forgiven.
>
> Luke 6:31–37

"But no one lives like this!" you say. "Followers of Jesus are anything but loving."

Really? How many hundreds (or thousands, or millions) of them do you know personally? How many Messianic Jews do you know who survived the Holocaust and *forgave* the very Nazis who killed or tortured their own parents, spouses, or siblings? I know some, and the love they have comes from Jesus the Messiah, without whom they would have been consumed with hatred and bitterness. How many Christian missionaries do you know who have had family members or friends killed by hostile members of another faith, only to give their own lives to reach such people? I know such people, and the fire that fuels their compassion is the fire of the Messiah's love.[81]

Let me give you just two examples that demonstrate the powerful, life-transforming effect of the message of the good news of the Messiah, examples that show how God's love for us—expressed through Yeshua—in turn produces supernatural love for others. And remember, these are merely two examples out of millions, and I mean that with no exaggeration.

Consider the stories of Sergeant Jacob DeShazer and Captain Mitsuo Fuchida, mortal enemies during World War II. DeShazer, an American, was downed in Japan during a bombing raid. Fuchida led the infamous Pearl Harbor attack in 1941. Both were soldiers at heart, and killing was their business during the war. But God had other plans.

The story begins in a prison camp and a five-foot-wide cell where DeShazer was kept after being shot down by the Japanese.

He was treated with the most horrible forms of cruelty. He developed an intense hatred for his Japanese guards. All he wanted was to get his hands on one of their throats to squeeze the life out of him. But they continued to torture him. Day by day his hatred grew until it became a veritable mountain. He lived for only one reason, and that was to seek revenge on his torturers.

One day a Bible was brought into the prison. It was passed around and finally came to DeShazer. He read it. He devoured it eagerly! And he came across the words of Jesus, who said [as he was being crucified!], "Father, forgive them, for they do not know what they do" (Luke 23:34a). The love of Christ melted that mountain of hatred inside of Jacob DeShazer and filled him with the joy of Jesus Christ. He said, "My heart was full of joy. I wouldn't have traded places with anyone." Soon after that a guard slammed the cell door on DeShazer's bare foot and began kicking him at the foot with hobnailed boots. DeShazer said nothing but thought of Jesus' words, "Love your enemies." That guard's attitude changed substantially.[82]

Upon his release after the war, DeShazer had the opportunity to return to Japan, and he did, but not as a soldier. Rather, he went as a missionary, sharing the message of the Messiah's love with the Japanese people. So wonderful was his story that it was printed as a tract in Japanese. But that was only the beginning:

> One day a Japanese man who was disheartened, broken, dejected, and hopeless was given that tract by an American stranger. He read that tract, and his heart was touched. He sought out Christian missionaries and the Bible. He too was converted. His name was Captain Mitsuo Fuchida. He was the Japanese officer who spearheaded the 1941 attack on Pearl Harbor on December 7. The very man who had declared, "Tora! Tora! Tora!" [Japanese for "Tiger! Tiger! Tiger!"] gave his heart and life over to Jesus Christ. He, too, began to preach the gospel of Jesus Christ to people all over Japan and America. He even came back to Pearl Harbor on the twenty-fifth anniversary of the attack with a gift in hand for the survivors: a Bible with Luke 23:34a inscribed in it ("Father, forgive them, for they do not know what they do"). Fuchida asked for forgiveness, for he had acted a quarter century earlier in moral ignorance.[83]

This is the infectious power of the Messiah's love! In fact, because examples such as these can so easily be multiplied, the Jewish objection I hear from those who work with true followers of Jesus around the world is generally the *opposite* objection of the one being raised here, namely, "It's unnatural to turn the other cheek and love your enemies. Christianity doesn't allow for a healthy expression of human emotion!"[84]

To the contrary, there is a wonderful, cleansing, liberating, God-ordained emotional release that comes through forgiveness and love. This divinely empowered, unconditional love helps explain why there is a direct correlation between the spread of true Christianity and dramatic increases in health care, education, and acts of kindness to the suffering and poor. There is no denying the profound, humanitarian effect that the gospel message has made around the world.

To this day, most major efforts in feeding the hungry, caring for the sick, and alleviating human suffering are financed and carried out by Christian organizations (see further vol. 2, 3.25). The true New Testament faith is a good tree, and that's why it has produced so much good fruit.

How then do we explain the substantial amount of bad fruit that Christianity has produced through the centuries? Let's take a minute to think this through, going back to Yeshua's own words. In Luke 6:43–44, he taught, "No good tree bears bad fruit, nor does a bad tree bear good fruit. Each tree is recognized by its own fruit. People do not pick figs from thornbushes, or grapes from briers."

What does this mean? Well, it is possible that a good tree might produce some rotten fruit from time to time, but its overall fruit will be good. A bad tree, however, will never produce truly good fruit at all. If a tree has borne lots of good fruit through the years—even if there have been some "rotten apples" along the way—the bad fruit would be the obvious exception that proved the rule. It would actually *stand out* because it was so unusual. This is the case with Jesus the Messiah: His coming into the world has produced an almost indescribable amount of wonderful fruit in the lives of countless millions who have truly embraced him. The ugly things done by some of his followers stand out because they are so contrary to the example set by Yeshua and his disciples. As expressed in a recent book, there is a difference between Christianity (meaning the true expression of the Messianic faith) and Christendom (meaning the humanly organized structure that has often strayed from the faith).[85]

At this point I can hear someone saying, "Nonsense! You are just copping out with this 'occasional bad fruit from a good tree' argument."

I'm prepared to answer your point. But remember this: We both agree that a truly *bad* tree will not produce truly *good* fruit, right? Keep this in mind as we analyze your argument.

It is often claimed that Christianity grew out of Judaism, and that the religion of Moses, the prophets, and the Rabbinic sages provided the soil out of which the religion of Jesus and the apostles grew.[86] What then does that say about Judaism? According to the logic being used against us here, the Rabbinic Jewish tree must have been bad because it produced the bad fruit of Christianity!

Of course, you would say, "Not at all! In fact, it is because Jesus and his followers broke away from their good Jewish roots that they produced such bad fruit." Well, aside from the fact that Yeshua and his followers did *not* break away from their biblical Jewish roots, you must realize that you have just stated to me my very argument to you. Christianity has produced bad fruit only when those who professed to follow Jesus the Messiah broke away from their good, New Testament roots.

According to your logic, since Christianity grew out of Jewish soil, and since Christianity has produced some bad fruit, then Judaism must be a bad tree since it produced the bad fruit of Christianity. The logic is clearly faulty.

I could also ask you what fruit the Torah has produced in the lives of our people during the last thirty-five hundred years. You might say, "That's easy to answer! It has produced the fruit of righteous living, integrity, devotion to God, and respect for the earth and for humanity as a whole."

Not quite! These things hold true only for those who have *adhered* to the words of Torah. For those who *rejected* the law—and that applies to the great majority of our people who have been born since the Torah was given—the Torah has produced unspeakable suffering for our people, beginning with the death of three thousand Israelites just days after Moses received the Commandments on Mount Sinai (see Exodus 32), and resulting in the deaths of one entire generation in the wilderness less than forty years later (see Numbers 13–14). This is because we *rejected* the words of the Torah.

Once again, the way to judge a tree is to see what fruit is produced by those who hold to its principles and live out its ideals. Just as it would be unfair to judge traditional Judaism by the actions of a religious Jew such as Baruch Goldstein, who massacred thirty praying Muslims at Hebron (although he is considered to be a hero and holy martyr by many ultra-Orthodox Jews living in Israel today) or by an irreligious Jew such as Karl Marx, whose writings helped birth the modern monstrosity called communism, so also it would be unfair to judge Jesus or the New Testament faith as a whole by the actions and words of those who sometimes served as leaders in the church while rejecting the teachings of Jesus, the very foundation of the church.

"But I still don't understand why so many Christian leaders have been such virulent anti-Semites. This doesn't make any sense, and to me, it calls into question your whole point here. If the Christian tree is good, it should surely have borne good fruit in terms of loving—not hating and persecuting—our people. Obviously, you judge a tree by the *general pattern* of the kind of fruit it produces."

Actually, I agree with your premises here. This time, it is your facts that are wrong. Of course, it is true that there has been somewhat of a double whammy when it comes to the question of the church and the Jews. On the one hand, we Jews have suffered for *our sins* for the last two thousand years, sins that include our continued rejection of

Jesus the Messiah. On the other hand, we have suffered for *the church's sins*, namely, their attacking us and discriminating against us because we didn't believe their message. This affair is so ugly that it breathes the very spirit of a satanic conspiracy, and I will devote the next three questions to the subject of "Christian anti-Semitism" (see 2.6–2.8).

The reason, however, that I differ with your facts is simply because true Christianity is often marked by philo-Semitism (that is, special love for the Jewish people) as opposed to anti-Semitism (for more on this, see especially, 2.7). In other words, during the Holocaust, the true followers of Jesus were *not* the Ukrainian S.S. officers whose belts read, "In God we trust," nor were they the Polish priests who urged their parishioners to expose and betray their Jewish friends and co-workers. No. They were the so-called "righteous Gentiles" who risked their lives to protect and save their Jewish neighbors, people like the ten Boom family in Holland, made famous through the movie *The Hiding Place*.[87]

The fact that the true followers of Jesus have always been a relatively small remnant—in contrast with the larger numbers represented by Christendom as a whole—should occasion no surprise, since there was only a faithful remnant of Israelites during the biblical period, and there has only been a faithful remnant since then, even according to Orthodox Jews. Even today, as the message of the good news of the Messiah spreads around the world (see above, 2.2), true believers in Yeshua represent only a portion of those who call themselves Christian, a portion, I might add, that is often persecuted and mistreated.

In any case, the wonderful fruit produced by the life, death, and resurrection of Jesus the Messiah continues to flood the world, and because of him, to this very day, terrorists are laying down their weapons, serial killers in prison are finding a new way of life, idol worshipers are turning to the one true God, drug addicts and alcoholics are being set free from their addictions, child abusers are changing their ways, prostitutes are no longer plying their trade, and broken families are being restored.[88] It is because of Jesus that countless medical missionaries continue to labor sacrificially in the midst of horrific conditions, massive shipments of food continue to be sent to the poor and needy, and schools and hospitals continue to be erected. Why? Because Yeshua's followers really care!

Of course, Christianity is not the only world religion active in these ways, but it is certainly the world leader, inspired as it is by the very example of its founder,[89] the one who not only spoke about love but demonstrated it as well:

> This is how we know what love is: Jesus Christ laid down his life for us. And we ought to lay down our lives for our brothers. If anyone has material possessions and sees his brother in need but has no pity on him, how can the love of God be in him? Dear children, let us not love with words or tongue but with actions and in truth.
>
> 1 John 3:16–18

The tree is very good, and therefore, the fruit is very good. Why don't you find out for yourself? As the psalmist wrote many centuries ago: "Taste and see that the Lord is good; blessed is the man who takes refuge in him" (Ps. 34:8).

2.6. Jesus himself taught that he did not come to bring peace but a sword. We Jews have felt the edge of this sword for more than fifteen hundred years now!

> Jesus was actually referring to the Hebrew Scriptures when he said that he did not come to bring peace but a sword (see Micah 7:5–6 and Matt. 10:34). That same passage is quoted in the Mishnah with reference to family conflicts that will come with the advent of the Messianic age. In any case, what Jesus and Micah were talking about was bringing division into families over the issue of loyalty to God and his Messiah. As for literally taking up swords for the faith, Jesus utterly renounced this.

In a previous answer, I stated that one reason the Messiah, the Prince of Peace, did not usher in an age of peace is because we rejected him as a nation (see above, 2.4). Let me expand on this. The New Testament Scriptures record that when the Messiah was born in Bethlehem twenty centuries ago, a host of angels announced the event to shepherds who were watching their flocks by night, proclaiming, "Glory to God in the highest, and on earth peace to men on whom his favor rests" (Luke 2:14). Yes, this was to be a time of peace for those whose hearts were right with God. In fact, before Jesus was even born, Zechariah, the father of John the Baptist, spoke these prophetic words about the Messiah, calling him "the rising sun [who] will come to us from heaven to shine on those living in darkness and in the shadow of death, to guide our feet into the path of peace" (Luke 1:78–79).

Tragically, just days before he was put to death, Yeshua wept over the city of Jerusalem saying:

> If you, even you, had only known on this day what would bring you peace—but now it is hidden from your eyes. The days will come upon you when your enemies will build an embankment against you and encircle you and hem you in on every side. They will dash you to the ground, you and the children within your walls. They will not leave one stone on another, because you did not recognize the time of God's coming to you.
>
> Luke 19:42–44

It happened just as he said it would. Our holy city was ransacked by the Romans in 70 c.e., and tens of thousands of Jewish lives were lost. Yes, the Messiah *did* come to bring peace, but as a people, we missed the opportunity to receive him as our King, and we have been suffering the consequences ever since. Should we fault Jesus, our righteous Prophet and Savior who warned us in advance, or should we fault those of our forefathers who failed to listen to him? The sad fact is *we missed our time of peace.*

"Hold on!" you say. "What about Jesus' own words? What about the fact that he himself said he did not come to bring peace but a sword? How do you explain that?"

Let's take a look and see exactly what Jesus said, remembering his words we just cited: "If you, even you, had only known on this day what would bring you peace—but now it is hidden from your eyes" (Luke 19:42). He offered peace, but we missed the opportunity, resulting in great calamity for our people, our land, and our city (Jerusalem). Yet none of this caught Jesus by surprise. He knew he would be rejected and killed, and he knew many of his followers would suffer a similar fate, warning them about this repeatedly.

On one occasion, after telling his disciples "that he must go to Jerusalem and suffer many things at the hands of the elders, chief priests and teachers of the law, and that he must be killed and on the third day be raised to life," he said to them, "If anyone would come after me, he must deny himself and *take up his cross* and follow me. For whoever wants to save his life will lose it, but whoever loses his life for me will find it" (Matt. 16:21, 24–25). In other words, "I'm not the only one who's going to die!" If the Master would be rejected, his servants would also be rejected:

> If the world hates you, keep in mind that it hated me first. If you belonged to the world, it would love you as its own. As it is, you do not belong to the world, but I have chosen you out of the world. That is why the world hates you. Remember the words I spoke to you: "No servant is greater than his master." If they persecuted me, they will persecute you also. If they obeyed my teaching, they will obey yours also. They will treat you this way because of my name, for they do not know the One who sent me.
>
> John 15:18–21

It was in a similar context that Yeshua made his famous—and quite ironic—statement that he had not come to bring peace but rather a sword, simply meaning that the effects of his coming would not bring earthly peace but rather a sword of separation. That is the plain and unmistakable meaning of his words. Just look at the extended context:

> I am sending you out like sheep among wolves. Therefore be as shrewd as snakes and as innocent as doves. Be on your guard against men; they will hand you over to the local councils and flog you in their synagogues. On my account you will be brought before governors and kings as witnesses to them and to the Gentiles. . . .
>
> Brother will betray brother to death, and a father his child; children will rebel against their parents and have them put to death. All men will hate you because of me, but he who stands firm to the end will be saved. . . .
>
> A student is not above his teacher, nor a servant above his master. It is enough for the student to be like his teacher, and the servant like his master. If the head of the house has been called Beelzebub [meaning "the devil himself"], how much more the members of his household! . . .
>
> Do not suppose that I have come to bring peace to the earth. I did not come to bring peace, but a sword. For I have come to turn "a man against his father, a daughter against her mother, a daughter-in-law against her mother-in-law—a man's enemies will be the members of his own household" [Micah 7:5–6]. Anyone who loves his father or mother more than me is not worthy of me; anyone who loves his son or daughter more than me is not worthy of me; and anyone who does not take his cross and follow me is not worthy of me.
>
> Matthew 10:16–18, 21–22, 24–25, 34–38

No honest person reading these words could question for a moment what Yeshua was saying: His servants would *not* be the ones taking up the sword. Rather, the sword would be taken up *against them* in the form of persecution, family separation, imprisonment, and death. Any other interpretation of the Messiah's teaching here is simply impossible.

To reiterate: Jesus was not telling his followers that they would be putting people to death by the sword, he was warning them that *they* would be put to death by the sword![90] Rather than being the persecutors—no true follower of Jesus would violently persecute another human being—the Messiah's people have been the persecuted, right to this very hour.

Think back to the Messiah's first followers, men such as Peter (his Aramaic nickname was Kepha, rock), Thomas (Greek for the original Aramaic Thoma), and Paul (whose Hebrew name was Saul). What happened to these men? All of them were killed for their faith! According to the traditions we have, Peter was crucified upside down for following Jesus (he requested that he be crucified in this fashion, since he didn't feel worthy of being crucified in the same manner as was Yeshua); Thomas was speared to death after preaching for years in India; and Paul was beheaded by Nero. (And remember: If Paul had continued his career as a budding, Rabbinic leader, he could have enjoyed a relatively peaceful life. Instead, he was treated like a criminal because of his faith in Jesus the Messiah.) Such was the pattern for several centuries, and that's why Paul could write that *"everyone who wants to live a godly life in Christ Jesus will be persecuted"* (2 Tim. 3:12).

The Messiah's followers were consistently persecuted for their faith, often laying down their lives as martyrs. In fact, our word *martyr* comes from the Greek word for *witness (martys, martyros).* This was because so many faithful witnesses for Yeshua sealed their testimonies with their deaths that the concepts of "witness" and "martyr" became almost interchangeable, quite an amazing phenomenon. (Think of joining a religion in which being loyal to your faith was synonymous with being killed for your faith![91]) Again, this gives a vivid picture of what the Messiah's followers, both Jew and Gentile, suffered then and what they suffer to this day, still being sent out like sheep among wolves, still being the persecuted not the persecutors.[92]

"But," you ask, "what about the church's violent persecution against our people? What about all the Jewish blood that has been spilled in Jesus' name?"

Did you know that for several hundred years after the Messiah's death and resurrection, there is not a single example in a single recorded source, be it a Jewish source, a Christian source, or a secular source, of a single Jewish person being put to death because he or she refused to believe the gospel? Not one. And yet, during this same time period, thousands of Jewish and Gentile followers of Jesus were put to death or imprisoned or tortured for refusing to renounce their faith.[93] Once again, the conclusion is unmistakable: The religion of Yeshua was *not* a religion to be advanced by violence or coercion.

This pattern continues to this very day: Although the Messiah's followers number approximately one billion people today, as many as one hundred thousand to three hundred thousand believers are killed for their faith every year. That is an overwhelming statistic! The fact is, we who follow Jesus are *not* the ones taking up swords against our enemies, imprisoning and torturing our religious opponents, and forcing them to convert under the penalty of death. Rather, it is the true followers of Jesus—despite our great numbers—who are despised, rejected, beaten, and martyred for their faith, just as Jesus said it would be.

Here are just a few examples of persecution against Christians today: In Africa, as many as one million Sudanese Christians have been killed by Sudanese Islamic extremists during the last decade of the twentieth century. They have been isolated in desert regions and starved, burned alive in church buildings, or brutally slaughtered in grotesque fashion. Christian men have been crucified, nursing mothers have had one breast chopped off, daughters have been sold into slavery or prostitution, while sons have been deported to Islamic schools. This is happening today.[94]

In Egypt, Coptic Christians have been beaten, tortured, and abused in the most horrific ways. According to a report sent out via e-mail by Charles Colson on November 12, 1998,

> During a government crackdown on Egypt's Coptic Christian community two weeks ago, a thousand Christians were manacled to doors, then beaten and tortured with electric shocks to their genitals. Teenage girls were raped. Even babies were not spared. Mothers were forced to lay their infants on the floor and watch helplessly while police struck them with sticks. And in a scene right out of ancient Rome, Christian men were nailed to crosses. It was a grisly example of a grave problem in the Middle East: the persecution of Christians by Arab governments—including governments like Egypt that America supports financially.

Such scenes are increasingly common in Islamic nations, including Indonesia, where Christian survivors have lived to describe what it felt like to have their entire families butchered and raped in front of their eyes.[95]

In communist countries such as China and Vietnam, Christians are still subject to imprisonment, beatings, and even death for "crimes" such as preaching the gospel, holding Christian meetings in homes, and baptizing new converts. The widow of a Vietnamese pastor who was shot to death by the government for his faith actually received a bill for the bullet!

Richard Wurmbrand tells the story of Victor Belikh, a Ukrainian Christian bishop who was kept in solitary confinement for twenty years, with only a straw mat put in his cell each night for seven hours. Every day, for seventeen hours, he was made to walk around the cell continuously, like a horse in a circus.

> If he stopped or broke down, they threw buckets of water on him or beat him and he was forced to continue. After twenty years of such a regime, he was sent to forced labour in northern Siberia, where the ice never melts, for another four years.
>
> I asked him, "How could you bear this suffering after the years in solitary confinement and a starvation diet?"
>
> He replied by singing a song he composed: "With the flames of love's fire that Jesus kindled in my heart, I caused the ice of Siberia to melt. Hallelujah!"[96]

Such accounts of victory in the midst of unbelievable suffering are being written even as you read these words, as Christians around the world suffer for their faith, just as Jesus said they would. And so I reiterate: True Christians will always be the persecuted not the persecutors!

As for Jewish people being persecuted for rejecting the message of Jesus, no Jew has ever been killed for rejecting the message I am declaring to you. No Jew has ever been put to death for refusing the New Testament message of the love of God. None of our forefathers were put to death as a result of rejecting this good news I'm sharing with you. Not one! Our Jewish people have been persecuted, abused, expelled, and even killed for rejecting a *counterfeit* message of a *counterfeit* Christ preached by a *counterfeit* church—and there is blood on the hands of that church.[97] None of our people, however, have ever suffered persecution for rejecting the *true* message of the *true* Messiah preached by the *true* people of God. (I'll discuss this further in the next answer.)

To state it again: For hundreds of years after Jesus came into this world, there was no such thing as violent, Christian persecution of Jews (although there was some Jewish persecution of fellow Jews who followed Yeshua). This horrific aberration came about only by a process of departing from the true Messianic faith: First, in the second and third centuries of this era, a number of Gentile Christian leaders began to express hostility toward the Jewish people for rejecting Jesus, departing from the explicit teaching of the Messiah and his emissaries. Then, in the fourth and fifth centuries, when the Roman Empire became officially "Christian," church leaders with political power began to act prejudicially against the Jewish people, occasionally advocating acts of violence against the Jews (or specifically, the synagogues). Finally, when the church bore almost no resemblance to the New Testament faith (it was really a cultural, political monstrosity better called "Christendom" than "Christianity," and it actually persecuted Christians who *adhered to* the New Testament writings), angry mobs—called Crusaders—began to turn against the Jewish people en masse.

The first church-inspired violent persecutions of Jewish people by Christians took place toward the end of the fourth century, but such actions were hardly regular occurrences. (One of the more notable actions took place in 388 c.e. in Callinicum, a small town in Mesopotamia, when, "The Christian population of the town, prompted by the bishop, set fire to the synagogue"—and were then defended strongly by Ambrose, a prominent church leader.)[98] Examples of forced conversion of Jews are almost nonexistent for the first one thousand years of church history.[99] (Remember also that there are examples of Jews forcing Gentiles to convert—and this meant forcing the men to be circumcised—as happened with John Hyrcanus and the Idumeans in the second century b.c.e.)[100]

The first examples of sustained violent persecution are found in the Crusades, beginning at the end of the eleventh century, and they are a complete and total aberration, a total misrepresentation of what the gospel is really about. (We'll take this up in even greater depth in the next answer, 2.7). Still, the fact that virtually no acts of violence were committed against the Jewish people by the church—even an apostate, false church—for several hundred years after Jesus' coming is enormously significant. Allow me to give you this illustration.

Let's say that the European settlers who came to America worked side by side with the Native Americans (incorrectly dubbed "Indians" by the settlers), never fighting a war with them or driving them off their land, but rather making and keeping peace treaties with them. Let's say that this went on for 350 years—longer than the United States has existed—despite some misunderstandings, occasional hostile sentiments, and rare displays of ill will. Then, after this long period of relatively peaceful coexistence, let's say that the distant descendants of the original settlers decided to reinterpret or even discard the peace treaties, launching a terrible persecution against the Native Americans. This would *not* tell you anything about the original settlers or about their peace treaties. Rather, it would tell you about those who departed from the pattern and commitment made by the original settlers. In the same way, it was only an aberrant, political church that could *order* people to believe and be baptized under the threat of death. This is a complete denial of the New Testament faith.

Returning, then, to the saying of Jesus that we have been discussing—that he didn't come to bring peace but a sword—it's also important to remember that it was not Christian teachers who misinterpreted his words about not bringing peace but a sword. Instead, it has been a few Jewish rabbis and anti-missionaries who have misrepresented and misused the Messiah's teaching.[101] In fact, to the best of my knowledge, no recognized church leader *ever* used this verse as a justification for taking up the sword against nonbelievers.

What makes this all the more interesting is that Jesus was simply quoting the words of the Jewish prophet Micah written seven hundred years earlier: "For a son dishonors his father, a daughter rises up against her mother, a daughter-in-law against her mother-in-law—a man's enemies are the members of his own household" (Micah 7:6). And it was this very verse—in fact, this was the one and only verse—that was cited in the Mishnah (compiled around 200 c.e.) regarding the days preceding the advent of the Messiah. In other words, there was a Jewish interpretation current in the days of Jesus (and continuing for some time after that) associating family upheaval with the coming of the Messiah (m. Sotah 9:15). This was part of a scenario predicted by the rabbis in which the moral fabric of society would disintegrate in the days immediately preceding the advent of the Messiah.

Yeshua quoted this very same verse in the context of the family divisions that his coming would cause, divisions that would bring a "sword" of separation between father and son, mother and daughter, daughter-in-law and mother-in-law. This pattern continues in our day when, for example, a young Hindu woman renounces her idols and puts her faith in Jesus the Messiah. Her own mother may turn against her. In fact, similar situations have sometimes arisen when secular Jewish couples have become Orthodox, resulting in separation between parents and children (or even grandchildren).[102]

That is all Jesus was teaching, a fact that is supported not only by honest biblical interpretation but by history as well.

"History?" you say. "I thought that history proved the *opposite!*"

To the contrary, as we just stated, there are hardly any examples of church-organized violence against the Jewish people—in other words, "the sword"—for the first one thousand years of church history, even though Christendom had long since forgotten its Jewish roots. We'll take this up in more detail in the next answer.

I do, however, want to leave you with an important spiritual truth. Although Jesus did not establish world peace when he came to earth two thousand years ago, he is still rightly hailed as the "Prince of Peace" (see Isa. 9:6[5]). He brings peace between man and God as people turn from their sins and receive cleansing and forgiveness, and he brings peace between man and man, as people who were once hostile enemies become part of the same spiritual family. That's why he could say to his followers, "Peace I leave with you; my peace I give you. I do not give to you as the world gives. Do not let your hearts be troubled and do not be afraid" (John 14:27).

In spite of the sword of separation and persecution that often comes *against* the Messiah's people, both Jew and Gentile, in him we have peace, and when the Messiah returns to establish his earthly kingdom and root out the wicked and the rebellious, the whole world will be filled with peace.

2.7. Christians have always hated and persecuted the Jewish people.

It is true that many false followers of Jesus have hated and persecuted the Jewish people and that many true followers of Jesus have been stained with an ugly anti-Semitic spirit, thereby making a mockery of the very faith they profess. This is tragic and reprehensible. But there is far more to the story than you know. Multitudes of true followers of Jesus—in our day and throughout history—have loved,

helped, and defended the Jewish people, thereby demonstrating the reality of the faith they profess. Also, there
is a history of Jewish hatred of Jesus and his followers,
including some violent persecution too. Many of the
problems that arose were political more than religious.
Consequently, things are not as simple as you might
imagine.

Rather than *you* rehearsing the horrible history of "Christian" anti-
Semitism with me, how about if I rehearse it with you?

Shall I recount the harsh rhetoric of the *Adversos Judaeos* literature written by prominent church leaders in the second to sixth centuries? Rabbi Dan Cohn-Sherbok notes that "according to these writers, just as Jews were guilty in the past of indecency, so they have
continued to be a lawless and dissolute people. For this reason all
future promises apply solely to the Church."[103] The Jews are cursed
as a people, their wandering in exile serving as a sign of God's dis-
pleasure with them for rejecting the Messiah, but the Christians are
blessed.

But there's more. Shall I recount the passionate words of the influential fourth-century leader John Chrysostom in his seven sermons
against the Jews?[104] His ferocious accusations have thundered through
the centuries. The Jews are "inveterate murderers, destroyers, men
possessed by the devil" who "know only one thing, to satisfy their gul-
lets, get drunk, kill and maim one another." The synagogue is "a repair
of wild beasts . . . the domicile of the devil, as is also the soul of the
Jews," and the Jewish religion is "a disease." Yes, the Jews are
accursed because of their "odious assassination of Christ," a crime
for which there is "no expiation possible, no indulgence, no pardon."
Indeed, God hates the Jews and has always hated the Jews, a sentiment that Chrysostom also embraced with zeal: "I hate the synagogue
precisely because it has the law and prophets" (yet rejects that biblical witness), and "I hate the Jews because they outrage the law."[105]
Hate is clearly the operative word here.

No wonder Rabbi Cohn-Sherbok could claim that "for Chrysostom and other writers of this period the Jews were not human
beings—they were demons incarnate, an apostate and immoral nation
who have been cast off by God into utter darkness."[106]

Yet there's more still! Shall I recount the anti-Jewish legislation
that became all too common in the ancient world after Christendom
came to power? From the late fourth century on, it was common for

Jews to be deprived of the rights to trade, work certain jobs, or travel freely, at times even having their property confiscated. It was also common for them to be forced to listen to church sermons preached in their synagogues, and the sermons were intended to convert the Jews to Christendom!

And yet there is more! Shall I recount the murderous Crusades, first launched in 1096 when Christian mobs in Europe decided to liberate the Holy Land from the "infidels," meaning the Muslim Turks. Yet as the Crusaders marched through Europe they found even worse infidels right in their own backyard: the Jews, the Christ-killers! It was there, for the first time in history, that Jews were given the choice of baptism or death. Many of them chose death. Then, in the summer of 1096, when the Crusaders took Jerusalem, Jews were herded into the great synagogue and burned alive while the Crusaders, with crosses emblazoned on their uniforms, marched around the building and sang, "Christ, we adore thee."[107]

And yet there is still more! Shall I recount the vicious, medieval blood libels in which Jews were accused of killing Christians and using their blood to make unleavened bread for Passover? These Jews were then made to pay with their own blood for crimes they never committed. Or shall I recount the ridiculous charge of "desecration of the host," beginning in the thirteenth century when the Catholic Church decreed that the communion elements (i.e., the wafer and wine) actually became the body and blood of Jesus? According to this libel, Jews stole these communion elements (called "the host") and tortured them (in other words, they tortured the wafer and wine) in order to get back at Jesus and attack him again. Yet as preposterous as this sounds, Jews were burned at the stake over such nonsense.[108]

Yet there remains still more to tell! Shall I recount the utterly abhorrent baptismal formulas that Jews were required to recite in order to join the church in the late medieval period? They were forced to renounce all connection with the synagogue, forced to renounce any celebration of the biblical holy days, forced to renounce the rabbis, forced to believe in the supremacy of the Virgin Mary, and forced to embrace the eating of pork.

And still there is more! Shall I recount the horrors of the Inquisition (actually, Inquisitions, since several of these "witch-hunts" occurred over a period of almost four hundred years in various European countries), during which the church sought to uncover Jews who outwardly converted to Christianity while continuing to practice some Jewish customs and traditions? These Jewish Catholics were systematically hunted, mercilessly tortured, and then horribly mistreated or (more often than not) executed.

Yet there is still more! Shall I recount the forced, *national* expulsions of all Jews who refused to be baptized? Although most Americans think of 1492 as the year Christopher Columbus discovered America, most Jews think of 1492 in entirely different terms: It was the year that all non-baptized Jews were expelled from Spain—the very country from which Columbus sailed. And Spain was not the only country from which non-baptized Jews were exiled; other countries share the shame.

And yet there is more! Shall I recount the shocking words of Martin Luther, a man once called "John the Baptist of Adolf Hitler"? It was Luther who in 1543 wrote the tractate entitled *Concerning the Jews and Their Lies*, a treatise that remains popular to this very day in neo-Nazi circles. There Luther penned his infamous recommendations for solving the Jewish problem: Jewish synagogues should be set on fire; their homes should be broken down and destroyed; they should be deprived of their prayer books and Talmuds; their rabbis should be forbidden to teach under threat of death; passport and traveling privileges should be absolutely forbidden to all Jews; they should be stopped from charging interest on loans; the young and strong Jews and Jewesses should be given the flail, the ax, the spade, the distaff, the spindle, so that they will earn their bread by the sweat of their noses. "We ought to drive the rascally lazy bones out of our system." So wrote the great Martin Luther.[109]

And still there is more! Shall I recount the destructive pogroms launched against our people in Europe, often after inflammatory Easter sermons urged Christians to attack "the Christ-killers"? Jews were beaten and killed, homes were ransacked, properties were destroyed—and all too often this was carried out in the name of Christianity.

Yet again, there is still more! Shall I recount the views of "Christian" theologians during the Holocaust? The influential New Testament scholar Gerhard Kittel wrote an entire study devoted to dealing with the Jews. Extermination would not be moral or practical; repatriation to Palestine was out of the question, since there were too many Jews to fit there and the Arabs would not be happy with it. The only viable solution was for the Jews to become second-class citizens, deprived of many of their essential rights and relegated to the inferior status that they deserved. Other scholars such as Walter Grundmann sought to prove that Jesus was not actually Jewish.[110]

And still there is more! Shall I recount the fact that after the Holocaust some Polish Jews who survived the concentration camps returned to their homes and villages, only to be killed by angry Catholic neighbors?

And yet there is still more to be told! Shall I recount the fact that some church leaders in our day have consistently sided *with* the PLO and *against* the Jewish people in virtually every land and security-related issue in the State of Israel?

Obviously, I know this history well, but I also know this is *not* the whole story, nor is it even a truly representative telling of the story. In fact, the real story that needs to be told reflects the *opposite* end of the spectrum. However, before presenting you with the rest of the story, let me give you an indication of just how far the church that persecuted the Jews had strayed from its biblical roots.

This church—or rather, this man-made, politically oriented, sometimes-corrupt religious institution—became so contaminated that when John Huss exposed the sins of his fellow clergymen, he was burned at the stake.

This church departed so far from its biblical roots that it completely lost sight of one of the fundamental doctrines of the New Testament, namely, that a person comes into right standing with God by faith and not by works, excommunicating and hunting like criminals those who began to teach this doctrine. This would be like Rabbinic Jews completely forgetting that they believed in an Oral Torah and then killing rabbis in later centuries who sought to recover that belief. That's how far this church had strayed during much of the period just described, especially during medieval times.

This same church actually *forbade* the translation of the Bible into the language of the people, condemning John Wycliffe for translating it into English in the fourteenth century and killing William Tyndale for making a fresh English translation in the sixteenth century. (He was strangled and then burned at the stake—by the church!)[111]

This same church completely repudiated Jesus' commandments forbidding his followers from acts of violence and hatred against others (see above, 2.4), to the point that at times it sanctioned the torture of alleged heretics and dissenters.

This same church completely lost touch with its Jewish roots, even forbidding its Jewish members to have any contact with the synagogue or to observe the biblical feasts and holy days, as we mentioned above.

At times, this church probably killed as many true Christians for refusing to follow its traditions as it killed Jews for refusing to follow its traditions. It is not difficult to see, therefore, that this church was hardly *the* church—in other words, it was hardly the true congregation of genuine believers in the Messiah.

How did this happen? Paul sternly warned Gentile believers in Jesus *not* to think they had replaced the Jewish people as God's special favorites, as if they were now "in" and the Jews were now "out." Rather, using the analogy of an olive tree, he wrote, "They were broken off because of unbelief, and you stand by faith. *Do not be arrogant, but be afraid.* For if God did not spare the natural branches, he will not spare you either" (Rom. 11:20–21). Continuing with this line of reasoning, Paul not only gave these Gentile believers a warning, he also assured them that Jews would actually be especially likely to put their faith in the Messiah in days to come:

> Consider therefore the kindness and sternness of God: sternness to those who fell, but kindness to you, provided that you continue in his kindness. Otherwise, you also will be cut off. And if they do not persist in unbelief, they will be grafted in, for God is able to graft them in again. After all, if you were cut out of an olive tree that is wild by nature, and contrary to nature were grafted into a cultivated olive tree, how much more readily will these, the natural branches, be grafted into their own olive tree!
>
> Romans 11:22–24

Yes, the natural branches (the Jewish people) will all the more readily be grafted back into their own olive tree. But Paul has one more warning—and promise—to bring: "I do not want you to be ignorant of this mystery, brothers, so that you may not be conceited: Israel has experienced a hardening in part until the full number of the Gentiles has come in. And so all Israel will be saved" (Rom. 11:25–26).[112]

Unfortunately, over the ensuing centuries, many Gentile Christians did not heed Paul's warning, becoming conceited and arrogant, imagining that Israel's hardening was both universal and permanent, and thinking that they, the church, were now the sole recipients of God's covenant love. How wrong they were. In their arrogance, many of them cut themselves off from his mercy and favor, just as Paul warned: "If you don't continue in God's kindness, you also will be cut off!"

And what was this kindness to consist of? Showing mercy to the Jewish people, praying for them and loving them, even if they opposed the message of Jesus the Messiah. As Paul explained, "As far as the gospel is concerned, they are enemies on your account; but as far as election is concerned, they are loved on account of the patriarchs, for God's gifts and his call are irrevocable" (Rom. 11:28–29). So says the apostle Paul, the writer of more than half the New Testament.

Therefore, he exhorts, "Just as you [Gentiles] who were at one time disobedient to God have now received mercy as a result of their [i.e., the Jewish people's] disobedience, so they too have now become disobedient in order that they too may now receive mercy as a result of God's mercy to you" (Rom. 11:30–31).

Based on this absolutely clear teaching—the lengthiest and the most direct of its kind anywhere in the New Testament—we can safely state that only a deviant church, a straying church, a church in name more than in reality could persecute, attack, malign, or kill Jews. True Christians would treat Jews with compassion.

"Then where were the true Christians? It looks like there never were any at all!"

I'll respond to this in a moment, but I'm still not finished explaining something important to you about the history of "Christian" anti-Semitism: First, church persecution of Jews, especially violent persecution, was hardly the norm through the centuries; and second, there was hostility both ways, Jews against Christians and Christians against Jews. But where Christendom conquered politically, it could enforce its hostile feelings more easily. Let me expand on these two points before returning to your question about where the true Christians have been over the last two thousand years.

You see, I have actually been highly selective in recounting the deplorable history of so-called "Christian" anti-Semitism, summarizing in a few paragraphs some of the most atrocious examples of a bloody saga that is more than fifteen hundred years old. But this means you might have a false and exaggerated impression of this history, as if Jews have continually and universally suffered violent persecution at the hands of professing Christians. This is simply not true.

Consider the fact that it was 350 years—as we stated above (2.6), longer than the existence of the United States—before there were any recurring examples of church-sanctioned or church-approved acts of violence against Jewish people or Jewish synagogues, and from this we can deduce three things: (1) Christians (in name alone or in reality) were not dominated and driven by anti-Jewish sentiments (as many of them were at the time of the Crusades), otherwise there would have been at least *some* violent acts carried out; (2) while there were many polemical words written, typical of the rhetoric of the day, those words did not lead to hostile actions; and (3) Christians did not believe in forcing people to convert.[113]

Things began to change when the Emperor Constantine converted to Christianity, leading to the Christianizing of the Roman Empire.[114] Obviously, something like this can spell doom for any religious faith, since power often corrupts.[115] It was at this time—and not before— that a church leader was recorded to have put forward the doctrine that the state might be justified in *forcibly* keeping people within the church. (The leader who argued for this was Augustine, one of the most influential thinkers in church history. He based his thinking on Jesus' words in Luke 14:23: "And the lord said unto the servant, Go out into the highways and hedges, and compel them to come in, that my house may be filled."

According to Phillip Schaff, one of the greatest church historians in modern times,

> Starting with a forced interpretation of the words, "Compel them to come in," in Luke 14:23, [Augustine] enunciates principles of coercion which, though in him they were subdued and rendered practically of little moment by the spirit of life which formed so large an element in his character, yet found their natural development in the despotic intolerance of the Papacy, and the horrors of the Inquisition.[116]

Commenting on these writings of Augustine, Schaff continues:

> These works are the chief patristic authority of the Roman Catholic doctrine of the Church and against the sects. They are thoroughly Romanizing in spirit and aim, and least satisfactory to Protestant readers. Augustin[e] defended in his later years even the principle of forcible coercion and persecution against heretical and schismatics by a false exegesis of the words in this parable "Compel them to come in" (Luke xiv. 23).[117]

Yet once again, there are several important observations that we must make: (1) It was almost four hundred years before any Christian leader clearly put forward the idea of using force to keep people within the faith, and if not for the Christianizing of the Roman Empire, it is unlikely that such a view would ever have been espoused; (2) even with this false interpretation of Jesus' words, Augustine did not advocate using force to bring people into the church but rather using force against church heretics and others who sought to leave or divide the Christian community; and (3) with regard to Jews who did not believe in Jesus, he was emphatic: Force is *not* to be used against them![118]

It was also Augustine who urged his fellow Christians not to "boast proudly against the broken branches" (meaning Jews who did not believe in Jesus the Messiah, thereby making room for Gentiles to be grafted into Israel's olive tree). "Let us rather reflect by whose grace and by what great mercy, and to what root we are connected."[119] This was also expressed by Augustine's contemporary Jerome: "We are connected with the same root; we are the branches, and they are the root. We should not curse our roots, but pray for our roots."[120] Yes, these sentiments also existed among prominent church leaders in the fourth and fifth centuries of this era.

Returning to the policy of *not* using force to convert Jewish people, we find a similar line of reasoning with Thomas Aquinas, the most prominent Catholic theologian of the Middle Ages, a man who lived during the very period of the Crusades and blood libels described above. According to John Hood,

> Aquinas has nothing to do with anti-Jewish violence that accompanied the Crusades or with executions and lynchings based on paranoid fantasies ... and he believed that conversion should "in no way" be coerced. ... Only on the issue of usury did Aquinas's ideas represent a direct threat to the security of European Jews. In every other facet of his social teaching on Jews, Thomas firmly supported the principle of *Sicut Iudaeis* [This was the protective and basically benevolent "Jewish Constitution" drafted by Pope Calixtus in the early twelfth century]: Just as Jews should not be granted new privileges, neither should those they possess be taken from them.[121]

Now, Aquinas was hardly a hero of the Jewish people, but as Hood observes,

> Thomas harbored no special malice towards Jews; he was not ... obsessed with converting Jews or whipping up popular enthusiasm against them. Even his demands that usury be suppressed were based on a moral conviction that usury was wrong rather than on any hatred of Jews as such. On most other issues—tolerating Jews, allowing them freedom to worship and the right to raise their children as they saw fit, while also discriminating against them and maintaining hedges against their influence—he was representative of an older tradition, a tradition

rooted in *Sicut Iudaeis* [see n. 121, immediately above, for details], Gregory the Great, Augustine, and ultimately Paul.[122]

Thomas Aquinas, therefore, perhaps the greatest and most influential Catholic theologian in history, was *not* a promoter of anti-Semitism.

Lest the significance of all this escapes you, let me recap what I have been saying: Christian acts of violence and hate against the Jews were virtually nonexistent for more than three hundred years after Jesus' death and resurrection. After that, they were quite sparse and sporadic for the next eight hundred years until the Crusades at the end of the eleventh century—and *that* murderous, destructive representation of Christianity bore *no* resemblance to the real Christian faith. We also need to remember that even though Christendom ruled in Europe, influential leaders from Augustine to Aquinas did *not* advocate violent persecution of Jews or forcible conversion of the Jews, in spite of the church's political power. In fact, the church at times offered the Jewish people protection. As a result, the story of "Christian" anti-Semitism is not as simple as many assume.[123]

To drill this point home, I'll share something that will really surprise you. In fact, it has to do with Martin Luther. Until the twentieth century, it was his *pro-Jewish* writings that were influential, while his vicious *anti-Jewish* writings were either rejected (as happened in his own day), or neglected (as happened through the centuries), or refuted (as happened last century), or repudiated (as happened after the Holocaust). And it was colleagues of Luther, followed by Lutheran church leaders and scholars, who either rejected, neglected, refuted, or repudiated his anti-Jewish work.

Let me briefly review what transpired. In 1523, Luther wrote a small book entitled *That Jesus Christ Was Born a Jew*, hoping to win the Jewish people to faith in Jesus by repudiating the atrocious behavior of many church leaders as well as by pointing out that Jesus himself was Jewish. He also argued that guilt for the death of Jesus should be assigned to the sinful human race as a whole and not to the Jewish people. In fact, as noted by Professor Carter Lindberg, "Luther's Roman Catholic opponents frequently considered Luther to be a friend of the Jews."[124]

In this book he wrote these amazing words:

If the apostles, who also were Jews, had dealt with us Gentiles as we Gentiles deal with the Jews, there would never have been a Christian among the Gentiles. Since they deal with us Gentiles in such brotherly fashion, we in our turn ought to treat the Jews in a brotherly manner in order that we might convert some of them. . . . When we are inclined to boast of our position we should remember that we are but Gentiles, while the Jews are the lineage of Christ. We are aliens and in-laws; they are blood relatives, cousins and brothers of our Lord. . . . God has also demonstrated this by his acts, for to no nation among the Gentiles has he granted so high an honor as he has to the Jews.[125]

I ask you: Were you aware that such writings proceeded from the pen of Martin Luther?

Unfortunately, during the 1530s and 1540s, when there was no major influx of Jews into the faith, and when Luther was shown some exceptionally vulgar, anti-Christian writings disseminated by Jews, he reacted with anger, writing the infamous tractate *Concerning the Jews and Their Lies*, along with some other anti-Jewish works.[126] But these harsh writings were not well received by many of his colleagues. As explained by Lindberg, "The rejection and condemnation of Luther's anti-Jewish writings is not a modern phenomenon but began already among his evangelical contemporaries." He further notes that "the history of Lutheran reception of Luther's anti-Jewish texts is still not fully researched, but initial studies indicate that they were rejected and ineffective until rediscovered by the racial ideologues of the Third Reich."[127]

Luther's closest colleague, Philipp Melanchthon, was very unhappy with these venomous writings, while another colleague, Andreas Osiander, wrote an anonymous apology for them, and Luther's Latin translator, Justus Jonas, actually changed the text when he translated it. In each of the succeeding centuries—the sixteenth through the nineteenth—Luther's hateful, anti-Jewish writings were repudiated, while his earlier, pro-Jewish writings proved to be the more influential.[128] This is an integral part of the story that is often untold.

The verdict of Lutheran theologian Friedrich Lezius, written in 1892, sums up the feelings of many Lutheran leaders during a period of more than 350 years of Lutheran practice and belief:

It is obvious that Luther does not argue in accordance with the spirit of the New Testament and the Reformation. . . . The Protestant Church has therefore rejected the errors of the aging reformer as not binding for the church and only regards Luther's treatise "That Jesus Christ Was Born a Jew," which was published in 1523, as the true expression of the spirit of the Reformation.[129]

Do you grasp the significance of these words? According to Lezius, the spirit of the *New Testament* and the spirit of the *Protestant Reformation*—which was launched by Luther—is a philo-Semitic spirit. True Christianity and anti-Semitism are therefore utterly incompatible—and this sentiment expresses the views of countless church leaders over the last five hundred years. What happened to Luther's anti-Jewish writings? They fell into virtual oblivion until they were utilized afresh by the Nazis.[130]

Of course, there is absolutely no excuse for Luther's hate-filled polemics, and I am not trying to make any excuse for them. Rather, I am simply pointing out that these writings did not reflect the sentiments of many of his contemporaries and colleagues who considered them to be aberrant and un-Christian from the start. Recent repudiations of these writings by Lutheran Church bodies simply follow in the footsteps of previous church leaders in the preceding centuries.[131] It may also be worth mentioning that both Hitler and most of his officers came from Austria—a country largely untouched by the Protestant Reformation—while Lutheran countries such as Norway and Denmark fought to save Jews during the Holocaust.[132]

Reverend David Read, a Scottish Christian leader involved in gracious and respectful interfaith dialog with Jewish leaders, makes an observation that Jews need to hear: Growing up in Presbyterian Scotland, a country "which has no record of anti-Jewish legislation or forced expulsion of the Jews," learning of the Jewish people through the Scriptures and through church-based classes, he was *not* exposed to anti-Semitism:

> I recall hearing as many sermons based on the Old Testament as on the New; and in the public school system . . . every child was exposed to the Ten Commandments and the history of Israel with its stories of memorable characters as well as its songs and proverbs. . . .
>
> In the Bible hour at school, from which the few Roman Catholics were excused, we were not only exposed to the teaching and stories of the Old Testament, but some attempt was made to explain Jewish devotion and ways of worship. . . . We were told that Jesus was a Jew, but never once did I hear the accusation that Jews were Christ-killers and therefore accursed. Those who have been led to believe that all Christians are indoctrinated with this accusation may be surprised to hear that I never heard it until I went to Europe during my student years. Neither at home nor at school was this crude accusation of deicide part of my upbringing as a WASP.[133]

This was part of Pastor Read's Scottish Christian heritage, a Protestant tradition dating back to John Knox in the sixteenth century. (By the way, Knox was fiercely persecuted by the church because of his opposition to its moral corruption and its departure from its biblical roots.)

All this clearly demonstrates that it is an overstatement to claim "Christians have always hated and persecuted the Jewish people." Hardly! In fact, it would be far more accurate to say that throughout history some Christians have hated and persecuted Jews and some Jews have hated and persecuted Christians.

"Jews hating and persecuting Christians? What are you talking about?"

For the sake of fairness and balance, I'll answer your question, but I don't want to get too far away from your initial claim that Christians have always hated and persecuted the Jews. Therefore, I'll give only the briefest of surveys of Jewish hostilities against followers of Jesus.

As we noted above (2.6), the New Testament records the martyrdom or persecution of Jewish believers at the hands of fellow Jews (see, e.g., Acts 7, 14, 17). This is the first recorded persecution suffered by Jews relative to Jesus, and it was *not* his followers who were doing the persecution. To the contrary, as we have emphasized, they were the persecuted.

"But why should I believe what the New Testament says?" you ask.

Well, not only have the New Testament authors been proven to be historically reliable,[134] but the Talmud itself recounts a similar event, describing how five of Yeshua's (Jewish) disciples were brought before the judges and sentenced to death (b. Sanhedrin 43a). The first-century Jewish historian Josephus also describes the martyrdom of Jacob (James), Yeshua's brother and a highly respected Jewish leader—even among the non-Messianic Jews. He was stoned by other, hostile Jews, apparently because of his outspoken allegiance to Jesus.[135]

There are other negative references in the Talmud to Messianic Jews (cf., e.g., t. Hullin 2:22–23), and by the end of the first century of this era, some leading sages had instituted the use of the so-called *Birkat HaMinnim*, the malediction against the heretics, cursing sectarian believers in their midst—and that included (or specifically targeted) Messianic Jews.[136] Yes, there *was* anti-Jesus hostility among many first-century Jews.

The learned historian Marcel Simon summarizes for us the predicament faced by Jewish followers of Yeshua in the first centuries of this era:

> They were driven from Jerusalem on the eve of the first war, harassed from time to time by the religious authorities, anathematized in the Synagogue liturgy, and persecuted during the second war by Bar Cochba's troops. . . . They were regarded as dissidents, sectarians, by both Synagogue and Church. By professing Christianity, as the gentiles did, they had classed themselves as gentiles in the eyes of the Synagogue.[137]

In addition to this, in a number of accounts of martyrdom in the early church, Jews are depicted as actively siding against the Christians, even encouraging the authorities to put them to death,[138] and on other occasions, as a result of Christian mobs attacking synagogues, Jews subsequently retaliated against the Christians.[139]

Edward Flannery, in his powerful exposé on anti-Semitism in the church, also notes some of the Jewish hostility against Christians:

> Sufficient incidents of Jewish violence against Christians are recorded to show that that Jewish hatred was widespread and, while sporadic, often intense. In 117 C.E., under Trajan, Jews participated in the death of St. Simeon, bishop of Jerusalem. During his revolt (132–135 C.E.), Bar Kokba massacred [Jewish] Christians who refused to deny Christ. In 155 at Smyrna, when St. Polycarp was condemned to be burned, Jews gathered faggots for the pyre "as is usual with them." In Smyrna, a century later, St. Pionius, burned under Decius, addressed the Jews that derided him before his death:
>
> > I say this to you Jews . . . that if we are enemies, we are also human beings. Have any of you been injured by us? Have we caused you to be tortured? When have we unjustly persecuted? When have we harmed in speech? When have we cruelly dragged to torture? . . .
>
> It appears from this text that the Jews were not direct participants in the martyrdom but rather its active supporters. The same may be said of the martyrdom of St. Philip of Heraclea and Hermes the deacon, in 304.[140]

Here then we see another side to the story that is often forgotten, and that is the side of Jewish persecution of the followers of Jesus, be they Jewish or Gentile.

And to the lasting shame of our Jewish people, a whole body of anti-Jesus literature arose during the first one thousand years of

church history, vilifying Jesus as a bastard, a magician, an idol wor-
shiper, and an arch deceiver, now suffering unspeakable torment in
hell. Of course, some of this was written as a result of the despicable
actions of so-called Christians, but some Christian hostility toward
Jews came about as a result of this literature. And it can be argued
that some of these slanderous charges against Yeshua pre-dated the
earliest persecution of Jews by the church. In any case, it has been a
vicious cycle, to say the least.[141]

What is especially interesting is that for the last two millennia, outside the modern State of Israel, Jews have not been the ruling powers in a country occupied by Christians, and so there is no way to tell
how power would have corrupted Judaism (as it corrupted some
branches of Christianity)—until now, that is. You see, the ultra-Orthodox in Israel have waged a major intimidation campaign against Jewish followers of Jesus in the land, and at times it has been violent.

In 1998 alone, ultra-Orthodox Jews in Israel (called Haredim)
sought to pass legislation that would make all attempts at proselytism
punishable by imprisonment; vandalized and ransacked the apart-
ment of three Christian women in the religious quarter of Jerusalem
called Mea Shearim; and surrounded a Messianic Jewish meeting
place in Beer Sheva, pelting it with rocks, threatening to burn it down,
and refusing to comply even with police orders. As an e-mail news
flash indicated, "A mob of several hundred Haredim (ultra-Orthodox
Jews) attacked and besieged a Messianic Jewish congregation meeting in this southern Israeli town today, trapping some 30 worship-
pers inside for about four hours."[142] According to Natan Adrian, a lecturer in history at Ben-Gurion University and a man *not* known as
sympathetic to Messianic Jews, the scene was reminiscent of Eastern Europe, except that the tables were now turned. "I witnessed a
pogrom, there can be no other word for it."[143]

In fact, such acts of violence are becoming more common in Israel.
An e-mail alert sent out in the fall of 1998 contained this shocking
account (I have changed the names to protect the safety of the victims):

This is an emergency email. Moshe X and his helper, Sasha, a young
Russian believer, had their tent burned down by the Ultra-Orthodox a
week or so ago at Samuel's Tomb, which property he owns. Now again
tonight, 3 November 1998, Moshe and Sasha were attacked and beaten
by the Orthodox. Moshe's arm was injured, but Sasha's skull and eye
were crushed and he is now entering into emergency surgery.

Please pray for his total restoration, especially for Sasha's brain and eyesight and whatever the enemy meant for evil God would turn around for good for the salvation of those who attacked them. Also pray for protection, as the Orthodox said they were coming back again in two days and for God's direction for wisdom regarding security for Moshe and those working for him. Also pray that God will send at least three Joshua's and Caleb's, fearless men, to come and hold up his arms immediately from whatever place God may call them.

What has been the official Haredi response to some of these recent acts of violence? "Don't judge the whole community by the actions of a few!"

This is exactly what I have been saying to you about the subject of "Christian" anti-Semitism!

"Well, I see your point, but all you have done is show that over the last two thousand years, there have been Christians who have hated and persecuted Jews and Jews who have hated and persecuted Christians (or Messianic Jews). Even if my initial objection was overstated, we *both* agree that many Christians have been anti-Semites. Therefore, they were no better than the Jews who were anti-Christian. Where is your wonderful religion of love?"

I'm ready to tell you. This is the best part of the story! Not only is it true that many Christians and church leaders through the centuries have *not* been anti-Semites, it is true that many Christians and church leaders, in ever-increasing measure, are philo-Semites—real lovers of the Jewish people, ready to die for them rather than kill them.

Shall I recount the words of the Puritan leader Samuel Rutherford penned more than three hundred years ago? He was known as one of the most deeply spiritual men of his generation, a man who longed to see the return of his Master, Jesus the Messiah, but he also longed to see the day when Jesus and his Jewish people would be reconciled.

O to see the sight, next to Christ's Coming in the clouds, the most joyful! Our elder brethren the Jews and Christ fall upon one another's neck and kiss each other! They have long been asunder; they will be kind to one another when they meet. O day! O longed-for and lovely day-dawn! O sweet Jesus, let me see that sight which will be as life from the dead, Thee and Thy ancient people in mutual embraces. . . . I could stay out of heaven many years to see that victorious triumphing Lord act that prophesied part of His soul-conquering love, in taking into His kingdom the greater sister, that kirk [assembly] of the Jews.[144]

Not surprisingly, John Owen, the greatest of the Puritan theologians, stated that "there is not any promise anywhere of raising up a kingdom unto the Lord Jesus Christ in this world but it is either expressed, or clearly intimated, that the beginning of it must be with the Jews."[145]

Or to quote one more Puritan witness, Robert Leighton,

> Undoubtedly, that people of the Jews shall once more be commanded to arise and shine [referring to Isa. 60:1], and their return shall be the riches of the Gentiles (Romans 11:12), and then shall be a more glorious time than ever the Church of God did yet behold.[146]

So much for the notion that Christians have always believed that the Jewish people were forever condemned because of their rejection of Jesus, never to be favored by God again. Rather, as these Puritans so beautifully articulate, God's purposes cannot possibly be fulfilled *without* the Jewish people.

This assurance that the Jewish people would once again be recipients of the Lord's grace was found in the early centuries of Christian history as well. Listen to the testimony of Ambrosiaster, writing in the late fourth century:

> However seriously the Jews may have sinned by rejecting the gift of God . . . nevertheless, because they are the children of good people, whose privileges and many benefits from God they have received, they will be received with joy when they return to the faith, because God's love for them is stirred up by the memory of their ancestors.[147]

Or consider the words of Cyril of Alexandria, writing one century later:

> Although it was rejected, Israel will also be saved eventually, a hope which Paul confirms [in Rom. 11:26] by quoting this text of Scripture [viz., Isa. 59:21]. For indeed, Israel will be saved in its own time and will be called at the end, after the calling of the Gentiles.[148]

Or listen to the words of a nineteenth-century Christian leader, Bishop H. G. C. Moule:

> The great event of Israel's return to God in Christ, and His to Israel, will be the signal and the means of a vast rise of spiritual life in the uni-

versal church [meaning, among all believers], and of an unexampled ingathering of regenerate souls from the world.[149]

All these witnesses join their voices to testify to one and the same fact: The Jewish people, because they have been specially chosen by God, will receive his favor in the end and will lead the way in faith in the Messiah, sparking a worldwide spiritual revival. Without their elder brothers, the Jews, Gentile Christians will not be complete.

As explained in the nineteenth century by the Scottish Presbyterian Andrew Bonar—and thus long before Israel's regathering and statehood in the twentieth century,

> Israel is the "everlasting nation" who are to be life from the dead to all nations. And the sure word of prophecy declares, "He that scattereth Israel shall gather them." "I will give them one heart and one way, that they may fear Me for ever." "Yea, I will rejoice over them, and will plant them in their own land, assuredly, with all My heart, and with all My soul."

> Crowned with her fairest hope, the Church
>   Shall triumph with her Lord,
> And earth her jubilee shall keep,
>   When Israel is restored.[150]

Attitudes such as these spawn love and respect for the Jewish people rather than persecution, hatred, or mistreatment. I tell you again: True Christians around the world are utterly shocked to learn that anyone in history who claimed to be a follower of Jesus the Messiah could ever hate or persecute the Jews.

Well do I remember eating a meal with a Christian family in Andhra Pradesh, India, in 1993. The wife had not slept all night because she was so excited about preparing a meal for visiting Jews (there were three Jews in our party, including my wife and a friend), but it was her husband's greeting that still rings in my ears: "You are the second Jew to come to my house. The first was Jesus Christ!"

It was on that same trip that I met Indian Christians who had regularly fasted and prayed for God's blessing on Israel and the Jewish people for more than ten years, considering it their sacred duty as Christians, although they had never before met a Jew in their lives. This was similar to my encounter with a young Kenyan Christian named Shadrach. It was his large backpack that caught my attention when we met in the city of Mombasa in 1989. What was it he carried with him? Copies of cassette tapes from America teaching that Christians are called to bless and pray for the Jewish people worldwide. He had given his life to distributing these tapes at no charge to Kenyan Christians everywhere—even though I was the first Jew he had met.

This was similar to my experience in Seoul, Korea, in 1991, when a group of Korean Christians literally soaked my manuscript on anti-Semitism in the church, *Our Hands Are Stained with Blood*, with their own tears, agonizing over the suffering of the Jewish people, both past and present. Among this group was the young Malaysian Christian woman to whom I referred in the introduction. She sobbed for Israel as we prayed together before telling me afterward in her broken English, "My people [meaning her tribal Christian people] don't know much about the Jews. We just know that we love them!" (Remember also that Malaysia is a predominantly *Muslim* nation.)

I think also of the Italian pastor I met in Sicily who told me, "There is not a service we hold in our church at which we do not pray for the Jewish people, and there is not a meal we have in my home at which we do not pray for the Jewish people, and there is not a time I get on my knees to pray when I do not pray for the Jewish people."

This reminds me of yet another Gentile Christian leader I know whose heart beats for the Jewish people. This soft-spoken minister often addresses large crowds—sometimes over one hundred thousand people—in Africa and Asia. When he calls on them to put their faith in Jesus to save them from their sins, he also gives them a solemn charge, saying, "I want you to commit to say a prayer for the Jewish people with every meal and to fast one day a week for God's blessing to be on his ancient covenant people." I kid you not! For these new Asian and African Christians to learn that there is such a thing as "Christian" anti-Semitism would be the shock of their lives. For them, loving Jesus and loving his Jewish people go hand in hand.[151] As an Iranian Christian said to me years ago in Maryland—he himself was baptized in Iran by a Jewish Christian—"If someone hates the Jews, he is not a Christian." It was that simple!

In fact, I hold before me a letter dated June 10, 1998. It was forwarded to me by a Messianic newspaper for Russian readers after the paper printed an excerpt from *Our Hands Are Stained with Blood*. The writer of this letter was a Ukrainian Gentile, raised in an anti-Semitic home, although he states that Jews were always considered as human as all other peoples. Therefore, it was with horror that the writer (identified by the initials M. K.) witnessed the events that transpired when the Nazis entered Galicia (Western Ukraine) and "thieves, drunkards, and bandits" helped the Nazi murderers purge all Jews from the area: The Jews were carted off to the woods, shot, and thrown into a huge pit.

While in the army, M. K. had a fine Jewish commander named Joseph, and watching Joseph suffer mistreatment at the hands of his fellow officers, M. K. began to look at the Jewish people "with respect and dignity." Then the turning point came:

> About seven years ago I met another Jew, my Lord Jesus Christ. His love for me influenced my love towards Israel and towards all Jewish people. The long-suffering nation, and the nation that has been vital in the scientific and technical development of the world, the nation that changes the destinies of other nations, makes history, carries and preserves the Word of the Living God. Let this letter of mine be my confession before the God of Israel, God of Abraham, Isaac and Jacob, my God: before you, my brothers in Christ, and before all the Jewish people.

My friend, I tell you the truth in the sight of God, *this* is the spirit of the true church, the spirit of philo-Semitism not anti-Semitism. Where a true expression of the New Testament faith has dominated the church, philo-Semitism—not anti-Semitism—has been the rule. In fact, it is no more possible to speak of *Christian* anti-Semitism than it is to speak of dry water or a godly murderer or a two-eyed Cyclops. The adjective *Christian* does not fit with anti-Semitism. And that's why Bible-believing Christians—called evangelicals—are Israel's staunchest and most loyal supporters today.[152]

This Christian spirit of love of the Jewish people is not just sentimental, nor is it tied in only with some expected endtime conversion of the Jews. Rather, it is tangible, it is committed for the long haul, and it is often sacrificial.

It is this spirit that motivates Finnish Christians to offer their services to Jews in the former Soviet Union, doing whatever they can do to help displaced Jews get back to the land of Israel. One Finnish woman I met several years ago goes to Israel for up to nine months at a time, volunteering her services as a nurse in an Israeli hospital while her husband works in Finland. When I asked the husband why he and his wife were willing to make such a sacrifice, he replied matter of factly, "Well, we love the Jews." That was it! Nothing more needed to be said. That said it all.

It is this same spirit that motivated a large church in Sweden to actually acquire and operate a ship—and I mean a ship, the size of some cruise vessels—with the sole purpose of transporting Jews from the former Soviet Union to Israel. This is the expression of their love for God's ancient people.

This is the spirit that motivates the multiethnic workers of the International Christian Embassy, based in Jerusalem but active in many nations. Day and night they give themselves to humanitarian aid to Jews in need, and they do it with a proviso: None of their workers are allowed to try to convert Jews to Christianity.

Do these Christian embassy workers believe that Jewish people should believe in Jesus? Absolutely! Do they want the Jewish people they help to believe in Jesus? Without a doubt. But they refuse to allow a single Jew to ever think that they are showing Jews love in order to win them to the faith, and they want to demonstrate that they will not stop showing these Jewish people love regardless of whether they ever believe in Jesus. No, these workers are showing love because that's what Christians do, and in light of Christendom's horrible history of anti-Semitism, they feel that helping the Jewish people in a tangible way is the least they can do.

I will say it again: True Christianity shines with Jewish love— unconditional and sacrificial. This is the spirit that characterizes a black Christian congregation in the Washington, D.C., area, a congregation that holds its services in a Conservative Jewish synagogue. That's right! An African American church rents space from a Jewish congregation, and in one joint meeting they held together, the pastor of the church—a personal friend of mine—stood up before the Jews in attendance and stated clearly, "The members of my church want you to know that if you are ever threatened in any way, we are committed to lay down our lives on your behalf."

It was only fifty years earlier that Christians got to act on such sentiments, risking their own lives to save Jews from the Nazis. Why did they do such things? As one of these "righteous Gentiles" remarked, "By staying idle at a time when we are the last resort for innocent people condemned to die, we blaspheme against God's commandment against killing."[153] *That* is Christianity! In fact, over and over, when questioned about why these Christian men and women did what they did, they responded with lines such as, "I did nothing special; anyone would have done it," or, "You must understand that it was the most natural thing in the world to help these people."[154]

And so, in answer to your charge that Christians have always hated and persecuted the Jewish people, I reply, "No, no, and a thousand times no!" In fact, I would encourage you to get to know some real, sincere Christians and find out for yourself. You'll be pleasantly surprised to see how gracious and respectful they are toward you when they find out that you, like their Savior, are a Jew. They may even thank you, since many Christians feel a special indebtedness to the Jewish people, recognizing that their Scriptures come from the Jews, their Messiah is a Jew, and without the faithful witness of Jewish people to Jesus the Messiah, there would be no Gentile Christians in the world today.

If they want to share their faith with you, it's just an expression of love, their way of repaying their debt to you. How could they do anything less?

2.8. The origins of anti-Semitism can be traced to the pages of the New Testament. From the negative depiction of the Pharisees to the charge of deicide, anti-Semitism is a Christian plague.

It is commonly recognized among scholars today that anti-Semitism existed in various forms in the ancient world long before a single page of the New Testament was written. Further, the New Testament documents primarily reflect friction between Jewish groups—differences between Messianic Jews and non-Messianic Jews (including Pharisees, Sadducees, etc.)—just like the Dead Sea Scrolls reflect legal and religious arguments between different Jewish groups. It is a mistake to read the later history of "Christian" anti-Semitism back into the New Testament. As for passages in the New Testament that have helped fuel anti-Semitism in the church, you need to remember that passages from our own Hebrew Bible have often been used against us Jews by anti-Semites, while alleged anti-Semitic texts in the New Testament, when properly translated and understood, are really not anti-Semitic at all. In fact, Israel's greatest support today comes from those who read the New Testament as the literal Word of God. For them, it is the source of philo-Semitism not anti-Semitism.

The first thing you need to realize is that anti-Semitism is not a Christian phenomenon. Even if you are convinced that the New Testament itself is terribly anti-Semitic, a subject we'll come to in a moment, there is no denying the fact that anti-Semitism was known long before Jesus came into the world, and it exists today in countries that are anti-Christian. There is more to anti-Semitism than you may realize.

The earliest recorded example of anti-Semitism is found in our very own Scriptures, in the Book of Esther, where Haman's hatred for one Jew, Mordechai, quickly grew into a hatred for an entire people. So fierce was this hatred that Haman succeeded in persuading the Persian king, Xerxes, to pass an edict calling on all peoples in the kingdom to "destroy, kill and annihilate all the Jews—young and old, women and little children—on a single day, the thirteenth day of the twelfth month, the month of Adar, and to plunder their goods" (Esther 3:13).

What was Haman's rationale? He informed the king that "there is a certain people dispersed and scattered among the peoples in all the provinces of your kingdom whose customs are different from those of all other people and who do not obey the king's laws; it is not in the king's best interest to tolerate them" (Esther 3:8). In other words, "The Jews are different! The Jews are troublemakers! It's in your best interest to get rid of them." Now *that* is anti-Semitism!

Similar accusations against our people are recorded elsewhere in the Hebrew Bible. For example, when the Jewish exiles returned from Babylon and began to rebuild Jerusalem, their opponents sent this letter to the Persian king Artaxerxes:

> The king should know that the Jews who came up to us from you have gone to Jerusalem and are rebuilding that rebellious and wicked city. They are restoring the walls and repairing the foundations. Furthermore, the king should know that if this city is built and its walls are restored, no more taxes, tribute or duty will be paid, and the royal revenues will suffer. Now since we are under obligation to the palace and it is not proper for us to see the king dishonored, we are sending this message to inform the king, so that a search may be made in the archives of your predecessors. In these records you will find that this city is a rebellious city, troublesome to kings and provinces, a place of rebellion from ancient times. That is why this city was destroyed.

> Ezra 4:12–15

Somehow, this perception that the Jews were different from other peoples persisted into the Greek and Roman culture before the time of Jesus, leading to numerous expressions of anti-Semitism. The respected historian Peter Schäfer recently devoted an entire book entitled *Judeophobia* to the subject of anti-Semitism in the ancient world, providing strong evidence that anti-Semitism originating in Hellenistic Egypt (300 B.C.E.) was "the 'mother' of anti-Semitism."[155] His research bears out the observation of Rabbi Samuel Sandmel that "hostility to Jews in the Greco-Roman world predates Christianity."[156] In our day, anti-Semitic strains have been found in radical Islamic nations, non-Christian countries such as Japan, and thoroughly atheistic, communist regimes. Clearly, Christianity is not to blame here.[157]

It is simply not accurate, therefore, to say that the New Testament is the main cause and main carrier of anti-Semitism around the world. You should also consider that anti-Semites have drawn from the pages of the Hebrew Scriptures as much as they have drawn from the pages of the New Testament. Let me give you a representative sampling. And remember, these are not the words of Adolf Hitler or some apostate, medieval church leader. They are the words of the Lord and his prophets as recorded in the Tanakh. (All citations are taken from the NJPSV.)

> Say to the Israelite people, "You are a stiffnecked people. If I were to go in your midst for one moment, I would destroy you."
>
> The Lord's words to Moses, Exodus 33:5

> Know, then, that it is not for any virtue of yours that the LORD your God is giving you this good land to possess; for you are a stiffnecked people. Remember, never forget, how you provoked the LORD your God to anger in the wilderness: from the day that you left the land of Egypt until you reached this place, you have continued defiant toward the LORD.
>
> The words of Moses to his people Israel, Deuteronomy 9:6

> Well I know how defiant and stiffnecked you are: even now, while I am still alive in your midst, you have been defiant toward the LORD; how much more, then, when I am dead! Gather to me all the elders of your tribes and your officials, that I may speak all these words to them and that I may call heaven and earth to witness against them. For I know that, when I am dead, you will act wickedly and turn away from the path that I enjoined upon you, and that in time to come misfortune will befall you for having done evil in the sight of the LORD and vexed Him by your deeds.
>
> The words of Moses to his people Israel, shortly before his death, Deuteronomy 31:27–29

Now,
Go, write it down on a tablet
And inscribe it in a record,
That it may be with them for future days,
A witness forever.
For it is a rebellious people,
Faithless children,
Children who refused to heed
The instruction of the Lord.

> The words of the Lord to the prophet Isaiah, Isaiah 30:8–9

O mortal, I am sending you to the people of Israel, that nation of rebels, who have rebelled against Me.—They as well as their fathers have defied Me to this very day; for the sons are brazen of face and stubborn of heart. . . . Do not be afraid of their words and do not be dismayed by them, though they are a rebellious breed. . . . Mortal, go to the House of Israel and repeat My very words to them. For you are sent, not to a people of unintelligible speech and difficult language, but to the House of Israel—not to the many peoples of unintelligible speech and difficult language, whose talk you cannot understand. If I sent you to them, they would listen to you. But the House of Israel will refuse to listen to you, for they refuse to listen to Me; for the whole House of Israel are brazen of forehead and stubborn of heart.

> The words of the Lord to the prophet Ezekiel,
> Ezekiel 2:3–4, 6; 3:4–7

How do you feel after reading such verses? God himself called our people stiff-necked, rebellious, faithless, brazen, stubborn, and disobedient, even describing these ugly traits as *characteristic.* Why then are verses such as these not considered to be primary theological sources of anti-Semitism? Why is it only the New Testament verses— none of which make such wide-ranging charges—that are supposedly anti-Semitic? Why not argue that *God himself,* along with the prophets he inspired, was anti-Semitic?

"That's easy!" you say. "The Hebrew Bible is *our* Bible. It was written *by* Jews *for* Jews, whereas the New Testament was written mainly to Gentiles, even if its authors were almost all Jews. In the case of the Tanakh, we have family conflicts recorded for family hearing alone; in the case of the New Testament, our dirty laundry is being hung out for the entire world to see—and in unfair, exaggerated terms at that."

Not quite! You see, our Hebrew Scriptures were never meant to be ours alone. Jews were called to be a light to the nations (see above, 1.2), spreading the knowledge of the one true God around the world.

According to ancient Jewish tradition, it was a group of seventy-two Jewish scholars who made the first translation of the Torah (the Five Books of Moses) into the Greek language at the behest of the Greek king Ptolemy.[158] It is this same Torah that includes some negative statements about our people, as we have just seen. (The Books of Exodus and Deuteronomy, from which verses were cited above, are the second and fifth books of the Torah, respectively.)

Also, some Jewish groups (before and after the time of Jesus) openly invited Gentiles into their synagogues,[159] and thus, *by our own choice,* the Gentile world became exposed to our sacred Scriptures, Scriptures that refer to the Israelites as chosen and elect, loved and cherished by the Lord, as well as stiff-necked and rebellious, the special objects of his wrath. This parallels the New Testament description of the Jewish people: They are a divinely chosen people who often rejected the messengers of the Lord but who, nonetheless, would not be rejected forever by the Lord. Rather, they would be instrumental in bringing his salvation to the world.

The plain truth about the New Testament is that it is a thoroughly Jewish book. It tells the wonderful news about Jesus—the Jewish Messiah—and all of its authors, save one, were Jews. Its pages are filled with citations from the Hebrew Scriptures—there are approximately three hundred direct quotations from the Tanakh and well over one thousand allusions to the Hebrew Bible in the New Testament[160]— and most of the religious conflicts it records (such as debates about healing on the Sabbath) can be understood only on the basis of Jewish law and tradition. Take the Jewishness out, and the Gospels make no sense. After all, the one most frequently addressed as Rabbi in the New Testament is Jesus.[161] In fact, this manner of address was so deeply instilled in Yeshua's followers that when Judas betrayed him, he called him Rabbi (see Matt. 26:49; see also Mark 9:5; 10:51; 11:21; 14:45; John 1:38, 49; 3:2, 26; 4:31; 6:25; 9:2; 11:8).

The New Testament begins with Israel (its opening words are "This is the genealogy of Yeshua the Messiah, son of David, son of Avraham")[162] and ends with Israel (its closing chapters give a description of the heavenly city called the New Jerusalem). In fact, according to the New Testament author Yohanan (John), the final destiny of all the redeemed will be a city whose twelve gates are inscribed with the names of the twelve tribes of Israel and whose twelve foundations bear the names of the twelve Jewish apostles. Even heaven is Jewish in the New Testament!

Let me give you a striking illustration of the Jewishness of the New Testament. Yechiel Lichtenstein was a nineteenth-century Hungarian rabbi who despised Christianity, believing—to cite his own words—that "Christ himself was the plague and curse of the Jews, the origin and promoter of our sorrows and persecutions."[163] With his own eyes he witnessed so-called Christians committing murderous acts against his people, acts committed in the name of Christ. Yet he also read passionate defenses of the Jewish people by others who called themselves Christians and who utterly renounced anti-Semitism—also in the name of Christ.

This led him to pick up a copy of the New Testament that forty years earlier he had angrily hurled into the corner of his study where it lay on the ground, covered with dust. He was in for the shock of his life. He wrote:

> I had thought the New Testament to be impure, a source of pride, of selfishness, of hatred, and of the worst kind of violence, but as I opened it I felt myself peculiarly and wonderfully taken possession of. A sudden glory, a light flashed through my soul. I looked for thorns and found roses; I discovered pearls instead of pebbles; instead of hatred love; instead of vengeance forgiveness; instead of bondage freedom; instead of pride humility; conciliation instead of enmity; instead of death life, salvation, resurrection, heavenly treasure.[164]

And what of the *Jewishness* of the New Testament? Listen once more to this rabbi's articulate description:

> From every line in the New Testament, from every word, the Jewish spirit streamed forth light, life, power, endurance, faith, hope, love, charity, limitless and indestructible faith in God, kindness to prodigality, moderation to self-denial, content to the exclusion of all sense of need, consideration for others, with extreme strictness as regards self, all these things were found pervading the book.[165]

It is little wonder that this noble rabbi became an outspoken follower of Yeshua the Messiah, despite persistent persecution inflicted on him by his fellow Jews. It is also no wonder that this rabbi recognized at once just how Jewish the New Testament writings were. To this day, an increasing number of Jewish scholars are involved in rediscovering the Jewish roots of Jesus and the New Testament, arguing that Yeshua and his followers can be properly understood only when placed in their first-century Jewish context.[166]

You might also be surprised to know that the New Testament has many positive things to say about our people. Yeshua himself taught that "salvation is from the Jews" (John 4:22), and Paul (Saul) said that the Jewish people were "loved [by God] on account of the patriarchs" (i.e., Abraham, Isaac, and Jacob; Rom. 11:28). In fact, Paul claimed that from a spiritual standpoint there was much advantage "in every way" in being born Jewish (Rom. 3:1–2), and that the Gentiles owed the Jewish people a material blessing, since they had partaken of the Jews' spiritual blessing (Rom. 15:27). Of his kinsmen according to the flesh he said, "They are Israelites, and to them belong the adoption, the glory, the covenants, the giving of the law, the worship, and the promises; to them belong the patriarchs, and from them, according to the flesh, comes the Messiah, who is over all, God blessed forever" (Rom. 9:4–5 NRSV).

This is hardly anti-Semitic rhetoric! On the contrary, it is statements such as these that are hated by anti-Semites, since the sentiments expressed here *validate* the idea that the Jews are chosen by God in a unique way and play a special role in his plan of redemption for humankind as a whole. Thus, the New Testament authors follow in the footsteps of the authors of the Tanakh, portraying the people of Israel as chosen by God yet rebelling against that calling, resulting in divine judgment and retribution. Let me show you some of the parallels in language and expression:

- The author of 2 Chronicles indicts our people with stinging words, explaining why Jerusalem was destroyed in 586 B.C.E.: "The LORD, the God of their fathers, sent word to them through his messengers again and again, because he had pity on his people and on his dwelling place. But they mocked God's messengers, despised his words and scoffed at his prophets until the wrath of the LORD was aroused against his people and there was no remedy" (2 Chron. 36:15–16). More than six hundred years later, Yeshua brings a similar charge against our people, explaining why Jerusalem was about to be destroyed again in 70 C.E.: "O Jerusalem, Jerusalem, you who kill the prophets and stone those sent to you, how often I have longed to gather your children together, as a hen gathers her chicks under her wings, but you were not willing. Look, your house is left to you desolate. . . . I tell you the truth, not one stone here will be left on another; every one will be thrown down" (Matt. 23:37–38; 24:2). God pitied our nation and did everything he could to bring us to repentance, but we refused, making judgment inevitable. So say the Scriptures, both Old and New Testaments.

• The accusation that our people consistently rejected the law and the prophets was fairly common in the Tanakh, and it was repeated in the New Testament. According to the Lord's words spoken through Jeremiah, "From the time your forefathers left Egypt until now, day after day, again and again I sent you my servants the prophets. But they did not listen to me or pay attention. They were stiff-necked and did more evil than their forefathers. . . . Therefore say to them, 'This is the nation that has not obeyed the Lord its God or responded to correction.' Truth has perished; it has vanished from their lips. Cut off your hair and throw it away; take up a lament on the barren heights, for the Lord has rejected and abandoned this generation that is under his wrath. . . . [For] the whole house of Israel is uncircumcised in heart" (Jer. 7:25–26, 28–29; 9:26). Again, more than six hundred years later, after most of our leaders rejected Yeshua, Stephen, a powerful Jewish preacher, brought a similar accusation to the Jewish ruling council: "You stiff-necked people, with uncircumcised hearts and ears! You are just like your fathers: You always resist the Holy Spirit! Was there ever a prophet your fathers did not persecute? They even killed those who predicted the coming of the Righteous One. And now you have betrayed and murdered him" (Acts 7:51–52).

• Both the prophets of Israel and the Jewish followers of Jesus had broken hearts because their people were lost. Listen to the words of Jeremiah, followed by the words of Paul: "Since my people are crushed, I am crushed; I mourn, and horror grips me. Is there no balm in Gilead? Is there no physician there? Why then is there no healing for the wound of my people? Oh, that my head were a spring of water and my eyes a fountain of tears! I would weep day and night for the slain of my people" (Jer. 8:21–9:1 [8:21–23]). "I speak the truth in Christ—I am not lying, my conscience confirms it in the Holy Spirit—I have great sorrow and unceasing anguish in my heart. For I could wish that I myself were cursed and cut off from Christ for the sake of my brothers, those of my own race, the people of Israel" (Rom. 9:1–4). I remind you again: These are not the words of an anti-Semite. This is especially significant when you remember that Paul is sometimes accused of being the father of anti-Semitism.[167]

• Both the prophets of Israel and the Jewish followers of Jesus were confident that in the end our people would turn back to God and be gloriously redeemed. Although the Lord rejected us for a season, he would not reject us forever. This time we'll compare the words of Isaiah with those of Paul: "'The Lord will call you back as if you were a wife deserted and distressed in spirit—a wife who married young, only to be rejected,' says your God. 'For a brief moment I abandoned you, but with deep compassion I will bring you back. In a surge of anger I hid my face from you for a moment, but with everlasting kindness I will have compassion on you,' says the LORD your Redeemer" (Isa. 54:6–8). "I ask then: Did God reject his people? By no means! . . . Again I ask: Did they stumble so as to fall beyond recovery? Not at all! Rather, because of their transgression, salvation has come to the Gentiles to make Israel envious. But if their transgression means riches for the world, and their loss means riches for the Gentiles, how much greater riches will their fullness bring! . . . Israel has experienced a hardening in part until the full number of the Gentiles has come in. And so all Israel will be saved, as it is written: 'The deliverer will come from Zion; he will turn godlessness away from Jacob. And this is my covenant with them when I take away their sins'" (Rom. 11:1, 11–12, 25–27, quoting Isa. 59:21).[168]

I ask you honestly and candidly, are these the sentiments and words of anti-Semites? Absolutely not!

"But," you say, "it's not so simple. That's why even Christian authors have written entire books documenting that it is the New Testament itself that is the seedbed for anti-Semitism, culminating in the Holocaust."

You're right—at least partially. It is true that professing Christian authors have written the very books of which you speak and that the question of anti-Semitism in the New Testament is not that simple. What you may not realize, however, is that further study and reflection have caused many scholars to say emphatically that the New Testament is *not* anti-Semitic in any way. Allow me to explain.

The years following the horrors of the Holocaust called for deep reflection and introspection, especially among professing Christians, and that's why in the last fifty years major studies have been written by both Jewish and Christian authors who claim that the roots of anti-Semitism are to be found in the New Testament writings themselves.[169] For this reason alone it is important for us to examine the major charges that have been brought against the New Testament, testing them carefully to see if any of them, in fact, are accurate.

But I am convinced it is extremely important that you first digest the facts I have just presented to you, since it is highly unlikely that an author will be a virulent anti-Semite in one breath and then a passionate lover of the Jewish people in the next breath. There is simply too much recognition of God's gracious purposes for the Jewish people in the

New Testament to give any credence to the sweeping claim that it is an anti-Semitic book.

It is also unfair to divorce the New Testament from its original, Jewish context and read it in the context of the Crusades and Inquisitions that occurred one thousand to fifteen hundred years later. As we saw in the previous answer, these false followers of Jesus actually persecuted and killed leaders who are revered as Christian heroes today. I would submit to you that it is only when the New Testament has been misinterpreted or misrepresented that it has been a vehicle of anti-Semitism.[170]

Let us therefore consider in detail the primary charges of anti-Semitism in the New Testament and see if, in fact, these passages have either been misunderstood or misused.[171]

- *Matthew makes all Jews—for all generations—responsible for the death of Jesus.* This charge is based on the account given in the Gospel of Matthew (Mattai), which informs us that the Roman governor Pontius Pilate told the assembled Jewish crowd that Jesus should be released since he was guilty of no crime. But the crowd kept shouting, "Crucify him!" Matthew then records, "When Pilate saw that he was getting nowhere, but that instead an uproar was starting, he took water and washed his hands in front of the crowd. 'I am innocent of this man's blood,' he said. 'It is your responsibility!' All the people answered, 'Let his blood be on us and on our children!'" (Matt. 27:24–25).

Tragically, this verse has been used by anti-Semites to justify all kinds of violent acts against our people, since, after all, we Jews asked for it! This was expressed in painful and poignant words by the rabbinic scholar C. G. Montefiore, who refers to Matthew 27:25 as a terrible verse whereby seemingly all the atrocities "wrought upon the Jews are accepted and invoked upon their own heads by the Jews themselves. This is one of those phrases which have been responsible for oceans of human blood and a ceaseless stream of misery and degradation."[172] But is the verse itself actually anti-Semitic? Is it a historical fiction, a creation of Matthew to get back at his own people for rejecting the Messiah? Hardly! The verse itself is quite believable historically, and the language is quite Jewish.

From a historical perspective, Raymond E. Brown, a brilliant and objective Catholic scholar who by no means assumes that what is written in the New Testament is historically accurate, makes four important points with regard to the possibility that there was, in fact, Jewish opposition to Jesus: First, he notes that "one must understand that religious people could have disliked Jesus"; second, "in Jesus' time, religious opposition often led to violence"; third, it is best to speak here of "responsibility, not guilt"; fourth, "the religious dispute with Jesus was an inner Jewish dispute."[173]

These observations help us better evaluate the accuracy of the Gospel accounts of Jesus' death as a whole, suggesting that what is recorded there may certainly be historically plausible. As to the possibility that an angry mob, stirred in part by some of their religious leaders, could have yelled out, "His blood on us and our children" (which is a literal translation of Matt. 27:25), Brown comments that, according to Matthew's representation, "They are not bloodthirsty or callous; for they are persuaded that Jesus is a blasphemer, as the Sanhedrin judged him."[174]

From a Jewish point of view, Samuel Tobias Lachs, professor of the history of religions at Bryn Mawr College, observes that the verse "has a Hebraic ring," referring to numerous parallel expressions in the Talmud.[175] Lachs explains that the basic Hebrew phrase is simply, "his blood will be on his own head" (cf. Josh. 2:19; b. Avodah Zarah 12b), meaning, "he alone bears the responsibility; he is guilty." This fits the context perfectly, since Matthew is simply stating that the Jewish crowd assembled claimed full responsibility for their actions. In other words, they were saying, "We take responsibility for rejecting this troublemaker named Jesus. He deserves to die!"[176] (Note also that the literal translation of this verse reminds us that this is *not* an imprecation in which the Jewish people called down a curse on themselves but rather a statement of responsibility.)[177]

As for the crowd involving their children in the scene—and remember, this is a crowd scene, meaning that words are being spoken in the heat of passion—Matthew is *not* claiming that the Jewish people called down a curse on all future generations. Rather, as the Christian scholar Scot McKnight explained, "It makes most sense for Matthew if the 'our children' of 27:25 literally means 'the physical descendants of those urging Jesus' crucifixion,' which then were those who suffered in the destruction with a generation."[178] In other words, the children of those who rejected the Messiah and turned him over to the Romans to be crucified suffered the consequences of their parents' sin when Jerusalem was destroyed forty years later.

"But that's where I have a problem!" you say. "The notion that the Jews played any role at all in the death of Jesus is utterly false. That's one of the New Testament myths that has caused us such pain through the years."

Really? What makes you think this is a New Testament myth? Do you deny that most of our leaders rejected Jesus as the Messiah when he was on earth? Do you deny that we have consistently rejected him since that time? Then why is it difficult to believe that we had some complicity in turning him over to the Romans to be crucified?

"Because," you argue, "it's one thing to reject him as Messiah. It's another thing to have him killed."

Then why do both the Talmud and Moses Maimonides speak freely of Jewish participation in Yeshua's death? The latter writes explicitly of "Jesus of Nazareth who aspired to be the Messiah and was executed by the court"—meaning the Jewish court, otherwise known as the Sanhedrin.[179] As explained by Rabbi Eliyahu Touger, "The Jews did not actually carry out the execution, for crucifixion is not one of the Torah's methods of execution. Rather, after condemning him to death, the Sanhedrin handed him over to the Roman authorities who executed him as a rebel against Roman rule."[180]

This is exactly what the New Testament teaches, and it is described three times in the Talmudic literature: "On the eve of Passover they hanged Jesus the Nazarene. And a herald went out before him for forty days, saying, 'He is going to be stoned, because he practiced sorcery and led Israel astray. Anyone who knows anything in his favor, let him come and plead in his behalf.' But, not having found anything in his favor, they hanged him on the eve of Passover" (b. Sanhedrin 43a; t. Sanhedrin 10:11; y. Sanhedrin 7:16, 67a).[181]

In light of all this we can state four things clearly: (1) Some Rabbinic sources indicate that Jewish leadership played a role in the death of Jesus; (2) the wording of Matthew 27:25 refers only to taking responsibility for the death of Jesus, not calling down a lasting curse on the nation; (3) from a historical standpoint, the picture painted by Matthew is certainly plausible; and (4) in and of itself, there is nothing anti-Semitic about Matthew 27:25. The fact that it has been utilized by anti-Semites is a terrible tragedy but certainly no fault of the New Testament itself. It should also be emphasized that this verse did not initially *cause* Jewish suffering; rather, its misuse provided an alleged theological *justification* for that suffering.[182]

• *The Jews are consistently demonized in the New Testament, especially in the Gospel of John.* According to this argument, John's Gospel, which may have been the last Gospel to be written, reflects a deep separation between church and synagogue, a separation so deep that Jesus and his followers are portrayed as virtually unconnected to the Jewish people.[183] As for "the Jews" (*hoi Ioudaioi* in Greek, occurring seventy-one times in John's Gospel), they are portrayed as children of the devil, hostile to the Messiah and to God. Is this charge true?

Once again, you're in for a surprise. In fact, a book written by a Jewish Catholic author in 1991 goes so far as to claim that the Gospel of John is actually a witness *against* anti-Semitism in that its account of the death of Jesus "suggests the likelihood of collusion between the Roman procurator Pontius Pilate and Caiaphas, the Jewish high priest, and gives no indication of participation by the [Jewish] people [as a whole]."[184] But if this assessment is correct, why then would John refer to the Jews in such scathing terms? On the other hand, why would this Gospel contain the remarkable statement from Yeshua's own lips that "salvation is from the Jews" (John 4:22)—as opposed to other peoples and groups?

In order to answer this question, we need to turn back to the Hebrew Scriptures. There we learn that the term "the Jews" (*hayehudim* in Hebrew) can be used in several different ways, sometimes meaning only "the Judeans," in other words, the inhabitants of Judea. This explains a verse in the Tanakh like Nehemiah 2:16, where Nehemiah, himself a Jew, refers to another group called "the Jews" (meaning those living in Judea), along with the priests, nobles, officials, "or any others who would be doing the work," all of whom were Jewish as well.[185] Similarly, when John speaks of "the Jews" in the New Covenant, he is generally referring either to the Jewish inhabitants of Judea in general (who were divided in their opinion about Jesus), or, in particular, to the Jewish religious leaders who were hostile to Jesus. Thus, the negative comments in the Gospel of John against "the Jews" are not meant to apply to all Jewish people but rather to specific Jewish leaders in Judea. Therefore, the issue is primarily one of improving our translations and interpretations as opposed to one of removing anti-Semitic statements. The *Jewish New Testament* of David Stern goes a long way in correcting these misapprehensions, as does the recent Christian translation called the *Contemporary English Version*.[186]

For example, most versions of John 7:1 read, "After this, Jesus went around in Galilee, purposely staying away from Judea because the Jews there were waiting to take his life," even though it's clear that "the Jews" here must mean the Judeans. (Remember: Jesus was among Jews in Galilee and didn't fear for his life there.) Stern has correctly translated, "After this, Yeshua traveled around in the Galil, intentionally avoiding Y'hudah [i.e., Judea] because the Judeans were out to kill him." Another clear example is found in John 9:22, where the *Jewish* parents of a *Jewish* blind man who had been miraculously healed were afraid of "the Jews" who controlled the synagogues, obviously meaning the Jewish religious authorities.[187] In fact, John makes this perfectly clear throughout the chapter, identifying these Jews with the religious leaders: "the Pharisees" (v. 13); "the Pharisees" (v. 15); "the Pharisees" (v. 16); "the Jews" (v. 18); "the Jews" (v. 22); "some Pharisees" (v. 40).

Concerning this last usage of *hoi Ioudaioi* (the Jews) in John's Gospel, Urban C. von Wahlde notes that "even the instances with the most hostile connotations are used in a way that is intended to refer to religious authorities rather than the entire nation."[188] As to the harshness of the polemic between these Jewish leaders and Yeshua, von Wahlde makes another important observation: Such language was typical of inter-Jewish debates in the first century of this era. In fact, he finds almost identical parallels between the rhetoric in John's Gospel—where Jesus tells the hostile Jewish authorities that they are walking in darkness, are blind, and have the devil as their father (see especially John 8:44)—and the rhetoric of the Dead Sea Scrolls, where rival Jewish groups are characterized as "sons of darkness" and "sons of the pit" who are under the dominion of Satan and do his works.[189] In this light, he rightly reminds us that "we must learn to listen to [the polemical statements in John] with first-century ears and not with twentieth-century ones."[190]

Professor Craig Evans, after comparing the language and tone of the Dead Sea Scrolls with that of the New Testament, offers some food for thought:

> The polemic found in the writings of Qumran surpasses in intensity that of the New Testament. In contrast to Qumran's esoteric and exclusive posture, the early church proclaimed its message and invited all believers to join its fellowship. Never does the New Testament enjoin Christians to curse unbelievers or opponents. Never does the New Testament petition God to damn the enemies of the church. But Qumran did. If this group had survived and had its membership gradually become gentile over the centuries and had its distinctive writings become the group's Bible, I suspect that most of the passages cited above would be viewed as expressions of anti-Semitism. But the group did not survive, nor did it become a gentile religion, and so its criticisms have never been thought of as anti-Semitic. There is no subsequent history of the Qumran community to muddy the waters. We interpret Qumran as we should. We interpret it in its Jewish context,

for it never existed in any other context, and thus no one ever describes its polemic as anti-Semitic.[191]

Evans also makes reference to the writings of the most famous Jewish historian of the first century, Flavius Josephus, noting that "Josephus's polemic against fellow Jews outstrips anything found in the New Testament."[192] Not only did this great historian slanderously attack Gentiles who had slandered the Jews (calling them "frivolous and utterly senseless specimens of humanity . . . filled with envy . . . folly and narrowmindedness"), he also maligned his own people. Speaking of the Zealots he writes, "In rapine and murder you vie with one another. . . . The Temple has become the sink of all, and native hands have polluted these divine precincts." Of the Sicarii he states, they are "imposters and brigands . . . slaves, the dregs of society, and the bastard scum of the nation." Such quotes could be easily multiplied, yet no one would ever accuse Josephus of anti-Semitism.

The verdict of the respected Jewish scholar Professor Ellis Rivkin really puts things in their proper perspective:

> As a historian who has spent a lifetime seeking to understand the interaction of the religious realm with the human realm and who has been especially concerned with the how and the why of anti-Semitism, I must conclude that however much the Gospel of John lent itself to anti-Semitic uses in later times, it cannot be considered anti-Semitic within its historical frame unless we are willing to apply the same measure to other intrareligious controversies. Did Josephus deride polytheism because he was anti-Thucydides, or anti-Plato, or anti-Stoic? Or did he mock polytheism because he considered its claims to be patently false? Did Jews and Muslims or Christians and Muslims tangle with each other because the former were anti-Arab or anti-Persian or because the latter espoused what Jews and Christians believed to be false teachings about God and his revelations? It is sad indeed that intrareligious and interreligious controversies mar the history of even the most liberating religions, but there is a difference between interreligious controversy that is sincerely generated, however unseemly, and the phenonemon of anti-Semitism, which, in my book, is a *deliberate manipulation of sacred texts to cause harm to the Jews so as to solve economic, social, political, and ecclesiastical problems.*[193]

Without hesitation, then, we can state that the (Jewish) Gospel of John is no more anti-Semitic than the (Jewish) Dead Sea Scrolls or the writings of the (Jewish) historian Josephus. Therefore, if the latter are *not* open to the charge of anti-Semitism (and they are not), neither is the Gospel of John.

• *The Jewish religious leaders, especially the Pharisees, are depicted as snakes and vipers, hypocrites who are rotten to the core, and men worthy of damnation.* As we just noted, first-century Jewish literature often contains harsh, in-house polemics between rival Jewish groups. In fact, some of the harsh rhetoric of the Dead Sea Scrolls was actually directed against Pharisees too. Even the Talmud, which continues in the traditions of the Pharisees, has a biting polemic against hypocritical Pharisees, even making reference to "the plague of the Pharisees."[194] Therefore, strong rebukes against hypocritical leaders, such as those found in Matthew 3:7–10 (the words of John the Baptist) and Matthew 23:1–37 (the words of Yeshua), should not surprise us.

The real question is this: Are they accurate? From this vantage point, we cannot prove or disprove their accuracy, and scholars who have studied the question in depth have come to widely different conclusions.[195] What we do know is this: In the Hebrew Bible, it was the religious leadership who often opposed the prophetic word. Just ask Jeremiah and Amos. (See, e.g., Jeremiah 26 and Amos 7:10–17.) We also know that two centuries before the time of Jesus, there were Sadducean high priests who were utterly wicked.[196] Therefore, it is certainly possible that there were hypocritical Jewish leaders in Jesus' day who considered this charismatic healer and miracle worker to be a threat to their religious establishment.[197]

After all, great crowds followed him wherever he went, hanging on his every word and bringing the sick and the dying for his healing touch. This kind of scene was repeated over and over during his ministry:

> When they had crossed over, they landed at Gennesaret and anchored there. As soon as they got out of the boat, people recognized Jesus. They ran throughout that whole region and carried the sick on mats to wherever they heard he was. And wherever he went—into villages, towns or countryside—they placed the sick in the marketplaces. They begged him to let them touch even the edge of his cloak, and all who touched him were healed.
>
> Mark 6:53–56

Can you imagine how threatening this would have been to his opponents? Sometimes so many people thronged around him that he would have to teach the people from a boat pushed off from shore.

There was even a time when temple guards were sent to arrest him only to return empty-handed. "No one ever spoke the way this man does," the guards explained (see John 7:32–47). This infuriated some of the temple leadership.

Human nature is such that jealousy, envy, and competition can easily influence our actions, and all too often, if I consider you a threat to my well-being or promotion, then I view your loss as my success and your defeat as my victory. Thus, from a strictly psychological viewpoint, if Jesus was as popular as the eyewitnesses claim, it's easy to understand why he received some hostile treatment from the other leaders and why, at times, other leaders were envious of him (see Matt. 27:18, where Pilate knew that it was "out of envy" that the leaders handed Jesus over to him; and note also Acts 5:12–17).

It's also important to remember that many of the disputes he had with the Pharisees were over matters of Jewish law, in other words, in-house legal disputes. For example, on one occasion "some Pharisees and teachers of the law came to Jesus from Jerusalem and asked, 'Why do your disciples break the tradition of the elders? They don't wash their hands before they eat!'" (Matt. 15:1–2). This was an in-house debate over the interpretation of legal intricacies.

On another occasion, Jesus healed a woman on the Sabbath, provoking a passionate discussion: "Indignant because Jesus had healed on the Sabbath, the synagogue ruler said to the people, 'There are six days for work. So come and be healed on those days, not on the Sabbath'" (Luke 13:14). Like many Jewish teachers of his day, this leader believed it was appropriate to save a life on the Sabbath and to perform emergency medical procedures on that sacred day, but to heal someone who could have been healed on any day of the week was unacceptable to him and constituted work.

Jesus replied sharply to this line of reason, viewing it simply as a cloak of hypocrisy:

> The Lord answered him, "You hypocrites! Doesn't each of you on the Sabbath untie his ox or donkey from the stall and lead it out to give it water? Then should not this woman, a daughter of Abraham, whom Satan has kept bound for eighteen long years, be set free on the Sabbath day from what bound her?" When he said this, all his opponents were humiliated, but the people were delighted with all the wonderful things he was doing.
>
> Luke 13:15–17

There are two things in this account that are believable, even to a skeptical reader. First, the religious leadership is guilty of majoring on the minors, ignoring the miracle of healing because it violated their tradition. This is something all too common. Just look at different factions within one particular religion and watch how they divide over the smallest, most insignificant issues, ignoring the large areas of common ground they share. Second, the people as a whole—in other words, synagogue-attending Jews—are delighted with this great prophet and healer named Jesus, while it is only a minority (specifically, the leadership) who oppose him. This, too, is all too common, since the people in general are being blessed while those who previously influenced them are feeling slighted.

Of course, the New Testament makes reference to key Jewish leaders who were sympathetic to Jesus the Messiah, recording that some even spoke out on his behalf (see John 7:40–52; 19:38–39 [in Mark 15:43, Joseph of Arimathea is described as a prominent member of the ruling council and a disciple of Jesus]; Luke 13:31; see also Luke 14:1). This reminds us that not all Pharisees (or Jewish leaders) were considered evil by the New Testament writers. In fact, some scholars (including contemporary Jewish scholars) have argued that Jesus himself was a Pharisee, differing primarily with other Pharisees over minor issues of legal interpretation, as we just noted.[198]

Nonetheless, it is true that the term *Pharisee* has become synonymous with *hypocrite* in the English language, and this is definitely a direct result of the New Testament usage. Still, as we have emphasized repeatedly, the fact that later readers used the New Testament documents to fuel the fires of anti-Semitism does not prove for a moment that the documents themselves were anti-Semitic. Craig Evans is therefore absolutely correct in stating that "these writings, though at times highly critical of Jews and Gentiles who for various reasons rejected the Christian proclamation, are not anti-Semitic."[199]

What about the general description of the Pharisees in the New Testament writings? We should first remember that Paul himself was a Pharisee and continued to refer to himself as a Pharisee long after putting his faith in Jesus as Messiah (see Acts 23:6; 26:5). Thus, we have firsthand testimony from a first-century Pharisee, although it is testimony that is, to a certain extent, critical of Pharisaism. Recent books on Paul have underscored his close relationship to Jewish law and tradition of his day.[200] In addition to this, the Gospel writings give us a picture of this important Jewish movement that is in keeping with the picture of the Pharisees painted elsewhere in contemporary Jewish literature.

You see, the New Testament writings are only one of several Jewish witnesses to the nature and character of the Pharisees. The historian Josephus and the rabbinic writings also give us a description of this group. Interestingly, all these witnesses have a number of key ingredients in common. As James D. G. Dunn summarizes: "A remarkably coherent picture emerges of Pharisees as a 'sect,' *airesis* [in Greek], whose most characteristic concern was to observe the law and ancestral traditions with scrupulous care, with a deep desire to maintain Israel's identity as the people of the law, as expressed not least in developing *halakoth* [laws] regarding the sabbath and particularly ritual purity."[201]

Of course, you might say, "That's fine and good. But I'm sure that the *negative* description of the Pharisees in the Gospels is unparalleled in those other writings you mentioned, and therefore, it must be questioned. In fact, in my view, it's just another proof of anti-Jewish bias in the Gospels."

I see your point, but again, I beg to differ. First, we have shown that religious resistance to the prophetic message of Jesus would be in keeping with similar religious resistance to prophetic figures in the Tanakh. Second, we saw in the previous answers (above, 2.6–2.7) that there were repeated acts of hostility by certain religious Jews against the first (Jewish) followers of Jesus. Third, such acts continue to this day, as Messianic Jews have been threatened, kidnapped, and even beaten by ultra-Orthodox Jews—in other words, by men who would not dare eat pork but who consider it their sacred duty to intimidate and attack Messianic Jews. I myself have been spat upon by such people, while other close friends of mine have been struck in the face, abducted, or assaulted. (For more on this, see above, 2.7.)

Does this prove that religious leaders did the same thing to Jesus? Certainly not! Does this prove that all ultra-Orthodox Jews (or all first-century Pharisees) are evil? No. But it *does* prove that *some* religious Jews can act violently toward fellow Jews who believe differently than they do and that *some* religious Jews may well have acted violently toward Yeshua. The fact that religious Jews in the land of Israel today are seeking to pass harsh legislation against all proselytism reminds us that this same aggressive, anti-pluralistic attitude can be found whenever a leading religious or political group feels threatened by another individual, group, race, or party. Islam has been guilty of it; Christendom has been guilty of it; and Judaism has been guilty of it.

Our people's disgraceful treatment of prophets such as Jeremiah and Ezekiel in the past, the disparaging Talmudic comments concerning Messianic Jews in the early centuries of this era, the persecution experienced by Messianic Jews at the hands of their fellow Jews in recent centuries (continuing right up to this day), and my own experiences as a Jewish follower of Jesus all cause me to take the Gospel descriptions of the Pharisees (meaning many Pharisees but by no means all Pharisees) seriously.

It's also worth noting that Rabbi Phillip Sigal, a respected Jewish scholar who was involved in Jewish-Christian dialog, accepted the description of the Pharisees in Matthew's Gospel at face value but claimed that these religious leaders were *not* the true predecessors of the later Talmudic rabbis.[202] While Sigal's proposal has not been widely accepted, it demonstrates how a Jewish scholar could find the New Testament descriptions of a particular, often hostile Jewish sect to be thoroughly plausible while at the same time allowing him to continue to revere and respect the later Talmudic rabbis, men who Sigal felt were leaders marked by a different spirit.

• *Paul told his Gentile readers that the Jews displease God, are hostile to all men, killed both the prophets and the Messiah, and are objects of God's wrath to the uttermost.* Let's begin by reading the specific passage in context. Paul was writing to the Thessalonians, Gentiles who previously worshiped idols but had now turned to the one true God through Jesus the Messiah. As a result of their newfound faith, they had suffered severe persecution from their own countrymen. Paul alluded to this several times in his two letters to them preserved in the New Testament, seeking to comfort them in the midst of their suffering. In fact, Paul himself had been threatened by his own countrymen when he first preached to the Thessalonians, since it was always his custom to begin in the synagogue, speaking to his Jewish people before taking the message of the Messiah to the Gentiles.

This is what happened when Paul began speaking in the city:

> When they had passed through Amphipolis and Apollonia, they came to Thessalonica, where there was a Jewish synagogue. As his custom was, Paul went into the synagogue, and on three Sabbath days he reasoned with them from the Scriptures, explaining and proving that the Christ had to suffer and rise from the dead. "This Jesus I am proclaiming to you is the Christ," he said. Some of the Jews were persuaded and joined Paul and Silas, as did a large number of God-fearing Greeks and not a few prominent women. But the Jews were jealous; so they rounded

up some bad characters from the marketplace, formed a mob and started a riot in the city.

Acts 17:1–5

It was quite a scene! As it turned out, the gospel message was hotly opposed in Thessalonica even after Paul left the city, and both Paul (in his ongoing travels) and the new Thessalonian believers continued to suffer harsh persecution. This, then, gives the background for some of what Paul wrote to them:

> You became imitators of us and of the Lord; in spite of severe suffering, you welcomed the message with the joy given by the Holy Spirit. And so you became a model to all the believers in Macedonia and Achaia. . . . You know, brothers, that our visit to you was not a failure. We had previously suffered and been insulted in Philippi, as you know, but with the help of our God we dared to tell you his gospel in spite of strong opposition. . . . We sent Timothy, who is our brother and God's fellow worker in spreading the gospel of Christ, to strengthen and encourage you in your faith, so that no one would be unsettled by these trials. You know quite well that we were destined for them. In fact, when we were with you, we kept telling you that we would be persecuted. And it turned out that way, as you well know. . . . Therefore, brothers, in all our distress and persecution we were encouraged about you because of your faith.

1 Thessalonians 1:6–7; 2:1–2; 3:2–4, 7

> Therefore, among God's churches we boast about your perseverance and faith in all the persecutions and trials you are enduring. All this is evidence that God's judgment is right, and as a result you will be counted worthy of the kingdom of God, for which you are suffering.

2 Thessalonians 1:4–5

As you can see, Paul wanted to encourage these new (Gentile) believers, telling them that the suffering they were experiencing was nothing unusual or unexpected. In fact, what they were going through was exactly what Paul was going through.

> For you, brothers, became imitators of God's churches in Judea, which are in Christ Jesus: You suffered from your own countrymen the same things those churches suffered from the Jews [or Judeans], who killed the Lord Jesus and the prophets and also drove us out. They displease God and are hostile to all men in their effort to keep us from speaking

to the Gentiles so that they may be saved. In this way they always heap up their sins to the limit. The wrath of God has come upon them at last.

1 Thessalonians 2:14–16

Some New Testament scholars have claimed that the language used here by Paul is not in keeping with his other letters, and they have suggested that these words were an addition written by another author. But there is little support for this proposal, and we must take Paul's words at face value.[203] Do they indict "the Jews" in general, and are they in fact anti-Semitic? The answer is no to both questions.

Paul was *not* saying that all Jews were guilty of killing Jesus any more than he was saying that all Jews were guilty of killing the prophets or that all Jews were guilty of driving him out of city after city. After all, he was making reference to the sufferings that were being experienced by Jewish believers in Judea from the hands of their own countrymen. That was his whole point. You (believing) Thessalonians are suffering persecution from your own (unbelieving) countrymen just like we (believing) Jews are suffering persecution from our own (unbelieving) countrymen. Just as it would be completely wrong to conclude that Paul was saying all Thessalonians were wicked, so too it would be wrong to conclude that he was saying all Jews were wicked.

"But," you say, "look at what he said about the Jews! He made a sweeping indictment against us as a people."

I can't agree with you. First, I remind you that Paul was speaking about *unbelieving* Jews, and he found a steady stream of such people throughout our history: those who killed the prophets, those who killed the Messiah, and those who hindered the Messiah's work from reaching the Gentiles.[204] The prophets dealt with this same kind of chronic unbelief and rebellion, stating,

The LORD was very angry with your forefathers. Therefore tell the people: This is what the LORD Almighty says: "Return to me," declares the LORD Almighty, "and I will return to you," says the LORD Almighty. Do not be like your forefathers, to whom the earlier prophets proclaimed: This is what the LORD Almighty says: "Turn from your evil ways and your evil practices." But they would not listen or pay attention to me, declares the LORD.

Zechariah 1:2–4

Like Zechariah, Paul was pointing out how consistently his people disobeyed the Lord, a fact he was struck with on several occasions when a hostile Jewish group followed him into a city, making his mission to the Gentiles difficult.[205] What he was saying is clear: Those same, unbelieving Jews who in previous generations killed the prophets and then the Messiah are now making life difficult for us Jews who do believe in Yeshua. "They displease God and are hostile to all men in their effort to keep us from speaking to the Gentiles so that they may be saved" (1 Thess. 2:15–16). This is hardly an indictment on all Jews.[206]

Second, it is possible that Paul was specifically speaking of the Judeans—meaning hostile, Jerusalemite leaders—who had a history of rejecting the prophets, who were instrumental in turning the people against the Messiah, and who now spearheaded the opposition to Paul's work. This is in keeping with Yeshua's own words about the city he loved so much: "O Jerusalem, Jerusalem, you who kill the prophets and stone those sent to you" (Matt. 23:37). This was often a sinful city. It could well be, then, that Paul was addressing an even more specific group, namely, unbelieving Jewish leaders in Judea.[207]

In any case, there is no possible way to think he indicted all Jews everywhere, since, as we have emphasized, in context he was contrasting believing Jews with unbelieving Jews.

As to Paul's closing comments that "the wrath of God has come upon them at last," this simply means that "wrath was determined against them, and would soon overtake them."[208] He was *not* saying Jews were doomed for all time. As we noted earlier, Paul declared that the day would come when *all Israel* would believe and be saved—something he wrote about no other nation or people. In fact, this was his constant prayer: "Brothers, my heart's desire and prayer to God for the Israelites is that they may be saved. For I can testify about them that they are zealous for God, but their zeal is not based on knowledge" (Rom. 10:1–2). Once more, we can say without question that these are not the words of an anti-Semite.

• *The New Testament charges the Jews with deicide—killing God. No wonder Christians turned on them so violently.* Where does the New Testament raise this charge?

"Well," you reply, "it says that the Jews killed Christ, and according to the New Testament, Christ is God. Therefore, it says that the Jews killed God."

Let's analyze this point by point. First, the New Testament authors make several clear statements regarding the death of Yeshua. Most importantly, they teach that Jesus the Messiah died for our sins (see, e.g., 1 Cor. 15:3), that is to say, he willingly died for us, for the ungodly (see Rom. 5:6–8). Thus, Jesus could state emphatically:

> I am the good shepherd. The good shepherd lays down his life for the sheep. . . . The reason my Father loves me is that I lay down my life— only to take it up again. No one takes it from me, but I lay it down of my own accord. I have authority to lay it down and authority to take it up again. This command I received from my Father.
>
> John 10:11, 17–18

Second, the New Testament authors indicate that the death of Jesus was ordained by God himself, referring to him as "the Lamb that was slain from the creation of the world" (Rev. 13:8). Thus, even when dealing with his fellow Jews regarding their complicity in the Messiah's death, Peter could say, "This man was handed over to you by God's set purpose and foreknowledge" (Acts 2:23).

Third, it is acknowledged that both Jew and Gentile conspired against Jesus, even in the most pointed New Testament statements. Continuing the verse just cited, Peter said to his people, "and you, *with the help of wicked men,* put him to death by nailing him to the cross" (Acts 2:23). This mentality is reflected in one of the first recorded prayers of the Jewish followers of Jesus shortly after his death and resurrection: "Indeed Herod and Pontius Pilate met together with the Gentiles and the people of Israel in this city to conspire against your holy servant Jesus, whom you anointed. They did what your power and will had decided beforehand should happen" (Acts 4:27–28; notice once again the emphasis on the foreordained nature of the Messiah's death).

Fourth, even when he was being crucified, Jesus uttered the unforgettable words, "Father, forgive them, for they do not know what they are doing" (Luke 23:34), a sentiment reflected elsewhere in the New Testament writings:

> Now, brothers, I know that you acted in ignorance, as did your leaders. But this is how God fulfilled what he had foretold through all the prophets, saying that his Christ would suffer. Repent, then, and turn to God, so that your sins may be wiped out, that times of refreshing may come from the Lord, and that he may send the Christ, who has been appointed for you—even Jesus.
>
> Acts 3:17–20

Even in passages where our people are held responsible for the death of Jesus, mercy is extended to them, since they acted in ignorance in handing over the Messiah to be crucified. As Paul declared while preaching in a synagogue one Sabbath, "The people of Jerusalem and their rulers did not recognize Jesus, yet in condemning him they fulfilled the words of the prophets that are read every Sabbath" (Acts 13:27). That's why he could boldly promise, "Therefore, my brothers, I want you to know that through Jesus the forgiveness of sins is proclaimed to you" (Acts 13:38). This is wonderful news!

In light of all this, you can see how misleading it is to claim that the New Testament says the Jews killed Christ. As to your next statement, that according to the New Testament Christ is God, and therefore, the New Testament says the Jews killed God, once again, you have not read the evidence clearly.

The New Testament emphasizes both the human nature and the divine nature of the Messiah, speaking of him throughout the Gospels as a fully human Jewish rabbi who at the same time was the Son of God. However, his divine nature is portrayed as a mystery, a gloriously veiled truth, and he never made overt statements such as, "I am God!" Rather, when speaking of God, he referred to him as "my Father and your Father . . . my God and your God" (John 20:17).[209] It was only little by little that his followers fully understood who he was, and even then, it required a good deal of reflection. After all, if God is one, how can he have a Son? The doctrine of God's tri-unity is deep and complex (see vol. 2, 3.1–3.4).

To this day, many religious Jews and Muslims (all of whom are staunch monotheists) incorrectly think Christians believe in three gods (Father, Son, Holy Spirit) rather than in one God. Thus, there is not the slightest notion that the New Testament authors felt that when their fellow Jews rejected the Messiah, they were killing God.[210]

"Can you prove this?" you ask.

You bet! Here are some key New Testament verses in which a Jewish speaker is addressing his own people regarding the death of the Messiah. You will see that his divine nature is never emphasized in any of them. In fact, if anything is emphasized, it is his humanity. Thus, the charge is simply, "You handed over the Messiah! You betrayed him!" The supposedly logical next step that you suggested—i.e., "Therefore you killed God!"—is never even hinted at anywhere in the New Testament. Read every line of every book, and you will not find the charge of deicide.

Here then are some of the most prominent statements (some of which have been quoted already):

> Men of Israel, listen to this: Jesus of Nazareth was a man accredited by God to you by miracles, wonders and signs, which God did among you through him, as you yourselves know. This man was handed over to you by God's set purpose and foreknowledge; and you, with the help of wicked men, put him to death by nailing him to the cross.

> Acts 2:22–23; notice that Jesus is twice referred to as a man

> Therefore let all Israel be assured of this: God has made this Jesus, whom you crucified, both Lord and Messiah.

> Acts 2:36; notice that God appointed Jesus to be Lord and Messiah[211]

> The God of Abraham, Isaac and Jacob, the God of our fathers, has glorified his servant Jesus. You handed him over to be killed, and you disowned him before Pilate, though he had decided to let him go.

> Acts 3:13; notice that Jesus is called God's servant

> If we are being called to account today for an act of kindness shown to a cripple and are asked how he was healed, then know this, you and all the people of Israel: It is by the name of Jesus Christ of Nazareth, whom you crucified but whom God raised from the dead, that this man stands before you healed.

> Acts 4:9–10; notice that the earthly origins of Jesus are emphasized and that, once again, rather than him being called God, it is stated that God raised him from the dead; see also Acts 5:30

From beginning to end, the accusation of deicide is false.

• *The real problem with the New Testament is the notion that God is finished with the Jewish people, that they are now the synagogue of Satan, having been replaced by Christians who are the true Jews and the New Israel.* Although it is easy to see how you came up with this idea, it is incorrect and without foundation. This doctrine, known as replacement theology or supersessionism, has been taught at times by many church leaders, but it remains an unbiblical view.[212] Again, I'll respond point by point for clarity's sake.

Does the New Testament say that God is finished with Israel? Absolutely not! As we saw earlier, Paul, in the fullest treatment of this question in the New Testament, emphatically rejected this notion. Rather, he explained to his Gentile readers that his people Israel had only stumbled temporarily, explaining that they were partially hardened (see Romans 9–11; for the concept of God hardening his people in the Tanakh, see Deut. 29:4; Isa. 6:9–10). The hardening was partial in at least two ways: (1) It was only temporary, and in the end, Israel as a nation would turn back in faith; and (2) it did not apply to all the people. After all, virtually all of Yeshua's first followers— amounting to many thousands—were Jews.

In keeping with this concept of Israel's final restoration, Jesus prophesied to his disciples that "at the renewal of all things, when the Son of Man [the Messiah] sits on his glorious throne, you who have followed me will also sit on twelve thrones, judging [or leading, ruling] the twelve tribes of Israel" (Matt. 19:28). The tribes of Israel will be part of God's endtime kingdom. It is *because* Yeshua's disciples knew this that shortly before he ascended to heaven they asked him, "Lord, are you at this time going to restore the kingdom to Israel?" (Acts 1:6). Rather than rebuking them and calling them stupid for thinking for a moment that God would ever restore the kingdom to Israel, he said, "It is not for you to know the times or dates the Father has set by his own authority" (Acts 1:7). In other words, it's none of your business to know when this will happen. Instead, he told them their job was to go into all the world and tell everyone that the Messiah had come (Acts 1:8).[213]

It is true that Jesus taught that "many will come from the east and the west [meaning Gentiles], and will take their places at the feast with Abraham, Isaac and Jacob in the kingdom of heaven. But the subjects of the kingdom will be thrown outside, into the darkness, where there will be weeping and gnashing of teeth" (Matt. 8:11–12). But this was saying nothing more than that many Jews, who should have been the first to recognize the Messiah, will be rejected and left out because of their unbelief, while many believing Gentiles will enjoy Israel's blessings in their stead. The entire context of Yeshua's ministry makes this clear.[214]

"But didn't Paul teach that the church was the new Israel?" Not at all. Rather, he taught that Gentile believers in the Messiah became fellow members of the household of God along with Jewish believers, but they remained Gentiles. Read through Romans 9–11, where Paul addresses Gentile believers as Gentiles, talking to them about his people Israel: "I am talking to you Gentiles. Inasmuch as I am the apostle to the Gentiles, I make much of my ministry in the hope that I may somehow arouse my own people [Israel] to envy and save some of them" (Rom. 11:13–14).

It is true Paul applied some of the spiritual descriptions of Israel to Gentile Christians, but he never said the church *was* Israel or, more importantly, that the church had *replaced* Israel. I have documented this in detail in my book *Our Hands Are Stained with Blood*.[215] As I noted there,

> Many people have feelings and impressions about what the Scriptures teach. But the facts are the facts: While the New Testament often describes Israel and the Church in similar terms—both are pictured as the children of God, the bride of God, the chosen people, etc.—*on no definite occasion does the New Testament ever call the Church "Israel."* In fact, out of the 77 times that the words "Israel" and "Israelite" occur in the Greek New Testament, there are only *two* verses in which "Israel" could *possibly* refer to the Church as a whole: Galatians 6:16, where Paul speaks of the "Israel of God" and Revelation 7:4, where John speaks of the 144,000 sealed from the twelve tribes of Israel. This is saying something! Seventy-five "definites" and only two "maybes." I wouldn't want to side with the "maybes"!
>
> As for the verses open to dispute, in Galatians 6:16 the King James Version, the New King James Version and the New American Standard Bible [important, contemporary Christian translations] all imply the same thing: "The Israel of God" does not refer to the whole Church. It refers to believing Jews. The same can be said for the description of the 144,000 sealed in Revelation 7:4. It most probably describes the final harvest of Jews worldwide. Elsewhere in the Book of Revelation "Israel" means "Israel" (Rev. 2:14) and the "twelve tribes of Israel" mean "the twelve tribes of Israel," as distinguished from the "twelve apostles" (Rev. 21:12–14).[216]

The same point can be made even more emphatically with regard to the use of the term *Jew* in the Greek New Testament: It occurs more than 190 times, referring in general to ethnic, national Jews, or specifically to Judean Jews or to Jewish leaders in Jerusalem.[217]

"What about Romans 2:28–29, where Paul says that those who are Jews outwardly (meaning in the flesh) are not Jews, whereas a true Jew is one who is a Jew inwardly (meaning spiritually)? According to Paul himself, if I don't believe in Jesus, even though both my parents are Jewish, I'm not a Jew, whereas a Gentile Christian is a Jew."

Again, your interpretation is wrong. In context, Paul is addressing Jews living in Rome, and his question has to do with who is a real Jew in God's eyes. Is it the Jew who is circumcised in body only, or the Jew who is circumcised in spirit as well? Thus the New International Version rightly translates these verses as follows: "A man is not a Jew if he is *only* one outwardly, nor is circumcision *merely* outward and physical. No, a man is a Jew if he is one inwardly; and circumcision is circumcision of the heart, by the Spirit, not by the written code. Such a man's praise is not from men, but from God" (Rom. 2:28–29).

Do you see Paul's point? It would be like me bringing three men before you, two from Africa and one from America. One of the Africans is a devout atheist, the other a devout Christian. The American is also a devout Christian. If I asked you, "Which of these men is the spiritual African?" you would reply, "The African Christian!" You wouldn't think for a moment that the American Christian was the spiritual African, would you? In the same way, if I brought before you a Jewish atheist, a God-fearing Jew, and a God-fearing Gentile Christian and asked you, "Which of these is a spiritual Jew?" you would say, "The God-fearing Jew."

That was Paul's point. *Between two Jews*, one who is circumcised in his flesh but does not know and serve the Lord, and one who is circumcised in his flesh and knows and serves the Lord, who is the true Jew, the real Jew in God's sight? Who is the spiritual Jew? You wouldn't think for a second he was speaking of a spiritual Gentile.[218]

"Okay, I'll admit your interpretation makes sense, but what about those verses in which Jews who oppose Christians are referred to as the 'synagogue of Satan'? If that's not anti-Semitic, nothing is."

Once again, I have no doubt that the verses to which you refer have been used by anti-Semites, just as verses in the Tanakh that call our people a "sinful nation, a people loaded with guilt, a brood of evildoers, children given to corruption" (Isa. 1:4) have been used against us. Still, you might be surprised with the facts behind the "synagogue of Satan" accusation.

This description is found just twice in the New Testament, Revelation 2:9, where Jesus comforts believers in Smyrna who were experiencing intense persecution and even martyrdom ("I know the slander of those who say they are Jews and are not, but are a synagogue of Satan"), and Revelation 3:9, where Jesus encourages suffering believers in the city of Philadelphia (in Asia Minor), assuring them, "I will make those who are of the synagogue of Satan, who claim to be Jews though they are not, but are liars—I will make them come and fall down at your feet and acknowledge that I have loved you" (Rev. 3:9).

On the one hand, there is the possibility that the people to whom Yeshua referred—and who were causing real hardship for these Christians in Smyrna and Philadelphia—were actually *not* Jews at all. This would be similar to a modern-day cult such as the Black Hebrews: They strongly oppose both Jews and Christians and claim to be the real Jews, the true Israel, when in fact they are not. As to being called a synagogue, it is important to remember that the Greek word used here could simply mean a meeting place, as in James (Jacob) 2:2— "Suppose a man comes into your meeting" (Greek, *synagoges*).

On the other hand, it could well be that Yeshua was speaking of his own kinsmen but using biting, prophetic hyperbole, just as when the Lord said through the prophet Hosea, "You are not my people, and I am not your God" (Hosea 1:9), and again, speaking of Israel as his wife, "Rebuke your mother, rebuke her, for she is not my wife, and I am not her husband" (Hosea 2:2). In both of these verses, God completely repudiates his people/wife Israel, only to immediately promise Israel's restoration (see Hosea 1:10; 2:16). The lesson we learn is that sometimes, when our people continually disobeyed the Lord and broke his covenant, he spoke of them as if they were not his people at all. In the same way, when the Messiah's own people actually tried to stop *Gentiles* from hearing about him (and this did happen; see, e.g., Acts 14:1–20), he could say of them, "You claim to be Jews but are not; you're really a meeting place of Satan."

"But that's so harsh!" you say.

Yes, it does seem harsh, but no harsher than the accusation in the (Jewish) Dead Sea Scrolls that Jews who opposed their (Jewish) group were part of the "congregation of Belial." (Belial was synonymous with Satan.) And it is certainly a lot less harsh than the Talmudic claim that Jesus is now in hell, burning in excrement (see b. Gittin 56b–57a).

In any case, this is where we get to the root of the problem. When the Dead Sea Scrolls were written, they were written primarily for their own believing community, consisting only of Jews. When the New Testament was written, it was written for a different believing community, consisting of Jews and Gentiles. Over the process of time, this community of believers (called the church) became increasingly Gentile and, hence, increasingly ignorant of its Jewish roots, the very thing Paul warned about (see Rom. 11:17–26 and the discussion above, 2.7). Ultimately, some of this church turned hostile to its Jewish roots, utilizing texts that at most provided evidence of a very selective anti-Judaism, and, more than eighteen hundred years later, were used to fuel the fires of racial anti-Semitism.[219]

As a follower of Jesus, I grieve over this misuse of my sacred Scriptures, and I stand against any so-called Christian who would misuse them in this way today. I also believe there should be a greater sensitivity in modern translations of the New Testament, not altering a word that was written but translating with special clarity in light of the terrible history of misinterpretation that we have described in part.

But that is only part of the grief I experience. You see, as a Jew, I agonize over the fact that our people as a whole missed the Messiah when he came, instead turning against him. How awful it is! We broke the Sinai covenant over and over again, we rejected prophet after prophet, even killing some, and then we rejected the Messiah, delivering him up to be crucified. So both the church and the Jewish people have sinned!

There is only one way to make things right: Let everyone who claims to be a Christian demonstrate it by showing the love of the Messiah to his own Jewish people, utterly repudiating even the slightest hint of anti-Semitism, and let every Jewish person turn back to Yeshua—our one and only Messiah—in repentance and faith.

Let me close this rather lengthy answer with an observation. As I mentioned earlier, I can honestly say that in almost thirty years in the church, I have rarely, if ever, met a "Christian" anti-Semite,[220] and when I have told Christians about the horrors of anti-Semitism in church history, they were utterly shocked. Moreover, when I shared with them that many Jews actually believe the New Testament itself is anti-Semitic, they were dumbfounded. These people who carefully studied the New Testament for years never came to any anti-Semitic conclusions. The thought of such interpretations never even dawned on them.

This should give you pause for thought, and it should help explain to you why, at this critical juncture in Jewish history, Israel's best friends are Bible-believing, New Testament–reading Christians.[221] I know this is the opposite of what you have been taught, but it's the truth. The gospel truth.

2.9. Without the long, ugly history of Christian anti-Semitism, the Holocaust would never have occurred.

Maybe so. Many so-called "Christians" and "Christian" leaders helped pave the way for the demonic and destructive atmosphere of the Holocaust, although it is important to remember that no church leader in history ever advocated exterminating Jews, that no church leader in history ever attempted to wipe out the Jewish people, that the church's historic anti-Judaism bore no resemblance to Hitler's racial anti-Semitism, and that the Holocaust itself was anti-Christian in every sense of the word. Still, there is blood on the hands of all anti-Semitic leaders who claimed to be Christians, and to this day, sincere Christians around the world agonize over the things that were done to the Jewish people by Nazis, communists, and other Jew-haters. As Jews, however, we have a different kind of soul-searching to do, since we must ask ourselves why such calamities overtook us if we were in good standing with God as a people. Why, in fact, was there a Holocaust? This is the real question that needs to be answered.

I'm not going to spend a lot of time arguing this point with you because, for the most part, I agree with you.[222] Where we differ is over the definition of who is a Christian and what is the church, as well as over the question of whether the New Testament itself is actually anti-Semitic. As we have stated previously (2.6–2.7), the true Christians during the Holocaust were the ones who rescued and helped Jews, not the ones who rounded up and hunted Jews. And the true church—in history and during the Holocaust—has often been marked by a special love for Israel, not a special hatred for our people. As for the New Testament, we have seen that it is no more open to the charge of anti-Semitism than is the Hebrew Bible.[223] Regarding the subsequent, anti-Judaic sentiments in early church writings, we have properly observed that such rhetoric "was in no way similar to nor has it directly been responsible for the racial anti-Semitism of this century that formed the rationale for the Holocaust of the 1930s and 1940s."[224]

In fact, in 1937, Pope Pius XI ordered that his encyclical *Mit brennender Sorge* (German for "With searing anxiety") be read from every Catholic pulpit in Germany. The document, which was smuggled into the country and caught the Nazis completely off guard, condemned Nazism "as fundamentally racist and anti-Christian."[225] As a result, the Nazi leadership "was infuriated and intensified its persecution of the [Catholic] Church and especially of its priests."[226]

I think you also need to come to grips with the fact that Messianic Jews in Europe—even if they were only one-quarter Jewish (meaning that only one of their grandparents was Jewish)—were slaughtered by the Nazis during the Holocaust. They too suffered the murderous madness of these killers, and the fact that they believed in Jesus and attended church did not change their lot one bit. This reminds us that the Holocaust was in no sense of the word "Christian." You could just as well say that Joseph Stalin was a God-fearing Jew as you could say that anything about the Holocaust was Christian.

The question that must be asked is why God allowed (or ordained?) millions of our people to die cruel deaths at the hands of the Nazis. Of course, that devastating and overwhelming question is, strictly speaking, outside the parameters of this book, and it deserves thousands of pages of in-depth, gut-wrenching, soul-stretching discussion. Still, I think it would be good for us to consider some religious Jewish responses to the Holocaust and compare them with some Christian reflections. We'll do this in the next answer.

2.10. Why did God allow six million Jews to die in the Holocaust? Before I could even think about believing in Jesus, I need an answer to *this* question.

This is an agonizing question that has been asked countless times by both Jews and Christians, but in many ways, it is more a question about man's sin against man than about God's silence during that sin. In other words, the Holocaust is something people did to other people. Why didn't God intervene? Some Orthodox rabbis would say it was because we, the Jewish people, had sinned against the Almighty and were therefore under his disfavor. The Holocaust, then, was a massive, overwhelming example of divine discipline, devastating for the moment but leading to health and healing in the end. To the extent that there is truth to this view, we must then ask what sins we had committed to merit such a fate (or to rob us of divine protection). Other Jewish leaders strongly disagree with this view, claiming that even godless Jews who died in the Holocaust were martyrs in some sense of the word, innocent victims of murderous injustice solely because they were Jews. Which view is correct from a biblical perspective? That is something we will consider, but let me suggest something you may never have entertained: The ultimate image of an innocent Jew suffering atrocities at the hands of godless murderers is not so much the image of a Jew dying in the Holocaust as it is the image of our Messiah, the best-known Jew of all time, beaten, flogged, humiliated, and nailed to a cross. He is a Messiah with whom we can identify—and who can identify with us.

Over the last thirty years, an almost endless stream of literature has been published delving into every imaginable aspect of the Holocaust, including detailed, meticulously documented studies that leave no stone unturned. Still, it is one thing to analyze the natural side of the Holocaust, tracing the political, economic, sociological, psychological, and ethnic factors that contributed to this time of unparalleled suffering. It is another thing to analyze the spiritual (and unseen) side, attempting to understand what God was or was not doing, what Satan was or was not doing, and what the religious dimensions of the Holocaust really were. Closely related to all this is the most fundamental of all questions: Why?

Do we even have a right to ask such questions? Limited as we are, can we really gain true insight into such deep, mysterious matters? Don't they belong to the realm of hidden things (see Deut. 29:29) that lie beyond the grasp of mortal, finite humans and are known only to God?

Perhaps there are dimensions of the Holocaust that will remain a mystery, and perhaps the motivation behind some of our questions is a wrong motivation. But it is impossible to think that people of faith—both Jews and Christians—would simply put their heads in the sand and not seek spiritual answers, no matter how painful the process may be. In fact, it can easily be argued that it is imperative that we ask some questions, either to learn whatever lessons must be learned from the Holocaust or to provide some assurance of the goodness of God in a time of such spiritual darkness.[227]

So much has been written and said. There have been countless books and articles devoted to the questions, Why did this happen? and Where was God? Is it possible to gain clarity in the midst of so many competing voices and conflicting ideas?

In order to make any headway, we need to step back and get as broad a perspective as possible. To help us do this, let me give you an overview of some of the more important religious Jewish responses to the Holocaust. Then I'll offer some biblical reflections on these responses. Finally, I'll present something that could radically affect your outlook concerning the Messiah.

The noted Jewish historian Steven Katz provided a useful summary reflecting major Jewish reflections on the Holocaust current as of 1975.[228] He enumerated them as follows:

(1) The Holocaust is like all other tragedies and merely raises again the question of theodicy and "the problem of evil," but it does not significantly alter the problem or contribute anything new to it.

(2) The classical Jewish theological doctrine of *mi-penei hata'einu*, ("because of our sins we were punished") which was evolved in the face of earlier national calamities can also be applied to the Holocaust. According to this account, Israel was sinful and Auschwitz is her just retribution.

(3) The Holocaust is the ultimate in vicarious atonement. Israel is the "suffering servant" of Isaiah (ch. 53ff.)—she suffers and atones for the sins of others. Some die so that others might be cleansed and live.

(4) The Holocaust is a modern Akedah (sacrifice of Isaac)—it is a test of our faith.

(5) The Holocaust is an instance of the temporary "Eclipse of God"—there are times when God is inexplicably absent from history or unaccountably chooses to turn His face away.

(6) The Holocaust is proof that "God is dead"—if there were a God He would surely have prevented Auschwitz; if He did not then He does not exist.

(7) The Holocaust is the maximization of human evil, the price mankind has to pay for human freedom. The Nazis were men, not gods; Auschwitz reflects ignominiously on man; it does not touch God's existence or perfection.

(8) The Holocaust is revelation: it issues a call for Jewish affirmation. From Auschwitz comes the command: Jews survive!

(9) The Holocaust is an inscrutable mystery; like all of God's ways it transcends human understanding and demands faith and silence.[229]

Let me encourage you to reread this brief summary and reflect on each of the responses. Do you find yourself in agreement with any of them? Do you find any of the views abhorrent? Perhaps you have a totally different view of your own.

Let's sharpen our focus and look at some related perspectives in a little more detail. In a compendium of Orthodox Jewish reflections on the Holocaust prepared by rabbis and students in Israeli yeshivas,

Yosef Roth discussed five principal responses, paraphrased below, some of which overlap with the positions presented by Steven Katz:[230]

1. *Hester panim* (Hebrew for "hiding of the face"; see 5 and 7 in Katz's list). According to this view, in order for God to allow real freedom of choice, he restrains himself from intervening in human affairs. Thus, to a point, he will allow evil to go on unchecked, even if it results in tragedy and loss of life. Otherwise, there would be no true freedom of choice and no real consequences for evil or good behavior.
2. *Holocaust and redemption.* Roth states, "According to this approach, the lack of proportion between the sin and its punishment is explained by the end of the Exile and the establishment of the State of Israel."[231] Therefore, the Holocaust is not seen as a punishment "but rather as a Divine 'treatment,' for lack of an alternative, intended to extricate the Jewish people from the Exile."[232]
3. *The birth pangs of the Messiah.* This view, too, does not see the Holocaust as a punishment. Rather, it is part of the final complex of events dubbed "the birth pangs of the Messiah" by the Talmudic rabbis, a period marked by unprecedented suffering and upheaval. (Cf. Matthew 24:4–13, where Yeshua also speaks of a period of time marked by calamity and upheaval called [v. 8] "the beginning of birth pains.")
4. *Fate and mission.* This view, articulated by Dr. Yonah Ben-Sasson, sees the explanation to the Holocaust "not in the context of sin and punishment, but as a necessary disruption of Jewish existence and as an imperative for the Jewish mission."[233] Somehow, then, the sufferings of the Holocaust were a necessary ingredient in the development and destiny of the Jewish people.
5. *Because of our sins* (see 2 in Katz's list). There are different theories as to what sins were being punished, including failure to observe the Torah and Jewish traditions (according to this view, the chief culprits here would be the Reform and secular Jews who, at that time, were especially prevalent in Germany and other parts of Eastern Europe); seeking to establish the State of Israel before the Messiah's coming and thereby trying to hasten the end by human (and even atheistic) means (this remains the conviction of anti-Zionist Jews, including the Satmar Hasidim, who blame the Holocaust on Jewish Zionists—including reli-

gious Jewish Zionists); the exact opposite view, namely, failing to heed the warnings of Zionist Jews who urged their people to come to the land before destruction broke out in Europe (this is the view of religious Zionists, who blame the anti-Zionist Jews—especially the religious—for the Holocaust).[234]

According to two contemporary Jewish leaders, Menachem Schneerson, the Lubavitcher Rebbe, and Rabbi Z. Y. Kook, a prominent Israeli thinker, the Holocaust is to be explained "as a healing process, as divine 'surgery' and 'treatment' performed on the body of the nation in preparation for its salvation."[235] As Rabbi Schneerson stated, "With all the horrifying pain of this tragedy, it is clear that 'no evil comes from Heaven,' and that within the very evil and suffering of the afflictions, a sublime spiritual good is embodied. . . . The Holy One, Blessed be He, as that professor-surgeon, did everything He did for good."[236] Or in the words of Rabbi Kook, the Holocaust was a "deep and hidden internal Divine treatment of the cleansing of impurity."[237] For the former, this painful divine process was primarily related to the spiritual salvation of those who died in the concentration camps, while for the latter, it related primarily to Israel's reestablishment as a nation. For both, however, there was a redemptive side to the sufferings of the Holocaust.

Of course, the problem with any of these answers—and I remind you that most of them come from traditional Jewish circles—is that it is easy to speak in the abstract about "divine purposes" or "redemptive" acts, but it is difficult to look in the faces of millions of victims and continue to speak in such terms. Naturally, these Jewish authors whom I have been quoting have looked into those faces. Some of them need only look in the mirror to see the face of someone permanently scarred by the Holocaust! Yet it is fair to ask, What would a religious Jewish response to the Holocaust sound like at the beginning of the Holocaust—when no one could have possibly anticipated the overall loss of lives—as opposed to a religious Jewish response after the Holocaust—when the staggering numbers became known?

One way to gain insight into this is to examine Orthodox Jewish reactions to Nazism as early as 1935, and thus, strictly speaking, before the Holocaust really began. It was in that year that the infamous Nuremberg Laws were instituted, resulting in harshly prejudicial treatment of the Jews, both socially and economically. As the Jewish press of the day demonstrates, there were mixed responses to these laws, with the Orthodox newspapers taking a surprising view:[238]

How did the Orthodox press react to the great test of German Jewry with the passage of the Nuremberg Laws in September 1935? "We do not want to admit that God has spoken, that the events . . . contain a call and appeal from God. We were like someone inebriated, we filled ourselves to bursting with the philosophy of the day then in vogue. . . . In the midst of this daze, the harsh language of the present has struck us in our stupor," wrote Rabbi Joseph Carleback in *Die Laubhütte.* "World history is the blast of the ram's horn of heaven, the voice of God, not the senseless voice of chance."[239]

The Nazi restrictions were seen as a divine wake-up call and a judgment for assimilation, intermarriage, and worldliness, among other things.[240] As expressed in *The Israelit:*

> We ourselves are to blame that we have any problems. When the ghetto gates fell [meaning when Jews could readily become part of the society at large] . . . it was our duty to demonstrate that Jews remain aware of their special character even when they are granted the opportunity to pursue the development of their external circumstances of life unimpeded—that they do not abandon the way of life based on the teachings and precepts of the Torah. Jews could have shown the entire world that it is certainly possible to acquire the treasures of culture such as art and science without abandoning the Jewish way of life. We have missed that opportunity of attaining a synthesis between Judaism and its eternal forms on the one hand, and the cultural assets of the surrounding world on the other.[241]

Thus, there was a perception among many Orthodox Jews that the first signs of Nazi persecution were, at least in part, acts of divine judgment, and such a perception had clear biblical foundations. What God-fearing Jew witnessing the destruction of Jerusalem by the Babylonians would fail to recognize the Lord's hand of chastisement on a sinning nation, especially if that Jew was familiar with the writings of Moses and the prophets (see above, 1.10)? Persistent and willful violation of God's covenant would result in divine judgment. The Scriptures are unmistakably clear on this point.[242]

In this vein, Rabbi Joseph Telushkin draws attention—with disapproval—to the writings of Rabbi Hayyim Elazar Shapira, an influential Slovakian Hasidic rebbe, dating to 1933 and the early days of Nazi power:

> When [the Nazis] imposed the boycott in Germany against Jewish business, I thought this was certainly not a reason to ordain a fast. For

nearly all [of the Jews] in Germany profane the Sabbath publicly by [keeping] their stores [open]. Now they are being paid back measure for measure [i.e., the closing down of their stores].[243]

Similarly—and on more of a gut level—Nobel laureate Elie Wiesel describes the religious reaction of many Jews upon first entering a concentration camp: "If I am here, it is because God is punishing me; I have sinned, and I am expiating my sins. I have deserved this punishment that I am suffering."[244] Such feelings are to be expected, since, if you are a religious person, you believe that nothing of significance happens to you simply by chance, and, because it is clear that something is terribly wrong right now, you conclude that you must have sinned.[245]

So we must ask, Is it scriptural to view the Holocaust, at least to some extent, as an act of divine judgment? The answer, as difficult as it is for many to handle, is yes—at least to some extent. God's Word—from the Torah through the Prophets through the Psalms and Wisdom Literature—is just too clear. As a nation, if we were in right standing with God, it is simply impossible to believe that such calamities could have overtaken us in such devastating fashion. Whether you believe that God was judging Jewish assimilation or departure from Rabbinic tradition or failure to return to the land or rejection of the prophets and the Messiah or human arrogance and self-will— whatever the specific causes of judgment were, there must be *some* recognition of judgment.

Now, please don't misquote me as saying that the Holocaust occurred because Jews did not believe in Jesus. That is not what I am saying, nor is it what I believe. To the contrary, although I am convinced by the Word of God that it is a sin for any Jew (or Gentile) to reject Jesus, I don't for a minute think that this particular sin took more than nineteen hundred years to judge. In other words, if Jewish suffering in the Holocaust was because of rejecting the Messiah, why did it take so long for judgment to come? Rather, I would say that our historic and continued rejection of Moses, the prophets, and the Messiah, and our attachment to this world more than to God, coupled with our desire to be like the other nations, along with our sins of greed, lying, immorality, and whatever other things polluted our lives when we forsook God's laws *all* contributed to taking us out of the place of divine favor and protection.

We must recognize that God was doing *something* during and through the Holocaust, since it is impossible to think he was completely uninvolved in an event of such great significance and magnitude, especially when you consider that his own covenant people, the Jews, were its chief victims. Therefore, I believe there was *some degree* of judgment or chastisement involved in this time of agony for our people.

To leave things here, however, would be unfair and incomplete. As articulated by Alexander Donat, who survived both the Warsaw Ghetto and the concentration camps,

> What had we done to deserve this hurricane of evil, this avalanche of cruelty? Why had all the gates of Hell opened and spewed forth on us the furies of human vileness? What crimes had we committed for which this might have been calamitous punishment? Where, in what code of morals, human or divine, is there a crime so appalling that innocent women and children must expiate it with their lives in martyrdoms no Torquemada [the Grand Inquisitor] ever dreamed of?[246]

Or to cite the well-known comments of Rabbi Irving Greenberg:

> God comforts the afflicted and afflicts the comfortable, whereas the devil comforts the comforted and afflicts the afflicted. . . .
> Moreover, summon up the principle that no statement should be made that could not be made in the presence of the burning children. On this rock, the traditionalist argument [viz., that the Holocaust was a divine judgment] breaks. Tell the children in the pits they are burning for their sins. An honest man—better, a decent man—would spit at such a God rather than accept this rationale if it were true. If this justification is loyalty, then surely treason is the honourable choice. If this were the only choice, then surely God would prefer atheism.[247]

Of course, I could see a biblical prophet taking issue with some of these statements, arguing that however fierce the judgment, it would be merited. After all, there were starving children and mutilated mothers when Jerusalem was sacked in 586 B.C.E., and that event was viewed as an act of divine wrath (just read Lamentations!). Still, one must reckon with the enormity of Jewish suffering in the Holocaust— clearly dwarfing anything in our past—and one must ask, Why at *this* time? Were the sins of the Jewish people any more ugly than they were in centuries past? Why such ferocious judgment now?[248]

Frankly, although the Scriptures force me to see clear elements of judgment in the Holocaust, those same Scriptures allow me to see something else: This was not merely judgment. Rather, it was also a satanic attack on our people, an attempt to wipe us out just before the time of national regathering. Thus, as happened before in our history, because we were not in right standing with God as a people, we came under a season of judgment. (It is commonly known that most German Jews before the Holocaust were more German than Jewish, and almost no one would argue that European Jewry as a whole was spotless or especially righteous.) But Satan exploited it by using wicked people to carry out his plans, plans which have always included the destruction of the Jewish people. After all, if he can destroy Israel, he can prove that God is not all-powerful, that his Word is not true, and that there is no reality to his promises. If he can stop the long-prophesied reestablishment of the Jewish people in their homeland, he can thwart one of God's greatest and most important covenantal pacts.

Did the devil know it was the eve of Israel's return to the land? I am quite sure he did! And just as Pharaoh was moved to kill all Israelite male babies at the time that Moses, their deliverer, was about to be born, and just as Herod was moved to kill all Jewish male babies in Bethlehem at the time that Yeshua, the Messiah, had been born there, so the devil tried to wipe out the Jewish people before the return. We can see, then, that the Holocaust reflects a spiritual battle of cosmic proportions, and the Jews, by virtue of their calling as the chosen people, were stuck in the middle of it all.[249] Therefore, to a certain extent, the Holocaust was a hideous, diabolical event, made possible, however, by a lack of divine covering over us as a people.

What about the human side of this? We have addressed the issues of divine activity and satanic activity, but in the end, we are left with the stark reality of debased, demented, and utterly depraved human activity. How could it be that so many people could commit so many wicked acts? How could it be that highly cultured and civilized Germans could conceive and carry out such an evil plan? (So much for human advancement after thousands of years of progress.) How could it be that such willing accomplices were found among the Poles and the Ukrainians and the Romanians and the Lithuanians? If people could sink so low, what hope is there for us as a race? If so many could participate in cold-blooded murder, could it be that such ugliness exists potentially in all of us?[250]

The answer to all these questions is disturbing, but it is one that Christians actually hold to as one of their core beliefs: Human beings, essentially, are not good; we are fallen and corrupt; by nature we do what is evil and wrong. (See further above, 1.10, and vol. 2, 3.20.)

That's why Christians believe people need to be saved—meaning, fundamentally, saved from sin.

Doing wrong is in our blood. All of us, without God's intervention, are capable of doing things we find repulsive, shocking, and reprehensible—and all too often, we do those very things! Unfortunately, we tend to go into denial, not recognizing the gravity of our sin, or else we fall prey to self-justification, explaining why our unclean thoughts and deeds are actually not that bad.

Nazism is just one extreme example of how far we can fall, and all the good deeds and kind acts in the world can never outweigh the sheer depravity of the Holocaust. The same can be said of the ruthless genocide carried out in Cambodia, or, on a more individual level, of the actions of a sexual predator such as Jeffrey Dahmer, who raped, tortured, killed, and then ate several dozen men. What good deeds can erase such sinfulness?

The problem, sadly enough, is that most religions—including Judaism—basically look to man himself (with God's help) to turn back and repent, not fully reckoning with how debased human nature really is.[251] And while Jews and Muslims are taught to ask for mercy and forgiveness in prayer, there are no sure grounds for atonement and no full recognition of the depth of human corruption.[252] It is one thing for the "average" person—who, supposedly, is not that bad—to improve in some areas and ask for forgiveness where he or she falls short, but how can a Nazi be forgiven? How can the murderer of babies be reformed? And, if similar manifestations of depravity lurk in all of us, how can any of us ever be truly righteous?

The Holocaust forces these questions on us and gives us, I believe, only one possible answer: God himself had to reach down into this deep pit of human evil to save us from our sins—including the sins of the Holocaust. Without him taking this initiative, we would be totally lost.

Lest my position strikes you as too Christian, let me point you back to the concept of Israel playing the role of Isaiah's servant of the Lord, suffering for the sins of the nations and dying that others might live. According to this view, the afflictions of the Jewish people should be understood as vicarious and substitutionary so that the nations of the world could receive healing through the wounds of the Jewish people.

Taking this one step further, Rabbi Ignaz Maybaum, an influential author on the Holocaust, actually suggested that the Holocaust represented the crucifixion of the Jewish people. Let me quote Professor Steven Katz at length as he explains Maybaum's interpretation (endnotes supplied in the following text are my own, for the purpose of clarification):

> With a profound insight into the relative world-views of Judaism and Christianity, Maybaum argues that for Judaism the central motif is the *Akedah* (the sacrifice of Isaac, [Gen. 22]), whereas for Christianity the central motif is the enormously powerful image of the Crucifixion.[253] The *Akedah* is a sacrifice which never happened. Isaac can grow to maturity, marry, have children, die normally. According to Maybaum there is no heroic tragedy in the *Akedah*, its message is: there can be progress without martyrdom and without death. Alternatively, the Crucifixion is a sacrifice that did happen. Jesus' life is foreshortened, he cannot marry, have children, die normally. Here is the stuff of heroic tragedy, its message is: martyrdom is required that others may live, vicarious death is needed so that the world may go forward. "The cross contradicts the *Akedah:* Isaac is sacrificed." As Maybaum understands it, the message of the Crucifixion is: "somebody had to die that others may live." With the Crucifixion as its model of Divine activity in history, the Christian world is unable to grasp the higher religious meaning of the *Akedah*. Tragic as this may be, for Judaism to speak to Christians it must speak in a language they understand—the language of the Cross. Thus the modern Jew collectively, as the single Jew of two millenia [sic] ago, must mount the Cross (undergo persecution, suffering and death) in order to arouse the conscience of the gentile world.
>
> So powerful is the hold on western consciousness of the image of the Crucifixion that progress can be made only when framed in terms assimilable to this pattern. The third *hurban* (the Holocaust),[254] like the earlier two, is a divine event which is meant to bring about humanity's advancement. It is framed in the shape of Auschwitz, an overwhelming reliving by the entire Jewish people of the Crucifixion of one Jew in order that it may be able to address the deepest sensitivities of modern Christian civilization: "In Auschwitz Jews suffered vicarious atonement for the sins of mankind." Pushing this interpretation of Jewish history to the utmost, Maybaum writes: "The Golgotha of modern mankind is Auschwitz. The cross, the Roman gallows, was replaced by the gas chamber. The gentiles, it seems, must first be terrified by the blood of the sacrificed scapegoat to have the mercy of God revealed to them and become converted, become baptized gentiles, become Christians."[255]

Now, I want to submit to you that there is something to Rabbi Maybaum's comparison of the Holocaust and the crucifixion, and I can easily see an important correlation between a crucified Jewish Messiah and an almost-exterminated Jewish people. In fact, even for Messianic Jewish author Arthur Katz, who strongly argues for the judgment aspect of the Holocaust, there is a distinct connection between the crucifixion of the Messiah, whom God judged for the sins of the world, and the attempted extermination of the Jews:

> The crucifixion of Jesus the Messiah was as much the judgment of God on sin as the Holocaust of the Jews under the Nazis was the judgment of God upon Israel. Both devastations were judgments. Both were equally deserved because God's judgments and God's wrath are not arbitrary. Both events have cost God greatly. He was not some passive observer looking down on the excruciating sufferings of the Jewish people, nor those of His own Son. He was in the midst of that suffering and was Himself afflicted. God is not cruel so that He takes malicious delight. Rather, "In all their affliction He was afflicted" (Isa. 63:9). *Can Judgment be God's final provision to obdurate and unwilling men, when every other grace to obtain our attention has failed?* If so, it is a grace and a mercy though it be a painful one.[256]

How interesting it is that Katz, a Messianic Jew, and Maybaum, a Reform rabbi, both compare the death of Jesus with the death of European Jewry, although their overall interpretations of the Holocaust could hardly be more different. Still, you might be wondering, what has all this got to do with the issues we have been discussing? How does this address the problem of the sinful nature of man? What, if anything, are we to make of the notion that Israel played the role of the suffering servant?

Let me propose to you that the key here will not be found in a reinterpretation of our people's suffering in the Holocaust but rather that our suffering in the Holocaust points us back to the Messiah's suffering and death, calling us to reinterpret that event. In other words, it is not the Jewish people as a whole who fulfilled the image of Isaiah's suffering servant, dying for the sins of others and suffering that they might be healed (see especially Isa. 52:13–53:12, and see vol. 2, 3.15, and vol. 3, 4.10–4.22), but rather it was one righteous Jew in particular—our Messiah—who fulfilled that image.

To make this point more clear, let me introduce you to another voice, the voice of a saintly Christian woman, a German woman, at that, and a passionate lover of Israel. It is the voice of Basilea Schlink (originally Dr. Klara Schlink), founder of the Evangelical Sisterhood of Mary. These words were originally written to her own German people in 1958.[257] Listen carefully to her anguish and consternation, both as a Christian and a German. Perhaps you have never been exposed to this kind of expression of Gentile Christian repentance and grief:

How are the Jews to believe in Jesus? Have not we ourselves blindfolded them? They cannot see Jesus because of our conduct. They cannot believe in Him, because in our lives we have not presented to them the image of Jesus; rather we have shown them the image of mercilessness. "Your deeds in Germany talk so loud that I cannot hear your words," a Jew of our times comments. Our words about Jesus must cut Jews to the heart, considering the cruelties we have perpetrated against them in the name of this Jesus from the time of the Crusades up to the present day. And not only that. How many acts of love have we neglected to do? Thus we share in the horrible guilt of our people in murdering six million Jews. This guilt still hovers over us like a cloud. (36–37)

For Basilea Schlink, her people could no longer go on with "life as normal":

Can we Germans really continue to walk under the open sky of our fatherland, in daytime in the sunshine and at night beneath the stars, enjoying it all without feelings of shame? Must we not remember that not long ago, under that same sky, in the midst of our people, gigantic flames ascended from the burning bodies of millions of people day and night? Were not these flames like a cry of desperation and a raised finger of accusation? (38)

We Germans were Satan's henchmen. In the midst of our people this hell was created. After reading the reports of those who survived it, we can only confess that never before in the whole span of history has a civilized nation been guilty of a crime such as has been committed here in Germany, a Christian country, a land of culture. . . . Within a few years, millions of people were murdered, gassed, burnt alive or tortured to death in every conceivable way. Who can still eat his fill at a nicely laid table without visualizing the emaciated forms of the thousands of victims in the extermination camps? (39–40)

We are personally to blame. We all have to admit that if we, the entire Christian community, had stood up as one man and if, after the burning of the synagogues [on Krystallnacht], we had gone out on the streets and voiced our disapproval, rung the church bells, and somehow boycotted the actions of the S.S., the Devil's vassals would probably not have been at such liberty to pursue their evil schemes. But we lacked the ardor of love—love that is never passive, love that cannot bear it when its fellowmen are in misery, particularly when they are subjected to such appalling treatment and tortured to death. Indeed, if we had loved God, we would not have endured seeing those houses of God set ablaze; and holy, divine wrath would have filled our souls. . . . Oh, that we as Germans and as Christians would stand aghast and cry out ever anew, "What have we done!" At every further evidence of our guilt may we repeat the cry. (42–43)

Oh, how can we now look upon German children playing happily and not think of the many, many thousands of children who screamed in anguish and terror when they were burnt alive or when they, either with or without their parents, choked to death in the gas chambers! May we not close our eyes but face up to what we have done, for these are the plain facts, and innocent blood cries for retribution: "If any one slays with the sword, with the sword must he be slain" (Revelation 13:10). Thus says Holy Scripture. (44)

These are convicting words! These are solemn indictments! These are words that can draw only a painful, deliberate sigh of affirmation from Jewish readers of every background—especially those who lost loved ones in the Holocaust—and draw a sorrowful admission of "It is so!" from every Christian reader. Surely, no one could possibly call Basilea Schlink insensitive or ignorant. She has taken the full weight of Germany's sin—including the sins of every professing Christian in the land—and she has confessed that sin, repented of that sin, and given her life to making restitution for that sin.

But there is something else you must see: In the suffering Jewish people, Schlink recognized a reflection of her Savior, Jesus the Messiah. Their rejection, anguish, and hardship mirrored the experience of the Son of God. Listen again to the one affectionately known to millions around the world as "Mother Basilea":

Woe betide us when we are called to account! Then it may turn out that Jesus finds His likeness in Israel and not in us. Two-and-a-half thousand years of immeasurable suffering have made her poor and wretched, so that she does indeed resemble the image of Jesus, "despised and rejected by men" [see Isa. 53:3]. (29–30)

Israel, unintentionally and unwittingly, has become a spectacle before heaven and mankind, because she bears the features of the Servant of God [from Isaiah 53]. The sight of her should continually remind Christians of Jesus, despised, destitute, covered with bruises, afflicted, hated, persecuted, tormented, and hounded to death. Even if these marks borne by the people of God also betoken the chastening hand of God stretched out in judgment upon sinners, the fact remains that by these very dealings God proclaims Himself to be the Holy One of Israel.

We as Christians are to hold in high esteem this people who bears such a close resemblance to Jesus. The sight of Jews as an oppressed and afflicted people crossing the face of the earth, despised and rejected, should make us think of those words of Jesus about the destitute and the needy: "Truly, I say to you, as you did it to one of the least of these my brethren, you did it to me" (Matthew 25:40). Who matches so accurately our Lord's description "the least of these my brethren" as His people Israel? Who has suffered so much contempt from all nations down through the ages? Who has been so rejected? From whom did men turn away their faces? Who has been persecuted and tormented with such burning hatred? Who has been wounded and tortured to death so often as this His people? Here, indeed, are the brethren of our Lord Jesus.

It may well be that He often feels closer to His people Israel than to those proud Christians who believe in Him and yet refuse to acknowledge their guilt towards the Jews, their heartlessness in passing by their brother in his desperate need. (33–34)

My Jewish friend, does this present a picture to you that you have never seen before?

Consider the image of a despised German Jew, stripped naked by the Nazis and then mocked, tormented, and beaten, before being taken away to die a very public, humiliating death. In a moment, he is shot in the back of the head and burned to ashes in a massive, flaming pyre. Then consider the image of Jesus our Messiah, flogged and beaten beyond recognition, ridiculed and mocked by the Roman soldiers as they push a crown of thorns deep into his scalp, then stripped of his clothes, nailed to a cross, and raised up to die a slow, agonizing, and very public, humiliating death, hanging naked alongside two common criminals.[258] And then hear him express the pain of his people through the ages, "My God, my God, why have You forsaken me?" We have much in common![259]

How strange it is that Jewish philosophers and religious thinkers could speculate that the Holocaust represented an act of vicarious, substitutionary suffering for our people, the experience of the servant of the Lord depicted in Isaiah 52:13–53:12, and yet these same philosophers and religious thinkers cannot conceive of our Messiah in such terms, nor can they find a point of identification between Yeshua and the Jewish people. Yet the identification is there! He is like us. He knows our pain. He can identify with our sufferings. He understands intimately what it means to be left alone in this world, abandoned and handed over to die a terrible death at the hands of wicked people. This was the fate of a crucified man: "Punished with limbs outstretched . . . they are fastened and nailed to the stake in the most bitter torment, evil food for birds of prey and grim picking for dogs."[260] How this resembles the horrors of the Holocaust!

In a deeply moving account, Elie Wiesel described the hanging of a young Jewish boy—a "sad-eyed angel"—who died an agonizingly slow death on the gallows in front of the whole concentration camp. As Wiesel and others watched in helpless horror, the question was asked, "Where is God now?" From within, Wiesel heard the answer: "Where is He? Here He is—He is hanging here on this gallows."[261] Yet Wiesel and other Jewish intellectuals who could see the reflection (or reality) of God in the face of that youth hanging on the gallows, can find no reflection (or reality) of God in the face of Yeshua hanging on the cross. Isn't it infinitely more appropriate to look at that bloody instrument of death and say, "There is God. He is hanging there on that tree, and he is dying for me"?

Now *that* is a powerful image, and one that brings hope as well, for while Wiesel's unforgettable picture of that struggling, expiring boy—dying as a Jew and hence, in a sense, as God's Son—evokes sympathy and pain, it brings no hope; the image of the agonizing, dying Messiah—dying as a Jew too and as God's Son in a special sense— brings life.[262] Please take time to think this through. My whole point is that Yeshua is the Messiah we need.

Would we prefer a lofty and powerful Messianic king who always triumphed in battle and exercised complete authority, never feeling the pangs of humiliation, never knowing what it was like to be under someone else's control, never knowing what it was like to be stripped, beaten, and led away to die? Would we prefer a Savior who could not possibly relate to the sting of public rejection and ridicule, who was never challenged, never misunderstood, never slandered, never repaid with evil for doing good? Is that the kind of Messiah we want? Or do we want a Messiah who suffers and then reigns, who dies and then lives again, who gives himself for us long before we give ourselves for him? The choice should be obvious.

More than nineteen hundred years ago, Jewish followers of Jesus were reminded of how far the Messiah came in order to reach out and save the Jewish people and the world:

> Since the children have flesh and blood, he too shared in their humanity. . . . For surely it is not angels he helps, but Abraham's descendants. For this reason he had to be made like his brothers in every way, in order that he might become a merciful and faithful high priest in service to God, and that he might make atonement for the sins of the peo-

ple. Because he himself suffered when he was tempted, he is able to help those who are being tempted.

Hebrews 2:14, 16–18

Therefore, since we have a great high priest who has gone through the heavens, Jesus the Son of God, let us hold firmly to the faith we profess. For we do not have a high priest who is unable to sympathize with our weaknesses, but we have one who has been tempted in every way, just as we are—yet was without sin. Let us then approach the throne of grace with confidence, so that we may receive mercy and find grace to help us in our time of need.

Hebrews 4:14–16

The horrors of the Holocaust should draw us *to* the side of the suffering Servant rather than drive us *away* from him. He can identify with us in our pain. And out of death (the Holocaust and the cross) came resurrection—the State of Israel and the raising up of the Messiah. There are some similarities here!

Yet we must recognize that there are some profound differences as well in these two experiences of suffering—the suffering of the Jewish people and the suffering of Yeshua—since by recognizing these differences, the work of our Messiah becomes all the more important, essential, and even appealing to us.

During the Holocaust, as Jews we suffered unwillingly. If we could have stopped the atrocities, we would have. But Jesus suffered willingly, telling his disciples not to fight on his behalf, since he came to die. He came to give his life as a ransom for us all:

Do you think I cannot call on my Father, and he will at once put at my disposal more than twelve legions of angels? But how then would the Scriptures be fulfilled that say it must happen in this way? . . . For even the Son of Man did not come to be served, but to serve, and to give his life as a ransom for many.

Matthew 26:53–54; Mark 10:45

This is the nature of the perfect Shepherd, the character of the ideal Messiah: Jesus said, "I am the good shepherd. The good shepherd lays down his life for the sheep" (John 10:11). Yes, of him it is written:

He committed no sin, and no deceit was found in his mouth. When they hurled their insults at him, he did not retaliate; when he suffered, he made no threats. Instead, he entrusted himself to him who judges justly. He himself bore our sins in his body on the tree, so that we might die to sins and live for righteousness; by his wounds you have been healed.

1 Peter 2:22–24

That is vicarious suffering!

In addition to this, we have noted that to some extent our suffering in the Holocaust was because of *our* sins as well as because of the sins of *others*. No doubt, we were victims who were viciously sinned against and abused, but we were not totally guiltless as a people—as recognized by some of the Jewish thinkers quoted above and as clearly taught in our Torah—and thus we suffered, to some degree, for our sins. Jesus, however, committed no sin, and he suffered entirely *because of* the sins of others as well as *for the sake of* the sins of others. People killed him, but he was dying for their sins. Again I say to you: Yeshua is our ideal Messiah, a righteous King forever imprinted with the marks of suffering.

What then of the view of many Jewish commentators and theologians who, through the centuries, have suggested that the suffering of our people at the hands of the nations was vicarious, as described most clearly in Isaiah 53 (v. 5: "he was pierced for our transgressions, he was crushed for our iniquities; the punishment that brought us peace was upon him, and by his wounds we are healed") and as articulated in the Talmudic formula "the death of the righteous atones" (see vol. 2, 3.15)? And what of the specific application of this theory to the Holocaust? Frankly, it doesn't work.

Our suffering in the Holocaust (and really, in history) has not brought healing to the nations that afflicted us. (Would anyone think that Germany has been healed through the Holocaust?)[263] Rather, our sufferings have brought judgment on the nations that so cruelly afflicted us. As they have treated us, so God has treated them in return. This was a recurring theme in the prophets: "Woe to you, O destroyer, you who have not been destroyed! Woe to you, O traitor, you who have not been betrayed! When you stop destroying, you will be destroyed; when you stop betraying, you will be betrayed" (Isa. 33:1).[264]

Yet the sufferings of Jesus have brought healing to countless millions of people, both Jews and Gentiles alike, who have found mercy, forgiveness, deliverance, redemption, and restoration through his wounds. His shed blood has become a fountain of purification and cleansing to all who will recognize his love. Can you grasp the weight of this? Is a new picture beginning to emerge?

You see, it is one thing to suggest with Ignaz Maybaum that Jewish suffering in the Holocaust was a Jewish, national "crucifixion." It is another thing to argue that it actually saved anyone. In reality, it did not improve human nature (just consider how many national atrocities have taken place since the Holocaust in Cambodia, in Russia, in the former Yugoslavia, in Rwanda), nor did it eradicate anti-Semitism (this virus is growing again in much of Europe—especially the former Soviet Union—and continues to intensify in the Islamic world), nor did it result in a cessation of wars and racial conflicts.

How then was it a redemptive "crucifixion"? It seems that it was not redemptive at all.

I recognize, of course, that in some Christian circles—including Roman Catholicism—the post-Holocaust era has been marked by a partial recognition and repudiation of anti-Semitism.[265] However, the overall tide of Jew hatred continues to rise worldwide, especially in Islamic lands. More importantly, there is no power in the Holocaust itself to change or redeem people. Those who survived it are, for the most part, not better because of it, and those nations that participated in it are no more humane than they were before. In fact, some of those nations have become world leaders in perpetrating historical revisionism, i.e., seeking to deny that the Holocaust even occurred.[266] In contrast with this, those who look to the Messiah's self-sacrifice on the cross encounter the love of God firsthand and meet with mercy and grace.

We must also admit that the Holocaust really provides no antidote for the reality of human evil. Yeshua's death on the cross, however, is the ultimate antidote: God himself, in the person of his servant the Messiah, exacted the full penalty for human sin and displayed the depth of that sin through the cross. After all, the closest the human race came to a face-to-face encounter with God was in the person of the Messiah, and we, fallen race that we are, killed him.

The cross says that people *are* capable of the basest forms of evil, that human beings *cannot* save themselves, and that only a drastic, radical form of atonement—the death of the Son of God—can possibly pay for our sins. Therefore, it is with complete justification that we call Jesus the Savior of the world. As the Letter to the Hebrews stated almost two thousand years ago, "He is able to save completely those who come to God through him, because he always lives to intercede for them" (Heb. 7:25).

Therefore, the cross means sacrifice, the cross means atonement, the cross means there is hope for the worst of sinners. And as I emphasized earlier (above, 2.6), the cross is not an image of triumphalistic pride or a symbol of a conquering Crusader. Rather, it is a symbol of humiliation and pain, of suffering and death, of being forsaken by God and man. That is the image for which our Messiah is known, and it is an image that should draw—not repel—our Jewish people, *especially* in light of the Holocaust.

Now, I fully recognize that there are dozens of fundamental questions about the Holocaust that I have not even raised, but my intent has not been to attempt to address every major question, nor do I claim to have full and complete explanations for them all. Instead, I want to encourage you to see Jesus and his relationship to the Holocaust—really, his relationship to our suffering through the centuries—in a whole new light. He is one of us. And when you see a photograph of a Jewish child being led naked to the crematorium, I want you to look again: Jesus is standing there too.

I pray that you hear his call: "Come to me, all you who are weary and burdened, and I will give you rest. Take my yoke upon you and learn from me, for I am gentle and humble in heart, and you will find rest for your souls. For my yoke is easy and my burden is light" (Matt. 11:28–30).

Isn't it time for you to put your heavy burden down—your burden of sin, of guilt, of sorrow, of pain, of confusion, of sadness, of alienation, of bitterness, of anger, of doubt, of unbelief, of whatever it is that weighs you down or separates you from God—and take the Messiah's burden instead? He has already carried the heavy part for you, all the way to the cross. Your burden can be light.

2.11. The main reason Christians are so zealous to convert Jews to their beliefs is to legitimize their faith. The fact that Jesus' own people rejected him is a real problem for Christianity.

I have never met a single Christian in my entire life—and I have met many—who felt that their own faith would be legitimized if they could convince a Jew to believe as they did. If anything, since the Hebrew Bible indicated to us that most of our Jewish people would reject the Messiah when he first came, it does not surprise us that our people did, by and large, reject him and that they still reject him today. The main reasons Christians are often especially zealous to win Jewish people to their faith are: (1) As followers of Jesus the Jewish Messiah, they have a special love for Jewish people; (2) it is especially painful for them to think of the People of the Book missing the Messiah of that Book, of Yeshua's own flesh and blood not recognizing him; and (3) many Christians believe that at the end of this age there will be a widespread turning of the hearts of our Jewish people back to God and his Messiah, ushering in the Messiah's return. Thus, they pray for this to take place and make every effort to help speed this process along by telling their Jewish friends and colleagues the good news about the Messiah.

I remember an incident that took place when I was traveling across the United States with my parents and sister in the summer of 1966. We went into a restaurant in Texas, and there on the menu was a steak advertised as a "New York Cut." My father commented, "I've lived in New York all my life"—he was about fifty-two at the time—"and have never heard of a New York Cut steak." He had to go to Texas to learn about it! Similarly, when I have been in restaurants elsewhere in the States and have seen a "Texas Cut" steak on the menu, I've wondered if Texans would know what this meant. I doubt it, simply because such a thing really doesn't exist.

In the same way, I never once heard about followers of Jesus (be they Jew or Gentile) needing to win Jewish people to their belief system so as to validate their own faith. I learned about this charge from the anti-missionaries! It's no more real than is the existence of a special New York cut of steak.[267]

It is true that church leaders in the first few centuries were frustrated that more Jews did not put their faith in Jesus. This, unfortunately, only confirmed to these leaders that Jewish people in their day were no different than Jewish people in the days of Moses, the prophets, and the Messiah, consistently rejecting the messengers of the Lord (see above, 2.8). As a result, rather than this Jewish rejection of Jesus changing their views about *the Messiah*, it actually confirmed their views about *the Jewish people*.

Of course, when you are part of a minority group, especially one that is persecuted for its beliefs, if a learned or influential person from the community that has excluded you has a change of heart and believes just as you do, you will be encouraged by this. For example, if you were raised as a highly intellectual, secular Jew and became Orthodox at the age of forty—to the shock and even ridicule of all your intellectual, secular Jewish friends—it would bring you real encouragement if one of these people (perhaps the most brilliant of them all) became convinced that traditional Judaism was true, becoming religious himself (or herself).

In the same way, I'm sure that Christians and Messianic Jews are blessed and heartened when they learn that an Orthodox rabbi or a brilliant Jewish agnostic has become born anew (see John 3:3, 5) and been radically transformed through Jesus the Messiah. But this hardly confirms or validates their own faith. If it did, they would hardly deserve to be called believers in the first place! Followers of Jesus around the world endure hardship, beatings, deprivation, imprisonment, torture, and even martyrdom rather than deny their Lord, and Jesus called his people to be faithful in spite of such suffering (see above, 2.6). He hardly countenanced a faith that would be so weak that it required the faith of other people (be they Jews or Gentiles) to confirm its reality.

Do many Christians especially try to reach Jewish people with the good news of the Messiah? Naturally, for the reasons stated above. In fact, there is a well-known anecdote involving Charles Simeon, a saintly leader at Cambridge in the nineteenth century and a great lover of the Jewish people:

> Once at a missionary meeting Simeon had seemed so carried away with the future of the Jews that a friend passed him a slip of paper with the question, "Six million of Jews and six hundred millions of Gentiles—which is the most important?" Simeon at once scribbled back, "If the conversion [turning] of the six is to be life from the dead to the six hundred, what then?"[268]

Thus, it is true that many Christians feel the return of the Jewish people to their Messiah is of real importance. Still, you must understand that of the vast majority of worldwide Christian outreach efforts, only the tiniest percentage of income and effort is expended on reaching the Jewish people. There are two billion people who have never even heard the name of Jesus, let alone the full message of his redeeming love. It is these people that receive special attention from Christian missions organizations, while the hundreds of millions of people who have only limited knowledge of the Messiah's grace are also high on the priority list.

"Then what about the vast amounts of money Christians donate to Jewish evangelism? How do you explain that?"[269]

Well, I did tell you that Christians are involved in seeking to reach Jews with the good news of the Messiah, and *some* money is given to this. But as far as "vast amounts of money" being donated by Christians for Jewish evangelism, where is it? Funds for Jewish ministry are notoriously scarce, and many Messianic Jewish congregations—in America and in Israel—run on shoestring budgets. The vast funding simply is not there. Once again, this is a myth.

I do, however, need to correct one last misconception, and that is the notion that Jews who become followers of the Messiah have converted to another religion and are no longer Jews (see above, 1.2–1.4). What do I mean? This example can speak for itself: When one of my Messianic Jewish friends was asked by a Christian how it felt to be a converted Jew, he said, "I don't know, because it's not a sin to be a Jew. I'm not a converted Jew, I'm a converted sinner!" I think you get the point.

2.12. Although Jews have been forced to hold public debates with Christians in the past, Jews have won every debate. You can even check the Christian records for verification.

To the contrary, the earliest records of debate and dialog between Jews on the subject of the messiahship of Jesus indicate that the followers of Jesus decisively won. Your facts are wrong here. Of course, there is no defense for the forced debates of the Middle Ages, and I would be more than happy if the rabbis won these debates against their theological opponents, since these Christian leaders were hardly faithful representatives of the Messiah. But let's put history aside for now, since none of us were there to witness any of the debates of the past. For years the Rabbinic community said that Jews who believed in Jesus were deceived and misled because of our ignorance and lack of scholarship, so we began to challenge rabbinic leaders to discuss the issues in public. Do you know what happened? These debates went so well that we widely distribute audio and video copies of these public forums to interested Jews of every background. The rabbis whom we debated do not.

The earliest records of debates between Jews who believed in Yeshua as Messiah and Jews who didn't are found in the New Testament Book of Acts. It includes several interesting accounts, all of which tell the same story: The Messianic Jews had the better arguments!

It is written of Saul of Tarsus (also called the apostle Paul) that immediately after recognizing that Jesus was the Messiah—before this he had been the most staunch opponent of Jesus among his Jewish contemporaries—"Saul grew more and more powerful and baffled the Jews living in Damascus by proving that Jesus is the [Messiah]" (Acts 9:22). This became the pattern of his work in every city he visited: "As his custom was, Paul went into the synagogue, and on three Sabbath days he reasoned with them from the Scriptures, explaining and proving that the [Messiah] had to suffer and rise from the dead. 'This Jesus I am proclaiming to you is the [Messiah],' he said" (Acts 17:2–3).

Interestingly, one of Paul's colleagues, a learned and eloquent Jewish man named Apollos, also engaged in debate and dialog in the synagogues. Of him it is recorded that "he vigorously refuted the Jews in public debate, proving from the Scriptures that Jesus was the [Messiah]" (Acts 18:28).

Now, you might simply say, "I don't accept these records. They are written from a biased perspective."

But you must remember two things: First, you claimed—as many religious Jews do—that history (specifically, Christian history) records that Jews who rejected Jesus won every debate with Jews who followed Jesus. I have shown you that (Christian) history does *not* support your statement. Second, I could easily say that it is *your* sources that are biased, since the accounts of important debates to which you refer have been transmitted by *traditional Jews*. Why should these be considered more reliable than Christian sources? Also, in some cases, the traditional Jewish records are the only ones we have, so we can't fully gauge their accuracy, while at other times the church sources provide a very different account.[270]

There is something else worth noting. Most rabbis make reference to the famous Barcelona debate between Rabbi Moses ben Nachman (known as the Ramban, or Nachmanides) and a Catholic Jew (renamed Pablo Christiani) as a prime example of the supremacy of the traditional Jewish position. But if the traditional Jews *always* won, why *always* point to this debate? Why accept the Ramban's version at face value while rejecting the Catholic version of the debate? And even if Ramban really did win the debate—which he may very well have done—we must remember that he was one of the greatest scholars in the history of Judaism. It would be no surprise if he proved the better debater.[271]

But let's put history aside for a moment. I have debated a number of rabbis myself—on college campuses, in synagogues (at the rabbi's request), on the radio, and on TV—presenting clear, biblical evidence that Jesus is the Messiah and refuting the arguments that he is not the Messiah. Some of my friends and colleagues have engaged in similar debates. What were the results? You can easily judge for yourself.

First, you can listen to these debates on audiotape or view those that were video recorded. Second, you can ask yourself a question: Why does my ministry organization actively distribute each and every recorded debate I have done with rabbis—some of whom are respected scholars or leading anti-missionaries—while those I debated virtually never distribute the debates? What does this tell you?[272]

In 1995, I was in Phoenix, Arizona, for a debate on the Arizona State University campus with Rabbi Dr. J. Immanuel Schochet, a well-known scholar of Jewish mysticism and messianism and an adamant opponent of Jesus as Messiah.[273] An older Jewish couple approached me a few days before the debate and said, "Our daughter believes in Jesus, and she has really been urging us to adopt her faith. What do you say?" I replied, "Go to the debate and listen carefully to Rabbi Schochet and to me, and make up your mind for yourself. I want you to hear the best of both sides before you come to any conclusions."

The reason I could respond in such a way was because Yeshua *is* the Messiah promised to our people in the Hebrew Scriptures, and honest debate and dialog can only confirm this conclusion. We have nothing to hide and nothing of which we should be ashamed. So study the Scriptures, review the arguments, and ask God to guide you into all the truth.[274]

2.13. Within two generations, the Jewish followers of Jesus (under the influence of Paul) had largely given up their Jewish practices, setting a precedent that has remained the same right up until

today: Jews who become Christians lose all connection to Judaism within two generations.

> Your facts are completely wrong. We know there were Sabbath-keeping, Hebrew-reading, Torah-revering Jewish followers of Jesus for at least the first four hundred years of church history. This was despite the fact that these Messianic Jews were excluded from the synagogue by Rabbinic Jews and misunderstood by Gentile Christians. In our own day, there are fourth and fifth generation Messianic Jews, some of whom have made *aliyah* and whose children now serve in the Israeli army. Again, this has happened despite pressure from the traditional Jewish community and occasional misunderstanding from Gentile Christians.

In previous answers (above, 2.6–2.7), I explained to you that the first followers of Jesus, all of whom were Jews, were often persecuted by fellow Jews who rejected him. Then, around the year 90 C.E., key rabbinic leaders decided that a prayer (actually an imprecation or curse) against the "heretics" would be recited in synagogues in order to weed out any possible Messianic Jews. Their identity would be known at once because they would not be able to recite a curse directed against themselves.[275]

What you must grasp is this: The Rabbinic leaders did this because these Jewish disciples of Yeshua were still attending synagogue more than sixty years after the Messiah's death and resurrection. That means that the *grandchildren* of some of the first Jewish believers had not yet exited the synagogues en masse. In fact, Jacob (James), the brother of Jesus, was a highly regarded Jewish leader whose stoning at the behest of a Sadducean high priest caused an uproar among many of the Jews.[276]

Of course, Jesus had warned his followers that such a time would come (see John 16:2, "They will put you out of the synagogue"), but the thing that should catch your attention is that these Jewish believers were put out by other Jews; they did not simply walk out.

In spite of this harsh treatment, which included painful social ostracizing, Jewish believers continued to be faithful to both their Messiah and their heritage, rejecting the binding authority of the traditions of the rabbis but holding to the written Scriptures.[277] As the church became increasingly Gentile—quite a natural development when you think of the thousands of Gentiles who came flocking to the God of Israel when they were told the good news about Jesus the Messiah—something very unnatural began to happen. The church began to forget its Jewish roots (how strange!), looking with suspicion at these Messianic Jews (called Nazarenes) who adhered to the gospel *and* the Torah. In spite of all this, these Jewish believers continued steadfast in their faith for centuries.

A number of prominent Gentile Christian leaders wrote about them, generally listing the same, key characteristics: They adhered to the Torah; some of their New Testament books were written in Hebrew (or Aramaic);[278] and they held to the fundamental teachings of Jesus and his emissaries.[279] It is false, therefore, to claim that Jewish followers of Jesus assimilated into the Gentile culture within two generations.

There are also some major political factors you need to consider. According to our best reconstruction of the events, when Jerusalem was being attacked by the Romans in the late 60s of this era, Messianic Jews fled to the city of Pella (now in Jordan), having been forewarned by Jesus that the city and temple would be destroyed. (Cf., e.g., Matthew 24:15–16: "So when you see standing in the holy place 'the abomination that causes desolation,' spoken of through the prophet Daniel—let the reader understand—then let those who are in Judea flee to the mountains.") This apparently was viewed with disfavor by other segments of the Jewish community, who considered it an act of betrayal.[280]

Sixty years later, when Simeon Bar Kochba launched his war against Rome in 132 C.E., it is possible that Messianic Jews would have been willing to join in the revolt, except for the fact that he proclaimed himself to be the Messiah. As a result, they could not fight on his behalf and were, in turn, severely persecuted by this valiant but ruthless general.[281] Thus, Yeshua's Jewish followers faced resentment, exclusion, opposition, and even violent persecution from their own people, yet many of them still remained loyal Jews.

Now, I have no question whatsoever that throughout history numerous Jews who have put their faith in Yeshua *have* assimilated into the surrounding (church) culture, but this was not the norm in the beginning, and it is changing again in our day. For example, in the last twenty years, many Messianic Jews have made *aliyah* to Israel, so that their children are now involved in every facet of society—including serving in the Israeli army—and their children's children will be native born (called *sabras* in Hebrew). We have also reached a point today, even in America, in which there are Messianic Jews whose parents, grandparents, great-grandparents, and great-great-grandparents have been Jewish followers of Jesus.[282]

In addition to this, true Christians around the world have not only begun to understand and appreciate their Jewish spiritual roots, they have done so with enthusiasm, recognizing the importance of Messianic Jewish congregations and doing things such as hosting Passover Seders in their churches and celebrating the Feast of Tabernacles. Yet the Jewish community, from ultra-Orthodox to Reform, has excluded Messianic Jews and deprived them of their rights as Jews, sometimes even refusing to allow their loved ones to be buried in Jewish cemeteries.

Well do I remember the grief experienced by dear Messianic Jewish friends of mine when their fifth child, a nine-month-old baby girl, died of a rare genetic disorder, and the officials of the Jewish cemetery refused to allow them to bury her there. Thankfully, the cemetery quickly reconsidered (albeit under pressure), and the tiny little treasure was laid in the ground in a deeply moving, God-glorifying gravesite service. The words of the father are still fresh in my ears: "I love my daughter very much, but I love God even more"—followed by his recitation of the ancient Jewish prayer called the Mourner's Kaddish. The mother's words were equally moving: "I feel very special today, because I have had the joy of being with my daughter for these nine months, and now I have given her to the Lord for him to enjoy." Does it sting you to think that such godly parents had to go through the scornful rejection of the religious Jewish community within hours of their daughter's passing?

Yet, this is not only painful, it is ironic too, since some of the rabbis who say, "Jews who follow Jesus lose all attachment to their people and their heritage," are the very ones who vigorously force us away from our people and our heritage. They tell us we have lost our Jewish roots, and then they call us deceptive when we try to be true to those very same roots. (See also 1.5.)

Of course, I could approach your objection here in a different way, pointing out to you that traditional Judaism is not necessarily God's Judaism—that is to say, it is not necessarily *the* true faith for our people. It has rejected both the Messianic believers as well as the Messiah, and it has even made void certain portions of the Scriptures (see vol. 3).

The right questions could really be: What does *God* require of us as Jews? What does *he* consider faithfulness to our heritage and calling? Perhaps these are the questions we should be asking ourselves as Jews.

2.14. Just look at the church! Who's right? The Protestants, the Roman Catholics, the Greek Orthodox, the Mormons, the Messianic Jews? Even so-called Christians can't agree among themselves.

I'm a little surprised at your objection, since there are several major variations in Judaism, ranging from Reconstructionist to ultra-Orthodox, and some branches don't even regard the others as truly Jewish at all. So how can you indict Christianity because of differences? Still, I'm happy to answer your question: First, not everyone who calls himself a Christian really is. Second, there is harmony around the world among true Christians regarding the fundamentals of the faith. Third, major disagreements tend to arise only when the authority of the New Testament is either denied or subjugated to human traditions and interpretations. When you get back to what Jesus and his followers taught, you can see who his real followers are today.

In the early 1980s, a Conservative rabbi invited me to have a public dialog/debate with him in his synagogue regarding Messianic prophecy, belief in Jesus as Messiah, and early Christianity (i.e., in the days of the New Testament, although the term *Christianity* did not exist at that time). This rabbi and I had been friends for some years, and we had both learned a lot from each other, so it was no surprise to me when this rabbi said during one of our exchanges, "One thing I've learned from Michael is that not everyone who claims to be a Christian is really a Christian. It's really only a small percentage of those who are born into the Christian faith who are genuine believers." Exactly!

You see, from the outside, it's easy to think there are endless varieties of the Christian or Messianic Jewish faith to the point that it's almost impossible even to define what makes someone a true Christian. But that is only a perception from the outside. From the inside, it's all very clear. In fact, Jesus himself warned his followers that false messiahs and false prophets would arise and deceive many, and several decades later, his followers warned other Messianic believers—both Jewish and Gentile—about deceivers who would lead God's people astray. These warnings—with clear guidelines—are recorded in the New Testament itself, which means that the New Testament itself tells us how to distinguish between false believers and true believers.

"But," you ask, "what about Christians who no longer accept the New Testament as divinely inspired? Surely you are aware that many Christian theologians don't believe what Paul and Peter wrote or what Matthew and Luke claim Jesus said."

Of course I'm aware of this. The problem is that these theologians are not Christians. If they deny the fundamentals of the faith—and again, I emphasize to you, there *are* clear fundamentals outlined in the Scriptures—then they have departed from the faith. In the same way, Orthodox Jews would say that Reform or Reconstructionist Jews who say that the Hebrew Scriptures were not divinely inspired and authoritative have deviated from the faith. The difference in this case is that no one is born a Christian (see above, 1.2) whereas people are born Jews. Therefore, in the case of someone who claims to be a Christian and rejects the historic Christian faith, that person is *not* a Christian. In the case of a Jew who denies the God of Israel and the Torah of Israel, that person would still be a Jew, albeit a God-denying, Scripture-rejecting Jew. Both of these people, however, would be guilty of departing from the faith.

Interestingly, many Jewish scholars today recognize that in the time of Yeshua there were actually several Judaisms—as opposed to one Judaism—and these Judaisms each had some claim to being a legitimate expression of the faith.[283] The thing that made them Judaisms was that there were several core principles that united them, including belief in one God, belief in the special calling of the Jewish people, and belief in the Torah of Moses. (By the way, one of the first-century Judaisms that had these core beliefs was Messianic Judaism![284] It continues to have these beliefs to this very day.) The variations had to do with such things as belief in the authority of the traditions of the sages or belief in the afterlife, to name just a few. But their core beliefs were the same.

On the other hand, even within one particular Jewish expression such as Pharisaical (or Rabbinic) Judaism, there were constant arguments about minor details and legal rulings. In fact, one entire tractate of the

Mishnah is devoted to disputed matters between the two leading Rabbinic schools.[285] How then did traditional Jewish scholars view these differences in their own traditions? According to Maimonides, they were like the tips of the branches of a tree. The tree and the branches were all united, and it was only the tips—in other words, the smallest minutiae of legal interpretation—that showed any divergences.[286]

With regard, then, to Jewish expressions of faith, there were major variations of Judaism in the first century of this era just as there are major variations in Judaism today, although some of today's versions have really departed from any claim to the name Judaism, since they deny some of the core principles of the Jewish faith. It is also true that even within one particular stream of Judaism, there have been differences and there remain minor, peripheral differences.

The same summary can be given regarding the Christian, or Messianic Jewish, faith: There are different expressions of the Messianic faith that agree on the fundamentals, there are expressions of the faith that are not worthy of the name (since they have denied the fundamentals), and even within one particular stream of the faith, there remain minor, peripheral differences. What is important to remember is that the first believers in Jesus—for centuries, in fact—held to one primary body of authoritative writings, and therefore, we can identify with certainty today those who remain loyal to those writings, in spite of some minor differences and variations.[287]

What then are the core beliefs of the Messianic (Christian) faith? Followers of Jesus believe that he is the Messiah of the Jewish people and the Savior of all humankind, that he came in fulfillment of the Hebrew Scriptures, that he shares both a human and divine nature (see vol. 2, 3.1–3.4 for detailed discussion of this), that he lived a sinless life, that he died for our sins and rose from the dead, that he will one day return and judge the world, that his sacrifice on our behalf is the only acceptable means of forgiveness, that through faith in him all people—even the worst of sinners—can be reconciled to God and begin a brand-new life, that true believers will be known by their good fruit, and that there will be a final heaven for believers and a final hell for those who refuse to believe. Those are just some of the core doctrines of the Messianic faith.

What I find amazing is that around the world, in every country I have visited, I have met Christians who experienced the same transforming power through faith in Jesus the Messiah, including former Hindus, Muslims, Buddhists, animists, atheists, terrorists, alcoholics, drug addicts, prostitutes—you name it—and who believe in the same fundamentals of the faith. Friends of mine who have spoken in as many as ninety different countries can attest to the same phenomenon: There is a supernatural unity among those who truly believe and who have come to know God through Yeshua. It's wonderful! This supernatural unity of the church is actually one of the best arguments for the Messianic faith, as opposed to being its Achilles' heel.

2.15. Christianity is just another great world religion, like Islam, Hinduism, or Buddhism. It is certainly not the true Messianic faith and the only way to find God. In fact, I find it to be the height of arrogance that Jesus claimed to be the only way to the Father. This is small-minded conceit at its worst.

Just as traditional Jews believe that God communicated his will for our people—his one and only will—through Moses, so also followers of Jesus believe that God communicated his way of salvation for all peoples—his one and only way—through the Messiah. While we recognize that there are many beautiful traditions and valuable ethical teachings to be found in all the religions of the world, we believe it is only through the Messiah—who is called the Savior of the world in the New Testament writings—that people can truly be saved from their sins. When you think of it, this is not really surprising: If there is only one God and we are his creation (as opposed to him being our creation), it makes sense that he will be the one to dictate to us how we can know him, serve him, and receive forgiveness from him. That's why Jesus the Messiah told his followers (all of whom were Jews in the beginning) to go into the whole world and tell everyone the good news that he had come and laid down his life as a payment for our sins.

At first, it would seem to be the height of arrogance and intolerance to claim that people can come into right relationship with God only through Jesus. After all, there are sincere, moral, deity-fearing people in every religion of the world. Why must Christians think their religion alone is right? Why not follow the teaching of traditional

Judaism that the righteous of every nation—not just Israel, or in this case, the church—have a place in the world to come?[288]

Let's think this objection through. In the natural world, we know there is often only one road that leads to a certain destination or only one correct answer to give on a test. Why should it be different in the spiritual realm? If there is only one God—something affirmed by Judaism, Islam, and Christianity—why is it so hard to imagine that he decides how people come into right relationship with him? Surely, if he is really there, it makes perfect sense that he is the one who sets the standards and calls the shots. In fact, it is certainly just as logical—actually, it is far more logical—to believe this than to believe that everyone makes his or her own way back to God (or the gods).

Is it possible that there are *any* truths that are absolute and universal? Is it possible that there are many *man-made* ways to get into right relationship with God but only one *divinely ordained* way to get right with him? Who says that we decide how to worship and serve the deity? Who says that our beliefs are right simply because we believe them to be right? If a man driving toward Los Angeles sincerely believes he is driving toward New York, that doesn't change the fact he is actually driving in the wrong direction. It's the same spiritually: Just because people sincerely believe their religion is right doesn't mean for a second that their religion is, in fact, right.

Now let's take this one step further. If different religions believe things that are mutually contradictory about the deity—e.g., he is one vs. he/she/they are many; or he must not be represented with graven images vs. he/she/they should be represented with graven images—then either one or all of them are wrong. But they cannot all be right. Therefore, if at least *some* of the world religions are wrong, then perhaps *one* of them is right. The very fact that these religions often contradict themselves in the most fundamental ways suggests that someone has missed the path somewhere.

But isn't it arrogant for Christians to say it is only through Jesus that people can get right with God? No more arrogant than it is for others to say that Jesus is one way among many—thereby declaring the beliefs of more than one billion Christians, the largest single religious group, to be wrong. For if there are many different ways to God/the gods, then Christianity is wrong. If Christianity is right, then the other faiths are wrong. Either way, millions of people are wrong in what they believe.

Even as far as the Jewish people go, the vast majority of today's Jews do not believe that God literally spoke to Moses on Mount Sinai or that the traditional Jewish lifestyle is the only Jewish lifestyle fully pleasing to God. But this doesn't stop Orthodox Jews from believing that their way is right—even though they are in the very small minority. All the different Jewish beliefs in the world today, from Reconstructionist to New Age, do not stop religious Jews from believing it is God's will *for every Jew* to follow the words of the Talmudic sages. In addition to this, we Jews believe that in some unique sense we are God's chosen people, with the full privilege and full responsibility of having a full revelation of God in the Torah. Isn't *that* the height of arrogance—to believe that *we alone* are specially chosen?[289]

It seems obvious, then, that the major issue is not whether it is arrogant and small-minded to believe there is only one way to God. The questions that must be answered are these: On what basis can we claim that faith in Yeshua alone brings people into right relationship with God? On what basis can we claim that he is the only legitimate way to the Lord? The answer is that only the Messianic work of Jesus—his life, death, and resurrection—provides a true antidote to the problem of sin.

You see, all religions recognize that human beings have somehow fallen short and become alienated from the Godhead (singular or plural). In most religions, the concept of sin is readily understood. The problem is how to receive forgiveness of sin and how to become reconciled with the Godhead. Some faiths emphasize good works and repentance, others emphasize the redemptive aspects of suffering, others emphasize strict moral codes. None of them, however, gives a definitive answer to the problem. On what basis does the deity forgive sin?

Muslims and Jews do their best and hope for mercy. Hindus patiently bear their lot, hoping for a better life next time around. Buddhists seek an ultimate nirvana. But if you ask them if they are *sure* they are accepted by the deity (or deities), all they have is *hope*. When the fasting and praying and repenting and sacrificing are over, these sincere believers are left without a definite assurance.

I have spoken to religious Jews immediately after Yom Kippur (the Day of Atonement), religious Hindus after a special fast for forgiveness, and religious Muslims seeking to please Allah, asking them if they *know* their past sins are forgiven. All of them have told me the same thing: "I'm not sure, but I certainly hope so!" When I asked the religious Muslims and Jews, both of whom believe in a day of judgment, if they *know* they will be accepted by God as righteous when they die, they too were not sure but could only hope for mercy.

This can be contrasted with the response of Jewish and Gentile followers of Yeshua who joyfully attest to the *certainty* of forgiveness of sins (which, of course, does not give them a license to sin) and their sure acceptance before God in this world and in the world to come. They *know* they already possess eternal life.[290]

Why? Because it is only through Jesus that sin is definitively addressed, and it is only through Jesus that there is a way for the worst of sinners to get right with God.

You see, it is not the moral teachings of Jesus that are totally unique, nor is it the concept of mercy that is so unusual, nor is it even the Savior's moral example that is absolutely different. Rather, it is the fact that he, the divine Son, took our place and paid the penalty for our sins, thereby satisfying the justice of God and definitively and absolutely securing eternal salvation for all who believe. By enduring the penalty for our sins, he purchased our redemption.

If there had been any other way for mankind to be forgiven, Jesus would not have died, and it is this fact alone—the necessary, efficacious, sacrificial death of the Son of God on the cross—that separates Christianity from all other religions. None of these religions have at their foundation a divine act that is unique and comprehensive for all people. That's why Jesus gave us the mandate to go into the whole world and bring the good news of his death and resurrection. And good news it is! No other religion in the world has its equal.

2.16. We dealt with Christianity nineteen hundred years ago. There were great Jewish leaders alive in Jesus' day and in the decades following. They watched him, they watched his followers, and they rejected the whole thing for good reason. There's nothing to discuss.

Then why are you reading this book? Why are Jewish scholars reevaluating their views about Jesus? Why have Jewish leaders and even rabbis become believers in Yeshua through the centuries? The fact is, our forefathers who rejected Yeshua made a wrong turn and got off track. Now, there's only one thing to do: Turn around!

Notes

Introduction

1. According to a report from the Task Force On Missionaries and Cults published in *The Jewish Press*, 1 September 1995, "From Chicago to Moscow, from Israel to the Ukraine, the so-called Hebrew Christians are capturing Jewish souls at a rate never before 'witnessed' in the 3,500 year history of the Jewish people."

2. The important, older study of A. Lukyn Williams, *A Manual of Christian Evidences for Jewish people* (New York: Macmillan, 1919), specifically refuting the classic, sixteenth-century work of Isaac Troki, *Faith Strengthened*, trans. Moses Mocatta (New York: Hermon, 1970) will be discussed in the projected one-volume reference edition of this work (see preface) in which we will provide a brief history of anti-missionary literature. The present book is unique in that (1) it deals with a wide range of objections that were not raised by Troki; (2) it is written by a Jewish believer in Jesus and is therefore especially sensitive to both traditional Jewish concerns as well as issues of importance to the church; (3) it is addressed, by and large, *to* the Jewish person who does not yet believe in Jesus, as opposed to merely supplying information to the interested Christian/Messianic Jewish reader, although such readers will easily benefit from the material compiled; and (4) it seeks to be faithful to both the Hebrew Scriptures and the New Testament, while using the best tools in biblical and Semitic scholarship as well as incorporating the Rabbinic writings (where relevant).

3. As mentioned in the preface, this is the first book in a three-book series, to be followed eventually by a one-volume reference edition. All citations such as "see 1.5" or "see vol. 2, 3.6" refer to the objections covered in this series: General and historical objections are numbered 1 and 2 respectively and are covered in this volume. Volume 2 will cover category 3, theological objections. Volume 3 will cover categories 4, 5, and 6, Messianic prophecy objections, New Testament objections, and traditional Jewish objections respectively.

4. It is true that the roots of Rabbinic Judaism are found in Pharisaic Judaism, going back one or two centuries before the time of Jesus. However, the distinctive elements of what became Rabbinic Judaism post-date the destruction of the Temple in 70 c.e. In that sense, Messianic Judaism is older than Rabbinic Judaism in terms of *some* of the latter's more important developments.

5. I write these words while sitting at my notebook computer in the house of some dear Christians in Lahti, Finland, who regularly use their home to help Jews from the former Soviet Union who are emigrating to Israel. They have taken in dozens of these Jewish strangers who are brought to Finland before flying to Israel, treating them with

hospitality and love, simply because these refugees are Jews. In fact, when this Finnish Christian family was laying the foundation to their home, one of their daughters asked, "Why are we building such a large house, since some of the children are older and are no longer living at home?" Her eighteen-year-old sister replied, "When the Jews start leaving Russia, this house will be used to take them in." Amazingly, no one in the family had heard of such a thing at that time, and it was one full year before the major Jewish exodus from Russia began. The eighteen-year-old spoke prophetically. Stories such as these could be multiplied throughout Finland, as well as in other parts of the world. Thankfully, an increasing number of Jews arriving in Israel from the CIS have met with genuine Christian love along the way, at times at great personal sacrifice and expense to the Christians.

6. Such claims are common in anti-missionary writing. Cf. these remarks by Beth Moshe (pseudonym), *Judaism's Truth Answers the Missionaries* (New York: Bloch, 1987), 250: The missionary "is driven by his own need to convince you that Jesus is the Messiah and Christianity is the successor to Judaism. . . . The missionary cannot emotionally accept Judaism's position and counter-claims, because if he did his entire religious survival might collapse. The missionary's view is that Christianity's unique salvation through belief in Jesus Christ rests on the supposition of Judaism's demise." Of course, one could ask whether the traditional Jew—or any committed person from a non-Christian religion—could "emotionally accept" Christianity's "position and counter-claims" without *his* "entire religious survival" being threatened. But Beth Moshe's point goes beyond this. She writes: "In fact, the missionary values the Jewish convert above all others, because in one fell swoop he believes he catches the soul, fortifies his own conception of salvation, and deals a blow to Judaism" (ibid., 3). In all candor, I can say that in almost thirty years as a Jewish believer in Jesus, I have not met one single "missionary" who holds to this, consciously or unconsciously, even though all of us are very grateful to God when we see his ancient people returning to him in repentance and faith and recognizing the real Messiah. Shouldn't we be?

7. For references see Michael L. Brown, *Our Hands Are Stained with Blood* (Shippensburg, Pa.: Destiny Image, 1992), 64–65. In 1997, a Japanese translation of this book was released, reflecting the wonderful spirit of philo-Semitism that is found among many Japanese Christians.

Part 1 General Objections

1. An important text in this regard for traditional Jewish thought is b. Sanhedrin 44a: "Even if [Israel] sins, he is still Israel," as explained by R. Abba with reference to a proverb, "A willow standing among willows is still named a willow, and people call it a willow." The Talmudic commentator Marharsha (an acronym for Rabbi Shmuel Edels) states that this applies even when one sins and transgresses against the entire Torah! Obviously, if you are a typical Orthodox Jew, you think I'm sinning by following Jesus, and you may even think I'm an idolater. Yet your tradition says that I'm still a part of Israel.

2. According to Moses Maimonides (Mishneh Torah, Hilkhot Melakhim 11:1), "Whoever does not believe in him [the Messiah], or does not look forward to his coming, denies not only the other prophets but the Torah and Moses, our Teacher." According to Rabbi Yehudah Chayoun, *When Moshiach Comes: Halachic and Aggadic Perspectives* (Southfield, Mich.: Targum; Springdale, N.Y.: Feldheim, 1994), 21, "Anyone who denies or doubts the coming of the Moshiach—whether he does so willingly, unwill-

ingly, intentionally, or unintentionally—has distanced himself from the Jewish people and is a heretic and an *apikores* [godless man]." See also ibid., 25–26, n. 5.

3. In the nation of Israel, the priests were called to teach and instruct the people concerning the things of God (Lev. 10:10–11). Among the nations of the world, we Jews are called to teach and instruct all peoples about the things of God. As to whether or not Jews actively engaged in "missionary" activity in the ancient world, see Scot McKnight, *A Light among the Gentiles: Jewish Missionary Activity in the Second Temple Period* (Minneapolis: Fortress, 1991); Robert Goldenberg, *The Nations That Know Thee Not: Ancient Jewish Attitudes towards Other Religions*, The Biblical Seminar 52 (Sheffield: Sheffield Academic Press, 1997). For recent discussion about Jewish outreach to other Jews, cf. Aryeh Kaplan, *Reaching Out*, 3d ed. (New York: Orthodox Union/NCSY, 1991); Moshe Weinberger, *Jewish Outreach: Halakhic Perspectives* (New York: Ktav, 1990).

4. Isaiah 42:1–7; 49:1–7 are key texts indicating that the Servant of the Lord (meaning Israel, fulfilling its destiny through the Messiah; see vol. 3, 4.10–4.12) will be a light to the nations. See also Isaiah 55:1–5. For a powerful argument that Jews (especially Messianic Jews) have been called by God to be a light to the nations, cf. Stuart Dauermann, "Motivating and Mobilizing for Messianic Jewish Outreach," *Kesher* 2 (winter 1995): 33–71.

5. For historical discussion, see Lawrence H. Schiffman, *Who Was a Jew? Rabbinic and Halakhic Perspectives on the Jewish-Christian Schism* (Hoboken, N.J.: Ktav, 1985), and see 2.7.

6. Already, in just the second century c.e., the church leader Ignatius could say that "if any one celebrates the Passover along with the Jews, or receives emblems of their feast, he is a partaker with those that killed the Lord and His apostles," cited in David A. Rausch, *A Legacy of Hatred: Why Christians Must Not Forget the Holocaust*, 2d ed. (Grand Rapids: Baker, 1990), 20. More broadly, Ignatius claimed that "it is wrong to talk about Jesus and live like the Jews. For Christianity did not believe in Judaism but Judaism in Christianity." See his Epistle to the Magnesians 10:3, cited in Samuel Bacchiocchi, *From Sabbath to Sunday: A Historical Investigation of the Rise of Sunday Observance in Early Christianity* (Rome: Pontifical Gregorian Univ. Press, 1977), 214. For the interesting view that the primary factor behind such polemicizing was the tendency of Christians to embrace Jewish people and Jewish forms of worship and ritual, see Oskar Skarsaune, "The Neglected Story of Philo-Semitism in Antiquity and the Early Middle Ages," *Mishkan* 21 (1994): 40–51.

7. For a sampling of some of these medieval baptismal formulas, cf. Brown, *Our Hands Are Stained with Blood*, 95–97, with references.

8. See 2.7; for important, recent studies on the Inquisition, cf. B. Netanyahu, *The Origins of the Inquisition in Fifteenth-Century Spain* (Ithaca, N.Y.: Cornell, 1995); idem, *Toward the Inquisition: Essays on Jewish and Converso History in Late Medieval Spain* (Ithaca, N.Y.: Cornell, 1997), esp. 183–200; Henry Kamen, *The Spanish Inquisition* (New Haven: Yale, 1998); and see the works cited in Brown, *Our Hands Are Stained with Blood*, 237.

9. For discussion of this "malediction against the heretics" (the *birkat hamminnim*), cf. Reuven Kimelman, "*Birkat Ha-Minim* and the Lack of Evidence for an Anti-Christian Jewish Prayer in Late Antiquity," in *Jewish and Christian Self-Definition*, ed. E. P. Sanders, A. I. Baumgarten, and Alan Mendelson, vol. 2, *Aspects of Judaism in the Graeco-Roman Period* (Philadelphia: Fortress, 1981), 226–44; and contrast with Schiffman, *Who Was a Jew?*, 53–61. For further references, cf. Anthony J. Saldarini, *Matthew's*

Christian-Jewish Community (Chicago: Univ. of Chicago, 1994), 18–19 (with n. 53 on 220–21), and see also 2.6–2.7.

10. I assure you, when Edith Schaeffer wrote her popular book, *Christianity Is Jewish* (Wheaton: Tyndale, 1977), or when the Italian scholar Gabrielle Boccaccini argued that Christianity is actually a Judaism (see his *Middle Judaism: Jewish Thought, 300 C.E. to 200 C.E.* [Minneapolis: Fortress, 1991]), neither of them was trying to pull the wool over anyone's eyes, nor did they write with any purposes of proselytizing. The former wrote her book to Christians, the latter to scholars of early Christianity and Judaism. See further the fine study of Marvin R. Wilson, *Our Father Abraham: Jewish Roots of the Christian Faith* (Grand Rapids: Eerdmans, 1989), widely read by both Jews and Christians.

11. See, e.g., Daniel C. Juster, *Jewish Roots* (Rockville, Md.: Davar, 1986); David H. Stern, *Messianic Jewish Manifesto* (Jerusalem/Baltimore: Jewish New Testament Publications, 1988); Michael Schiffman, *Return of the Remnant: The Rebirth of Messianic Judaism* (Baltimore: Lederer, 1992); Arnold Fruchtenbaum, *Israelology: The Missing Link in Systematic Theology* (Tustin, Calif.: Ariel Ministries, 1993); see also the lively discussion on the use of Rabbinic literature by Messianic Jews in *Mishkan* 8, no. 9 (1988): 25–74, between Avner Boskey, Daniel C. Juster, Chaim Pearl, and Larry Brandt (see also Beth Messiah's "Consensus Statement on Jewish Tradition," in ibid., 75–78). For a full-scale commentary on Romans from a Messianic Jewish perspective (and interacting thoroughly with Second Temple and Rabbinic Jewish literature), see Joseph Shulam with Hilary Le Cornu, *Commentary on the Jewish Roots of Romans* (Baltimore: Lederer, 1998).

12. Where we do have a difference with the Rabbinic calendar based on our interpretation of Scripture, we make changes accordingly. A good example would be our interpretation of the injunction to count fifty days from the "morrow of the Sabbath" after Passover (Lev. 23:11, 15). Most Messianic Jews interpret this to mean the first Sunday after the first day of Passover, whereas the rabbis understood the reference to "the Sabbath" to mean the first day of Passover, hence the "morrow of the Sabbath" would mean the second day of Passover. In this case, traditional Judaism follows the understanding of the Pharisees, while Messianic Jews find themselves siding with the interpretation of the Sadducees, Samaritans, and Karaites, all of whom rejected the authority of the Rabbinic traditions when those traditions conflicted with the plain sense of Scripture. For discussion of Leviticus 23:11, cf. Baruch A. Levine, *Leviticus*, The JPS Torah Commentary (Philadelphia: Jewish Pub. Society, 1989), 158, who observes that, while the traditional "interpretation resolves a difficulty in the text, it does not convey its simple sense." For the prophetic significance of First Fruits and Shavu'ot, which are the holy days related to the text in Leviticus 23, see 2.1.

13. For typical anti-missionary rhetoric on this, cf., e.g., Beth Moshe, *Judaism's Truth*, 212, who speaks of the need to "demonstrate the unreliability of the man [i.e., Paul] who actually formulated the break away from Judaism by the early Church. We have shown that Paul contradicted Jesus in important religious matters and made himself greater than his master. Now see who he is, by his own words [referring to 1 Cor. 9:20]. He admitted using trickery and deception to gain his ends. We can wonder whether his missionary effort was flawed with fiction throughout as well." According to Gerald Sigal, *The Jew and the Christian Missionary: A Jewish Response to Missionary Christianity* (New York: Ktav, 1981), 289–90, "By distorting the biblical word, Paul developed much of his teachings. How one came to faith, as he defined it, was of no importance. In fact, he considered deceit and pretense valid means for achieving his

goal (1 Corinthians 9:20–22; Philippians 1:18)." Similarly, Michoel Drazin, *Their Hollow Inheritance: A Comprehensive Refutation of the New Testament and Its Missionaries* (Jerusalem: Gefen, 1990), 18, claims that, "The authors of the New Testament had a powerful personality to emulate in Saul of Tarsus (Paul), who openly advocated 'pious fraud,'" with reference not only to 1 Cor. 9:20–23 and Phil. 1:18 but also, even more amazingly, to Rom. 3:7–8 and 2 Cor. 12:16.

14. For the view that Paul lived his entire life as a Pharisee, cf. most recently Brad H. Young, *Paul the Jewish Theologian: A Pharisee among Christians, Jews, and Gentiles* (Peabody, Mass.: Hendrickson, 1997); cf. also vol. 3, 5.26, 5.29.

15. See Acts 10–11 for the first recorded instance of a group of Gentiles becoming part of the fellowship of (hitherto all-Jewish) Messianic believers.

16. I recognize, of course, that there were many Jews, especially in past centuries, who forsook anything Jewish as a result of their "conversion." There are, however, several reasons for this: (1) In most cases, their "conversion" was more of a social change than a true, spiritual transformation, hence no awakening of their true Jewishness would follow from this. (2) Especially in the Middle Ages, there was little possibility that Jews who followed Christianity would thereby recover their Jewishness because they were often forced to renounce their Jewishness in the "conversion" (e.g., baptismal) process; see 2.8. Of course, the "Christianity" to which they converted was often less faithful to the Bible than the Judaism they left.

17. See Charles B. Chavel, ed. and trans., *The Commandments* (London: Soncino, 1967), 2:434, regarding idolatry.

18. I say *almost* one billion because, in the fifty years following the communist takeover of mainland China, there has been a remarkable spiritual revival among the Christians in that country, and they have grown from approximately one million to as many as one hundred million during that time, despite severe persecution and hardship. For the remarkable story of this church, shining in the midst of its sufferings, see now Danyun, *Lilies amongst Thorns: Chinese Christians Tell Their Story* (Ventura, Calif.: Gospel Light, 1993).

19. In one of the most beautiful verses in the Hebrew Bible (Isa. 53:6), the prophet wrote that, "*All of us* [Hebrew, *kullanu*], like sheep, have gone astray, each one has turned his own way, but the LORD has laid on him [i.e., the servant of the LORD, Jesus the Messiah] the iniquity of *all of us [kullanu]."*

20. Note the words of the prophet Isaiah, speaking of a time of future spiritual unity between Israel and some of its arch enemies: "In that day there will be a highway from Egypt to Assyria. The Assyrians will go to Egypt and the Egyptians to Assyria. The Egyptians and Assyrians will worship together. In that day Israel will be the third, along with Egypt and Assyria, a blessing on the earth. The LORD Almighty will bless them, saying, 'Blessed be Egypt my people, Assyria my handiwork, and Israel my inheritance'" (Isa. 19:23–25). Through Jesus our Messiah, we can see the beginning of the realization of passages like this, among others found in our Hebrew Scriptures.

21. See Romans 9–11; for further information, see 2.7.

22. The infamous Rabbinic collection of anti-Jesus fables, called *Toledot Yeshu*, is still studied in some ultra-Orthodox circles, although virtually all other Jewish scholars have long since repudiated the *Toledot*. These scurrilous writings, based in part on some Talmudic references, accusing Mary of fathering Jesus through a Roman soldier (or by rape), and portraying Jesus as an idolater, magician, and Israel's arch-deceiver, were the primary source of information about Jesus for many traditional Jews, especially in the Middle Ages. Of course, as noted by the *Oxford Dictionary of Jewish Reli-*

gion, ed. Geoffrey Wigoder (New York: Oxford, 1997), 695, "the work is an expression of vulgar polemics written in reaction to the no less vulgar attacks on Judaism in popular Christian teaching and writing." But as I have stated before, just as many Gentiles around the world have had a biased and inaccurate view of the Jewish people, so also have many Jews had a biased and inaccurate view of Jesus, the Jewish Messiah. For a representative sampling from the *Toledot,* see the excellent study of Walter Riggans, *Yeshua ben David: Why Do the Jewish People Reject Jesus as Their Messiah?* (Crowborough, England: Marc, 1995), 127–32. Interested readers of this present volume would do well to read Riggans as well.

23. For more on this, see Nahum Brodt, "The Truth about the Rabbi," in *Would I? Would You?,* ed. Henry and Marie Einspruch (Baltimore: Lederer, 1970), 8–10. For a fuller account of Wertheimer's faith, see Jacob Gartenhaus, *Famous Hebrew Christians* (Grand Rapids: Baker, 1979), 191–97.

24. This is not the first time in our history that God has hardened our hearts because we sinned against him. This is what God said to the prophet Isaiah more than twenty-five hundred years ago: "Go and tell this people: 'Be ever hearing, but never understanding; be ever seeing, but never perceiving.' Make the heart of this people calloused; make their ears dull and close their eyes. Otherwise they might see with their eyes, hear with their ears, understand with their hearts, and turn and be healed" (Isa. 6:9–10). The prophet was actually called to a ministry of hardening his people's hearts! It was as if God were saying, "Fine. If you want to be hard-hearted, refusing to believe me or obey me, I will give you over to your hardness and make you even harder." This is exactly what has happened to us regarding the Messiah: When so many of our people refused to follow him, God gave us over to our unbelief and obduracy to the point that through the centuries, we have become *especially* resistant to Jesus.

25. This well-known, anonymous tribute to Jesus, known as "One Solitary Life," puts things in perspective: "He was born in an obscure village. He worked in a carpenter shop until He was thirty. He then became an itinerant preacher. He never held an office. He never had a family or owned a house. He didn't go to college. He had no credentials but himself. He was only thirty-three when the public turned against him. His friends ran away. He was turned over to his enemies and went through the mockery of a trail. He was nailed to a cross between two thieves. While he was dying, his executioners gambled for his clothing, the only property he had on earth. He was laid in a borrowed grave. Nineteen centuries have come and gone, and today he is the central figure of the human race. All the armies that ever marched, all the navies that ever sailed, all the parliaments that ever sat, and all the kings that ever reigned have not affected the life of man on this earth as much as that one solitary life."

26. For the misguided attempt of some anti-missionaries to interpret some of Jesus' teaching as if he were, in fact, advocating physical violence against those who rejected him, cf. 2.6.

27. For a readable study giving both sides of the conflict, see Elijah Judah Schochet, *The Hasidic Movement and the Gaon of Vilna* (Northvale, N.J.: Aronson, 1994).

28. Yeshua said, "I tell you that anyone who looks at a woman lustfully has already committed adultery with her in his heart" (Matt. 5:28). This saying is also paralleled by the teaching of the rabbis. For example, Resh Lakish taught that if a man "commits adultery with his eyes he is also called an adulterer" (Leviticus Rabbah 23:12), while another Talmudic sage said that, "He who looks at a woman with desire is as one who had illicit intercourse with her" (Massekhet Kalla 1). See further Samuel Tobias Lachs,

Rabbinic Commentary on the New Testament: The Gospels of Matthew, Mark and Luke (Hoboken/New York: Ktav/Anti-Defamation League of B'nai Brith, 1987), 96–98.

29. For the question of whether the Holocaust was in any sense a divine judgment, see 2.10.

30. The Talmud also makes reference to some people going to eternal punishment; see, e.g., b. Rosh Hashanah 16b–17a (where it is stated that the "completely wicked" go down to Gehenna and don't come back up, with reference to Dan. 12:2); and cf. Dan Cohn-Sherbok, *Rabbinic Perspectives on the New Testament* (New York: Edwin Mellen, 1990).

31. Important biblical statements on this question include Romans 1–2, along with Romans 10:1–15; for recent discussion concerning this among evangelical Christians, cf. William V. Crockett and James G. Sigountos, eds., *Through No Fault of Their Own? The Fate of Those Who Never Heard* (Grand Rapids: Baker, 1991); John Sanders, *No Other Name: An Investigation into the Destiny of the Unevangelized* (Grand Rapids: Eerdmans, 1992); Ronald H. Nash, *Is Jesus the Only Savior?* (Grand Rapids: Zondervan, 1994); idem, Gabriel Fackre, and John Sanders, *What about Those Who Have Never Heard? Three Views on the Destiny of the Unevangelized* (Downers Grove, Ill.: InterVarsity, 1995).

32. Cf. some of the remarkable stories related in popular form in Don Richardson, *Eternity in Their Hearts* (Ventura, Calif.: Regal, 1984); cf., however, the strictures of Tite Tiénou, in Crockett and Sigountos, *Through No Fault of Their Own?*, 209–15.

33. I should note here that anti-missionaries are quick to quote this text when arguing that blood sacrifices are not necessary for true repentance and forgiveness. See, e.g., Sigal, *The Jew and the Christian Missionary*, 15–16. For my response to this argument, see vol. 2, 3.9, 3.12–3.13.

34. Jacob Neusner, "Repentance in Judaism," in *Repentance: A Comparative Perspective*, ed. Amitai Etzioni and David E. Carney (Lanham, Md.: Rowman & Littlefield, 1997), 60–75 (specifically 60–61).

35. Of course, there were still horrible consequences to Manasseh's sins, and, while he was *personally* forgiven, on a *corporate* level, his deeds could not be forgiven (see 2 Kings 24:1–4). This would be similar to God forgiving even a man like Hitler—if repentance could have been possible for him—while still punishing the nation because of its sins and the sins of its leader.

36. Important Jewish books on repentance (for the English reader) include Pinhas H. Peli, *Soloveitchik on Repentance* (New York: Paulist Press, 1984); Leonard S. Kravitz and Kerry M. Olitzky, eds. and trans., *The Journey of the Soul: Traditional Sources on Teshuvah* (Northvale, N.J.: Aronson, 1995). More broadly, cf. Adin Steinsalz, *Teshuvah: A Guide for the Newly Observant Jew* (New York: Free Press, 1987).

37. Important Christian books on repentance include Thomas Watson, *The Doctrine of Repentance* (Carlisle, Pa.: Banner of Truth, 1988); Basilea Schlink, *Repentance: The Joy Filled Life* (Minneapolis: Bethany, 1984); Charles Finney, *True and False Repentance* (Grand Rapids: Kregel, 1981); see further the references in Michael L. Brown, *Go and Sin No More: A Call to Holiness* (Ventura, Calif.: Regal, 1999).

38. For issues concerning sacrifice and atonement, see vol. 2, 3.9–3.16.

39. He is only referred to as James in English translations of the Bible, but this represents a corruption in pronunciation, since his name in either Hebrew or Greek is Jacob, not James. All the other translations of the New Testament into other languages that I have personally seen correctly call him Jacob (or its equivalent in their language).

40. This is not merely some point I am raising so as to make Christianity seem more attractive to you. Rather, I have emphasized this in preaching and teaching for many years now; see, e.g., my *How Saved Are We?* (Shippensburg, Pa.: Destiny Image, 1990); *Whatever Happened to the Power of God? Is the Charismatic Church Slain in the Spirit or Down for the Count?* (Shippensburg, Pa.: Destiny Image, 1991); *It's Time to Rock the Boat: A Call to God's People to Rise Up and Preach a Confrontational Gospel* (Shippensburg, Pa.: Destiny Image, 1993); along with the references to my writings above, n. 36.

41. Cf. titles such as *Jewish Martyrs of Pawiak* by Julien Hirshaut (New York: Holocaust Library, 1982), reflecting the common Jewish view that any Jew who died in the Holocaust should be designated a martyr, regardless of their religious beliefs or lifestyle.

42. These would be the sentiments of militant (ultra) Orthodox rabbis such as Yoel Teitelbaum, the Satmar rebbe (see his Hebrew work *Va'Yoel Moshe;* for excerpts in English see Allan Nadler, "Piety and Politics: The Case of the Satmar Rebbe," *Judaism* [spring 1982]: 135–52), or Avigdor Miller, *Rejoice O Youth* (Brooklyn: n.p., 1961).

43. For more details, see Joseph Shulam, "Rabbi Daniel Zion: Chief Rabbi of Bulgarian Jews during World War II," *Mishkan* 15 (1991): 53–57. Members of the Shulam family personally witnessed most of the events described here.

44. From *The Story of Bible Translations*, cited by Gartenhaus, *Famous Hebrew Christians*, 171. As we think of men such as Isidor Loewenthal (a German Jew who spread the good news about the Messiah in Afghanistan) and Joseph Schereschewsky, both of whom used their linguistic genius to translate the Scriptures into the language of unreached masses—ultimately making the sacrifice of life and limb for these poor souls who had no knowledge of the one true God—it is only fair to ask whether you think they fulfilled their God-ordained purposes as Jews. Does it make sense to you that these men used their God-given talents in educating the Gentile world concerning God and his Messiah, or would they have done better to have studied Talmud day and night, coming up with new twists on the meaning of the ancient rabbis?

45. Brodt, *Would I? Would You?*, 10.

46. Richard Wurmbrand, *Tortured for Christ* (Bartlesville, Okla.: Living Sacrifice, 1967), 41. See further idem, *From Torture to Triumph* (Eastbourne: Monarch, 1991).

47. For his own biographical reminiscences as a Jewish Christian, see Richard Wurmbrand, *Christ on the Jewish Road* (Middlebury, Ind.: Living Sacrifice Books, 1970); for his wife's remarkable story, see Sabina Wurmbrand, *The Pastor's Wife* (Middlebury, Ind.: Living Sacrifice Books, 1970) (note that Sabina too is a Jewish believer). For more of the shocking details of Pastor Wurmbrand's years in prison, see *In God's Underground* (London: W. H. Allen, 1968).

48. W. M. Christie, "A Tiberias Rabbi," in *Would I? Would You?*, 55; see further 50–57.

49. Ibid., 55.

50. See m. Sanhedrin 10:1 and b. Sanhedrin 100a for a potential basis for this view; cf. further Schiffman, *Who Was a Jew?*, 62–64.

51. See further, 2.12.

52. Nowhere have I found comments more extreme or unrelated to reality than in Gabriel Marzel's foreword to Michoel Drazin's anti-missionary book, *Their Hollow Inheritance*, 230, n. 13 in which he claims: "Many missionary cults use psychological indoctrination or 'brainwashing' techniques to obtain their quotas. This process usually begins by luring their victims to the cult's center, away from family, friends, and familiar surroundings. Upon arriving, they are assigned a 'companion' of the opposite sex, who is to program the cult's beliefs, accomplishments, and goals into their

thought processes by monotonous repetition day and night. Subjects are also deprived of sleep and food, thereby substantially lowering their mental and physical resistance. During this period, the other cult members make them feel loved, wanted, needed, and 'privileged' to help bring the cult's 'sacred' message to the world. Within a few days, each innocent victim is mentally and physically broken, and becomes one of them!" And who is it that these ruthless soul-stealers target? Marzel tells us: "It behooves [the missionary] to prey on such vulnerable individuals as the lonely, the elderly, the poor, the emotionally unstable, the naive, or those who are just untutored in Scripture."

53. For more on this, see Janet Avigad, *Return to Judaism: Religious Renewal in Israel* (Chicago: Univ. of Chicago, 1983), discussing the phenomenon of Israeli yeshivas for *ba'alei teshuvot* (i.e., "outreach" yeshivas for the newly Orthodox), yeshivas that quite explicitly target the young.

54. See M. Herbert Danzger, *Returning to Tradition: The Contemporary Revival of Orthodox Judaism* (New Haven: Yale, 1989), 194–95, with table A-6 on 345.

55. If you are an observant Jew, then you know the difference—at least in theory—between laws that are *mid'orayta'* (i.e., from the Torah, and hence divine in origin) and laws that are *mid'rabbanan* (i.e., from the rabbis, and hence human in origin). In reality, however, don't you really put more weight in the traditions of the rabbis, even when they seem to contradict the written Word?

56. Perhaps you would like to read about this from both sides, hearing the testimonies of Jews who have become Messianic as compared to the testimonies of Jews who have become traditional. Then read the following and compare. For the Messianic side, see any of the following collections: Ruth Rosen, ed., *Jesus for Jews: If Jesus Is the Messiah at All Then He Is the Messiah for All* (San Francisco: Jews for Jesus, 1987); Sid Roth, ed., *They Thought for Themselves* (Brunswick, Ga.: MV Press, 1996); Ben Hoekendijk, ed., *Twelve Jews Discover Messiah* (Eastbourne: Kingsway, 1992; this book is entirely devoted to testimonies of Jews living in Israel). There are not as many "testimony" books written from the traditional side, but some representative readers include Richard H. Greenberg, ed., *Pathways: Jews Who Return to God* (Northvale, N.J.: Aronson, 1997); Debra Renee Kaufman, *Rachel's Daughters: Newly Orthodox Jewish Women* (Rutgers, N.J.: Rutgers Univ. Press, 1991). I heard a tragic confession made by Rabbi Ben-Zion Kravitz on a tape from an anti-missionary conference in the early 1990s: He claimed to have pulled about one hundred Jews *away* from Jesus in his years as a leader in the Jews for Judaism movement (a figure that is quite suspect, by the way). But out of that one hundred, only a handful had become observant Jews! Thus, to the extent that his claims are true, he has succeeded in making Jews for Jesus into Jews for nothing.

57. Speaking of Jewish views of the Song of Songs, the biblical and Semitic scholar Marvin H. Pope notes that, "The Jewish interpretation saw the Song as depicting the relation of Yahweh and the Chosen People, Israel, as his bride. This interpretation is reflected in the Talmud spreading over the first half of the first millennium of the common era, and was fully developed a little later in the Targum as a historical allegory covering the highlights of Israel's experiences from the Exodus to the impending Advent of the Messiah. Essentially the same interpretation is offered by the Midrash Rabbah and by the great medieval commentators Saadia, Rashi, and Ibn Ezra." See his *Song of Songs* (Garden City, N.Y.: Doubleday, 1977), 89.

58. A copy of the audio tape of this debate is available through ICN Ministries; see below, part 2, n. 271 for information concerning the tapes that Rabbi Singer asked me *not* to release to the public.

Part 2 Historical Objections

1. For an in-depth study of the issues involved, with ample bibliography, see Mitchell First, *Jewish History in Conflict: A Study of the Major Discrepancy between Rabbinic and Conventional Chronology* (Northvale, N.J.: Aronson, 1997; note that First is a graduate of Yeshiva University); cf. also Judah M. Rosenthal, "Seder Olam," *Encyclopedia Judaica* 14:1091–93. For the Hebrew text with translation and commentary, cf. Heinrich W. Guggenheimer, *Seder Olam: The Rabbinic View of Biblical Chronology* (Northvale, N.J.: Aronson, 1998).

2. It should be pointed out that ancient Near Eastern and biblical scholars often begin their dating of the patriarchal period (i.e., beginning with Abraham) to roughly 2000 B.C.E., although there is no definite consensus. Cf., e.g., Mordecai Cogan, "Chronology," *Anchor Bible Dictionary* 1:1005, who notes that, "Many scholars would place the Patriarchs in the MB [Middle Bronze] I period (2000–1800 B.C.E.), a conjecture based on the putative similarities between their seminomadic lifestyle as described in Genesis and the Amorite movements known from archaeology and the Mari documents." In contrast, only "a few" scholars "place them in the LB [Late Bronze] Age (1550–1200 B.C.E.) . . ." (ibid.). Of course, as Cogan observed (ibid., 1:1004), "No absolute dates for the patriarchal age are available since the events related in Genesis and Exodus cannot be synchronized with extrabiblical chronology."

3. This is the expanded rendering of the Hebrew text by Aharon Feldman in *The Juggler and the King: The Jew and the Conquest of Evil. An Elaboration of the Vilna Gaon's Insights into the Hidden Wisdom of the Sages* (Jerusalem/New York: Feldheim, 1991), 146.

4. Ibid., 149–50.

5. Ibid., 151–52.

6. Abba Hillel Silver, *A History of Messianic Speculation in Israel* (New York: Macmillan, 1927), 7.

7. Ibid., 6, his emphasis.

8. Ibid., 19.

9. For more on the issue of sacrifice and atonement, see vol. 2, 3.8–3.17.

10. See also the commentary to Daniel 7:13–14 attributed to Saadiah Gaon, in which these verses are once again interpreted messianically, and see Rashi to the verses cited in Daniel and Zechariah.

11. For more on the glorious return of the Messiah, see Brown, *Our Hands Are Stained with Blood*, 165–73, and cf. vol. 2, 3.24; vol. 3, 5.15. Interestingly, the Lubavitcher Rebbe taught that *both* descriptions of the Messiah's coming could be fulfilled and that it was not necessarily a matter of either/or. See *From Exile and Redemption*, vol. 2, *Chassidic Teachings of the Lubavitcher Rebbe Rabbi Menachem Schneerson and the Preceding Rebbeim of Chabad on the Future Redemption and the Coming of Mashiach* (Brooklyn: Kehot, 1996), 6: "The Talmudic sages [b. Sanhedrin 98a] speak of two possible ways in which *Mashiach* can come: (a) *'m 'nny smy'*—'with the clouds of heaven' [Dan. 7:13]; (b) *'ny wrwkb hmwr*—as 'a poor man riding on a donkey' [Zech. 9:9]. It may be suggested that these are not mutually exclusive alternatives. Rather, *Mashiach* will be both powerfully exalted ('on the clouds of heaven') and humbly self-effacing ('a poor man riding on a donkey')." Of course, the problem with Rabbi Schneerson's interpretation is that it fails to do justice to the language of Daniel 7:13, which speaks of one *coming* with the clouds of heaven, also describing this individual as *gloriously* and *universally* exalted, receiving the adoration of the entire world.

12. While it is true that the immediate context in Haggai 2 speaks of physical splendor and earthly wealth, using the Hebrew word *kabod* (glory) in this sense, several factors militate against a purely physical explanation: (1) As stressed above, the term *kabod* when tied in with the temple or tabernacle (in particular in light of 2 Chronicles and Exodus 40 in which it occurs with the verb *male'*, "fill") cannot be limited to physical appearance alone. Just note some of these other verses in which the Hebrew Bible speaks of *filling* something with *glory*, all with reference to the manifest presence of God: 1 Kings 8:11; Ezek. 10:4; 43:5; 44:4, and see especially Exod. 29:42–43: "For the generations to come this burnt offering is to be made regularly at the entrance to the Tent of Meeting before the Lord. There I will meet you and speak to you; there also I will meet with the Israelites, and the place will be consecrated by my glory." The obvious question is, How much "glory" could there be in a beautiful, even splendid building devoid of the Shekhinah, the "down-to-earth" presence of God? See also Isa. 6:3–4; Hab. 2:14. (2) The fact that some sages (from the Talmud on) suggested that the greater glory was to be understood in terms of *duration* (hardly a compelling interpretation, to say the least) indicates that in their view, the contextual meaning of *kabod* of Haggai 2 did not clearly refer to physical splendor. (3) Even some refutationists, such as Isaac Troki in his classic work *Hizzuk Emunah: Faith Strengthened* (New York: Sefer Hermon, 1970), 169–73, rejected the standard Rabbinic interpretations, arguing instead that the references to "this House" in Haggai 2 actually referred to the *Third* Temple! Of course, such arguments become completely unnecessary when it is realized that the Messiah, bearing and revealing the glory of God and prophetically called "the Prince of Peace" (Isa. 9:6[5]), came to the Second Temple, right on schedule. See also immediately below, n. 13.

13. Isaac Troki also refutes this notion, stating, "For during the existence of the second temple no peace reigned in the land; but according to Daniel, 'the street and the entrenchment were to be built amidst the troubles of the times.' Much less can it be said that the glory of the temple was reserved for the days of Herod, for from his house contention never departed, and after his death sufferings never ceased with the Jews, until their final overthrow" (*Faith Strengthened*, 170). His further arguments against traditional Jewish interpretations of Haggai 2:9 are also worth quoting: "Nor can we admit that the glory of the second temple consisted in its longer duration—a point discussed in the Talmud (Baba Bathra), for the Scripture makes no mention of the glory being attributable to the length of the time during which the temple was constructed or lasted. And even if the duration of the second temple had exceeded by double the time of the first temple, the word *glory* could not have been assigned to this distinction" (ibid.). For Troki (ibid., 169–70), the "non-fulfillment" of the promise of peace in Haggai 2:9 sets aside the possibility that the greater glory referred to in this verse is merely one of material splendor. Interestingly, Abraham Ibn Ezra raises the possibility that the promise of Haggai 2:9 is *conditional:* "If they will be completely righteous, as Zechariah said, and if they will diligently hearken and obey." This interpretation certainly says a lot, since it basically admits that the standard Rabbinic views are not correct and that, therefore, the prophecy was never fulfilled. The alternative, of course, is obvious: Yeshua fulfilled the prophecies! See also immediately above, n. 12.

14. Outside of Malachi 3:1, the phrase is always *ha'adon yhwh*; see Exod. 23:17; 34:23; Deut. 10:17; Isa. 1:24; 3:1; 10:16, 33; 19:4. For the usage in Malachi 3:1, cf. Andrew E. Hill, *Malachi* (New York: Doubleday, 1998), 268.

15. It is ludicrous to argue that the coming of the Lord to his Temple did *not* refer to the Second Temple but rather to a Temple that is yet to be built, now twenty-four

hundred years after Malachi's words. There was, quite obviously, no way that the prophet himself would have conceived of such a thought, and the entire context of the Book of Malachi makes it clear that there was to be a time of divine judgment and visitation for the people who worshiped and served *at the Second Temple*. In fact, it is surprising that it even took four hundred years for this word to be fulfilled, since the coming of the messenger of the covenant was said to be *imminent* (cf. the NJPSV's "he is already coming"). It is also worth pointing out that Radak believed that this messenger who prepares the way of the Lord was either the Messiah or Elijah (in the former case, meaning that both figures are one and the same), whereas Metsudat David states only that it is Elijah (but in v. 1, Radak felt that it was a heavenly messenger, as in Exod. 23:25). According to Ibn Ezra, the messenger of v. 1a might refer to Messiah Ben Joseph, but the *'adon* in v. 1b did not refer to Yahweh but to the aforementioned messenger of the covenant. For the New Testament application of these verses and concepts, cf. especially Matt. 11:10; Mark 1:2–3; and cf. Matt. 3:10–12 with Mal. 3:1–4. According to Moses Maimonides, the words "he will sit as a refiner and purifier of silver" describe the work of the Messiah; see his Mishneh Torah, Hilkhot Melakhim 12:3.

16. For those who find references to the divine nature of the Messiah to be crass or "un-Jewish," I would point out that either the Messiah was a divine man who brought the presence of God to earth two thousand years ago and who will return with divine glory in the near future, or else Yahweh himself had to literally visit the Second Temple (according to Malachi 3) and will have to literally return and stand on the Mount of Olives in the future (according to Zechariah 14). In light of our forthcoming discussion (see vol. 2, 3.1–3.4, 3.22), only the former option (viz., the divine nature of the Messiah) is possible. See also John J. Collins, "Jewish Monotheism and Christian Theology," in *Aspects of Monotheism: How God Is One*, ed. Hershel Shanks and Jack Meinhart (Washington, D.C.: Biblical Archaeological Society, 1997), 81–105.

17. For further discussion of Isaiah 9, cf. vol. 2, 3.22 and vol. 3, 4.9; for more on the Messiah bringing peace, cf. below, 2.6.

18. Luke, a devoted Gentile follower of Yeshua (who some think may have been a Jewish convert), tells us that Zechariah, the father of John the Immerser and a Levite himself, prophesied that the Messiah would "guide our feet into the path of peace" (Luke 1:79), while the angels announcing his birth proclaimed to the startled shepherds, "Glory to God in the highest, and on earth peace to men on whom his favor rests" (Luke 2:14); for discussion of this phrase in the light of linguistic usage in the Dead Sea Scrolls, see Joseph A. Fitzmyer, "'Peace upon Earth among Men of His Good Will' (Luke 2:14)," reprinted in idem, *Essays on the Semitic Background to the New Testament* (Missoula, Mont.: Scholars Press, 1974), 101–4. Also, as we will see shortly, when Jesus came to Jerusalem shortly before his death, he cried out, "If you, even you, had only known on this day what would bring you peace—but now it is hidden from your eyes" (Luke 19:42). In other words, we rejected his offer of peace! See also Luke 4:18–19, where Jesus explained his mission with reference to Isaiah 61:1–3, but he ended the quote from Isaiah part way through the last verse, saying that he had come "to proclaim the year of the Lord's favor" and stopping before the words "and the day of vengeance of our God." In other words, his primary mission was to offer grace not bring judgment.

19. Interestingly, the NJPSV version renders here with "grant prosperity," understanding Hebrew *shalom* in a broader sense.

20. For further discussion of this passage, see vol. 3, 4.23–4.26.

21. Other renderings of this important phrase include, "the [or, an] anointed one will be cut off and have nothing"; or, "the [or, an] anointed one will be cut off, but not for himself." Note further that "anointed one" could also be rendered "Messiah."

22. For Rabbinic literature on the significance of the holy days, cf., e.g., S. Y. Agnon, ed., *Days of Awe: A Treasury of Jewish Wisdom for Reflection, Repentance, and Renewal on the High Holy Days* (New York: Schocken, 1995); Abraham P. Bloch, *The Biblical and Historical Background of the Jewish Holy Days* (New York: Ktav, 1978); Avraham Yaakov Finkel, *The Essence of the Holy Days* (Northvale, N.J.: Aronson, 1993); Moshe A. Braun, *The Jewish Holy Days: Their Spiritual Significance* (Northvale, N.J.: Aronson, 1996); Phillip Goodman, *The Rosh Hashanah Anthology* (Philadelphia: Jewish Publication Society, 1994); idem, *The Yom Kippur Anthology* (Philadelphia: Jewish Publication Society, 1994); idem, *The Sukkot and Simhat Torah Anthology* (Philadelphia: Jewish Publication Society, 1973); idem and Amy Goodman, *The Passover Anthology* (Philadelphia: Jewish Publication Society, 1994); see also the Messianic Jewish sources listed in the bibliographical supplement in Brown, *Our Hands Are Stained with Blood*, 234; cf. further the non-technical studies of Barney Kasdan, *God's Appointed Time: A Practical Guide for Understanding and Celebrating the Biblical Holidays* (Baltimore: Lederer, 1993); and Edward Chumney, *The Seven Festivals of the Messiah* (Shippensburg, Pa.: Treasure House, 1994).

23. For discussion of the counting of days from First Fruits to Shavu'ot, see above, 1.5, n. 12.

24. See b. Shabbat 86b.

25. Note also that, immediately after receiving the Holy Spirit, Peter stood up and spoke to a large crowd of fellow Jews who had just assembled, proclaiming to them the death and resurrection of the Messiah. As a result, three thousand more Jews put their faith in Jesus that very day and received eternal life through their repentance. Interestingly, shortly after the Lord gave our people the law on Mount Sinai, many of the people were guilty of idolatry, resulting in the *death* of three thousand Israelites. See Exod. 32:1–28; Acts 2:1–41.

26. Mishneh Torah, Hilkhot Teshuvah (Laws of Repentance) 3:4, as vibrantly translated by Finkel, *The Essence of the Holy Days*, 25.

27. For further discussion of this passage, see vol. 3, 4.36.

28. For the significance of the Feast of Tabernacles as an endtime Messianic event, as well as a foreshadowing of the final ingathering of the nations of the world into the kingdom of God, cf. Mitch and Zhava Glaser, *The Fall Feasts of Israel* (Chicago: Moody, 1987), along with the works referred to above, n. 22. Note also that the ancient rabbis stressed the universal importance of Tabernacles, believing that the seventy bulls sacrificed over the seven days of the feast (see Num. 29:12–38) represented the seventy nations of the world and Israel's intercession on their behalf; cf. Numbers Rabbah 21; b. Sukkah 55b; and Zech. 14:16–19.

29. For the deeply spiritual Jewish teaching that the death of the righteous atones, see vol. 2, 3.15.

30. For refutation of the idea that the authors of the scrolls expected only *one* Messiah of Aaron and Israel, see John J. Collins, *The Scepter and the Star: The Messiahs of the Dead Sea Scrolls and Other Ancient Literature* (New York: Doubleday, 1995); note also L. H. Schiffman, "Messianic Figures and Ideas in the Qumran Scrolls," in *The Messiah: Developments in Earliest Judaism and Christianity*, ed. James H. Charlesworth (Minneapolis: Fortress, 1992), 116–29. It is also noteworthy that in several other Qumran texts, there is reference to a Davidic Messiah *and* a priest (see Collins, *Scepter and*

the Star, 74–101); note further b. Sukkah 52b, interpreting Zech. 1:20 with reference to the two Messiahs, Elijah, and the righteous High Priest.

31. See conveniently Raphael Patai, *The Messiah Texts* (Detroit: Wayne State Univ., 1979), 191–92, for important excerpts. For full editions of the Testament of the Twelve Patriarchs, see James H. Charlesworth, ed., *The Old Testament Pseudepigrapha,* vol. 1 (Garden City, N.Y.: Doubleday, 1983), 775–828 (ed. and trans. by H. C. Kee, who dates the fundamental writing of the Testaments to around 100 B.C.E.); H. F. D. Sparks, ed., M. de Jonge, trans., *The Apocryphal Old Testament* (Oxford: Clarendon, 1984), 505–600.

32. For the sole reference in Rabbinic literature to a priestly figure in conjunction with the Messiah, cf. Avot d'Rabbi Nathan 34:6 (the two sons of oil are Aaron and the Messiah, but it is the Messiah who is more beloved *[habib],* based on Ps. 110:4); cf. also the reference to b. Sukkah 52b, above, n. 30.

33. Cf., e.g., Midrash Psalms 2:9; 18:29.

34. It is important to remember that King Saul, David's predecessor, got into big trouble by offering a sacrifice without priestly authorization (see 1 Sam. 13:14), while a later, godly king like Uzziah was stricken by God for daring to infringe on priestly ministry (in his case, burning incense in the Temple; see 2 Chron. 26:16–26).

35. The noun occurs 440 times in the singular and 310 times in the plural and always means "priest"—without exception; the Rabbinic commentators to 2 Samuel 8:17 struggle with the obvious meaning, which is confirmed by the fact that *kohanîm* also occurs in the previous verse (2 Sam. 8:16), and the meaning there is indisputably "priests." It is impossible to think that the same word is used two very different ways in the space of two verses in the same context, especially when it is *never* used in any sense except "priest" throughout the Bible. That the Spirit of God was hinting at something important in this verse is confirmed when we realize that the later parallel passage to 2 Samuel 8 (viz., 1 Chronicles 18) states that David's sons were "chief officials" (v. 17; *ri'shonim*). Thus, the special, intentional statement made in 2 Samuel 8:17 is clear: David's role as a priestly king is seen in the fact that some of his sons were also called priests.

36. This is universally recognized by traditional Jewish and Christian scholars; for key biblical references in which the Messianic king is actually called "David," cf. Jer. 30:8–9; Ezek. 34:20–24; 37:24–28; Hosea 3:5. Note also verses such as Isa. 9:5–6[6–7]; 11:1; Jer. 23:5; 30:20–26.

37. Targum Jonathan actually substitutes "Messiah" for "Branch"; see further the discussion in Ibn Ezra and Radak, in which the text is first applied to Zerubbabel (so also Rashi), and then, typologically, to the Messiah; note also that the figure most commonly called "my servant" in the Hebrew Bible is David (see immediately above, n. 36, for some of the references). For related discussion, see vol. 3, 4.12 (to Isa. 52:13).

38. Cf. the reference to Avot d'Rabbi Nathan 34:6, above, n. 32, in which these two "sons of oil" are interpreted to be Aaron and the Messiah.

39. We will comment on this important chapter at greater length later in our discussion of Messianic prophecy; see vol. 3, 4.10–4.22.

40. For more on this, see vol. 3, 4.1. It should also be remembered that during the days of the Second Temple, specifically during the Hasmonean Dynasty, the ruling king over the Jewish people was actually the high priest, and from the time of Simon (143/2–135/4 B.C.E.), the titles of high priest and prince were considered hereditary, passed on to John Hyrcanus I and II and then to Aristobulus (for the entire period in question, see Emil Schürer, *The History of the Jewish People in the Age of Jesus Christ*

[175 B.C.–A.D. 135], rev. Eng. ed. by Geza Vermes, Fergus Millar, and Matthew Black [Edinburgh: T & T Clark, 1973–1987], 1:137–242).

41. During a debate with Rabbi Dr. David Blumofe in 1993, I was challenged with a quote alleged to have come from the brilliant thirteenth-century rabbi known as Ramban (Rabbi Moses ben Nachman, also called Nachmanides), and that quote is relevant here. I was told that during his heralded debate with a Jewish Catholic named Pablo Christiani (Friar Paul), Ramban exclaimed, "Woe to the world if the Messiah has come," meaning, "If this is how the world looks *after* the Messiah has already come, woe to the world." Actually, as we have seen—and as I replied in the debate— a more accurate quote from the standpoint of the Hebrew Scriptures would have been, "Woe to the world if the Messiah has *not* come," since, if he didn't come when expected, we have no reason to believe that he will ever come. And would Ramban have thought for a moment that more than six hundred years after his debate the traditional Jewish Messiah *still* would not have arrived? Certainly not. In fact, in the debate he made it clear that he expected the Messiah to come in the next ninety-five years. See Rabbi Dr. Charles B. Chavel, ed. and trans., *Ramban (Nachmanides): The Disputation at Barcelona* (New York: Shilo Publishing House, 1983), 26; cf. further the works cited below, n. 269). Interestingly, when I actually checked the text of the Ramban-Pablo Christiani debate, I was surprised to see that the alleged quote was not found there.

42. *Genesis*, The JPS Torah Commentary (Philadelphia: The Jewish Publication Society, 1989), 89. Sarna, contrary to the general trend of past Jewish scholarship, favors a passive translation of the verb *bless* (meaning that all nations *will be blessed* through Abraham's seed), as opposed to a reflexive translation (meaning that all nations *will bless themselves* in the name of Abraham's seed, saying, "May God make you like the descendants of Abraham"). For a discussion of the grammatical and interpretative issues, cf. Michael L. Brown, *"brk,"* in *The New International Dictionary of Old Testament Theology and Exegesis*, ed. Willem VanGemeren (Grand Rapids: Zondervan, 1997), 1:757–67 (specifically 759–60).

43. Strangely, some anti-missionaries have appealed to verses such as Micah 4:5 ("All the nations may walk in the name of their gods; we will walk in the name of the Lord our God for ever and ever") or Deuteronomy 4:19 ("And when you look up to the sky and see the sun, the moon and the stars—all the heavenly array—do not be enticed into bowing down to them and worshiping things the Lord your God has apportioned to all the nations under heaven"), as if it is fine for Gentiles to worship idols, as long as Jews are faithful to the one true God; cf. Sigal, *The Jew and the Christian Missionary*, xvii–xviii.

44. Some of the more startling statistics in this regard include the following (current as of early 1998): "More scientific knowledge has been amassed since 1960 than was generated in the previous 5,000 years of recorded history. . . . [The general] fund of information doubles every 2 to 2.5 years . . . [and] by the time a child born today finishes college, the body of knowledge may have increased fourfold. By the time the person reaches 50 years of age, accumulated knowledge may have grown 32-fold. As much as 97 percent of all knowledge will have been created [perhaps "discovered" is a better word!] since that person was born" (taken from www.ibm.com/Stories/1997/01/future4.html).

45. By the "kingdom of God" I mean his active rule over someone's life, his bringing that person into submission to his will. Ultimately, that is the key to world peace and harmony: The Lord ruling over the earth!

46. I am not for a moment buying into the popular religious craze known as "millennial madness" (which is actually the title of a 1997 teaching video hosted by Bruce Marchiano; cf. also Timothy J. Dailey, *Millennial Deception: Angels, Aliens, and the Antichrist* [Grand Rapids: Chosen, 1995]). Nonetheless, this century has been the most momentous and eventful century in human history, and it is interesting to note that one of the greatest men of prayer in the history of the church, John "Praying" Hyde, an American Christian who gave himself to reach the people of India, wrote these words in the year 1901: "I hail in the twentieth century, the blessing of our age restored—a Church holy in life, triumphant in faith, self-sacrificing in service with one aim, to preach Christ crucified 'unto the uttermost part of the earth.'"

47. Among the countless books devoted to Jewish and Christian reflections on "God and the problem of evil," some recent studies of note include Richard Swinburne, *Providence and the Problem of Evil* (New York: Oxford, 1998); Joni Eareckson Tada, *When God Weeps: Why Our Sufferings Matter to the Almighty* (Grand Rapids: Zondervan, 1997); Edith Schaeffer, *Affliction* (Grand Rapids: Baker, 1993); D. A. Carson, *How Long, O Lord? Reflections on Suffering and Evil* (Grand Rapids: Baker, 1991); an older classic is C. S. Lewis, *The Problem of Pain* (New York: Macmillan, 1962). For Jewish reflections, cf. recently Reuven P. Bulka, *Judaism on Illness and Suffering* (Northvale, N.J.; Aronson, 1998); Shmuel Boteach, *Wrestling with the Divine: A Jewish Response to Suffering* (Northvale, N.J.: Aronson, 1995); see also David Charles Kraemer, *Responses to Suffering in Classical Rabbinic Literature* (New York: Oxford, 1994).

48. Cited in Michael L. Brown, *Let No One Deceive You: Confronting the Critics of Revival* (Shippensburg, Pa.: Destiny Image, 1997), 212, with references on 283, n. 19.

49. For Islam and violence, cf. Amir Taheri, *Holy Terror: Inside the World of Islamic Terrorism* (Bethesda, Md.: Adler & Adler, 1987); Emanuel Sivan, *Radical Islam: Medieval Theology and Modern Politics* (New Haven: Yale Univ. Press, 1985); Victor Mordecai, *Is Fanatic Islam a Global Threat?*, rev. ed. (Springfield, Mo.: n.p., 1996); for "Christianity" and the sword, cf. 2.6. In stark contrast with the New Testament admonition to love one's enemies and turn the other cheek (see 2.5), the Koran praises those who die "in the way of Allah" (see, e.g., in the Koran 3:156–59, 169–75; the reference to the "way [Arabic *sabila*] of Allah" speaks in particular of holy war; cf. John Penrice, *Dictionary and Glossary of the Koran* [London: Curzon Press, 1970], 66).

50. Cf. the similar statements in the Talmud relative to the calamitous times immediately preceding the Messiah's coming (b. Sanhedrin 97a; and note in particular R. Abbaye's rebuttal to the claim of R. Yoseph that such things have happened before: perhaps, but never in the manner or order predicted!).

51. The respected church statistician David Barrett, editor of the prestigious *World Christian Encyclopedia*, 2d ed. (New York: Oxford, 1999), is the primary scholar associated with the three-hundred-thousand martyrs-per-year estimate. For the most complete account of martyrdom of Christians in the twentieth century, offering a representative sampling of both the suffering of these believers and their triumphant faith, see James C. and Marti Hefley, *By Their Blood: Christian Martyrs of the Twentieth Century*, 2d ed. (Grand Rapids: Baker, 1996). Cf. also Paul Marshall and Lela Gilbert, *Their Blood Cries Out: The Untold Story of Persecution against Christians in the Modern World* (Dallas: Word, 1997); Nina Shea, *In the Lion's Den: Persecuted Christians and What the Western Church Can Do about It* (Nashville: Broadman & Holman, 1997).

52. He is referred to as "the devil" in later Jewish and Christian literature; for in-depth discussion about this figure as depicted in different religious traditions, see the four-volume study of Jeffrey Burton Russell, *The Devil: Perceptions of Evil from Antiq-*

uity to Primitive Christianity (Ithaca, N.Y.: Cornell Univ. Press, 1977); *Satan: The Early Christian Tradition* (Ithaca, N.Y.: Cornell Univ. Press, 1981); *Lucifer: The Devil in the Middle Ages* (Ithaca, N.Y.: Cornell Univ. Press, 1984); *Mephistopholes: The Devil in the Modern World* (Ithaca, N.Y.: Cornell Univ. Press, 1986). Note also Peggy Day, *An Adversary in Heaven: Satan in the Hebrew Bible* (Atlanta: Scholars Press, 1988), and see, more broadly, Bernard McGinn, *Antichrist: Two Thousand Years of Fascination with Evil* (San Francisco: HarperSanFrancisco, 1994).

53. This prophecy cannot be interpreted with reference to the time of the Babylonian exile, since it was not followed by the promised seeking of God and the Davidic king, nor can it refer to the time of the Second Temple, since during that time there were sacrifices being offered and at least some of the priestly functions being fulfilled.

54. The New Testament paints a picture of the end of this age that can be characterized as a time of parallel extremes, using images such as the separation of the wheat and the tares at harvest time (Matt. 13:24–30); the separation of the good fish from the bad fish after a large catch (Matt. 13:47–50); the separation of the sheep from the goats at the final judgment (Matt. 25:31–46); the shaking of everything that can be shaken so that only God's unshakable kingdom will remain (Heb. 12:25–29); Messiah's return resulting in the exultation of the righteous and the destruction of the wicked (2 Thess. 1:6–10). See further this statement from the last chapter of the last book of the New Testament: "Let him who does wrong continue to do wrong; let him who is vile continue to be vile; let him who does right continue to do right; and let him who is holy continue to be holy" (Rev. 22:11).

55. For further discussion of this, see vol. 2, 3.24.

56. Mordechai Staiman, *Waiting for the Messiah* (Northvale, N.J.: Aronson, 1977), front, inside cover, his emphasis. Of course, there are many well-known midrashim in the Talmud and later Rabbinic literature that speak, e.g., of the Messiah already being at the gates of Rome at the end of the Second Temple period (b. Sanhedrin 98a, waiting to be revealed) or being born on the day the Temple was destroyed (Bereshit Rabbati, 130–31; see conveniently Patai, *Messiah Texts*, 124–25).

57. See vol. 3, sect. 4 for discussion of the relevant prophecies.

58. In fact, the first major biography of the rebbe put out by Lubavitch contained the Rabbinic prayer, "May his death serve as an atonement," right in the front of the book; for more on this traditional Jewish concept that the death of the righteous atones, see vol. 2, 3.15.

59. Staiman, *Waiting for the Messiah*, 250.

60. Michael Shapiro, *The Jewish 100: A Ranking of the Most Influential Jews of All Time* (Secaucus, N.J.: Citadel, 1996); the reference to Menachem Schneerson is found on 365. Of course, this book only represents Shapiro's educated opinions, but they are opinions that, for the most part, reflect a fairly wide consensus. At the least, they remind us that it was *several Jews* intimately connected with "Christianity"—Yeshua, Saul of Tarsus, Miriam (Mary)—who mightily influenced the world and that their influence completely dwarfs—really, that is a vast understatement—the influence of Rabbi Schneerson. In fact, there are more *Jews* today who believe that Yeshua is the Messiah than those who believe that the Rebbe is the Messiah! This too is something worth considering. Interestingly, in the eyes of his admirers, the Rebbe has taken on colossal importance; see, e.g., the evaluation of *The Encyclopedia of Hasidism*, ed. Tzvi M. Rabinowicz (Northvale, N.J.: Aronson, 1996), 430, where Rabbi Schneerson is hailed as "the most phenomenal Jewish personality of the twentieth century."

61. I understand, of course, that in the time of Jesus there was not one, fixed Jewish view of what kind of man the Messiah would be and what exactly he would do. My point is that there were certainly Jews who were expecting a miracle-working Messiah, and his miracles would be part of the proof of his messiahship. On the diversity of Messianic expectations in the first century C.E., cf. Jacob Neusner, William S. Green, and Ernest Frerichs, *Judaisms and Their Messiahs at the Turn of the Christian Era* (Cambridge: Cambridge, 1987); Charlesworth, *The Messiah;* Collins, *The Scepter and the Star;* Craig A. Evans and Peter W. Flint, eds., *Eschatology, Messianism and the Dead Sea Scrolls* (Grand Rapids: Eerdmans, 1997); see also the important collection of older material in Leo Landmann, ed., *Messianism in the Talmudic Era* (New York: Ktav, 1979).

62. This is part of the text called the Messianic Apocalypse (4Q521, fragment 2), as translated in the standard scholarly edition of Florentino García Martínez, *The Dead Sea Scrolls Translated* (Leiden: Brill, 1994), 394. For discussion of this text and its striking parallels with some of the words and acts of Jesus, see the discussion in Collins, *The Scepter and the Star,* 117–22.

63. It is important to remember that, generally speaking, to the first-century Jewish community, the Judaism of the Dead Sea Scrolls was no more or less "normative" than the Judaism of the Pharisees or Sadducees, despite later Rabbinic reconstructions that give the impression that the other, non-pharisaical groups were completely marginal. This, of course, is not true. See Günter Stemberger, *Jewish Contemporaries of Jesus: Pharisees, Sadducees, Essenes,* trans. Allan W. Mahnke (Minneapolis: Fortress, 1995); and note Anthony J. Saldarini, *Pharisees, Scribes, and Sadducees in Palestinian Society* (Wilmington, Del.: Michael Glazier, 1988); cf. also above, n. 61.

64. See Genesis Rabbah 95:1 [Tanhuma Wayyigash 8] on this verse being fulfilled in the world to come.

65. For a discussion of Yeshua's miracles in the context of other contemporaneous miracle workers in Judaism, cf. Geza Vermes, *Jesus the Jew* (Philadelphia: Fortress, 1973), especially 69–80. According to Vermes, "It is necessary to remember that from the time of the prophet Elijah Jews believed that holy men were able to exert their will on natural phenomena."

66. With reference to various Messianic claimants in the first five centuries of this era, Patai, *The Messiah Texts,* xli, notes, "The belief in these self-proclaimed Messiahs and in their power to perform miracles could be so strong that it could override all normal instincts of self-preservation."

67. See Schürer, *History of the Jewish People,* 1:544–45.

68. I refer here especially to Maimonides's classic description of the Messiah that has become normative for many Jews, in which he actually downplayed the idea that the Messiah would be a miracle worker (cf. Mishneh Torah, Hilkhot Melakhim 11:3). In context, however, Maimonides used this description to deny any true Messianic credentials to Jesus, known by both friend and foe as an exceptional miracle worker. Interestingly, Joseph Klausner, *The Messianic Idea in Israel,* trans. W. F. Stinespring (London: George Allen, 1956), 506, stresses that "*the Messiah*—and this should be carefully noted!—*is never mentioned anywhere in the Tannaitic literature as a wonder-worker* per se" (his emphasis; his point was that it was God who performed the miracles at the time of the inbreaking of the Messianic kingdom). This can easily be viewed as a reaction of sorts to the emphasis on Yeshua's miracles in early Messianic Jewish circles, a period contemporaneous with the Tannaim (i.e., first to second centuries C.E.). It is worth pointing out that the Talmudic rabbis spoke of all kinds of miraculous, almost

cosmic transformations taking place in the Messianic age, and yet somehow downplayed miraculous healings. For further thoughts on the Rabbinic downplaying of the supernatural elements of messianism, cf. Jacob Neusner, *Messiah in Context: Israel's History and Destiny in Formative Judaism* (Philadelphia: Fortress, 1984); note also Vermes, *Jesus the Jew*, 80–82, who explains why, by their very natures, Pharisees and "charismatic" Jews would have certain fundamental conflicts, observing quite tellingly that, "Since *halakhah* became the corner-stone of rabbinic Judaism, it is not surprising that, despite their popular religious appeal, Jesus, Hanina, and the others [referring to sages alleged to have miraculous powers; see above, n. 65], were slowly but surely squeezed out beyond the pale of true respectability."

69. Obviously, I am not guaranteeing that you will be healed of disease if you become a follower of Jesus. I am simply saying that it is unrealistic for you to deny that healing and miracles are of importance to you. When the rubber meets the road and calamity hits home, you will find yourself seeking "faith" answers more than you expect. In fact, it is a common saying among ministers that many an atheist has suddenly become a profound believer on his or her deathbed!

70. For the whole story, see Roth, *They Thought for Themselves*, 11–23.

71. For the appeal to Psalm 44 as an apparent contradiction of the Sinai covenant (cf. Ps. 44:17, "All this happened to us, though we had not forgotten you or been false to your covenant . . ."), see vol. 3, 4.11, with reference to Isa. 52:13–53:12.

72. Meir Simcha Sokolovsky, *Prophecy and Providence* (Jerusalem/New York: Feldheim, 1991), 79–80.

73. See Brown, *Our Hands Are Stained with Blood*.

74. Cf. also Sokolovsky, *Prophecy and Providence*, 63–64, with reference to Deuteronomy 28:64; Sokolovsky notes that the Ramban in his *Letter to Yemen* "explains this curse as meaning that the Gentiles will coerce Jews to worship their gods. And so it was. From the time of the expulsion nearly two thousand years ago, there has hardly been a generation which has not been subject, in one land or another, to decrees of *shemad* (forced conversion), when Jews were commanded to renounce their faith and worship other gods on pain of death." See also his reference to Rashi's interpretation, ibid., of Deut. 28:36; 4:28. Of course, for this Orthodox Jewish author, following Christianity means worshiping other gods, an incorrect concept to which we will give considerable attention. See vol. 2, 3:1–3.4.

75. According to Rashi, the "nation of fools" refers to deniers of the faith *(koperim)*, in accordance with Psalm 14:1 ("The fool says in his heart, 'There is no god'"). Cf. also W. Gunther Plaut, ed., *The Torah: A Modern Commentary* (New York: Union of American Hebrew Congregations, 1985), 1559, explaining the reference to "no-folk" in v. 21 as "meaning either a people who are hardly worth mentioning or who are so uncivilized that they do not deserve the name 'people.' The poet may not have had any particular nation in mind, his statement meaning that when the time came God would use even barbarians for His purpose."

76. This is the Rabbinic concept of *middah keneged middah*, meaning that we are repaid by God "measure for measure." Cf., e.g., b. Shabbat 105b; b. Nedarim 32a; b. Sanhedrin 90a; note also a clear biblical example such as Hosea 4:6.

77. See also below, the end of 2.7, for a picture of true Christianity and its relation to the Jewish people.

78. For the Orthodox Jewish persecution of Messianic Jews in Israel today, see 2.7. If someone would say that it seems that whoever is in the majority (or has the political upper hand) does the persecuting, then that would indict *neither* side (i.e., neither

Christian nor traditional Jewish) in and of itself. However, examples could be pointed to (such as America, past and present) that were clearly a "Christian" majority but remained largely tolerant of Jewish expressions of faith, being given to some degree of pluralism and religious freedom; see, however, Leonard Dinnerstein, *Antisemitism in America* (New York: Oxford, 1994); Frank E. Eakin Jr., *What Price Prejudice: Christian Antisemitism in America* (New York: Paulist, 1998). For a more narrowly focused study on a positive side of the story, see David A. Rausch, *Zionism within Early American Fundamentalism, 1878–1918* (New York: Edwin Mellen, 1979); cf. also idem, *Fundamentalist-Evangelicals and Antisemitism* (Valley Forge, Pa.: Trinity, 1993).

79. Note that Rashi and Ramban explain the reference to a "no-folk" in Deuteronomy 32:21 (cited above, and see n. 75) to the Babylonians (literally, Chaldeans).

80. See, e.g., the seriously flawed work of Christian author Gary North, *The Judeo-Christian Tradition* (Tyler, Tex.: Institute for Christian Economics, 1990), esp. 86–88 (or more broadly, 73–130); North's work is generally of a much higher caliber than what is reflected here, and I do not intend here to classify him as an anti-Semite. Cf. also James McKeever, *Claim Your Birthright* (Medford, Ore.: Omega Publications, 1989), 265–79; McKeever's work, too, is generally of a much better quality than that found in the volume cited. Most deplorable of all—and completely devoid of sound scholarship—is Theodore Winston Pike, *Israel: Our Duty . . . Our Dilemma* (Oregon City, Ore.: Big Sky Press, 1984), 20–105, 296–324. For a summary, see Brown, *Our Hands Are Stained with Blood*, 68–69, with references on 199–200 and 235–36.

81. I have made reference to Richard and Sabina Wurmbrand (1.13). Sabina met *and forgave*—with many tears—the Nazi murderer of her family, shortly after he had repented of his sins and received mercy from God through Jesus the Messiah. For a classic example of a godly woman who returned to reach out to the very people who killed her husband, living among them for years and bringing them to faith in Jesus, see Elisabeth Elliot, *Through Gates of Splendor*, rev. ed. (Wheaton: Tyndale, 1986). Elisabeth's husband, Jim Elliot, along with four other missionaries, was killed by the Auca Indians in Ecuador in 1956.

82. D. James Kennedy and Jerry Newcombe, *What If Jesus Had Never Been Born? The Positive Impact of Christianity in History* (Nashville: Thomas Nelson, 1994), 196–97.

83. Ibid., 197.

84. See vol. 3, 5.19.

85. See Kennedy and Newcombe, *What If Jesus Had Never Been Born?*, 209–11 (part of a very honest, self-critical chapter entitled "The Sins of the Church," 205–23).

86. Of course, it is more accurate to say that both the Messianic Jewish and traditional Jewish faiths developed out of the Hebrew Scriptures, and that Christianity and Rabbinic Judaism are thus siblings, which is actually the title of a recent book by Rabbi Hayim Goren Perelmuter, *Siblings: Rabbinic Judaism and Early Christianity at Their Beginnings* (New York: Paulist, 1989). He correctly observes (ibid., 16) that "Both Rabbinic Judaism, the form in which Judaism survived the destruction of State and Temple by the Romans, and Christianity were shaped at approximately the same time." See also Hershel Shanks, ed., *Christianity and Rabbinic Judaism: A Parallel History of the Origins and Early Development* (Washington, D.C.: Biblical Archaeology Society, 1992), and note Ellis Rivkin, "A Jew Looks at the New Testament," in idem, *What Crucified Jesus? Messianism, Pharisaism, and the Development of Christianity* (New York: UAHC Press, 1997), 133–51, who sees Rabbinic Judaism and Christianity as "mutations" (divinely accepted, at that) of the religion of Israel, although still recognizing Judaism

as the mother and Christianity as the daughter (ibid., 3). In any case, for the present, I'll accept at face value the generalization that Christianity arose out of Judaism.

87. See Corrie ten Boom with John and Elizabeth Sherrill, *The Hiding Place* (Old Tappan, N.J.: Chosen, 1977); more broadly, see the excellent summary in Rausch, *Legacy of Hatred*, 147–54.

88. The most dramatic conversion story of which I am aware is that of David Berkowitz, the notorious Son of Sam serial killer, who, along with a group of Satanists, terrorized New York City in 1977. We have documented this gripping account, which displays the amazing mercy and grace of God, in a video entitled "Son of Sam, Son of Hope" (ICN Ministries, 1998).

89. In contrast with this, one can point to Shiite Islam, consistently more violent than the much larger Sunni branch, following in the footsteps of *its* turbulent origins. Thus, the violence that marked the founding of Shiite Islam has been perpetuated through the centuries.

90. This was clearly articulated by Riggans, *Yeshua ben David*, 197: "What Jesus is really saying, then, is that when Jewish people become believers in Jesus they will end as *victims* of aggression. They will *suffer* the violence, not perpetrate it!"

91. To help grasp the significance of this, let's say that so many Hasidic Jews were killed for their faith during a fifty-year span that, over a course of decades, the word for martyr in our language became *hasid*, as in, "Let me tell you how many of our people have been *hasids* for their faith!" That would be an equivalent linguistic phenomenon.

92. For the theological underpinnings behind this, cf. Joseph Ton (Tson), *Suffering, Martyrdom, and Rewards in Heaven* (Lanham, Md.: Univ. Press of America, 1997).

93. Similarly, many Rabbinic (i.e., Pharisaic) Jews were imprisoned, put to death, or tortured by the Romans for refusing to renounce their faith.

94. For heartrending details, see now Cal R. Bombay, *Let My People Go!* (Portland, Ore.: Multnomah, 1998). There is also a powerful video put out by Voice of the Martyrs, "Mission Sudan: Running to Help," with some graphic footage.

95. On October 10, 1996, an anti-Christian mob of twenty attacked the family of an Indonesian Christian named Petrus Kristian, trapping his father, mother, sister, cousin, and a church worker in a house—and then burning them to death. Amazingly, he had this to say shortly after the tragedy: "In my opinion, because we have Jesus it is not difficult to be a Christian although there are many oppressions" (cited in "The Voice of the Martyrs," July 1997, 7). *That* is the spirit of true Christianity.

96. Richard Wurmbrand, *The Overcomers* (Tunbridge Wells: Monarch, 1993), 18–19. This entire book is filled with similar examples of remarkable faith in the midst of persecution for the faith. While such examples are known to many evangelical Christians, I fear the average Jewish reader is unaware of such accounts, perhaps having read only of Jewish heroism in the midst of suffering.

97. It is this church that we previously referred to as "Christendom" in order to distinguish the worldly, political, and sometimes violent expression of Christianity from the real thing.

98. Marcel Simon, *Verus Israel*, trans. H. McKeating (London: The Littman Library of Jewish Civilization, 1996), 226. His entire discussion on 224–33 is important.

99. For the conversion of the Jews in Minorca in 418, see Scott Bradbury, ed. and trans., *Severus of Minorca: Letter on the Conversion of the Jews* (New York: Oxford, 1996).

100. See Schürer et al., *History of the Jewish People*, 1:207, 538; 2:3–6, 10.

101. See Troki, *Faith Strengthened*, 173: "Jesus himself admitted, that his object was not to afford peace; for he says in Matthew x. 34, 'Think not that I am come to send peace on earth, I came not to send peace, but a sword.'"

102. For more thoughts on this, cf. above, 1.9.

103. Dan Cohn-Sherbok, *The Crucified Jew* (Grand Rapids: Eerdmans, 1997), 25. For an interesting perspective on this literature, see Oskar Skarsaune, "The Neglected Story of Philo-Semitism in Antiquity and the Early Middle Ages," *Mishkan* 21 (1994): 40–51.

104. This church saint was so articulate a preacher that, after his death, he was dubbed "Chrysostom," meaning, "Golden Mouth." For a good biography, see J. N. D. Kelly, *Golden Mouth: The Story of John Chrysostom, Ascetic, Preacher, Bishop* (Grand Rapids: Baker, 1998).

105. I have excerpted these writings from the useful summary in Edward H. Flannery, *The Anguish of the Jews: Twenty-Three Centuries of Antisemitism* (New York: Paulist, 1985), 50–52.

106. Cohn-Sherbok, *Crucified Jew*, 28.

107. See Brown, *Our Hands Are Stained with Blood*, 89–97, with references; for an overview of the Crusades, cf. Jonathan Riley-Smith, *A Short History of the Crusades* (New Haven: Yale, 1987), along with the works cited in Brown, 238. As horrifying as these mob actions were, some of them proved quite convenient, since many of the "Christians" were heavily in debt to Jewish moneylenders (one of the few professions open to the Jews at that time), and if these Jews could be killed, the debts could be eliminated. For church opposition to the murderous deeds of the Crusaders, cf. the words of Bernard of Clairvaux, cited in Rausch, *Legacy of Hatred*, 27. Bernard was an advocate of the Crusades but *not* of their violent persecution of the Jews.

108. See again Brown, ibid., 59–63, with references on 195 and 235–36.

109. For references, cf. Brown, ibid., 14–15; see further the works cited immediately below, n. 110, and cf. Heiko A. Oberman, *The Roots of Antisemitism in the Age of Renaissance and Reformation*, trans. James I. Packer (Philadelphia: Fortress, 1981).

110. See Charlotte Klein, *Anti-Judaism in Christian Theology*, trans. Edward Quinn (Philadelphia: Fortress, 1978), 11–13 (amazingly, Grundmann continued to write and teach without interruption after World War II, and his writings—both pre- and post-Holocaust—continued to be used by the scholarly community); see further Robert Kittel, *Theologians under Hitler* (New Haven: Yale, 1985); Alan Rosen, "'Familiarly Known as Kittel': The Moral Politics of the *Theological Dictionary of the New Testament*," in *Tainted Greatness: Antisemitism and Cultural Heroes*, ed. Nancy A. Harrowitz (Philadelphia: Temple Univ. Press, 1994), 37–50; for Martin Buber's response to Kittel's proposal concerning the Jews—which Kittel actually sent to Buber!—see the important collection edited by Frank Ephraim Talmage, *Disputation and Dialogue: Readings in the Jewish-Christian Encounter* (New York: Ktav/Anti-Defamation League of B'Nai Brith, 1975), 49–54, "An Open Letter to Gerhard Kittel," addressed throughout by Buber as "werter Herr Kollege" (worthy colleague). Talmage has introduced this selection with the painful title of "A Reply to a Christian Nazi" (49), words which should send chills down the backs of all truly Christian readers.

111. For an in-depth, appreciative study of Tyndale, see David Daniell, *William Tyndale: A Biography* (New Haven: Yale, 1994).

112. For discussion of this text, see below, 2.7. Interestingly, it was Pelagius, a "non-orthodox" Christian in the fifth century who commented here, "All that follows is designed to prevent the Gentiles from being filled with pride toward the Jews." See

Gerald Bray, ed., *Romans*, Ancient Christian Commentary on Scripture (Downers Grove, Ill.: InterVarsity Press, 1998), 298.

113. In point of fact, throughout its history, Christendom never officially approved converting people by force, something that is, in fact, an accepted—and justified—practice in some expressions of Islam (and cf. above, n. 49). It is also important to remember just how intense *written polemics* can actually be, without any physical violence associated with those words. For an interesting, related perspective, see Miriam S. Taylor, *Anti-Judaism and Early Christian Identity: A Critique of the Scholarly Consensus*, Studia Post-Biblica 46 (Leiden: E. J. Brill, 1995), who argues that it was primarily "symbolic Judaism" that was under attack in the early church literature.

114. Flannery, *Anguish of the Jews*, 46, is circumspect regarding the existence of anti-Semitism in the church in the pre-Constantinian era: "Did antisemitism exist in the Church during the first three centuries? Opinions differ. It is difficult, on our part, to categorize as antisemitic: hostile Christian writings or actions effectively provoked by Jews; theological or apologetical treatises or teachings which expounded an anti-Judaism more or less integral to the dogmas of the Church; or the indignation of pastors gravely worried about the dangers Judaism posed for their often superficially Christianized congregations. . . . The first three centuries served as a warning that theological or pastoral anti-Judaism could take either of two directions: one toward a benign, even benevolent, separation and disagreement . . . or wax to a level of negation and virulence that would erase that line which differentiates it from antisemitism pure and simple." For a sampling of anti-Jewish rhetoric from the second and third centuries (that is, in the period before Constantine), see Rausch, *Legacy of Hatred*, 20–22.

115. For the interfacing of politics and religion in the Constantinian era, cf. Ramsay MacMullen, *Christianizing the Roman Empire (a.d. 100–400)* (New Haven: Yale, 1984).

116. Phillip Schaff, ed., *The Nicene and Post-Nicene Fathers*, First Series, vol. 4 (Albany, Ore.: Sage Software, 1996), 766.

117. Phillip Schaff, ed., *The Nicene and Post-Nicene Fathers*, First Series, vol. 1 (Albany, Ore.: Sage Software, 1996), 33.

118. See further Flannery, *Anguish of the Jews*, 53. Of course, for Augustine, in keeping with the views of other church leaders, the Jews were destined to wander the earth under divine judgment, a continuing proof of their rejection by God.

119. Cited in Simon, *Verus Israel*, 231 (with translation on 512).

120. Ibid.

121. John B. Y. Hood, *Aquinas and the Jews* (Philadelphia: Univ. of Pennsylvania Press, 1995), 107–8. Of course, usury (i.e., lending money with interest) was especially important for Jewish livelihood, since it was sometimes the only major profession allowed Jews in society. For a summary of the *Sicut Judaeis*, cf. ibid., 29–31.

122. Ibid., 111.

123. At the conclusion of a study that must be evaluated with caution, Elaine Pagels, *The Origin of Satan* (New York: Random House, 1995), 184, rightly points out that, "Many Christians . . . from the first century through Francis of Assisi in the fifteenth century and Martin Luther King, Jr., in the twentieth, have believed that they stood on God's side without demonizing their opponents. Their religious vision inspired them to oppose policies and powers they regarded as evil, often risking their well-being and their lives, while praying for the reconciliation—not the damnation—of those who opposed them."

124. Carter Lindberg, "Luther's Attitudes toward Judaism," in Harrowitz, *Tainted Greatness*, 22 (the entire article runs from 15–35).

125. I follow here the convenient and representative sampling cited by Lindberg, ibid., 17–18.

126. For some of the historical background, as well as for some of Luther's other anti-Jewish publications written at the same time, see Graham Keith, *Hated without a Cause? A Survey of Anti-Semitism* (Carlisle: Paternoster, 1997), 149–74; Oberman, *Roots of Antisemitism*. I should note, of course, that the situation of the Jews in much of Europe was hardly better than that outlined in Luther's measures. Also, his coarse and base descriptions of the Jews as a people paralleled his descriptions of papal leaders (and really, all of his other opponents!), whom he also vilified in the crudest of terms. For an English translation of the basest of Luther's anti-Jewish writings, *Vom Schem Hamphoras*, most of which is spent refuting perceived Jewish beliefs against Christianity, see Gerhard Falk, *The Jew in Christian Theology* (Jefferson, N.C.: McFarland, 1992). Note also that Luther, like some other Christian leaders in history, was concerned about Jewish influence on Christianity (in Luther's case, the influence of Jewish interpretation of the Bible infiltrating the church, as if this would have been some grave danger), also explaining why he attacked and denigrated the Jewish faith in such harsh terms. It was to "protect" the Christians! For the argument that Luther's last (and harshest) anti-Jewish writings were the product of old age and disease, see John Warwick Montgomery, "Luther, Anti-Semitism, and Zionism," in *Christianity Today* (8 September 1978), 79–80.

127. *Tainted Greatness.*

128. Cf. Lindberg, "Luther's Attitudes," for further details.

129. Cited in ibid., 25.

130. Because of this, it has been debated whether Luther's works actually influenced Hitler at all. Rather, they may have simply provided him with another foil for his madness. Cf. again ibid., 25, with references.

131. Cf. this statement made in 1984 by the World Lutheran Federation: "We cannot accept or condone the violent verbal attacks that the Reformer made against the Jews. The sins of Luther's anti-Jewish remarks and the violence of his attacks on the Jews must be acknowledged with deep distress, and all occasion for similar sin in the present or the future must be removed from our churches. . . . Lutherans of today refuse to be bound by all of Luther's utterances against the Jews." See *Our Hands Are Stained with Blood*, 180–81, n. 20, for further details.

132. As mentioned above, however, some prominent German Lutheran theologians were Nazis, reflecting the fact that they followed Luther's anti-Jewish writings in contrast with other Lutheran theologians in other countries.

133. David H. C. Read, "Reflections of an Imported Wasp," in *Removing Anti-Judaism from the Pulpit*, ed. Howard Clark Kee and Irvin J. Borowsky (Philadelphia: American Interfaith Institute, 1996), 62–63 (the entire article runs from 60–66).

134. For a study of the historicity and accuracy of the Gospels, which, traditionally, have come under the greatest attack and scrutiny, cf. Craig L. Blomberg, *The Historical Reliability of the Gospels* (Downers Grove, Ill.: InterVarsity Press, 1987).

135. The account of Josephus, confirmed by early church records as well, is accepted by most historians today. For references, see below, n. 276. Interestingly, James was so highly esteemed and his killing so outrageous to many Jews, that the early church leader Hegesippus claimed that the destruction of Jerusalem in 70 C.E. occurred not

as a punishment for the crucifixion of Jesus—a view commonly held in the early church—but because of the killing of James! See Simon, *Verus Israel,* 67–68.

136. See above, 1.4, n. 9. According to William Horbury, *Jews and Christians: In Contact and Controversy* (Edinburgh: T & T Clark, 1998), 110, the *birkat haminnim* "was not decisive on its own in the separation of church and synagogue, but it gave solemn liturgical expression to a separation effected in the second half of the first century through the larger group of measures to which it belongs." For a contemporary perspective on this malediction, cf. the comments of the Artscroll Siddur, cited by Weinberger, *Jewish Outreach,* 149, n. 2: "Chronologically this is the 19th blessing of Shmone Esrei; it was instituted in Yavneh during the tenure of R. Gamliel II as Nasi of Israel, some time after the destruction of the second Temple. The blessing was composed in response to the threats of such heretical Jewish sects as the Sadducees, Boethusians, Essenes, and the early Christians. They tried to lead Jews astray through example and persuasion and they used their political power to oppress observant Jews and to slander them to the anti-Semitic Roman government. In this atmosphere R. Gamliel felt the need for a prayer against the heretics and slanderers and to incorporate it into the Shmone Esrei to make the populace aware of the danger. Despite the disappearance from within Israel of the particular sects against whom it was directed it is always relevant because there are still non-believers and heretics who endanger the spiritual community of Israel."

137. Simon, *Verus Israel,* 66–67. Of course, these first Jewish believers would hardly have seen themselves as "professing Christianity," as if it were some novel, new religion. Rather, they saw themselves as simply embracing the Messianic faith long anticipated by their forefathers. In this regard, the observation of Scot McKnight, "A Loyal Critic: Matthew's Polemic with Judaism in Theological Perspective," in *Anti-Semitism and Early Christianity,* ed. Craig A. Evans and Donald A. Hagner (Minneapolis: Fortress, 1993), 55–79 (here 57, n. 5), is quite relevant: "The early Jewish Christians, it seems to me, thought of themselves as true Jews and saw nonmessianic Jews as false Jews. But these early Jewish Christians saw themselves, then, as *for Judaism* (defined messianically). Thus, they were 'anti-nonmessianic Judaism' or 'anti-disobedient Judaism' but not simply 'anti-Judaism' (which kind?)," with reference also to L. T. Johnson, "The New Testament's Anti-Jewish Slander and the Conventions of Ancient Polemic," *Journal of Biblical Literature* 108 (1989): 419–41 (specifically 423–30). I have added the emphasis in the quote from McKnight, which deserves serious scholarly consideration and stands in stark contrast to the inaccurate and emotionally charged statements in Moshe, *Judaism's Truth,* 3: "Hand in hand with the determined destruction of Judaism, which is rooted in the New Testament, is found a hatred of Jews. . . . Paul shaped the Church in a manner which stripped away all links to Judaism and cursed it at the same time. The New Testament says Judaism is bad and abandoned by God, while Christianity is good and beloved." Joseph Klausner gives us a more accurate picture here, noting that while Paul opposed a certain form of Judaism, "he considered his teaching as true Judaism, as the fulfillment of the promises and assurances of authentic Judaism" (*From Jesus to Paul,* trans. William F. Stinespring [New York: Macmillian, 1943], 591, cited in Evans and Hagner, ibid., 129, n. 2, along with other important references).

138. The evaluation of James Parkes in his important, ground-breaking study, *The Conflict of the Church and the Synagogue: A Study in the Origins of Antisemitism* (New York: Atheneum, 1985), 121–50, virtually exculpating the Jews from any involvement in the martyrdom of Christians, has been judged by some scholars to be an example of

overly pro-Jewish scholarship, hence biased in the other direction. The evaluation of Flannery, *Anguish of the Jews*, is more accurate. For an important study on Parkes and his work, see Robert Andrew Everett, *Christianity without Antisemitism: James Parkes and the Jewish Christian Encounter*, Studies in Antisemitism (New York: Oxford, 1993).

139. See further Claudia J. Setzer, *Jewish Responses to Early Christians: History and Polemics, 30–150 C.E.* (Minneapolis: Augsburg-Fortress, 1994); and Stephen G. Wilson, *Related Strangers: Jews and Christians 70–170 C.E.* (Minneapolis: Fortress, 1995), especially 169–94, for evaluation of the evidence. Note also, Horbury, *Jews and Christians*, with special attention to early Jewish-Christian literature.

140. Flannery, *Anguish of the Jews*, 36. For discussion of the atrocities apparently committed by Bar Kochba, cf. above, n. 67.

141. For the background to *Toledot Yeshu*, see above, 1.8, n. 22; for its use and abuse by anti-Semites, cf. the works cited above, n. 80. The earliest recorded charges of bastardom with regard to Jesus can be dated to the second century, on the lips of Celsus (as related in Origen's *Contra Celsum*).

142. This notice was sent out by the staunchly Zionistic International Christian Embassy in Jerusalem, Saturday, 28 November 1998. The number of "demonstrators" reported varies between five hundred to one thousand ultra-Orthodox Jews, including the local chief rabbi, Yehuda Deri, who unashamedly called for the action on a Friday radio broadcast—the same day of the week, it has been observed, that Muslim radio preachers call for violent actions against Jews!—subsequently asking the police to help shut down the activities of the Messianic Jews. See "Maoz Israel," January 1999 (this is the newsletter of Ari and Shira Sorko-Ram).

143. Cited in the *Jerusalem Post*, as reported by Bradley Antolovich, "News Report from Jerusalem" (e-mail), 2 December 1998. A further quote from Adrian carried by the *Jerusalem Post* (4 December 1998) read, "This wasn't a demonstration; this was a mob." They had gathered because a bogus rumor was spread that the Messianic Jews were bringing two busloads of Jewish children and infants to be baptized that day. Of course, there were *no* busloads, nor did the congregation practice the baptism of children or infants!

144. Brown, *Our Hands Are Stained with Blood*, 21.

145. Ibid., 20.

146. Ibid.

147. Cited in Bray, *Romans*, 299. In light of this understanding, Ambrosiaster, who may have had a strong influence on Augustine, wrote (with reference to Romans 11:31), "Paul recalls the unbelief of the Gentiles so that being ashamed of it they may not insult the Jews who have not believed but rejoice when they accept the promise of God." Cited in ibid., 300.

148. Cited in ibid., 298–99.

149. Cited in Brown, *Our Hands Are Stained with Blood*, 25.

150. Ibid., 23.

151. In truth, I could expand on this theme for hours, since my book *Our Hands Are Stained with Blood* has been translated into numerous languages, including Korean, Japanese, Finnish, Swedish, Norwegian, Dutch, Russian, Romanian, Hungarian, Italian, and German, as a result of which, we have received feedback from Christian readers around the world who were absolutely horrified to hear of something called "Christian" anti-Semitism. In all their years in the church, they had never met a Christian who hated or despised or mistreated a Jew! Rather, what we would normally hear from our readers is that as soon as they became "born-again" through faith in Jesus, they

felt a special love for the Jewish people. Note also the reference to "nearly four thousand letters" received by David Rausch from a period from 1984, when the first edition of his *Legacy of Hatred* was published, until 1990, when the second edition was published (preface, ix).

152. For a brief, interesting survey, see Timothy P. Weber, "How Evangelicals Became Israel's Best Friend," *Christianity Today* (5 October 1998), 39–49, and cf. also Rausch, *Zionism within Early American Fundamentalism* (New York: Edwin Mellen Press, 1979).

153. These were the words of Pieter Miedema, quoted in André Stein, *Quiet Heroes: True Stories of the Rescue of Jews by Christians in Nazi-Occupied Holland* (New York: New York Univ. Press, 1988), 93.

154. See Rausch, *Legacy of Hatred*, 148, 153, for further details and bibliographic references. Henri de Lubac, *Christian Resistance to Anti-Semitism: Memories from 1904–1944*, trans. Elizabeth Englund (San Francisco: Ignatius Press, 1990), 15, makes reference to an outspoken, French Catholic leader, who, "heedless of the abuse that poured in on him," continued to speak out on behalf of the Jews. His reason? In substance, it was this: "I defend Israel because Jesus was the descendant of David. I defend Israel because I am a Christian; as a Christian, I have the duty to come to its aid."

155. Peter Schäfer, *Judeophobia: Attitudes toward the Jews in the Ancient World* (Cambridge: Harvard Univ. Press, 1997), 11.

156. See Samuel Sandmel, *Anti-Semitism in the New Testament?* (Philadelphia: Fortress, 1978), 1. For Sandmel's clear distinctions between "pagan anti-Semitism" and "Christian anti-Semitism," cf. ibid., 5.

157. For the diabolical forces behind anti-Semitism, cf. Brown, *Our Hands Are Stained with Blood*, 155–64.

158. Cf. Sydney Jellicoe, *The Septuagint and Modern Study* (Oxford: Clarendon, 1968), 29–171, for discussion of the mythical and real origins of the Septuagint.

159. See McKnight, *A Light among the Gentiles*.

160. For detailed discussion, see Walter C. Kaiser Jr., *The Uses of the Old Testament in the New* (Chicago: Moody, 1985), 2–4. He notes that the United Bible Society's Greek New Testament text "lists over 2,500 NT passages from nearly 1,800 OT passages," while Henry M. Shirer, in his 1974 study (*Finding the Old Testament in the New*, Westminster), found a total of "1,604 NT citations of 1,276 different OT texts," including 239 direct quotes "drawn from 185 different OT passages." And this is all the more extraordinary when one realizes that the entire New Testament contains less than 8,000 verses! See further Gleason L. Archer and Gregory Chirichgno, *Old Testament Quotations in the New Testament* (Chicago: Moody, 1983), for a verse-by-verse analysis in Hebrew and Greek; and cf. G. K. Beale, ed., *The Right Doctrine from the Wrong Texts? Essays on the Use of the Old Testament in the New* (Grand Rapids: Baker, 1994). Interestingly, the Book of Revelation, the last book of the New Testament, contains 404 verses, more than half of which (approximately 278 verses) are drawn from the imagery of the Hebrew Scriptures, although Revelation does not directly quote one verse from the Tanakh. More broadly, cf. Steven Thompson, *The Apocalypse and Semitic Syntax*, SNTSMS 52 (Cambridge: Cambridge Univ. Press, 1985).

161. The only other figure called Rabbi is John the Immerser (John 3:26).

162. The popular Christian author Philip Yancey recently noted that such a genealogy would be the equivalent of calling someone in America today "the son of Abraham Lincoln, the son of George Washington." That's about as American as you can get! In

the same way, there could be nothing more Jewish than identifying someone as "son of David, son of Abraham," a fact that struck Yancey in a fresh new way as he worked on his best-selling book, *The Jesus I Never Knew* (Grand Rapids: Zondervan, 1995).

163. See Gartenhaus, *Famous Hebrew Christians*, 124.

164. Ibid.

165. Ibid., 125. Note also the description of Rivkin, *What Crucified the Messiah?*, 107, as to what someone finds upon opening the New Testament: "One is struck by the framework of Judaism that encloses all that is recorded in the Synoptic Gospels, Acts, and the Epistles of Paul. There is scarcely a page that does not have some proof-text drawn from the Old Testament: Abraham, Moses, David, and Elijah are the spiritual heroes; Jesus is a Jewish teacher who frequents the synagogue, visits the Temple, refutes the Sadducees, parries the Pharisees, evokes Scriptures, and ends his life on the cross under a *titulus* bearing the inscription Jesus, King of the Jews. Like Jesus, all his disciples are Jews because he seemed to be to them the Son of man, the Messiah, the scion of David, preaching the gospel of God's kingdom to the people of God. Paul, the most gifted preacher of the risen Christ, had been as to the Law a Pharisee, as to righteousness under the Law blameless."

166. Some of the top Israeli scholars are involved in the Jerusalem School of Synoptic Research, and their conclusions regarding the Jewishness of the Gospels are often even more positive than mine! For a major collection of essays by one of the Jerusalem School's Jewish leaders, see David Flusser, *Judaism and the Origins of Christianity* (Jerusalem: Magnes, 1988); see also idem, *Jesus* (Winona Lake, Ind.: Eisenbraun, 1997).

167. Cf. the statement of Moshe, cited above, n. 137; in contrast with this, the eminent historian Marcel Simon noted that, "There is no shadow of anti-Semitism in St. Paul. He was disappointed in his countrymen but incapable of hating them." See *Verus Israel*, 207. Simon's comment is especially noteworthy in light of his beliefs that "anti-Jewish feeling" can be found in John's Gospel (ibid.).

168. For the citation from Isaiah 59 at the end of Romans 11, see vol. 3, 5.1.

169. Recent works, some of which espouse extremely controversial theories (e.g., Maccoby), include Rosemary Radford Reuther, *Faith and Fratricide: The Theological Roots of Anti-Semitism* (New York: Seabury, 1974); Sandmel, *Anti-Semitism in the New Testament?*; A. T. Davies, ed., *Anti-Semitism and the Foundation of Christianity* (New York: Paulist, 1979); Hyam Maccoby, *Judas Iscariot and the Myth of Jewish Evil* (New York: Free Press, 1992); George M. Smiga, *Pain and Polemic: Anti-Judaism in the Gospels* (New York: Paulist, 1992); Sidney G. Hall III, *Christian Anti-Semitism and Paul's Theology* (Minneapolis: Fortress, 1993); Norman Beck, *Mature Christianity: The Recognition and Repudiation of the Anti-Jewish Polemic of the New Testament*, expanded and rev. ed. (New York: Crossroad; World Alliance/The American Interfaith Institute, 1994); Lillian C. Freudman, *Antisemitism in the New Testament* (Lanham, Md.: Univ. Press of America, 1994); John Dominic Crossan, *Who Killed Jesus? Exposing the Roots of Anti-Semitism in the Gospel Story of the Death of Jesus* (San Francisco: HarperSanFrancisco, 1995); Pagels, *Origin of Satan*. On the broader subject of Christianity and anti-Semitism, which has fostered an enormous amount of literature, some of the key works in English include: Jules Isaac, *The Teaching of Contempt: Christian Roots of Anti-Semitism*, trans. Dorothy and James Parkes (New York: Holt, Rinehart and Winston, 1964); idem, *Jesus and Israel*, trans. Sally Gran (New York: Holt, Rinehart and Winston, 1971); Malcolm Hay, *The Roots of Christian Anti-Semitism* (New York: Liberty Press, 1981), also published under the titles *The Foot of Pride* and *Europe and the*

Jews; Frank E. Manuel, *The Broken Staff: Judaism through Christian Eyes* (Cambridge: Harvard Univ. Press, 1992); William Nichols, *Christian Antisemitism: A History of Hate* (Northvale, N.J.: Aronson, 1993); Frederick Gladstone Bratton, *The Crime of Christendom: The Theological Sources of Anti-Semitism* (Santa Barbara: Fithian Press, 1994); see further Peter Richardson and David Granskou, eds., *Anti-Judaism in Early Christianity,* vol. 1 (Waterloo, Ontario: Wilfred Laurier Press, 1986); Stephen G. Wilson, ed., *Anti-Judaism in Early Christianity,* vol. 2 (Waterloo, Ontario: Wilfred Laurier Press, 1986); Clark M. Williamson and Ronald J. Allen, *Interpreting Difficult Texts: Anti-Judaism and Christian Preaching* (Philadelphia: Trinity, 1989); note also the previously cited works of Parkes, *Conflict of the Church and Synagogue;* Simon, *Verus Israel;* Flannery, *Anguish of the Jews;* Falk, *The Jew in Christian Theology;* Rausch, *Legacy of Hatred;* Cohn-Sherbok, *Crucified Jew;* Klein, *Anti-Judaism;* Keith, *Hated without a Cause?,* On the more general subject of Christian responses to the Holocaust, see Steven L. Jacobs, ed., *Contemporary Christian Religious Reponses to the Shoa,* Studies in the Shoa (Lanham, Md.: Univ. Press of America, 1993); note also Jacob Jocz, *The Jewish People and Jesus Christ after Auschwitz: A Study in the Controversy between Church and Synagogue* (Grand Rapids: Baker, 1981). The bibliography in Taylor, *Anti-Judaism,* should also be consulted.

170. According to Graham Keith, Jules Isaac, the Jewish historian who lost most of his family in the Holocaust, "insisted that the Christian church was primarily responsible for the anti-Semitic legacy on which Nazis capitalized. But he did so without impugning the New Testament itself. Instead, he claimed the church had misunderstood its own Scriptures and its own founder." See Keith, *Hated without a Cause?,* 34, with reference to Isaac's two important works, *Jesus and Israel* and *The Teaching of Contempt.*

171. Along with the references cited in the following notes, see the listing of works in Brown, *Our Hands Are Stained with Blood,* 230–31. Cf. also L. H. Feldman, "Is the New Testament Anti-Semitic?" *Humanities* 21 (1987): 1–14.

172. Cited in R. E. Brown, *The Death of the Messiah,* 1:831, n. 22, with reference to Montefiore's work, *The Synoptic Gospels,* 2:346.

173. Brown, *The Death of the Messiah,* 1:391–97; for Crossan's arguments with this, see *Who Killed Jesus?,* although Brown's work seems to treat the evidence much more evenhandedly.

174. Ibid., 838–39.

175. Cf. Lachs, *Rabbinic Commentary,* 428, with reference on 429, n. 13, to b. Avodah Zarah 12b; b. Yoma 21a; Sifra 24.14; b. Avodah Zarah 30a; Pirkei d'Rabbi Eliezer 10; y. Berakhoth 7:6, 11c [61]; b. Pesahim 111a; b. Megillah 17a.

176. Cf. also the words of the Jewish leadership in Acts 5:28, addressing the Jewish followers of Jesus: "Yet you have filled Jerusalem with your teaching and are determined to make us guilty of this man's blood." Note also the repeating of Matthew 27:24–25 in the apocryphal Acts of Pilate (IV:1, then again in IX:4, then once more in XII.1); see also Tertullian, *Ante-Nicene Fathers,* vol. 3, 580 (Five Books against Marcion, book 2, chapter 16); Hyppolytus (Sage, vol. 5, briefly); Augustine (Sage, commenting on Pss.); Cyril (Sage).

177. Cf. Brown, *Death of the Messiah,* 2:839.

178. See McKnight in Evans and Hagner, *Anti-Semitism and Early Christianity,* 76, n. 79. According to McKnight, who is terribly anguished over anti-Semitism in Christian history and who believes that anti-Semitism in any form is actually "an enemy of Christianity" (ibid., 79, quoting A. T. Davies, *Anti-Semitism and the Christian Mind:*

The Crisis of Conscience after Auschwitz [New York: Herder, 1968], 33), Matthew "needs no apology, for he is not anti-Semitic. He is no more anti-Semitic than Amos or Jeremiah. Those who have read Matthew so, I believe, have surely misread him. . . . But having said this, I maintain that the only apology that needs to be made is 'the deeper form of apology that every Christian owes to every Jew for the part which historic Christendom has played in the shaping of modern anti-semitism'" (ibid., 78, again quoting Davies, ibid., 18).

179. Rabbi Eliyahu Touger, trans., *Maimonides Mishneh Torah: Hilchot Melachim U'Milchamoteihem (Laws of Kings and Their Wars)* (New York: Maznaim, 1987), 234–35.

180. Ibid., 235–36.

181. For a dated, although still valuable discussion of this text (along with other related material from the Rabbinic texts), see R. Travis Herford, *Christianity in Talmud and Midrash* (London: Williams & Northgate, 1903).

182. To my knowledge, the first church leader on record to misuse this verse was Origen in the second century. This shows how early the verse was being misappropriated, also underscoring how shocking it was for Christians to think that key Jewish leaders, along with a crowd of Jewish people, handed their Messiah over to be crucified. For a clear and concise study of Matthew 27:25 by a Messianic Jew, see Michael Rydelnik, "His Blood Be Upon Us," *Mishkan* 6, no. 7 (1987): 1–9, who concludes that "only on the surface does Matthew 27:25 present a problem. When properly understood as a local acceptance of guilt and viewed from the perspectives of Matthew, the crowd and the early church, it is impossible to prove a deicide charge against the Jews from this text."

183. Some would also point to verses such as John 10:34, where Jesus speaking to "the Jews" says, "Is it not written in *your* Law, 'I have said you are gods'?" as if he was saying, "This is your Law, not mine!" However, such an understanding of this text is completely untenable for the following reasons: (1) Elsewhere in John, Jesus insisted that it was *the whole Bible* in general, and *the law of Moses* in particular, that bore witness to him: "You diligently study the Scriptures because you think that by them you possess eternal life. These are the Scriptures that testify about me, yet you refuse to come to me to have life. . . . But do not think I will accuse you before the Father. Your accuser is Moses, on whom your hopes are set. If you believed Moses, you would believe me, for he wrote about me. But since you do not believe what he wrote, how are you going to believe what I say?" (John 5:39–40, 45–47; see also John 8:32, where *continuing in God's Word*—meaning the Hebrew Bible!—is the prerequisite for being a true disciple). (2) When dialoging with Jewish leaders, Jesus alluded to Moses as part of their shared heritage; see, e.g., John 3:14–16; 7:19–23. (3) Jesus' own disciples are credited with seeing him as the fulfillment of Moses and the prophets: "We have found the one Moses wrote about in the Law, and about whom the prophets also wrote—Jesus of Nazareth, the son of Joseph" (John 1:45). (4) The verse from "the law" cited by Jesus in John 10:34 is actually from Psalms (82:6), indicating that Jesus used "the law" (i.e., "Torah") in the broader sense of the Scriptures as a whole, something that was quite common in Jewish usage. Certainly no one would argue that Jesus was rejecting *the Psalms* as something foreign and alien! Rather, what he was saying here would be the equivalent of one Christian minister saying to another hypocritical minister, "Look at what is written in *your own New Testament.* You're not even living by your own book!"

184. Philip S. Kaufman, *The Beloved Disciple* (Collegeville, Minn.: Liturgical Press, 1991), 12. For a similar observation regarding John's narrative of the death of Jesus, cf. Urban C. von Wahlde, "The Gospel of John and the Presentation of Jews and Judaism," in *Within Context: Essays on Jews and Judaism in the New Testament*, ed.

David Efroymson, Eugene J. Fischer, and Leon Klenicki (Collegeville, Minn.: Liturgical Press, 1993), 81. Note that this interfaith collection of essays is foreworded by two noted Jewish leaders, Irvin J. Borowsky, founder and chairman of the American Interfaith Institute, and Rabbi Leon Klenicki, director of the Department of Interfaith Affairs, Anti-Defamation League of B'nai B'rith. The question of alleged anti-Semitic bias in the trial of Jesus will be discussed in vol. 3, 5.20.

185. In other contexts (such as 2 Kings 16:6), such usage is typical, as reflected in English translations that render with "men of Judah" (so the KJV and NIV) or "Judeans" (so the NRSV) rather than "Jews." For striking examples, see also Jeremiah 32:12, where Jeremiah, Baruch, and Hanamel—all "Jews"!—are distinguished from "the Judeans"; Jeremiah 38:18, where the Jewish king Zedekiah tells Jeremiah, "I am afraid of the Judeans who have deserted to the Chaldeans . . ." (wrongly rendered in the NIV here with "the Jews"); similarly, cf. Jer. 40:11–15; 41:3; 1 Chron. 4:27.

186. See Dr. David G. Burke, "How the Contemporary English Edition Avoids Anti-Judaism," *Explorations* 12, no. 2 (1998): 8. He points out that "where the Greek text reports that 'the Jews' plotted against Jesus, there would be no one among the original audiences who would have assumed that all Jews (whether in Jerusalem, Judea, or anywhere) were involved in some sort of monolithic conspiracy, but they would have understood this to indicate that certain leaders did oppose Jesus and the movement that formed around him" (ibid.).

187. Cf. also John 7:13, "where people who are Jewish by nationality are said not to talk openly about Jesus 'for fear of the Jews.'" See von Wahlde, "The Gospel of John and the Presentation of Jews and Judaism," 74.

188. Ibid., 81.

189. Cf. ibid., 80 (with references also to the Testament of Levi); cf. Lawrence H. Schiffman, *Reclaiming the Dead Sea Scrolls* (Philadelphia: Jewish Publication Society, 1994), 249–52. It should also be emphasized that, according to the New Testament, *all people who reject Jesus,* whether Jew or Gentile, are understood to be under the dominion of Satan and in the kingdom of darkness; see, e.g., 2 Cor. 4:6; Eph. 2:1–2; Col. 1:13; 1 John 5:19.

190. Ibid., 82. Interestingly, in context, John 8:44 ("You are of your father the devil") is not addressed to Jews in general (as is sometimes alleged), but actually to those Jews who believed (see John 8:31–32), although only to a point (see John 8:33ff.).

191. *Anti-Semitism and Early Christianity,* 8.

192. Ibid., with reference to Johnson, "The New Testament's Anti-Jewish Slander and the Conventions of Ancient Polemic," 419–41. Remember also that Josephus wrote for both Roman readers and Jewish readers, and therefore, the argument cannot be raised that he was a Jew writing only to Jews about Jewish matters. Rather, both Josephus and John wrote for both a Jewish and Gentile audience, the main difference being that John wrote first and foremost to believers in the Messiah, be they Jew or Gentile.

193. Rivkin, "Anti-Semitism in the New Testament," in *What Crucified Jesus?,* 124 (see in full, 107–29), his emphasis; for the references to Josephus, see Johnson, "Anti-Jewish Slander," 434–36. Rivkin, ibid., 108, also notes tellingly that if we disregard how the New Testament texts were used later for anti-Semitic purposes, "one would conclude that we have here a record of bitter religious controversy, exarcerbated by the fact that the individual around whom the controversies centered had been subjected to a painful death, and from which, according to his disciples, he had been resurrected. The parties to the controversy are at one another's throats over issues that would make sense only to those who were members of a community that shared the

same basic ideas, concepts, and assumptions. God, revelation, Israel, prophetic visions, Messiah, resurrection—concepts so charged with sanctity and so fraught with life and death—could mean nothing to one who had not been nurtured in Judaism or one who had not been taught its doctrines. . . . Now it is true that some very harsh acts are reported, some very harsh words are blurted out, and some very harsh feelings are expressed. But, the historian must ask, how could it have been otherwise?"

194. See b. Sotah 22b (with parallels in y. Berakhoth 67a); m. Sotah 3:4 (the Hebrew here literally speaks of the "smitings of the Pharisees").

195. Cf. the literature cited above, n. 63, with the assessment in James D. G. Dunn, *Jesus, Paul and the Law: Studies in Mark and Galatians* (Louisville: John Knox/Westminster, 1990), 61–88, and note the ongoing and sometimes intense debate between Jacob Neusner and E. P. Sanders regarding the Pharisees and the development of Jewish law; among the myriad works of Neusner, cf. most pointedly, *Judaic Law from Jesus to the Mishnah: A Systematic Reply to Professor E. P. Sanders*, South Florida Studies in the History of Judaism 84 (Atlanta: Scholars Press, 1994); for Sanders's most forceful statement, see *Jewish Law from Jesus to the Mishnah: Five Studies* (Philadelphia: Trinity, 1990), 309–31.

196. For the period in question, cf. the reference to Schürer et al., *History of the Jewish People*, above, n. 40.

197. I remind you of the religious Jewish persecution of Messianic Jews in our day, as discussed in 2.7, immediately above. See further Rivkin, "Anti-Semitism in the New Testament," 117–21, for insightful remarks on why and how the Jewish religious leaders, the Jewish crowds, the Jewish disciples of the Messiah, and Pontius Pilate all did what they did. (To the extent that Rivkin accepts the Gospel narratives as factual, I find myself in fundamental agreement with his observations.) For an interesting study of the potential threat that prophetic religion presents to traditional religion (here = Pharisaical/Rabbinic authority), see Frederick E. Greenspahn, "Why Prophecy Ceased," *Journal of Biblical Literature* 108 (1989): 37–49 ("By rejecting the holy spirit's presence, the rabbis, whose own legitimacy rested on the interpretation of previous revelation, protected themselves from those claiming a more direct link to the divine while undermining the theological basis for such figures' anti-establishment activities," ibid., 49). According to Greenspahn, this was the only way Judaism could have survived, and he finds parallel reactions against prophetism in both Christianity and Islam.

198. For more on this, along with the general question of the Jewishness of Jesus, see vol. 2, 3.25–3.26 and vol. 3, 5.19, 5.21, 5.28; cf. also James H. Charlesworth and Loren L. Johns, eds., *Hillel and Jesus: Comparative Studies of Two Major Religious Leaders* (Minneapolis: Fortress, 1997).

199. Ibid., 17. Most of the polemic in the epistles is against the "Judaizers"—i.e., against Jewish believers in Jesus who were requiring *Gentile believers* to be circumcised and keep the entire law.

200. E.g., Young, *Paul the Jewish Theologian;* Peter Tomson, *Paul and the Jewish Law: Halakha in the Letters of the Apostle to the Gentiles* (Assen/Minneapolis: Van Gorcum/Fortress, 1990). See vol. 3, 5.26, 5.29 for extensive references.

201. Dunn, *Jesus, Paul and the Law,* 71.

202. See Phillip Sigal, *The Halakha of Jesus of Nazareth according to the Gospel of Matthew* (Lanham, Md.: Univ. Press of America, 1986).

203. Cf. Hagner, "Paul's Quarrel with Judaism," in Evans and idem, *Anti-Semitism and Early Christianity,* 128–50 (specifically 130–36).

204. Note that Paul's own people were willing to hear him out until he stated that God had called him to go to the Gentiles. *This* they couldn't handle. See Acts 22:1–22.

205. See Acts 14:8–19; in Israel, anti-missionary groups such as Yad L'Achim (or now, Lev L'Achim) have sometimes followed Messianic Jews from city to city, seeking to harass them and hinder their work. Although it is unpleasant to report such things, they are, nonetheless, true. Of course, these anti-missionaries are often men who feel deeply that Messianic Jews who seek to win other Jews to their faith are worse than Hitler, "since," they say, "he only wanted to kill our bodies, but you want to kill our souls!" With this kind of thinking, it's easy to understand why they get so upset!

206. According to Hagner, "Paul is righteously indignant concerning Israel's opposition to the plan and purposes of God," and, following I. Broer, Hagner believes that "it is probable that Paul's words quite consciously reflect a Deuteronomistic-type judgment oracle against the Jews in general" (*Anti-Semitism and Early Christianity*, 134).

207. If this is the case, then it is proper to speak of the "anti-Semitic comma" found here in most translations after the word "Jews" (or "Judeans"), as cited above in the NIV: "You suffered from your own countrymen the same things those congregations suffered from the Jews, who killed the Lord Jesus and the prophets . . ." (1 Thess. 2:14–15). If this comma is removed (which, of course, was not part of the original Greek), the text then makes a clear and direct reference to one specific group of people, namely, the Judeans, with a history of hostility toward God and his prophets. Cf. G. E. Okeke, "1 Thessalonians 2:13–16: The Fate of the Unbelieving Jews," *New Testament Studies* 27 (1980–81): 127–36.

208. As expressed concisely by Matthew Henry, *Matthew Henry's Commentary on the Bible* (Peabody, Mass.: Hendrickson, 1991). According to I. H. Marshall, *1 and 2 Thessalonians*, New Century Bible (Grand Rapids: Eerdmans, 1983), 81, possible meanings include: (1) "at long last" or "finally"; (2) "completely," "to the uttermost"; (3) "for ever," "to the end," i.e., "lasting for ever"; and (4) "until the end" qualifying "wrath," i.e., "the wrath that leads up to the End."

209. For a comprehensive discussion of these issues, see vol. 2, 3.1–3.4.

210. Even in the parable of the vineyard taught by Jesus, in which he compared himself to the vineyard owner's son, as opposed to simply one of his servants, he was not overtly identifying himself with God (the vineyard owner in the parable) but only with his son, worthy of better treatment than the prophets (the servants in the parable). See, e.g., Matt. 21:33–46.

211. In the preceding verses quoted (viz., Acts 2:22–23), Peter explains clearly what his people had done: with the help of wicked men (the Romans, in this case), they nailed the Messiah to the cross. Thus, he says, "you crucified him," similar to Nathan's rebuke of David in 2 Samuel 12. David had Uriah killed in battle, but Nathan said to him: "*You struck down* Uriah the Hittite with the sword" (2 Sam. 12:9).

212. A useful compendium of short studies can be found in *Mishkan* 21 (1994): Walter C. Kaiser Jr., "An Assessment of Replacement Theology," 9–20; Ray Pritz, "Replacing the Jews in Early Christian Theology," 21–27; Ole Anderson, Menachem Benhayim, Tuvya Zaretsky, Albrecht Haefner, Kenichi Nakagawa, "Replacement Theology—Anti-Replacement Theology (Five Statements)," 28–39. See also Jeffrey Siker, *Disinheriting the Jews* (Louisville: John Knox/Westminster, 1991).

213. For further discussion, see C. K. Barrett, *The Acts of the Apostles*, International Critical Commentary, vol. 1 (Edinburgh: T & T Clark, 1994), 75–77.

214. In Matthew 21:43, when Jesus said, "Therefore I tell you that the kingdom of God will be taken away from you and given to a people who will produce its fruit," he

was *not* saying that Gentiles would take the place of Jews in God's kingdom. Rather, he was saying that the current Jewish leadership, marked by hypocrisy, would be replaced by faithful people (in the first place, referring to his own emissaries, and then to those who received their message). Matthew makes this perfectly plain: "When the chief priests and the Pharisees heard Jesus' parables, they knew he was talking about them. They looked for a way to arrest him, but they were afraid of the crowd [meaning the Jewish crowd!] because the people [meaning the Jewish people!] held that he was a prophet" (Matt. 21:45–46).

215. See esp. 127–41, and cf. the references to further literature cited above, n. 211.

216. Ibid., 129–30.

217. Ibid., 131.

218. See also Shulam and Le Cornu, *Jewish Roots of Romans*, 101–13.

219. See the lengthy and carefully nuanced selections from Marcel Simon, below, n. 224, which can be contrasted with the more negative verdict of Jules Isaac, viz., that "Christian anti-Semitism is the powerful, millenary, and strongly rooted trunk upon which (in the Christian world) all other varieties of anti-Semitism are grafted, even those of a most anti-Christian nature" (cited in Talmage, *Disputation and Dialogue*, 49).

220. To the best of my memory, I encountered only one such person, but he was so unstable and his beliefs so unusual that I have serious doubts as to whether he was really a Christian. Of course, I am aware of a number of professing Christians who are presently engaged in aggressive, even vicious, anti-Semitic rhetoric, using the New Testament to support their claims (along with the Old Testament and the Talmud, of course). In fact, I confronted them directly in *Our Hands Are Stained with Blood*. But if such people are, in fact, true Christians, they are the tiny (and ugly!) exception to the rule. As for alleged Christians who are so anti-Israel that they virtually cheer for terrorist groups like Hamas, they are the modern-day equivalent of the Crusaders and Inquisitors. In other words, they are apostate Christians who have no connection with true Christianity.

221. See immediately above, 2.7, and n. 126.

222. It was Raul Hillberg, one of the foremost historians of the Holocaust, who pointed out that most of the anti-Jewish measures passed by the Nazis (with the exception of the plan to exterminate our people) had their parallels in earlier church legislation. See his classic study, *The Destruction of the European Jews* (New York: Holmes & Meier, 1985).

223. Lillian Freudman expressed the views of many Jews when she made reference to "nineteen-and-a-half centuries of Jewish suffering and the martyrdom of millions of Jews sacrificed on the altar of Christian antisemitism"; see her *Antisemitism in the New Testament*, xii. Of course, one might ask *what* Jewish suffering she was referring to that dated back to the mid first century of this era, as well as what relationship that alleged suffering had with Christianity, since it was the followers of Jesus who were being persecuted at that time. It would also be fair to ask how accurately Nazi altars of death can be described as "Christian." This illustrates how passionately our people feel about the subject of "Christian" anti-Semitism, even to the point of making exaggerated and unsupportable statements in the preface of what attempts to be a scholarly, careful study.

224. Lee Martin McDonald, in Evans and Hagner, *Anti-Semitism and Early Christianity*, 225, with reference to Simon, *Verus Israel*, 397–402. Although Simon documented in detail the early history of "Christian" anti-Semitism and was eminently aware of its development right up until this century, he still states: "But to argue from this that

the Church must bear the essential responsibility, even though it be an indirect responsibility, for the Nazi atrocities, or to see the gas chambers of Auschwitz as the natural result of the Church's teaching—this is to take a step that the historian will hesitate to regard as legitimate. It seems hardly likely, on a priori grounds, that in an age as secularized as ours, and even more so, under a regime as utterly hostile to Christian ideas as that of the Nazis, it should be the theological components of anti-Semitism that are the determining factors in it." He adds, "It must not be forgotten, when the attempt is made to connect the Nazis' anti-Jewish persecutions too closely with Christian teaching, that the Jewish massacre was not the only example of genocide engaged in by the Third Reich. Other 'inferior' races and malefactors were hunted down by the Nazis in the name of the same biological principle; the Gypsies for example" (397–98). Finally, Simon notes that, "From the Church's point of view, at any period, a Jew was characterized by his religion. If he was converted, he ceased to be a Jew [of course, this view was one of the *errors* of the church], and the ultimate aim was just that, the conversion of Israel. . . . For Hitler's anti-Semites, a Jew turned Christian was still a Jew, because a Jew was characterized by his race, and it was neither desirable nor possible to change his ethnic characteristics. Total extermination was the only solution. This, in my opinion, marks a fundamental difference that forbids us to establish any very definite or close connecting link or continuity between the two" (398).

225. Richard P. McBrien, *Lives of the Popes* (San Francisco: HarperSanFrancisco, 1997), 362.

226. Ibid. As to the question of why Pius XII, the next pope, was not more outspoken against the Nazis, see the fair discussion in ibid., 364–65. More broadly, cf. Klaus Scholder, *A Requiem for Hitler: And Other New Perspectives on the German Church Struggle* (Philadelphia: Trinity Press, 1989).

227. In this regard, Arthur Katz, a Messianic Jew whose whole life has been shaped by the Holocaust, rightly observes, "When something of this proportion takes place in history, the interpretation of it, or the *lack* of an interpretation, is enormously consequential. The most tragic thing would be that the event itself should not be properly understood as God intended." See *The Holocaust: Where Was God?* (Pensacola, Fla.: Mt. Zion Publications, 1998), 1, his emphasis.

228. An excellent, systematic, and judicious summary of Jewish religious responses to the Holocaust is provided by Barry Leventhal, "Theological Perspectives on the Holocaust," *Mishkan* 6, no. 7 (1987): 10–48. For a representative sampling of essays, cf., e.g., Steven L. Jacobs, ed., *Contemporary Jewish Religious Reponses to the Shoa*, Studies in the Shoa (Lanham, Md.: Univ. Press of America, 1993); Bernhard H. Rosenberg and Fred Heuman, eds., *Theological and Halakhic Reflections on the Holocaust* (Hoboken, N.J.: Ktav, 1992); and see also the works cited in the following discussion, as well as those listed in Brown, *Our Hands Are Stained with Blood*, 232–33 (under the rubric of books on "Jewish piety during the Holocaust").

229. Steven T. Katz, "Jewish Faith after the Holocaust: Four Approaches," in *Encyclopedia Judaica Year Book 1975/6*, 93, cited in Leventhal, "Theological Perspectives," 18.

230. See Yosef Roth, "The Jewish Fate and the Holocaust," in *I Will Be Sanctified*, ed. Rabbi Yehezkel Fogel, trans. Edward Levin (Northvale, N.J.: Aronson, 1998), 49–60.

231. Ibid., 51.

232. Ibid., 54.

233. Cited in ibid., 56.

234. Cf. also Katz, *The Holocaust: Where Was God?* who devotes a chapter to the question of "What Sin Was God Judging?"

235. Aviezer Ravitzky, "The Messianism of Success in Contemporary Judaism," in *Encylopedia of Apocalypticism*, vol. 3, *Apocalypticism in the Modern Period and the Contemporary Age*, ed. Stephen J. Stein (New York: Continuum, 1998), 223 (the article runs from 204–29).

236. Cited in ibid.

237. Cited in ibid.

238. For the historical background, cf. Leni Yahil, *The Holocaust*, trans. Ina Friedman and Haya Galai (New York: Oxford, 1990), 67–72; for the response in the press, cf. Herbert Freeden, *The Jewish Press in the Third Reich*, trans. William Templer (Providence: Berg, 1993), 117–28.

239. Freeden, *The Jewish Press in the Third Reich*, 117.

240. See further, ibid., 117–18.

241. Ibid., 119.

242. This is one of the primary arguments of Katz, *The Holocaust: Where Was God?*

243. *Jewish Wisdom* (New York: William Morrow, 1994), 306. His concise discussion concerning "Jews and God after the Holocaust" (ibid., 303–15) is relevant to our topic here.

244. "Eichmann's Victims and the Unheard Testimony," *Commentary* 32 (December 1961): 515, cited in Leventhal, "Theological Perspectives," 26.

245. Based on insights from the psalms, we see that this was the typical reaction of an Israelite stricken with a severe illness, especially if the illness proved agonizing or debilitating; see Michael L. Brown, *Israel's Divine Healer*, Studies in Old Testament Biblical Theology (Grand Rapids: Zondervan, 1995), 119–49, with extensive references.

246. From *The Holocaust Kingdom: A Memoir*, cited in Leventhal, "Theological Perspectives," 16.

247. "Cloud of Smoke, Pillar of Fire: Judaism, Christianity, and Modernity after the Holocaust," in *Auschwitz: Beginning of a New Era?*, 34, cited in Leventhal, ibid., 28–29.

248. For a recent Orthodox rejection of the judgment theory, see Rosenberg and Heuman, *Theological and Halakhic Reflections*.

249. This, of course, bears at least some resemblance to the biblical story of Job; for an overview, see Brown, *Israel's Divine Healer*, 165–81, with references to other important studies; see also R. Dedmon, "Job as Holocaust Survivor," *Saint Luke's Journal of Theology* 26 (1983): 165–85, although I would take exception to some of the author's positions on the Book of Job. Note also the title of the recent book by Alan Berger, *Children of Job: American Second Generation Witnesses to the Holocaust* (Albany: State Univ. of New York, 1997). On the subject of the Holocaust followed by the "resurrection" of the State of Israel, cf. the brief observations of Rabbi Abraham R. Besdin, "The Holocaust and the State of Israel: Are They Related?" in Rosenberg and Heuman, *Theological and Halakhic Reflections*, 137–43.

250. As expressed chillingly by Yossel Rakover, the fictional—but deeply real and thoroughly representative—victim of the Warsaw Ghetto uprising created by Zvi Kolitz, "It is not true that there is something beastly in Hitler. He is, I am deeply convinced, a typical child of modern man. Humanity as a whole has spawned him and reared him, and he is the frankest expression of its innermost, most deeply buried wishes." See Zvi Kolitz, *Yossel Rakover Speaks to God: Holocaust Challenges to Religious Faith* (Hoboken, N.J.: Ktav, 1995), 14.

251. It is true, of course, that one of the daily prayers of an observant Jew includes the petition for repentance (the fifth benediction of the Shemoneh Esreh), in which

God is asked to "turn us back," "draw us near," and "cause us to return." Nonetheless, the emphasis in Jewish teaching on repentance is clearly on human responsibility, while traditional Judaism's evaluation of the nature of man is far more positive than that of Messianic Judaism and Christianity.

252. See 2.15 on the uniqueness of the message of forgiveness and salvation through Jesus the Messiah.

253. Cf. Louis A. Berman, *The Akedah: The Binding of Isaac* (Northvale, N.J.: Aronson, 1997); Aharon (Ronald E.) Agus, *The Binding of Isaac and Messiah: Law, Martyrdom, and Deliverance in Early Rabbinic Religiosity* (Albany: State Univ. of New York, 1988).

254. The Hebrew *hurban* (or *horban*) means "destruction" and refers specifically to the destruction of the First and Second Temples; hence the reference here to the "third *hurban*."

255. Katz, "Jewish Faith after the Holocaust," is quoting here from Maybaum's book *The Face of God after Auschwitz*, 36. Some Jewish readers may not know that "Golgotha" refers to the place of Jesus' crucifixion (it was also known as Calvary).

256. Katz, *The Holocaust*, 65.

257. Basilea Schlink, *Israel, My Chosen People: A German Confession before God and the Jews* (Old Tappan, N.J.: Chosen, 1987). See also idem, *For Jerusalem's Sake I Will Not Rest* (London: Marshall Pickering, 1969); note that this was written shortly after the Six Day War; for her autobiography, see idem, *I Found the Key to the Heart of God: My Personal Story* (Minneapolis: Bethany, 1975). The above three books are available from Evangelical Sisterhood of Mary, 9849 North 40th Street, Phoenix, AZ 85028-4099.

258. According to S. T. Lachs (to Matt. 27:35), "The condemned were crucified naked, and the executioners were allowed to divide their clothing and property among them" (*Rabbinic Commentary*, 432, with ref. to Artemidorus Daldianus, Onirocriticus 2.61). Also commenting on Matthew 27:35, Strack and Billerbeck note that, "Das Verteilen der Kleider setzt voraus, dass Jesus unbekleidt gekreuzigt worden ist. Das entsprach auch judischer Sitte" ("The dividing of the clothes presupposed that Jesus was crucified naked. This also corresponds to the Jewish setting"), with reference to m. Sanhedrin 6:3; see Hermann L. Strack and Paul Billerbeck, *Kommentar zum Neuen Testament aus Talmud und Midrasch* (München: C. H. Beck, 1924), 1:1038. Note also that Melito of Sardis, who died around 190 c.e., wrote, "He who hung the earth [in its place] hangs there, he who fixed the heavens is fixed there, he who made all things fast is made fast upon the tree, the Master has been insulted, God has been murdered, the King of Israel has been slain by an Israelite hand. O strange murder, strange crime! The Master has been treated in unseemly fashion, his body naked, and not even deemed worthy of a covering that [his nakedness] might not be seen. Therefore the lights [of heaven] turned away, and the day darkened, that it might hide him who was stripped upon the cross" (Pass. 96–97, cited by Gerald G. O'Collins in *Anchor Bible Dictionary* 1:1012). See further Brown, *Death of the Messiah*, 2:952–53.

259. Joel Marcus, a Jewish Christian scholar, makes a similar point in his short collection entitled *Jesus and the Holocaust: Reflections on Suffering and Hope* (New York: Doubleday, 1997), 15: "No, I do not really know what the Holocaust was like. I don't know what it's like to see my child, or my parent, or my friend swept off to death or murdered before my eyes (God grant that I may never know). But neither do I know exactly how a crucifixion feels. Yet on Good Friday one says something about crucifixion. And in the fiftieth year after the end of the Holocaust, one says something about

the Holocaust. And when those two things come together, one tries, however inadequately, to say something about their mysterious relation to each other."

260. This is Brown's "free rendition" of Pseudo-Manetho (third century C.E.), *Apotelesmatica* 4.198–200; see *Death of the Messiah*, 2:954, with reference also to Martin Hengel, *Crucifixion*, 9.

261. Elie Wiesel, *Night*, trans. Stella Rodway (New York: Hilland Wang, 1960), 75–76.

262. I think of the words of Charles Wesley from his celebrated hymn "Arise, My Soul Arise," in which one stanza describes the Messiah's wounds as actually offering prayers of intercession of lost sinners: "Five bleeding wounds he bears, received on Calvary; They pour effectual prayers, they strongly plead for me. Forgive him, oh forgive they cry, forgive him, oh forgive they cry, nor let that ransomed sinner die."

263. While it is true that Germany has become much less militaristic since the Holocaust, the nation has certainly not advanced morally or spiritually since that time. Just think: For more than forty years, the nation was divided into East and West, the Eastern part being an atheistic police state; racism is rampant throughout Germany today; neo-Nazism is rapidly rising again; the post-Kohl government refused to invoke God's help in the oath of office; sexual promiscuity and alcoholism are rife in the land. Sadly, Germany has not experienced moral or spiritual healing through the Holocaust. (The interested reader might want to hear a message I preached in Duisberg in 1995, entitled, "Who Will Weep for Germany?" available through ICN Minstries.)

264. See further Isaiah 10:5ff., especially vv. 5 and 12: "Woe to the Assyrian, the rod of my anger, in whose hand is the club of my wrath! . . . When the Lord has finished all his work against Mount Zion and Jerusalem, he will say, 'I will punish the king of Assyria for the willful pride of his heart and the haughty look in his eyes.'" Zechariah 1:14–15 says, "Then the angel who was speaking to me said, 'Proclaim this word: This is what the LORD Almighty says: "I am very jealous for Jerusalem and Zion, but I am very angry with the nations that feel secure. I was only a little angry, but they added to the calamity."'" In point of fact, the nations among whom the Jewish people were scattered were promised especially severe judgment, while our people were promised ultimate preservation: "'I am with you and will save you,' declares the LORD. 'Though I completely destroy all the nations among which I scatter you, I will not completely destroy you'" (Jer. 30:11).

265. Cf., e.g., Eugene J. Fischer, *Faith without Prejudice: Rebuilding Christian Attitudes toward Judaism* (New York: Paulist, 1977), and note also the relevant works cited above, n. 169.

266. For the difficulties of dealing with the history of the Holocaust even in the former West Germany, see Richard J. Evans, *In Hitler's Shadow: West German Historians and the Attempt to Escape from the Nazi Past* (New York: Pantheon, 1989).

267. Cf. the statement of Beth Moshe, cited above, introduction, n. 4.

268. Cited in Brown, *Our Hands Are Stained with Blood*, 24.

269. Such statements are quite common in anti-missionary fund-raising literature, and they are designed to put fear into the hearts of Jewish people, making them feel as if there is some vast conspiracy targeting them for conversion. There is even a myth that missionaries get special bonuses for every Jew they can convert (not to mention the ludicrous notion that someone is paying them "by the convert"!).

270. For discussion and sampling of these debates, see especially Hyam Maccoby, ed., *Judaism on Trial: Jewish-Christian Disputations in the Middle Ages* (London/Washington: Littman Library, 1993); note also Robert Chazan, *Barcelona and Beyond: The*

Disputation of 1263 and Its Aftermath (Berkeley: Univ. of California Press, 1992); idem, *Daggers of Faith: Thirteenth-Century Christian Missionizing and Jewish Response* (Berkeley: Univ. of California Press, 1989).

271. To be perfectly candid, if the debate actually went as recounted by Ramban, then I would be the first to admit that his Catholic opponents did very poorly and that his arguments were, for the most part, superior.

272. Of my two debates with the anti-missionary Rabbi Tovia Singer, one held at a private residence in Maryland and the other held live over a New York/New Jersey radio station, our ministry distributes only the second. This is because Rabbi Singer asked me *not* to distribute the first debate, which was held quite unexpectedly at the home of an inquisitive Russian Jew who had scheduled the debate without Rabbi Singer or me having any real idea that it was coming. What happened was that this man, who was a new believer in Yeshua, invited Rabbi Singer and me to his home, along with several other anti-missionaries and Christian guests (Rabbi Singer and I had never met before), and then surprised us with a three-hour program for the debate! Both parties informally recorded the proceedings, but Rabbi Singer was not at all happy with the debate, and as a result, he asked me to cease distributing any of the tapes. Of course, since we had no formal agreement, I complied with his request. Still, there was lasting fruit that came from that night: A Jewish woman who had been living an observant Jewish lifestyle for more than six years and who was a close friend of Rabbi Singer had accompanied the group that traveled from New York to Maryland that night. She was so shaken up by the debate that she ultimately became a believer in Jesus the Messiah, even working for a year in Messianic Jewish ministry in the former Soviet Union. When asked who led her to the Lord, she replied, "Tovia Singer!"

273. For a sampling of some of his rhetoric, see Riggans, *Yeshua Ben David*, 63–64; for an example of his academic work on Jewish messianism, see his study entitled *Mashiach: The Principles of Maschiach and the Messianic Era in Jewish Law and Tradition*, 3d ed. (New York/Toronto: S.I.E., 1992). Note that Schochet merited an entry in the *Encyclopedia of Hasidism*, 433, as "an acknowledged authority on Jewish philosophy and Jewish mysticism."

274. Asking God to guide you is a good Jewish thing to do! See, e.g., Pss. 119:18; 143:10; Prov. 3:5–6; and note God's promise to those who take refuge in him: "I will instruct you and teach you in the way you should go; I will counsel you and watch over you" (Ps. 32:8).

275. For discussion and background, see 1.4, n. 9; for the definition and usage of Hebrew *mîn/minnîm*, heretic, schismatic, cf. Herford, *Christianity in Talmud and Midrash*, along with the more recent discussions in Schiffman, *Who Was a Jew?*

276. Cf. Josephus, *Antiquities*, 20.9.1; for detailed historical analysis, cf. Schürer et al., *History of the Jewish People*, 1:428–41. In this last-cited work, the authors tellingly note, "That various Pharisaic circles entertained friendly relations with Jewish Christians for a long time after the crucifixion is attested, not only by the report on the resentment caused by the stoning of Jesus' brother at the order of a Sadducaean High Priest, but also by the significant fact that certain communal Christian traditions of Palestinian provenance . . . depict various Pharisees or other Jews not members of Jesus' own companionship as harbouring feelings and intentions of friendship for Jesus and maintaining social contact with him" (ibid.).

277. See Ray A. Pritz, *Nazarene Jewish Christianity: From the End of the New Testament Period until Its Disappearance in the Fourth Century* (Jerusalem/Leiden: Magnes/Brill, 1988). He describes the Nazarenes as "Law-keeping Christians of Jew-

ish background" who were "basically trinitarian" and "did not reject the apostleship of Paul" (108–9). However, they "refused to accept the authority established by the Pharisaic camp after the destruction of Jerusalem, and in so refusing they adjudicated their own isolation from the converging flow of what we call Judaism" (110).

278. For bibliography and discussion, cf. Michael O. Wise, "Languages of Palestine," in *Dictionary of Jesus and the Gospels*, ed. Joel B. Green and Scot McKnight (Downers Grove, Ill.: InterVarsity Press, 1992), 434–44; further references are provided in Michael L. Brown, "Recovering the Inspired Text? An Assessment of the Work of the Jerusalem School in the Light of *Understanding the Difficult Words of Jesus*," *Mishkan* 17, no. 18 (1992): 38–64.

279. See A. F. J. Klijn and G. J. Reinink, *Patristic Evidence for Jewish-Christian Sects* (Leiden: E. J. Brill, 1973); Pritz, *Nazarene Jewish Christianity;* Bellarmino Bagatti, *The Church from the Circumcision* (Jerusalem: Franciscan Printing Press, 1984); and note the works cited by Juster, *Jewish Roots*, 289–94; an important older study is Fenton John Anthony Hort, *Judaistic Christianity*, ed. J. O. F. Murray (Grand Rapids: Baker, 1980).

280. For discussion and evaluation of this tradition, cf. Pritz, ibid., 122–27, and see further C. R. Koester, "The Origin and Significance of the Flight to Pella Tradition," *CBQ* 51 (1989): 90–106, along with the additional works cited in John Nolland, *Luke 18:35–24:53*, Word Biblical Commentary (Dallas: Word, 1993), 2:985. According to Simon, *Verus Israel*, 261, "This act, committed in such serious circumstances, took on a symbolic significance. It immediately placed them outside the community of Israel and exposed them to the rancor and hatred of the nationalists." He adds, however (480, n. 93), "It was nevertheless not this act which provoked the hostility in the first place. It rather presupposes the existence of such hostility. That this already existed is shown by the martyrdom of James, and it was probably in order to avoid fresh acts of cruelty that the community left the city." For a sociological approach to the general first century conflict, see Jack T. Sanders, *Schismatics, Sectarians, Dissidents, Deviants: The First One Hundred Years of Jewish-Christian Relations* (Valley Forge, Pa.: Trinity, 1993); for the theological schism, see James D. G. Dunn, *The Parting of the Ways: Between Christianity and Judaism and Their Significance for Christianity* (Philadelphia: Trinity Press, 1992); note also Vincent Martin, *A House Divided: The Parting of the Ways between Synagogue and Church* (New York: Paulist, 1995).

281. For scholarly evaluations of the evidence surrounding these events, cf. Schürer et al., *History of the Jewish People*, 1:543–45.

282. To give just one example, the Messianic Jewish scholar Dr. John Fischer comes from such a family. He is, moreover, a strong advocate of Messianic Jews adhering to a scriptural Jewish lifestyle and utilizing Rabbinic traditions wherever appropriate.

283. This was expressed in the title of the important study cited above (n. 61), edited by Neusner, Green, and Frerichs, *Judaisms and Their Messiahs*, and is commonly accepted by the great majority of Jewish and Christian scholars. As stated simply by B. Pixner (in Charlesworth and Johns, *Hillel and Jesus*, 193), "The Judaism of the Second Temple period, and in particular the Judaism at the time of Jesus and the primitive church, was not monolithic in its religious attitude, but rather pluralistic." One of the conclusions reached by the contributors to this volume was that, "Both Hillel and Jesus set in motion perspectives, commitments, and means of adhering to and inculcating traditions that founded respectively Rabbinic Judaism and Christianity" (460–61).

284. As noted in 1.5, n. 10, Gabrielle Boccaccini has recently argued that Christianity be recognized as a Judaism (see his *Middle Judaism*, with some strictures in the

foreword by J. H. Charlesworth, xviii), citing the judgment of scholars who underscore the Jewishness of early Christianity (see esp. 13–18); cf. also the challenge of Geza Vermes, *Jesus and the World of Judaism* (Philadelphia: Fortress, 1983), 87–88, for a new "Schürer-type *religious* history of the Jews from the Maccabees to A.D. 500 that fully incorporates the New Testament data." See also Marvin R. Wilson, *Our Father Abraham: Jewish Roots of the Christian Faith* (Grand Rapids: Eerdmans, 1989).

285. It is called Eduyot (meaning, "Testimonies"). According to Rabbi Adin Steinsaltz, *The Essential Talmud* (New York: Bantam, 1976), 91, Eduyot is a "compilation of testimonies on ancient *halakhah* that was in danger of falling into oblivion and on unusual aspects of *halakhah*, apparently amassed at a special session of the Yavneh court." See also H. L. Strack and G. L. Stemberger, *Introduction to the Talmud and Midrash*, trans. Markus Bockmuehl (Edinburgh: T & T Clark, 1991), 129.

286. Cf. Maimonides's introduction to his commentary on the Mishnah for a detailed defense of the essential unity and harmony of the Rabbinic traditions.

287. So, for example, despite their claims to the contrary, Mormons are in no sense of the word Christian, since they base their beliefs more on the Book of Mormon than on the Bible and they deny certain fundamental tenets of Christianity. See James R. White, *Is the Mormon My Brother? Discerning the Differences between Mormonism and Christianity* (Minneapolis: Bethany, 1997).

288. Cf. Seder Eliyahu Zuta, 20, where righteous Gentiles are likened to Israel's high priest.

289. In the Siddur (the Jewish prayer book), prayers such as this are typical: "Blessed are You, O Lord our God, King of the universe, who chose us from all peoples and gave us His Torah. Blessed are You, O Lord, giver of the Torah." To the outsider, such prayers could appear arrogant; to the religious Jew, they are reminders of a solemn calling and responsibility.

290. Of course, this certainty of faith does not prove they are right, but it raises a question: Since every religion strives for acceptance by the deity and divine forgiveness for misdeeds, why are the practitioners of the other world religions unable to convince themselves that they *have* received that forgiveness and acceptance? Could it be that deep down they know their "account" with God has not yet been settled?

Glossary

Babylonian Talmud. The foundational text for Jewish religious study, it consists of 2,500,000 words of Hebrew and Aramaic commentary and expansion on the **Mishnah.** It includes much **Halakha** as well as **Haggada,** and thus it touches on virtually every area of life, religion, custom, folklore, and law. It reached its final form between 500 and 600 C.E., and it is mainly the product of the Babylonian sages. *See also* **Palestinian Talmud.**

Five Scrolls. (Hebrew, kha-MESH me-gi-LOT) The biblical books of Song of Songs (Song of Solomon), Ruth, Lamentations, Ecclesiastes, and Esther. They were read in the synagogues on special holidays. *See also* **Ketuvim.**

Haggada. (Sometimes spelled Aggada) Nonlegal (i.e., nonbinding) Rabbinic stories, sermons, and commentaries relating to the **Tanakh** and Jewish life. *See also* **Halakha** and **Midrash.**

Halakha. A specific legal ruling ("What is the Halakha in this case?") or Rabbinic legal material in general. The word **Halakha** is interpreted as meaning "the way to go." *See also* **Haggada.**

Humash. (pronounced KHU-mash) Another name for the Five Books of Moses. *See also* **Written Torah.**

Ibn Ezra. Abraham Ibn Ezra (1089–1164). He was one of the three greatest Jewish medieval biblical commentators, especially famous for his careful attention to Hebrew grammar. *See also* **Radak** and **Rashi.**

Jerusalem Talmud. *See* **Palestinian Talmud.**

Kabbalah. The general term for Jewish mystical writings and traditions. It literally means "that which has been received." *See also* **Zohar.**

Ketuvim. Writings. This refers to the third division of the Hebrew Bible (*see* **Tanakh**) and includes Psalms, Proverbs, Job, the **Five Scrolls,** Daniel, Ezra-Nehemiah, and 1 and 2 Chronicles.

Masoretic Text. The term for the closely related Hebrew text editions of the **Tanakh** transmitted by the Masoretes ("transmitters") from the sixth to the eleventh centuries. All translations of the **Tanakh** (including the King James and *all* modern versions) are primarily based on this text. (*Note:* There is not *one* Masoretic Bible; there are thousands of Masoretic manuscripts with almost identical texts.)

Midrash. Rabbinic commentaries on a verse, chapter, or entire book of the **Tanakh**, marked by creativity and interpretive skill. The best-known collection is called Midrash Rabba, covering the Five Books of Moses as well as the **Five Scrolls.**

Mishnah. The first written collection of legal material relating to the laws of the **Torah** and the ordinances of the sages. It provides the starting point for all subsequent **Halakha.** It was compiled approximately 200 C.E. by Rabbi Judah HaNasi (the Prince) and especially emphasizes the traditions of the rabbis who flourished from 70 to 200 C.E. *See also* **Babylonian Talmud, Palestinian Talmud,** and **Halakha.**

Mishneh Torah. Systematic compilation of all Jewish law by Moses Maimonides (also called Rambam; 1135–1204). It remains a standard legal text to this day. *See also* **Shulkhan Arukh.**

Mitzvah. Commandment. The foundation of Jewish observance consists of keeping the so-called 613 commandments of the **Torah.**

Nevi'im. Prophets. This refers to the second division of the Hebrew Bible (*see* **Tanakh**) and consists of Joshua, Judges, 1 and 2 Samuel, 1 and 2 Kings (together called the Former Prophets), and Isaiah, Jeremiah, Ezekiel, and the Twelve Minor Prophets (together called the Latter Prophets).

Oral Torah. All Rabbinic traditions relating to the **Written Torah** and various legal aspects of Jewish life. The traditions were first passed on orally before they were written down.

Palestinian Talmud. Similar to the **Babylonian Talmud** but based primarily on the work of the sages in Israel. It is shorter in scope, less authoritative, and therefore, studied less than the **Babylonian Talmud.** It reached its final form in the Land of Israel approximately 400 C.E.

Radak. Acronym for *R*abbi *D*avid *K*imchi (pronounced kim-KHEE; 1160–1235). He wrote important commentaries on much of the **Tanakh.** *See also* **Ibn Ezra** and **Rashi.**

Rashi. Acronym for *R*abbi *Sh*lomo *Y*itschaki (pronounced yits-KHA-ki; 1040–1105), the foremost Jewish commentator on the

Tanakh and **Babylonian Talmud**. Traditional Jews always begin their studies in Bible and **Talmud** with Rashi's commentaries as their main guide. *See also* **Ibn Ezra** and **Radak**.

Responsa Literature. (Hebrew, she-ey-LOT u-te-shu-VOT, "Questions and Answers") A major source of **Halakha** from 600 C.E. until today, it consists of the answers to specific legal questions posed to leading Rabbinic authorities in every generation. *See also* **Oral Torah**.

Shulkhan Arukh. The standard and most authoritative Jewish law code, compiled by Rabbi Joseph Karo (1488–1575). *See also* **Mishneh Torah**.

Siddur. The traditional Jewish prayer book, containing selections from the **Tanakh** as well as prayers composed by the rabbis.

Talmud. *See* **Babylonian Talmud** and **Palestinian Talmud** (Jerusalem Talmud).

Tanakh. Acronym for *Torah, Nevi'im, Ketuvim*, the Jewish name for the Old Covenant in its entirety. Although the order of the books is different from that of the Christian Old Testament, the contents are the same.

Targum. Literally, "translation." This refers to the expansive Aramaic translations of the Hebrew Bible that were read in the synagogues where biblical Hebrew was no longer understood. They were put in written form between 300 and 1200 C.E. The most important Targum's are Targum Onkelos to the Five Books of Moses, and Targum Jonathan to the **Nevi'im** (Prophets).

Torah. Literally, "teaching, instruction, law." It can refer to: (1) the **Written Torah** (the first division of the Hebrew Bible; *see* **Tanakh**); or (2) the **Oral Torah** in its entirety (this of course includes the **Written Torah** as well).

Torah She-be-al-peh. *See* **Oral Torah**.

Torah She-bikhtav. *See* **Written Torah**.

Tosephtah. An early collection of Rabbinic laws following the division and order of the **Mishnah** but containing parallel legal traditions not found in the **Mishnah**.

Written Torah. The Five Books of Moses (the Pentateuch). *See also* **Humash**.

Zohar. The foundational book of Jewish mysticism. It was composed in the thirteenth century, although mystical tradition dates it to the second century. *See also* **Kabbalah**.

Subject Index

Josephus, Flavius, 159, 163
Joshua, 26
Josiah, king of Judah, 26
Judah, 89
Judaism, 27, 54, 138
Judas, 149
Judeophobia (Schäfer), 147
judgment, 94–95, 151–53
  coming, 32
  divine, 41
  of Jews, 22
  of nations, 108

Kahane, Martin (Meir Kahane), 13
Kaplan, Rabbi Aryeh, 10
kashrut (traditional dietary laws), 11, 15
Katz, Arthur, 187–88
Katz, Steven, 179–80, 186–87
Kittel, Gerhard, 127
Knox, John, 136
kohanim (nation of priests), 5, 86
Kook, Rabbi Z. Y., 181

Lachs, Samuel Tobias, 155
Lake of Huleh, 49
Lamentations, Book of, 30, 42, 184
languages, with Word of God, 92
legislation, anti-Jewish, 125–26
Leighton, Robert, 140
Levites, 25
Leviticus, Book of, 29
Lezius, Friedrich, 134–35
Lichtenstein, Yechiel, 150
lifestyle, biblical, 10
Lindberg, Carter, 133–34
literature, anti-Jesus, 137–38
Lithuanians, and Holocaust, 185
liturgy, Rabbinic, 11
love, 25, 112. *See also* philo-Semitism
loyalty, radical, 25
Lubavitch, ultra-orthodox movement,
  16, 53, 60–61, 100
Lubavitcher Grand Rabbi. *See* Schneer
  son, Menachem Mendel
Luke, the disciple, 99
Luther, Martin, 127, 133
  *Concerning the Jews and Their
  Lies*, 127, 134
  That Jesus Was Born a Jew, 133
Lutheran Church, 135

Maimonides, Moses, 83, 156, 207
Malachi, Book of, 77
Malaysia, 142
Manasseh, king of Judah, 37–38
Mandarin (language), 44
Mao Tse Tung, 91
Margolis, Rabbi Dr. Max, 45
martyr, 119. *See also* Holocaust
Marx, Karl, 114
Mary, the mother of Jesus, 98
mashiach, 6
Matthew, Gospel of, 154–56
Matthew, the disciple, 98–99
Maybaum, Rabbi Ignaz, 186, 195
McKnight, Scot, 155
Mea Shearim, 138
meek, the, 106, 110
Melanchthon, Philipp, 134
Melchizedek, 85–86
Messiah (Son of David), 12, 99
  belief in, 19
  as Branch, 86–87
  as Davidic king, 70, 80, 85–86, 95
  and German Jews, 191
  as God's messenger, 105
  and Hebrew Scriptures, 75–88
  and Jewish calendar, 81–84
  as king, 84–85
  overlooked, 84–85
  as Passover lamb, 81–82
  potential of, 96–97
  as priest, 84–85
  as Prince of Peace, 78
  second coming of, 88
  standard objection to, 69
  Talmudic traditions and, 74–75
  two, 85
  See also Jesus
Messiahs, false
  Messiah Bar Kochba, 73, 87, 100,
    203
  Messiah ben David, 100
  Messiah ben Joseph, 100
  Schneerson, Menachem Mendel
    (Lubavitcher Rebbe), 87, 96–98,
    181
  Shabbetai Zvi, 87
Messianic age, 70, 73, 100, 116
Messianic Jew, 6, 8, 10, 51, 107, 145

Index of Scripture and Other Ancient Writings

14:8–19 245 n. 205
15 3
17 136
17:1–5 164–165
17:2–3 200
17:30 39
18:28 200
20:21 39
22:1–22 245 n. 204
23:6 162
26:5 162
26:18 41
26:20 39

Romans

1–2 219 n. 31
2:28–29 172, 172–173
3:1–2 151
3:7–8 217 n. 13
5:6–8 168
9–11 171, 217 n. 21
9:1–4 152
9:4–5 151
10:1–2 167
10:1–15 219 n. 31
10:9–10 40
11 240 n. 168
11:1 153
11:7–8 22
11:11–12 153
11:13–14 171
11:17–26 174
11:20–21 129
11:22–24 129
11:25–26 129
11:25–27 23, 153
11:28 151
11:28–29 130
11:30–31 130
12:14 107
12:17 107
12:21 107
15:27 151

1 Corinthians

9:19–22 14
9:20 216 n. 13
9:20–23 217 n. 13
15:3 168
15:20–23 82
15:51–52 83

2 Corinthians

4:6 243 n. 189
12:16 217 n. 13
13:8 xxv

Galatians

6:16 172

Ephesians

2:1–2 243 n. 189,
    217 n. 13
1:29 9

Colossians

1:13 243 n. 189

1 Thessalonians

1:6–7 165
2:1–2 165
2:13–16 245 n. 207
2:14–15 245 n. 207
2:14–16 165–166
2:15–16 167
3:2–4 165
3:7 165
4:16 83

2 Thessalonians

1:4–5 165
1:6–10 229 n. 54

1 Timothy

1:13 34

2 Timothy

3:12 119

Hebrews

2:14 192–193
2:16–18 192–193
4:14–16 193
6:1 39
7 85
7:25 195
9:27–28 87
10:22 62
12:25–29 95, 229 n. 54
13:12–14 9

James

2:2 13, 174
2:18–26 40

1 Peter

2:21–24 107
2:22–24 193–194
4:16 6

2 Peter

3:9 39

1 John

3:14–15 107
3:16–18 116
5:19 243 n. 189

Revelation

2:9 173
2:14 172
3:9 173
7:4 172
11:15 83
12:12 95
13:8 168
13:10 190
21:12–14 172
22:11 229 n. 54

Mishnah

Avot

2:10 41

Sanhedrin

6:3 249 n. 258
10:1 220 n. 50

Sotah

3:4 244 n. 194
9:15 123

Tosephtah

Hullin

2:22–23   136

Sanhedrin

10:11 156